The Business of
BOOK PUBLISHING

The Business of
BOOK PUBLISHING

Papers by Practitioners

edited by Elizabeth A. Geiser
and Arnold Dolin, with Gladys S. Topkis

WESTVIEW PRESS / BOULDER AND LONDON

Copyright © 1985 by Westview Press, Inc., except for Chapter 4 (© Elisabeth Sifton); Chapter 10 (© Esther Margolis); Chapter 13 (© Mildred Marmur); Chapter 21 (© Lozelle DeLuz); Chapter 23 (© R. R. Bowker Company); Chapter 25 (© Arthur J. Rosenthal); and Chapter 30 (© Elizabeth A. Geiser)

Published in 1985 in the United States of America by Westview Press, Inc., 5500 Central Avenue, Boulder, Colorado 80301; Frederick A. Praeger, Publisher

Library of Congress Cataloging in Publication Data
Main entry under title:
The Business of book publishing.
    Bibliography: p.
    Includes index.
    1. Publishers and publishing. 2. Book industries and
trade. I. Geiser, Elizabeth A. II. Dolin, Arnold.
III. Topkis, Gladys S.
Z278.B96   1984   070.5   84-13230
ISBN 0-89158-998-8

Printed and bound in the United States of America

10   9   8   7   6   5   4   3   2   1

Contents

2266205

Tables and Figures

Preface

When the first University of Denver Publishing Institute came to a close in August 1976, all of us involved in its launching knew that we had a real success on our hands. And we knew it was due in great measure to an outstanding faculty of more than forty top publishing executives who had come to Denver during those four weeks to teach our students. How regrettable, it seemed, that their knowledge and expertise were available only to the eighty students handpicked for that first class. Fred Praeger, publisher of Westview Press, suggested a solution. "Do a book," he invited, "and let Westview publish the curriculum for others to share."

I loved the idea, but demurred, asking for time to refine and develop what was then a neophyte program. Three years later the Publishing Institute was well established both here and abroad, and I set forth on a task that was to last for four years. By late January 1980 I had outlined the book, identified topics to be covered, invited contributors to participate, and sent guidelines to all. Then I sat back—expectant and (as it turned out) naive—to await the flood of manuscripts scheduled for submission that spring.

It turned out to be a mighty long spring, with the last of the missing pieces not completed until the end of 1983. I knew that I had invited the best and the most experienced to contribute, but what I had failed to realize was that they were also the busiest.

As chapters arrived, they were edited, returned for revision, and frequently edited and revised again. As you well know if you are already in publishing, the writing and editing process usually takes longer than anticipated—and the result often falls short of the perfection the author and editor are seeking. Our goal was the definitive work on the business of book publishing, and although this collection may have some gaps and imbalances, it is clear that it also provides a lot of valuable information on most of the phases and functions of the publishing process. From the very beginning this has been a labor of love on the part of many people. We hope you will benefit from what they have to share with you and that you will agree with our decision to make it available without further delay.

Many of my friends in publishing have been generous with their help and advice. I would not have undertaken this project without the commitment of help from Arnold Dolin of New American Library, one of publishing's most gifted editors. He has brought his remarkable skills to work on most of the chapters in this book, and when his work load bogged him down, Gladys Topkis of Yale University Press stepped in and did an outstanding job of honing and sharpening a number of the contributions. Without the hard work and help of these two good friends and colleagues, our book would not have reached this stage in its publication process, and I am deeply grateful for their participation. I would also like to thank Samuel Vaughan of Doubleday, who reviewed and critiqued the general plan and first outline; Martin Levin of the Times Mirror Company, who read the entire manuscript and offered invaluable guidance; and the late Curtis Benjamin, who reviewed and commented upon many of the chapters. And a special note of gratitude to my friends at Westview Press and especially to Lynne Rienner, who showed patience beyond the call of duty and supplied encouragement and moral support at all the right and crucial moments.

To all these friends—both named and unnamed—my warmest thanks.

Elizabeth A. Geiser

The Business of
BOOK PUBLISHING

CHAPTER ONE

The State of the Heart

SAMUEL S. VAUGHAN

Toward Definition

American book publishing: What is, in the fashionable phrase, the state of the art?

Well, to start with, it's not an art, it's a business. That is—as this book's title proposes—the first fact to face. Then we can move more happily to a second. If at base publishing is a business, at its best it becomes a vocation.[1]

Strictly speaking, publishing is neither an art nor a profession. Though artists and professionals find careers in publishing (lawyers, accountants, M.B.A.'s, art directors, and so on), ours is only accidentally a profession and sporadically an art. It makes no formal professional demands for study, internship, admission by examination, or expulsion for violation. The best publishers are ethical and have standards, but the business has no fixed rules or ethical codes of conduct and you can dismay but not be disbarred by your peers.

To be an ounce more generous, there can be art in publishing as there is in carpentry or diplomacy or psychiatry (three fields not unrelated to ours). Nevertheless, publishing, though it derives in part from art, can be at times as mundane and repetitive as other forms of labor. It is no more an art than such kindred activities as librarianship or bookselling[2] and should not be confused with, say, either writing or printing, each of which can be an art or craft or simply workaday.

No, we profess no profession, claim no art. Our curious tribal customs and actions are to an extent, and increasingly, businesslike—though we are far from all business.

The irony is that publishers are regularly criticized for being too businesslike and for being poor at business. The sadness is that we have failed to clarify (just as publishing's critics seem unwilling to learn) the basic, tough truth: If we can't stay in business, we can't be good *or* bad publishers.

Ours can be a quiet or a spectacular business; it is surely an interesting

SAMUEL S. VAUGHAN is vice president and editor in chief, Doubleday Publishing Company.

and a quirky business. It may be frustrating or fulfilling, ethical or dubious, but the people who survive in publishing are those who have learned how to publish and how to run a business. The ones who will prosper, especially spiritually, are the individuals fortunate enough to find that what they have is not just a job but a vocation.

Paradox and Publishing

It does seem an unbusinesslike business. In several respects, book publishing is a business like any other, but in significant ways, it resembles no other business. Publishing is rife with paradox and rich with contradiction.

For one thing, it is more than one business. Apart from the varieties of publishing—textbook, professional and scientific, religious, reference, mail order, small press—each publishing house partakes of other businesses or professions. Among general publishers, such houses as Doubleday; Harper; Little, Brown; Morrow; Random House; Simon & Schuster; and Viking are involved in education, journalism, and the so-called information industry. They and their paperback customers or subsidiaries—Avon, Dell, Bantam, Ballantine, New American Library (NAL), Warner, Berkley, and others—are very much part of entertainment and show biz. Some houses like James Laughlin's New Directions, Fred Praeger's Westview, Braziller, Knopf, Pantheon, and Farrar, Straus, and Giroux, and such presses as Anchor, Black Sparrow, Bill Henderson's Pushcart, Atlantic Monthly, and the university presses are what Europeans call serious. Other imprints—Crown, A&W—are frankly commercial, interested mainly in books as "merchandise." Wiley, McGraw-Hill, Laidlaw, Houghton Mifflin, and Harcourt Brace do texts and technical treatises, journals, magazines, and much of the industry's total business. Many houses combine several of these characteristics.

Looked at in elementary economic terms, "trade" or general publishers use their own or someone else's money to produce seasonally a list of new books. The publisher then attempts to sell them, convinced that with effort, experience, expenditure, timing, and occasionally a little luck, several will sell well enough to more than cover their costs. A number of books will also be published without any hope of making money.

So it is argued that the winners pay for the losers. (At other times it is argued, in contradictory fashion, that the winning books get too much attention, while other books are left to languish.) It is said also that continuing sales of "backlist" (books that survive from among those published in previous years) help to underwrite investment in new books and authors.

If the few pay for the many and if the backlist lives, the publisher lives. If not, the house goes under—unless it is subsidized, intentionally run as a nonprofit operation, or absorbed by another, profitable house.

Like other industries, we have our equivalent of R&D (research and development). For us, it is the search for new authors and ideas, or educational techniques, as well as the continuous running of risks and experiments, plus nurture, care, patience. Some people use R&D to develop drugs or to design automobiles. We do it to help create books.

Which brings us to another basic: The single most important difference between publishing and other businesses is the unique importance and the presence, visible or not, of the author.

Many authors feel neglected or misunderstood by their publishers, but compared with what can happen to the creative output of automobile designers, playwrights and screenwriters, architects and commercial artists, the author is God. There is no doubt about who created the work—and alone. The publisher does not simply manufacture an object of industrial design, assembled by employees; the publisher brings forth a "product" that in the end, as in the beginning, belongs in the deepest sense to its author.

Diary or dictionary, treatise, novel or biography, a book is personal. What it looks like, the words used to describe it, what people think of it—such matters are of consummate importance to the person who wrote it. Therefore, good publishers often try to take the author's wishes into consideration, even if it is seldom possible to follow them to the letter. (Given the fact that most authors are demanding, and a few impossible to satisfy, the people who publish books learn to listen but not dance to the tune of those who write them.)

Therein lies a continuing source of dissatisfaction. The author would like (more) advertising; the publisher believes that (more) advertising will yield few further profitable sales. The author would like a blue binding; the publisher, unknowing, has bound the book in red and, hoping not to end up in same, declines to rebind the book. The book is not available in the author's home town; the local bookseller "explains" that the publisher's sales representative (1) never called or (2) called but never said anything about the book. The publisher does not like to explain that (1) the bookseller hasn't been able to pay his bill for six months or that (2) the author's tiny town falls 1,249,000 people short of being a metropolis and is not worth a traveler's time.

And so it goes—but the author, who at times feels powerless, remains a true power because without the author there would have been no book to read, to publish, or to fight about in the first place.

Another person of consequence in the process, invisible yet important and too often overlooked or underrepresented, is the reader. Book readers are discerning, even about books they have not read. Most books can be judged by their covers. A book has to be "good" to one kind of reader, even if "bad" or boring to another. A book must be satisfying to the reader or difficult in an intriguing, rewarding manner. Many businesses claim to be market oriented, to care about the customer, yet almost none attempt to be so responsive to so many audiences of such varying sizes, interests, tastes, and needs.

While we're comparing publishing to other businesses, there is the matter of monopoly. A publisher of books, like the manufacturer of light bulbs (both can illuminate), may not create a monopoly, but an author always does. The new poem by James Dickey or novel by James Michener has no competition, by and large. Yes, other books are published in the same season, vying perhaps for some of the same readers and dollars. Other forms of recreation and entertainment compete for time. But in his season, only one publisher, ordinarily, can offer the work of an author. The next Garry Wills book will be intensely interesting and provocative, but in no way a substitute for a new Arthur Hailey (or vice versa). Phyllis Whitney and Victoria Holt appear on our list in the same season, and they do not seem to be in competition with William F. Buckley's latest Blackford Oakes novel or Wilbur Smith's new adventure, though catholicity of enjoyment is a characteristic of the hard-core, hardcover reader. Thus, you can see how the individual author creates a benevolent monopoly.

One more major difference: The book, unlike many of its cultural cousins—the movie, the magazine, the play, the newspaper, the television show or series—is the work of an *individual.* Except for the occasional collaboration, one person has written it; except in schools or in public readings, one person at a time "uses" it. In a corporate, collaborative, conglomerating age, the book remains the stronghold of the individual.

Much of publishing defies easy, glib, or logical business analysis. Books involve *prodigious* amounts of energy, capital, skill, hope, work, and waste. They and their authors require recognition, conception, development. Publishing profits year in, year out are unimpressive by any aggressive capitalist standard, and the financial returns are unimpressive for the majority of authors. For publishing's employees, the pay is lean at the bottom, middling in the middle, and not tops at the top. Ours is a commercial occupation in which the fringe benefits are vastly better than the basic ones. (Thank God there is no tax on psychic income.) Books offer what some of us consider essential to the good, or at least the happily anxious, life. We find in them stimulation and stress, excitement and depression. Through publishing we pursue happiness, authors, agents, profits, prestige. Daily, we accept or reject and are ourselves accepted or rejected. Books provide for us—as they do for readers—sex, song, story, and spirit.

So, as big business goes, individual book-publishing firms seldom rank with the giants. For logicians, for those who insist that B follow A or the night the day, it presents problems. If you would woo the wealth of Araby, the odds are long. But in ideas, intrigue, mysteries, blessedness, wrong-headedness, in high taste and low cunning, book publishing has it all.

Who's Complaining?

Unsubsidized presses need to produce profits as well as publications, as noted. (Indeed, university presses, once profit proof, have to pay their way these days.) At times, and especially at the moment, profits are minimal or nonexistent. The need for profit does not justify everything we do—but without at least a moderate profit, a publisher can do nothing. Unless there are salable books to pay the rent, that is, overhead, including salaries, a house cannot publish other books, whether literature or "popcorn."

More than a few authors and book critics and journalists seem to hold the view that publishing should trouble itself only with literature, with perhaps a few other books thrown in (or thrown out) for contrast. Indeed, in general publishing we are always looking for the next Faulkner or Bellow or Colette. But the intervals between the appearance of a Shakespeare or a Proust, a Hemingway or a Styron, can be long ones. Meanwhile, the meter is ticking; publishing houses cannot sit silently, awaiting the genesis of genius. Other authors want to earn a living, as do publishing people, and readers want the results. Moreover, the publishing of entertaining stories more modest than classic, or of useful, practical books is an honorable and a needed occupation.

Yet misunderstandings about the business of publishing lie at the heart of the clash between publishers and people who are, in many respects, their natural allies: authors, librarians and literary critics, columnists, and agents.

Disparate and sometimes desperate essayists do not seem to (or want to) understand that publishing operates in several time perspectives. We have to be concerned with the immediate book, the one that will sell now; we are interested in the book that might work well over the middle distance, perhaps two to ten years; and we are always looking for the enduring work.

Even the most commercial house wants to publish great books. Again, paradox: The book that turns out to be a classic turns out to be, in the end, the most commercial.

A few years ago, the author-journalist Harrison Salisbury told book publishers that ours is, in many ways, the most important business of all. Rare praise, and welcome, but excessive. Not long before Salisbury spoke, the *Annals,* a scholarly journal, described us as "the gatekeepers of culture." A colorful description but passive. We are not simple toll takers on the turnpike of U.S. culture. True, we publish, for the most part, what is conceived and executed by others. But we also conceive, commission, sponsor, discover, and uncover.

The conflicts between culture and commerce, between publishers and critics, which cause such outbreaks of indignation inside and outside publishing houses, are not just inevitable, they are invaluable. They are, in fact, desirable, even essential.

What's a Book? What Is Publishing?

First things last. The verb *to publish* has many definitions. The best is short and sweet: *to make known.* Though the phrase doesn't begin to suggest either the dimensions or the dementia of the task, the three words point to the central job—which is to make an author's work known, to build the bridge between author and reader.

Fine. But what is a book? Dictionary definitions suggest that it is a number of printed sheets of paper bound together between covers. Such definitions fall short. Not everything of over a hundred pages or so, printed and bound, justifies being called a book. The book is distinguished by length, to be sure. A short work may be an excellent essay or polemic or pamphlet or short story, but it isn't a book. Still, a book's depth should count for more than its length. Look to its intent and accomplishment, as well as its binding and word count. What it *says* gives the book its importance, makes the medium continue to be consequential.

The book has certain other technological as well as cultural characteristics. In a media-minded age, when television, movies, and computers command much attention, the uniqueness of the book as a medium is worth reconsideration. The book as artifact, as a physical product, represents investments—of the author's time, talents, at times life. And of the publisher's money, time, and talents. The book is considerably more than a manufactured object, one reason why some publishing purists object to the word *product.* It is a mind-to-mind transmission, which can cross all boundaries (except the sad border of illiteracy). It is inexhaustible. As a device, the book is portable, compact, prerecorded, replayable. Small screen though it may seem, it is instead as illimitable as the imagination. Some books are in full color; others in glorious black-and-white; the most imaginative are in colors not yet cataloged.

Publishers continue to deal with both mass and "class" audiences, demonstrating one answer to the dilemma that has been confronting and confounding motion-picture and network television producers: how to produce works that do not always require maximum box office appeal to succeed. (Radio and magazines got around to solving this problem, under pressure, by addressing themselves to selected special interests.)

One distinction that we point to, with pride and passion, is that the book is free. Not in cost or price, of course—though there are libraries— but free as in *liberty*. The book has no advertisers, conforms to no party line, is not prescribed by government or proscribed by censors. Of course, there are exceptions. Here and there, troubled vigilantes send out a posse to pursue and shoot books down from shelves. Sometimes there are legal questions to inhibit publication. But by and large we publish freely in a free country.

Publishing as a *business* is regulated, to be sure, by state and local governments; by the Federal Trade Commission, Securities and Exchange Commission, and so on. But the book as medium goes unregulated by any agency: Happily, there is no Federal Communications Commission or Federal Aviation Administration to control our traffic. (It is, instead, aided and protected by the Registrar of Copyrights in the Library of Congress.) Despite recent shortsightedness in several courts, the book, its creators, and its readers are beneficiaries as well as guarantors of the First Amendment.

Even so, it helps to remember that the book, like the business, constantly presents contradictions. Valid but opposing ideas coexist about freedom and justice. The First and the Sixth amendments, for instance, are sometimes at odds. And the freedom authors and publishers refer to rightly or self-righteously is freedom to *read*, not just to write and publish. It is the public's right, even more than ours. The public also has the freedom not to read or not to like what we offer—and to say so. We must respect, even if we do not yield to, the objections of others.

If you would go into publishing, go prepared to respect and defend the freedoms.

Why Be in Publishing?

First, let us look at a little of what is going on. Second, I'll suggest some of the reasons why, despite scar tissue and occasional overdoses of stardust, I'm still in it. Then we'll look at what it might offer you.

In publishing, history has always been very much with us. Both the historical novel (Costain, Shellebarger, Kenneth Roberts) and "straight" history were staple. Over the last long decade or so, U.S. history seems to have fallen on hard times. Its decline began back in the late 1960s, I think, when many young Americans rejected conventional ideas about America's past, as well as its present, and did not like what they read as America's future.

Personal history, on the other hand, is flourishing, as is gossip. This is an age, as the sociologist David Reisman pointed out decades ago, when everyone wants to be an insider, backstage. Fewer people seem to be concerned with such niceties as good taste or documented fact. One potentially important debate concerns the dynamic but ethically disturbing overlaps of fiction, journalism, memoirs, and history. Such writers as Norman Mailer, Tom Wolfe, Gay Talese, David Halberstam, Arthur Schlesinger, Jr., and the Watergate chroniclers (accusers and accused) figure in these arguments.

Meanwhile, popular novelists who tell strong stories and offer genuine information—Michener, Stone, Uris, Hailey, Wouk et al.—prosper. Excellent scary novels are selling, viz., those by Stephen King. Feminist books succeeded black books in sympathetic attention. A number are outstanding; some simply ride the wave. All modish and opportunistic writing or publishing eventually declines while excellent books by authors of any color, creed, or sex will continue to be read.

There is criticism of editors: It is said that there are few good ones. Editorially, a first-rate editor today is what the best editors have always been: an alert, responsive reader, an analyst, an advocate. Fine editors are at work. But editors would stress that they have to be much more businesslike and entrepreneurial than (they suspect) editors were in the past.

The most dynamic changes have come from without. Book "packagers," many of them young—Delilah, Rolling Stone—and many English groups, prepare books for publishers to buy, at various stages, and see through to the market. Retail chains now offer hundreds more stores to sell standout books even as they offer a few new problems to go with that opportunity. The publisher's distribution system is always under fire. The industry's critics almost willfully fail to understand that publishers do not own or control the network of distribution. They are merely the start of the process.

In business, we are becoming somewhat more sophisticated. The computer is seen either as all-purpose splendid solution or ominous omnipresence (it is neither), and the desk calculator is at everyone's hand, including the editor's. Such economic issues as "cash flow" and "return on investment" are considered more frequently than before. So are interest rates, the cost of borrowing money to finance publishing—or to run a bookstore or book-wholesaling operation.

In the promotion of general books, television is used for publicizing (and advertising—although not as much as almost everybody would like). Frequently, the author is the main visible promoter—on the road, talking away, with publishers providing support in the form of logistic arrangements, tickets, automobiles, and meals.

The subsidiary rights markets have been electric for years, becoming less and less subsidiary. Much attention is given to the book in the original edition; at times even more is given over to its subsequent reuse—as paperback reprint, book-club edition, or translation. This is an exciting, dangerous, and dynamic situation. Reprint publishers are doing more "originals" and are suffering the same economic anemia as their hardcover counterparts.

There are other slow-burning trends. We worry about the further impact of photocopying, microfiching, and interlibrary lending, rather than the purchase of individual books; the decline of the once-extraordinary trade paperback in college markets, even as most people are proclaiming the trade paperback as the salvation of the future; the unforeseeable but undeniable impact to come of cable, cassettes, discs, fiche, and such; the economic demands of authors, booksellers, wholesalers; the rise in the retail prices of books; the decline in the numbers of books sold.

As for me, there are sobering personal considerations.

- I dislike having to disappoint so many people—to frustrate the dreams of would-be authors who will never be published, as well as falling short of the dreams of those who are.
- I don't much admire the tendency to divide publishing into two camps, of "we" and "they," with sales and financial people presumably arrayed against editors and authors. This is neither desirable nor the case. The best editors and authors care about audiences and markets and rewards, just as the best of my business-minded colleagues give a damn about books and not just the ones they balance.
- I regret that I haven't made myself, my family, my colleagues, and more of my authors rich and famous.
- I wish I were better at my job.
- I do not enjoy saying no so often. Being in publishing means always having to say you're sorry.

Meanwhile, there is much more to like:

- I like a great many of the books we publish—and sharing in some of their success: critical, commercial, or both.

- I like the fact that just about everybody in our business reads them, including, as mentioned, the so-called brass and "business" marketing people who are often characterized, unfairly, as caring more about the bottom line than the printed line.
- I like the associations—with authors, agents, other publishers, with my colleagues and not a few of our competitors and customers. By and large, I like spending my life with the people who populate it.
- I like the constant call for optimism. The business is based on discovery and delight. Optimism must spring eternal, especially in the face of frequent failure.
- I like knowing that some books satisfy existing appetites, while others create them. Certain books are written for definable markets. Others, as Eric Larrabee wrote, come about only because the performer creates the audience.
- I'm even beginning to like the constant misunderstandings. If everybody understood this peculiar business, anybody could do it.
- And I like the fact that we get to say "Yes," "Congratulations," "Well done," "Nice going," and "Thanks."

Still, such satisfactions could have nothing to do with the question of why (or if) you should be in publishing. Or even why you should read a book about it. (I am appalled at the number of otherwise bright young job applicants who have never read a book about books. The literature of publishing is uneven and not easily available. Yet it would seem to be worth reading about books if you ever hope to work with them.) We are, after all, mere men and women sitting around in offices, reading the paperwork of others, and creating more paper. Worrying about inventories and unearned advances and the apathy or seeming semiliteracy of the public. Growling about booksellers, who growl back, grousing about the perfidy of agents. Lamenting the loss of loyalty in authors, laying plans to snare someone else's author.

Much of the work is routine and not a little difficult, including editing, selling, printing, promoting, managing, negotiating, and the fabled—or infamous—expense account lunch, which offers some of the world's most expensive, least-tasted food. In or out of the office, the hours can be ridiculous.

On lackluster Tuesdays, one worries about being part of an industry with more underlying faults than California and as much science as alchemy.

To be sure, if Tuesdays were the whole story, publishing would not be worth your time—or mine. But that is hardly where it stops. Or even begins. Here is where the sense of vocation, the state of the heart, comes in.

For publishing offers each of us a chance regularly to test our ideas and opinions, our judgment, our abilities and beliefs; to face moral, commercial, or artistic dilemmas; to rise to an occasion. And publishing, any kind of publishing, offers more occasions to rise to than baking or ballooning.

The valuable papers contributed by others to this volume will parade facts, opinions, assertions, procedures, and contradictions before your eyes. Cherished illusions about books and authors and publishers may soon lie like fallen confetti around your ankles. But once you have been part of the parade, even for a moment, you will never be the same. If you choose not to be in publishing but elsewhere in the community of the book—in the school or university, the library or the bookstore, in a room alone as a writer or researcher or reader—you will find yourself as a result of what you read here more understanding and discerning.

Furthermore, the informed audience becomes part of any creative process. Judgments about what is published are too important to be left to publishers alone. Knowledgeable readers are enough to keep writers and publishers on their toes, trying to do their best work.

Enough. As you will learn, publishing is a world not unlike, say, the theater: always changing, while much remains the same; always in delicate health and apparently immortal; often annoying, frustrating, or imitative and once in a while admirable.

Our form of show biz, too, includes the roses and the footlights and the sweeping up after elephants.

If, as others have said, this is a business where you get paid for doing what you enjoy doing anyhow, publishing could sound suspiciously like the world's oldest profession. But much of the time it is the real thing. It is love.

Notes

1. "Vo-ca-tion . . . *n* . . . 2. a call to, or fitness for, a certain career. 3. The work or profession for which one has or believes one has a special fitness"—*The Doubleday Dictionary* (advertisement).

2. To be sure, the inspired bookseller or librarian who creates ways to bring together the author and the reader, who buys with taste and foresight, who devises new forms of accessibility, atmosphere, and service may be something of an artist. The librarian *is* a trained professional; the bookseller is in business, is a retailer.

CHAPTER TWO

The Structure and Functions of the Book Business

CHANDLER B. GRANNIS

"Structure" may be too static a term for such a variegated, fluid endeavor as book publishing. Nevertheless, the actions necessary to get any book published follow a fairly natural pattern that applies to all books, and publishing houses generally fall rather easily into groups according to the kinds of books published, the constituencies served, the markets sought, and the styles of business or institutional structure involved.

"Business," too, may be a not quite sufficient term to describe an enterprise in which the commodity is the product of human thought and creativity. Publishing assuredly is a business in the full sense, but it is also something more, because it concerns all the responsibilities and opportunities of communication.

Many publishing operations are recognized as "commercial"; many are considered "noncommercial." Some firms seek to "maximize profit" as a primary goal; many feel fortunate to achieve what could be called reasonable profits; and some exist not primarily (or at all) to make a profit but to meet some defined need (social, scholarly, or religious, for example) on a break-even or subsidized basis. But whether they are "in business" or not, all publishers, if they are to carry out their chosen purposes, have to be businesslike.

Writers about the book industry (including this one) have said over and over that the publishing of books can be a business, a profession, a gamble, or all three, and that for many people it is a vocation or calling. Herbert S. Bailey, Jr., suggested another choice of terms to describe the industry by calling his book *The Art and Science of Book Publishing*. Still another term, "the accidental profession," was used by Samuel S. Vaughan for his contribution to *To Be a Publisher*, the Association of American Publishers' book about education for publishing.

One can notice all these characteristics at different points and with different intensities throughout the publishing industry. First, there is

---

CHANDLER B. GRANNIS, former editor in chief at *Publishers Weekly*, is currently a contributing editor to the magazine.

the basic structure or common procedure that brings all books into being: a sequence of creating, producing, and disseminating them, along with financial management and administration. Accordingly, in publishing houses large, medium, or small, the functions are those of (1) planning a program, commissioning or selecting manuscripts and book projects, evaluating the material, and editing it for printing; (2) designing, specifying, and overseeing manufacture; (3) marketing in all its aspects; and (4) managing and coordinating these activities.

Currently reshaping arrangements in every department of publishing—in editorial, production, marketing, financial, and administrative operations and even in authorship—is the electronic factor seen especially in the swiftly proliferating use of in-house data-processing and word-processing equipment. The essential functions of publishing are the same as before, but the procedures and order of events are being sharply changed, and mastery of the new tools has become vital.

A second aspect of book-industry structure can be seen in the categories into which the industry divides itself by types or broad fields of publishing. These fields have been grouped into certain divisions for statistical treatment and analysis. Thus, the Association of American Publishers (AAP) issues an annual report showing, among other actual and estimated figures, the receipts of U.S. publishers in total and for each division. In 1982, the aggregate net receipts of all U.S. publishers from domestic and foreign sales came to about $7.999 billion. The divisions accounting for this sum are as follows, with a figure derived from the AAP report to show each division's approximate share of the total net receipts:

Adult Trade: general books of fiction and nonfiction of the kinds sold in most bookstores and circulated in public libraries: hardcover, 8.4 percent; paperbound, 5.7 percent (not mass market)

Juveniles (children's books): hardcover, 2.3 percent; paperbound, 0.6 percent

Religious: 4.9 percent (including Bibles, 2.3 percent)

Technical and Scientific: 5.4 percent

Business and Other Professional: 6.7 percent

Medical: 3.4 percent

Book Clubs (sales to subscribers): 7.4 percent

Mail Order Publishing (other than clubs): 7.6 percent

Mass-Market Paperbounds (pocket or "rack size" only): 10.3 percent

University Presses: 1.2 percent

Elementary and High School Texts ("el-hi"): 13.2 percent

College Texts and Materials: 14.3 percent

Standardized Tests: .9 percent

Subscription-Reference (encyclopedias and so forth sold by subscription): 5 percent

Audio-Visual and other Media (primarily for schools): 1.9 percent
Other Sales (unbound printed sheets, miscellaneous merchandise): .3 percent

Overall publishers' receipts in the middle 1980s were increasing at a rate of about 9 to 10 percent per year.

From the standpoint of dollars received, therefore, the biggest divisions of publishing are Trade (Adult, Juvenile, and some Religious combined), about 22 percent; Professional (Technical, Scientific, Business, and Medical combined), almost 15.5 percent; College, 14 percent; El-Hi Texts, 13 percent; and Mass-Market Paperbounds, 10 percent.

So much for publishers' sales in dollars. The total numbers of copies that account for those dollars divide up rather differently. The figures have been estimated by the Book Industry Study Group (BISG), a nonprofit industry service organization. John P. Dessauer, for BISG, sets the 1982 unit sales by U.S. publishers at about 1.901 billion books. Calculations made from the BISG report suggest that Adult and Juvenile Trade books accounted for about 23.7 percent of all units sold; Religious, 5.7 percent; all Professional, 3.5 percent; Book Clubs, 9.7 percent; Mail Order, 2.9 percent; Mass-Market Paperbounds, 34.9 percent; University Presses, .6 percent; El-Hi Texts, 13.3 percent; College Texts, 5.7 percent; Subscription-Reference, under .1 percent. High-priced categories often involve fewer books; for example, compare dollars and unit ratios of the Mass-Market category with those of the Professional group.

Still another aspect of the structure of publishing can be seen by examining the total numbers of titles published in major subject classifications. Title counts and estimates of average prices are made in cooperation with the Library of Congress by the R. R. Bowker Co., primarily. The Bowker reports, appearing in a spring annual summary issue of *Publishers Weekly* and in a reference book, the *Bowker Annual of Library and Book Trade Information,* show a yearly output of over fifty-three thousand titles in the middle 1980s. Roughly 85 percent of these are brand-new books; the rest are new, revised, or specially reprinted editions. Probably about a third of the forty-eight thousand titles are in paper covers of one kind or another. Bowker reports the numbers under twenty-three topical headings selected through consultation with library and publishing people.

One very important way to view the structure of publishing is to look at its markets. In fact, the processes of editing and producing books all point to the final step: making the book public. How publishers identify and develop their markets, how these efforts are structured, and how they affect the pattern of the publishing house are topics described in detail in at least three books: Nat Bodian's *Book Marketer's Handbook* (for scientific, scholarly, medical, and other professional books and journals); Robert Carter's *Trade Book Marketing Handbook;* and the American Booksellers Association's (ABA's) updated *Manual on Bookselling* edited by Robert Hale, Allan Marshall, and Jerry Showalter (see Books About the Book Industry).

What proportions of publishers' sales are made to what markets? Each firm, group of books, or title calls for its own analysis, but in the overall structure of book publishing, some idea of the proportions in very broad areas can be gained from studies made by AAP and BISG. From the latter's reports it is possible to calculate the following rounded-off estimates of sales ratios in U.S. book publishing in 1981: General Retailers, 25 percent of all the sales; College Stores, 15 percent; Libraries and Institutions, 8 percent; Schools, 16 percent; Direct to Consumers, 26 percent; Other Domestic Sales (unbound sheets and miscellaneous merchandise), 1 percent; Export, 9 percent. Widely different ratios appear, of course, in the reports of the individual divisions—Adult Trade, Professional, College, and so on. The same holds true for estimates of the proportion of sales that go through wholesalers to the above markets; for the industry overall, 22 percent of the sales pass through wholesalers.

An important role is played in marketing by certain associations other than those of publishers. Large annual meetings accompanied by domestic and foreign book exhibits, and important regional meetings as well, are held by the big umbrella group of book retailers, the ABA; by the National Association of College Stores (NACS), made up of private, institutional, and cooperative stores on campuses; and by the evangelical Christian Booksellers Association. The great annual conferences and exhibits of the American Library Association (ALA) are opportunities to present trade and professional books. The many academic and professional association conferences also present book displays and, in addition, facilitate contacts with authors and experts in many fields.

It goes almost without saying that the industry's reference tools are essential in its book-marketing structure. They also give an idea of the industry's size and scope. The 1984 edition of *Books in Print* (*BIP*), Bowker's multivolume annual index, lists more than 618,000 books. In the annual *Subject Guide to Books in Print,* the *BIP* listings are rearranged under more than 60,000 topical headings and subheadings. In 1984, *BIP* named some 15,200 publishers of the listed books.

The number of consistently active publishers is much smaller, however—more like the approximately two thousand U.S. publishers named, with departments and personnel, in Bowker's 1983 *Literary Market Place* (*LMP*). This annual directory also cites great numbers of service firms, agents, manufacturers, suppliers, reviewers, associations, and other categories of book-related activity other than book retailers and libraries, which are covered in other directories.

The business structures within which all the book-publishing functions exist are of many kinds. The activities of any publishing house are of course influenced by the nature of the business structure, which may determine whether a department has close or distant relations with management, what levels of costs and profits are demanded, and what the policies are regarding risk taking, cost controls, author relations, and overall goals. Business changes in recent years have certainly changed structures: Control has shifted in many cases from book-oriented to financially oriented people; mergers have proliferated; publishing companies and their parent companies have grown in size and complexity.

On the other hand, there have been divestitures and cutbacks and some countertrends. Some editorial imprints have survived, at least for a time, by working within a large house that performs the noneditorial functions. Some writers and editors have formed cooperatives that prepare and produce projects that are handled under a publisher's imprint. Most important, hundreds of small partnerships and individual or family-owned enterprises have sprung up nationwide over the past two decades, and scores have survived. They have built their own structure of cooperative service devices, including wholesalers and trade associations—especially the Small Publishers Association—that give practical advice and assistance and hold book fairs that have proved popular in many cities.

For the more established publishers, industry associations have long been important in the structure of the industry. The booksellers' associations, as noted, are vital to trade publishing. For the publishers themselves, the AAP represents the broadest spectrum of publishers of all kinds; it frequently works with the Association of American University Presses (AAUP). The AAUP represents most of the scholarly publishing houses on university campuses. The Society for Scholarly Publishing is made up primarily of individuals in academic, scientific, governmental, and other presses and institutions. The Children's Book Council brings together the people in "juvenile" publishing for the exchange of professional and business information and for cooperative promotion.

The major production interests are represented in the Book Manufacturers' Institute, which relates to publishers on the association and management levels. Many rank-and-file production people in publishing belong to various design and technical groups.

Local and special-interest clubs abound in the book field, and some have national membership. Many hold instructional programs, and all present discussions of industry problems and opportunities. There are groups made up of literary agents; women in publishing; people in small firms; young publishers; and people who work in religious publishing, publicity, advertising, library marketing, domestic sales, foreign sales, translating, editing in specialized areas, illustration, typography, and design. There are peripheral groups whose interests range from reading and literacy to book collecting and the history of printing and publishing. Many people in publishing work with or in organizations of authors: for example, regional writers, science writers, science-fiction writers, mystery writers, romance writers, and the important national societies, the Authors Guild and the American Center PEN, the international literary society of poets, playwrights, editors, essayists, and novelists.

Education for publishing has been increasingly recognized as a needed element in the industry. Local workshops and university extension programs are held in many places, and the important summer institutes, especially the pioneering Radcliffe program and the even more intensive University of Denver program and the New York University courses, have produced valuable recruits for the industry. The AAP has assisted many programs and has held traveling seminars.

Finally, the book industry, through its associations, finds itself involved at many points in the loose structure of national groups serving the public interest. Important examples are library associations, civil-liberties groups, organizations of educators, groups concerned with reading skills, child development associations, urban and rural community interests, and professional societies in the sciences and humanities.

Notably since the 1930s and increasingly since the 1950s the book industry has worked with appropriate groups on—to name a few major issues—postage rates for books, reading for the armed forces, promotion of the reading habit, reduction of barriers to the international flow of intellectual materials, international and domestic copyright reform, federal funding to expand the library system, federal aid to education, defense against censorship of books and authors, the fight to widen access to public documents of public concern, and the growing problem of functional illiteracy. Efforts such as these clearly illustrate the close identity of the book industry with the public interest.

These, then, are the principal structures that make up the book-publishing industry. Most of the people in it are concerned most of the time with the operational structures. But it is interesting, rewarding, and sometimes very important to have a view of the entire scene. This book should help serve that purpose.

PART ONE

Editorial

CHAPTER THREE

The Editorial Process: An Overview

HUGH RAWSON AND ARNOLD DOLIN

Editor and *publisher* may not be synonymous, but the editor who thinks of himself as a one-person publisher won't go far wrong. Good editors are involved in all phases of a book's publication, including design, manufacturing, and marketing as well as the acquisition and actual editing of the book. Moreover, the editor's efforts continue long after publication, extending through the entire selling life of the book. In this way, editors build up their own backlists just as companies do. Finally, the editor's critical sense must be balanced with a good business sense—a knowledge of what is profitable and what isn't—for no editor, and no publisher, can run in the red for very long and still survive.

Few editors actually are independent entrepreneurs, of course. Even those who are fortunate enough to have their own imprints usually have to rely upon others for capital—and a short purse string can be an effective leash on editorial independence. Typically, an editor is part of one department within a company that may in turn be part of some large business organization, often a conglomerate whose activities extend into many other fields besides publishing.

The Editorial Department

Most medium to large editorial departments are headed by an editor in chief or editorial director. In a smaller house this person may also have the title of publisher or president. Beneath the editor in chief, there may be an executive editor and one or more senior editors, charged primarily with acquisitions (bringing books into the house). The next echelon consists of editors (sometimes including assistant and associate editors), manuscript editors, and copy editors, who handle various aspects

---

HUGH RAWSON, a consultant on backlist and reference books to New American Library, is editor of the Authors Guild *Bulletin*. ARNOLD DOLIN is vice president and editor in chief, Plume, Meridian, Mentor, and Signet Classic, New American Library.

of the actual editing. Copy editors may be part of the editorial department or the production department, and depending on the house, they may be expected to rewrite and reorganize manuscripts or to perform routine styling for the printer. There is usually a managing or administrative editor who supervises the copy editors and coordinates and expedites the flow of manuscripts through the publishing process.

The entry-level jobs in the editorial department are held by editorial assistants. Much of their work is secretarial, but frequently editors ask their assistants to review manuscripts, handle permissions, do picture research, and perform other editorial functions under their supervision. If there is sufficient editorial turnover in the house, editorial assistants may eventually be promoted to the level of assistant editor, copy editor, or manuscript editor. At the upper levels, it probably is more common for people to promote themselves by moving to other companies.

The relationship of the editorial department to other departments in the firm varies a great deal from one house to another and also varies with the kind of publishing the house does—trade, textbook, or scholarly. In some houses, the production department is more or less expected to march to the editorial department's drum, but in others production is an entirely separate corporate division moving at its own, often stately, pace. In some firms editors make all the crucial editorial decisions and take the attitude that it is then up to marketing to figure out a way to sell the books. In other cases, the company's marketing department has an important say in deciding which projects to sign up and what kind of backing to give them.

Whatever the form of corporate organization, most important decisions surrounding the publication of any book will be discussed by a number of people both within and outside the editorial department. In some cases, though, one person—the president or the publisher—in effect makes those decisions after listening (usually) to staff arguments pro and con. The key decision that editors ordinarily make—whether to offer a contract—almost certainly will be subject to ratification by a superior.

Though individual authority is limited by the rest of the publishing apparatus, the editor remains very much the focal point in the development and selling of any book. From the time a book is acquired to the time it finally goes out of print, the editor (at least the editor who remains in the publisher's employ) will serve as the principal contact between the author and the company. The editor will be the first person the author turns to for answers to the myriad questions that can arise about distribution, publicity, royalty statements, and so on. The editor also will be the first person the publisher turns to if someone threatens a libel suit, or if reviewers unanimously agree that this book shouldn't have been published.

The Editor's Roles

Throughout the editorial process, the editor plays several different roles, each to a different audience. There is the editor-as-advocate, the editor-as-parent (or psychotherapist), the editor-as-manager, and the editor-as-marketer. Each role has its own tensions, and each conflicts to a certain degree with the others.

The editor usually starts with the advocate's role—as the chief lobbyist within the house for the particular books and authors he is sponsoring. In this role, the editor will attempt to convince others that the books of his choice should be published by the house and he will strive for good advances for the authors, better quality and a better schedule in book making, wide distribution, more support from the publicity and advertising departments, and so on.

While serving as the author's representative within the publishing house, the editor also acts as the firm's principal conduit to the author of policy and procedures, praise and criticism, moral support and money. In this role, the editor necessarily looms as a parental figure. The editor not only personifies an otherwise faceless corporation but is often the author's only real link with it. This is one of the reasons authors usually are distressed when their editors leave for other jobs and why they sometimes move with them, bringing their books to the editor's new publishing house. The fear—sometimes well founded—is that a book will not get the attention it deserves in the absence of its principal (and perhaps only) in-house advocate. Worse, once the sponsoring editor leaves, the company may decide it doesn't want the book at all and cancel the contract. Such things don't always happen, of course. An author may be fortunate enough to inherit a new, no less enthusiastic editor. Or the house's investment in a book may be so large that it simply has to be published well, whether or not the original editor is still on the premises. Nevertheless, the risks are real, and any author who has lived through the experience of working with two or three editors on a single book—a not uncommon occurrence in contemporary trade publishing—is almost certain to feel like an orphan caught in a storm.

The editor-as-manager is the administrator at the center of the publishing process. The manager's life is measured out in a series of deadlines. The period of gestation for a book, from delivery of the completed

TABLE 3.1 TYPICAL TRADE-BOOK EDITING AND PRODUCTION
SCHEDULE (IDEALIZED)

1 January	Author delivers manuscript.
1 February	Editor returns edited manuscript to author with comments.
1 March	Author returns revised manuscript to editor.
8 March	Editor delivers edited manuscript to copy editor, with duplicate copy to production deparment for estimating and design, and prepares in-house editorial bulletin and memo for jacket artist.
20 March	Presales conference.
8 April	Copy editor returns copyedited manuscript to editor.
10 April	Editor sends copyedited manuscript to author.
16 April	Catalog copy due.
20 April	Jacket design approved.
24 April	Author returns copyedited manuscript to editor.
26 April	Editor sends copyedited manuscript to production.
2 May	Jacket flap copy due (to be copyedited).
15 May	Fall sales conference.
25 May	Galleys arrive from the typesetter. Editor sends one set to author; proofreader (usually freelance) begins reading master set against original manuscript.
10 June	Author returns corrected galleys.
13 June	Author's corrections are transferred to master set, and galleys are returned to typesetter.
25 June	Bound galleys are received, and copies sent to selected list of people who may provide blurbs.
30 June	Page proofs are received from typesetter. One set is sent to indexer.
10 July	Corrected page proofs and manuscript of index are sent to typesetter; copy of index sent to author.
24 July	Typesetter finishes corrections and makes films.
7 August	Printing of books is completed.
28 August	Binding is completed.
4 September	Books reach company warehouse and shipping begins.
15 October	Publication day.

manuscript to publication, is about the same as for any other baby—
about nine months (see Table 3.1). During this period, a series of tasks
has to be performed, including the basic editing, collection of any
artwork, caption writing, copy editing, design of the book and the jacket,
composition, proofreading of galleys and pages, printing and binding,

and shipping. At each stage, the manager has to make sure that the author delivers the manuscript and proofs on time and that the copy editors, designers, and production people are giving the book the attention it deserves. Delays tend to cascade. Printers, for example, may put a book aside if galleys are not returned on schedule. In this way, a three-day delay in returning proofs to production can easily lead to a two-week delay in the return of corrected proofs from printer to publisher. Almost before anyone realizes what is happening, the book is four weeks late coming from the bindery, and it may have missed a valuable part of the selling season. The blame for this can be apportioned only so far; ultimately, the editor-manager is responsible for riding herd on everyone else.

Finally, the editor metamorphoses into a marketer. The person who knows most about a book often is its best sales promoter. It is the editor's responsibility, first, to make sure that the people in the marketing department understand the book and its sales potential and, second, to supply them with all the information and material they need for an effective selling job. Editors who wash their hands of this part of the job are doing their authors a disservice. Most books need all the help they can get. Some books may succeed despite editorial inattention, but success usually is the result of someone working hard to make it happen.

The Acquisition Process

The editor's involvement as advocate for a book begins some time before the work is formally acquired by the publishing firm. The idea for the book may be broached to the editor in various ways, perhaps in the form of a letter from an author or in a conversation with a literary agent. If the editor likes the idea, he then will encourage a submission. This might consist of a memo or letter but more usually will be an outline and several sample chapters.

Editors also supply ideas *to* authors. Few editors are able to build successful lists out of what falls into their laps. Generally, editors have to help create the kinds of books they know their house needs and can sell effectively. Their ideas may grow out of their lives, their interests, and their activities, not only in the office, but in their so-called leisure time. They emerge from the editors' voracious reading of newspapers, magazines, books, cereal boxes, and whatever else is at hand; from dinner-table conversations; from their natural curiosity; and from their developed sense of what interests other people. More difficult than finding ideas is matching the right idea with the right author at the right time. Therein lies much of the art—and the pleasure—of being an editor.

Regardless of the source of the idea, the proposal for any new book will have to pass a series of hurdles before a contract is offered. The decision-making process varies from company to company, but the first hurdle is always the editor. If the editor likes a proposal or manuscript and decides to become its sponsor, other people, as has been noted, probably will have a say in the final decision. These may include other editors, the sales or marketing manager, the subsidiary rights director, and the publisher. In many trade editorial departments, the editors meet regularly to discuss new projects, and such meetings frequently are attended by the key marketing people too. All participants will feel free to give their opinions, though not everyone will have read all the proposals or manuscripts at hand.

While few editors can offer a contract to an author on their own initiative, they are almost always free to say no. And that is what most of them say most of the time. The reasons are various: The manuscript is poorly written; it is on a subject of little interest to the audience for which the house publishes; the company has a competing title on its backlist or under contract; several other books are already available on the subject, including one or two that are excellent; a similar book was published three years ago and was a dismal failure; the subject is good, but the style is somewhat dull and the presentation disorganized; the manuscript presents too many problems, and the editor simply doesn't have the time or inclination to take on another complicated editorial project; the author has the reputation of being a difficult person to deal with. And so on.

When editors are attracted by a manuscript, they will ask themselves certain questions about why it *is* publishable. Is the proposal or manuscript written in an acceptable style? Is the idea for the book exciting, and is the author likely to be able to carry it off? Is there an identifiable audience for the book? Is there a need for it, a reason for its existence, and will people or institutions really want to buy it? If the answers to these questions are positive, the editor must try to visualize the finished book, ascertain its sales potential, and obtain an estimate of the cost of producing it. Can the company sell it for a price that will be attractive to the intended audience, pay the author a royalty, and still make a profit? And finally, does the company have the marketing expertise to reach the target audience and sell enough copies to make the whole endeavor worthwhile? In effect, is this book right for this house, or would it be better published elsewhere?

Editors normally get help in answering at least some of these questions. In some houses, for example, a submission is typically read by more than one person in the house and perhaps by one or more outside readers as well. The number of readings depends in part on the seniority and track record of the sponsoring editor, whether the subject is so specialized that hardly anyone but the sponsoring editor is qualified to render an opinion, the length of the submission (short proposals are likely to receive more readings because they take less time to read), and the size of the prospective investment for the house (a book that can be signed up for an advance of five thousand dollars probably will not be considered in as much detail or by as many people as one that will require an advance of fifty thousand dollars or more).

Often the trade editor will solicit opinions from other departments— from sales and subsidiary rights in particular—even when this is not formally required. The sales manager's estimate of the advance (or prepublication) sale of the book usually determines not only the economic viability of the project but how large a royalty advance can be offered the author—an important factor if several other publishers are competing for the title. The subsidiary rights manager's assessment of the chances of making a book club or paperback reprint sale also weighs heavily at most companies. The publicity department may also be consulted if it appears that the book's success will depend largely on the promotional effort. In some cases, the author may be brought in for an interview so that the publicity manager can offer an informed opinion about how well this writer will come across on TV or radio.

Negative appraisals from one or even all of the noneditorial departments may not be enough to kill a project (depending, of course, on the procedures and pecking orders within the company), but the editor nevertheless will usually woo these colleagues. Not many editors have the clout to override an experienced sales manager, and the prophecies of sales managers tend to be self-fulfilling.

If the proposed project is approved, the editor will be authorized to negotiate a contract with the author or the author's agent. Typically, the editor will be empowered to offer an advance up to a certain maximum, with the understanding that an attempt will be made to persuade the author or agent to accept less. Throughout the negotiations, as well as at later stages in the publishing process, the editor must walk a very thin line. On the one hand, it is crucial that he build a relationship of mutual trust with the author, and to some extent the editor's efforts to see that the author receives an advance that truly reflects the quality and sales potential of the manuscript will affect their future dealings. On the other hand, the editor is duty bound to act in the best interests of the house. This means conserving the company's capital and maximizing profits by minimizing expenses.

The Editor's Work Load

Once the contract is signed, the project becomes part of the flow in the editor's pipeline. Despite all the emphasis often put on acquiring, the editor's work has actually only now begun. Acquisitions are easy for company managers to count when the time comes to hand out promotions or pay raises, and they are obviously important. But to measure editorial effectiveness only in terms of acquisitions or title output is to exhibit a misunderstanding of what it is that editors do. The typical editor handles, in one way or another, from forty to perhaps one hundred or more titles and authors a year. And the longer the editor has been on the job, the higher the total will be.

Because an editor is responsible for all phases of a book's creation, it follows that at any one moment he is overseeing a large number of books at different stages of development. Some will be virtually completed, with the editing and copyediting done and ready to go to press. Others will be finished manuscripts, neatly boxed and sitting on a shelf or in a briefcase, waiting to be read. Some will be partial manuscripts, whose authors are impatient for editorial comments—and for payment of the advance installments that may be due at the halfway mark. Others will be in the proposal stage, and more will just be ideas, still in search of authors. Altogether, these books may represent a two- to three-year supply above and beyond the fifteen or so titles per year on the typical trade editor's list of publications.

Even this does not exhaust the editor's work load. Early in a book's life, long before actual publication, the editor will start beating the drums within the house, trying to get publicity, sales, rights, and advertising people to give attention to a title that might otherwise be lost in the shuffle. If books aren't in stock in Cleveland when the author hits town on a publicity tour, the editor is likely to hear about it before anyone else—often at the top of a frustrated author's voice. Six months to a year after publication, it will be the editor who is saddled with the chore of explaining the mysteries of the royalty statement, tracking down the missing check from a specialty book club, and trying to respond to the author's anguished complaint that the book is no longer available in bookstores. It may also be at just about this time that the editor is involved in discussions with the author about her next book.

Three to five years later, in the case of a nonfiction book that has shown staying power in the market, the editor will consider the possibility of issuing a new updated edition. If this proves feasible, then the whole process will begin anew. On the other hand, if the book goes out of print—and the selling life of many a trade book is less than a year nowadays—it will be the editor's unhappy task to inform the author. Thus the editor who helped give birth to the book may often find himself presiding over the last rites: delivery of a specified number of copies to the author (usually ten, assuming someone at the warehouse has thought to save them); retrieval of the films used for printing the book, if the author wishes to purchase them (a common contractual right, sometimes forgotten by production people); and whatever nagging is necessary to ensure that the contracts department produces on demand a formal letter canceling the original agreement and returning the publishing rights to the author.

The editor does all these things for the books of the past and for the books of the future, while somehow managing to get to press the books of the present. And every year, as new books are published and the editor's personal backlist grows, the total obligations mount too. The more books, the more things can go wrong. Each problem lands first on the editor's desk, and each takes time to resolve. Letters and telephone calls are likely to be received every day that will necessitate some kind of action on behalf of one or more of the previously published books that remain in the editor's care. This is one of the main reasons that editors are chronically behind in their work. It also helps explain why they do so much of their reading and editing at home. Office hours tend to be taken up with letter writing, phone calls, meetings, and follow-up on the physical details of overseeing so many books. Hence, the bulging briefcase for taking the manuscripts home, where most of the real editorial work is done.

The Editing Process

The dynamics of the author-editor relationship tend to cast the editor, no matter how young and green, in a parental role, as previously pointed out. It is perhaps not so surprising then that some editors occasionally treat authors as though they were children—and not very bright ones at that. This is of course a serious error. To the extent that the editor assumes the parental role, that role must be one of a very wise parent indeed. And this gets to the heart of the editorial process.

The chief function of the editor is to help the author write the best book of which she is capable. The editor may advise, suggest, cajole, criticize, and praise, but has to remember at each step of the way that it is the author's book, not the editor's, and that it is the author's name and reputation that are on the line.

The wise editor will carefully define each editorial problem that has been identified, explain why a particular solution might be a good one, and try to persuade the author to make the change in her own words. If the editor's reasoning is sound and the comments are made with tact, most authors will adopt most of the suggestions or will at least recognize the problem and devise other, often better solutions. Sometimes the editor may find it necessary, for one reason or another, to play a more active role—to rewrite parts of the manuscript, for example. Again, this must be done as unobtrusively as possible and in the author's own style and vocabulary.

Reviewers may notice poor editing or lack of editing, but when the editing is good, only the author should know. The other side of this coin, alas, is that good manuscript editors seldom receive real recognition. Because their best work is seamless, in effect, it may be difficult for corporate managers—unless they also have served as editors—to appreciate just how valuable good editing is. Even for editors themselves, good editing becomes almost an act of faith. One assumes that good editing does count even though it is invisible.

LEVELS OF EDITING

There are different levels of editing, but the principles just discussed apply to each of them. Whether the editor is doing substantive editing, line editing, or copy editing, the prime object should be to make sure that the author's voice comes across as clearly and forcefully as possible. Theoretically, substantive editing concentrates on the content and overall shape, organization, or conception of a book—on the big things, in other words. Line editing proceeds more methodically, focusing on details of content and style page by page, paragraph by paragraph, line by line. Copy editors are charged with final preparation of manuscripts for the printer, including responsibility for spelling, punctuation, fine points of grammar, consistency of style, incidental fact checking, and minor polishing and tightening to eliminate ambiguities, unnecessary repetitions, and so on.

In practice, distinctions among the different levels of editing tend to be blurred, depending on the styles of different houses and individual editors. Many so-called manuscript or substantive editors spend much time going through the text line by line, and many copy editors are alert and caring enough to ask substantive questions that the editors themselves somehow overlooked. Styles vary even among acquisition editors: Some of them work closely with authors throughout all phases of the creation of a book; others focus only on signing up new projects and turn over the nitty-gritty manuscript work to junior editors, outside free lances, or copy editors.

When a contracted manuscript comes into the house, its safe arrival should be acknowledged promptly. If the editor does not already know the author, this is a good time to introduce himself and to set the tone of friendly, interested cooperation for the relationship that will develop between them. The editor should also try to give the author at least a rough estimate of when to expect to receive editorial comments.

Then the editor should examine the book contract and the file, especially if he himself did not initiate or acquire the project, so as to determine how well the author has fulfilled the goals established at the outset. For example, has the manuscript come in at the right length? Were any changes in the plan for the book agreed upon while it was being written? Is the author obligated to deliver any artwork? And how much (if any) additional advance money is due once the editor has determined that the manuscript is acceptable for publication?

The actual process of editing may take anywhere from several weeks to several months, depending on the size and complexity of the manuscript and on the editor's work load and priorities. A common rule of thumb is that editing of relatively well prepared manuscripts proceeds at the rate of about ten pages an hour. This is a very rough average, of course. An editor may whiz over twenty pages in an hour, only to spend a great deal of time agonizing over a single page, paragraph, sentence, or even word. And the editing itself usually moves by fits and starts; rarely will an editor have the luxury of devoting several hours at a stretch to work on a particular manuscript. In general, nonfiction probably consumes more editorial time than fiction, especially if the editor feels obliged to double-check facts. But every manuscript is unique, and each presents a unique set of editorial problems.

EDITORIAL TECHNIQUES

There probably are as many editorial techniques as there are editors. Some editors make notes in the margins of manuscripts. Others would be lost without a supply of gummed tags, which can be attached with messages to the pages of a manuscript. Still others like to prepare long memos or critiques for the author, discussing a manuscript page by page as well as in overall terms.

The preferred approach is to skim the entire manuscript, or a large portion of it, to get an overview of the book before going back to page one and beginning to make detailed notes. This method helps the editor to see and evaluate the author's organization, pace, and style before beginning to focus on details.

It is important that the editor commit all comments to writing. Otherwise there is the possibility that the editor will forget at least some of what he meant to say or that the author will manage to hear only what she wants to hear—or indeed that both parties will misunderstand each other. The author will benefit much more from written comments that can be pondered in solitude than from spoken ones. At the same time, if a manuscript is seriously deficient and in danger of being rejected, the editor must—in fairness to the author and for legal reasons as well— begin creating the kind of written record that will justify a contract cancellation.

Editors usually choose to transmit their comments to authors in stages, especially if the manuscript is lengthy and if the editor and author have not worked together before. The author's reaction to the editing on the initial section of the manuscript, usually accompanied by a general memo or letter discussing any overall problems the editor has identified, will guide the editor in completing the task. The editor will have learned how much leeway exists in making changes in the manuscript, how well the author accepts criticism, and whether or not author and editor really have the same conception of the book and its intended audience.

Some editors try very hard to make their authors into friends; others prefer to erect a firm barrier between their professional and personal lives. But whatever the editor's style in this regard, he must be very careful about the tone in which advice and especially criticism are given, remembering also to give praise where it is due. In particular, the editor should avoid the temptation to lecture the author or to deliver a string of judgmental decrees. All editorial comments should be clearly and carefully explained so that the author will at least understand the editor's reasoning and, better, realize that the editor's suggestion will strengthen the work. If all has gone reasonably well in this initial phase, the editor will have created a feeling of confidence and trust on the author's part, and this should be the beginning of a good working relationship.

In addition to examining the manuscript for content, organization, and style, the editor will simultaneously bear in mind certain other concerns: Does this manuscript present any legal problems? For example, has one of the characters in a novel been modeled so closely after a real person that there may be a threat of libel? If the author of a nonfiction work has quoted extensively from other published sources, has there been proper crediting of the sources, and should permission be obtained for these extracts or do the quotations fall within the hazy realm of fair use?

While reading the manuscript for content, the editor asks himself a variety of other questions: Does the manuscript cover the subject fully or has something been left out? What is the quality of information presented—is the manuscript the product of original research or thinking or just a tired rehash of what everyone already knows? Is the level of exposition right for the intended audience?

It helps, of course, if the editor has at least passing familiarity with the subject under discussion, but most editors are generalists: They know a little bit about everything. Often, therefore, they will have to rely on their powers of logical analysis to determine if and when the author is going astray. When authors are on shaky ground, internal contradictions almost always start appearing in their manuscripts. It is up to the editor to spot these—to realize that a statement on page 193, say, contradicts what was being reported on page 16. If the editor finds many flaws of this sort or if the manuscript is in a particularly technical or controversial area, it may be wise to have it vetted for factual accuracy by an outside expert.

Throughout, the editor should be continually looking for and seeking to repair mistakes or misstatements. A reader who has found the author out in one error will begin doubting everything else, no matter how well founded. The same rule applies to fiction, where a single misstep can shatter the reader's belief in the world the author has created. In either case, the editor, like a good squire, will try to ensure that there are no chinks in the author's armor of credibility.

The editor also must worry about organization. Does one point follow logically from another? Would the manuscript be improved if material in chapter 10, say, were transferred to chapter 20? Has the author omitted any links in the chain of reasoning that extends throughout the book?

The editor should try to take the position of the reader who may come to the book knowing nothing at all about the subject beforehand. This means that the editor should not hesitate to question the author about anything that seems unclear, even if the questions sound somewhat simpleminded, since these are often the same points that could trouble the reader. In a real sense, the editor is here acting in yet another role—that of the reader's advocate.

Obviously the manuscript should be clearly and grammatically written, and it should be a pleasure to read as well. An editor can make a manuscript correct in form, but cannot impart good style to a manuscript that lacks it. Even for novice writers, style is as personal and individual as fingerprints. A writer's manner of expression reflects that person's cast of mind and outlook on the world. It is beyond the editor's province to tamper with a writer's style, other than to comment on ways in which it might seem unsuited to the subject at hand. In this sense, style almost has to be accepted, or rejected, in toto.

Significant improvements in exposition can be made, however, by helping the author to tighten, polish, and rearrange sentences and thoughts. Much of this work may be entrusted to a good copy editor. Among the things the editor or copy editor will look for are the following:

- Does the author know how to construct a paragraph effectively, leading off with a topic sentence?

- Has the author missed opportunities to balance sentences and thoughts with parallel clauses?
- Are there times when the author has chosen a word that does not express the thought precisely?
- Does the author have a tendency (as most do) to overuse certain words, phrases, or constructions so that they lose their rhetorical punch?
- Does the manuscript suffer from mixed metaphors, malapropisms, or other infelicitous phraseology?
- Are transitions from one thought to another logical and smooth?

Weeding out flaws of this sort will not automatically produce a book with elegant style, but it should result in one that is more pleasurable to read and easier to comprehend. The author's thesis, whatever it is, will be strengthened at least to the extent that linguistic distractions are removed.

When working on a manuscript, the editor has to be quite certain that all changes he makes are genuine improvements. Manuscripts can be disimproved, too. It is all too easy to recast a cloudy sentence and in doing so distort the author's meaning or introduce a factual error. When changing a particular word for another, the editor must check to see that the new word does not appear two sentences later. More important but much more difficult to explain, the editor must see that any changes in words or construction are in the author's voice, that the editing, once again, is "invisible."

The primary question for the editor is how well the author has accomplished what she set out to do. Vague dissatisfaction on the editor's part is not sufficient cause for making a change in a manuscript or for requesting that one be made. The editor may not be called upon to articulate each problem precisely and justify the proposed change to the author, but it should be theoretically possible to do this.

While avoiding the temptation to make changes for changes' sake, the editor also must be sure to let the author know in detail exactly what has to be done. The editor cannot pass silently by a passage that needs work, hoping that the author will recognize the trouble and make the necessary revisions. To the contrary, the author will interpret silence as acceptance. In this respect, the editor serves to some extent as the author's conscience. Writing is hard work, and it is only human for tired authors occasionally to submit copy in the hope that it will pass the editor even though they know in their hearts that it does not represent their best efforts.

Only in the most extreme cases should the editor actually run part of a manuscript through his own typewriter. Unless the editor is very skilled at duplicating the author's style, rewriting to this extent tends to introduce too much change into the manuscript. And it also takes time—more time, probably, than the editor can rationalize spending on most manuscripts.

If a manuscript is so seriously deficient that much rewriting is required, the editor usually should try to get the author to do it—bearing in mind, however, that the chances of obtaining an acceptable manuscript tend to diminish with successive tries. If the author doesn't succeed on the first or second try, the editor probably should be thinking of more radical solutions, such as bringing in a free-lance editor/writer to help or rejecting the manuscript as unsatisfactory and canceling the contract.

Again, the editor has to realize that he is distinctly fallible. Not all editorial suggestions will be equally good, and the editor has to count on the author's ability to separate the wheat from the chaff. In fact, the author's acceptance of every suggestion may well be a sign of trouble, indicating that she is uncertain about what she is doing or—worse—that she simply doesn't care about the book.

COPYEDITING

Occasionally a manuscript will present so few problems that it can be sent directly to the copy editor. Then, after copyediting is completed, the author can answer whatever questions the copy editor has raised along with the editor's minor queries, all in one operation. Usually, however, there are enough editorial questions to require that the manuscript be sent to the author so that they can be resolved before copyediting begins.

When returning the manuscript to the author, the editor should establish several guidelines. First, the author should be asked to respond to all queries, preferably by making legible changes directly on the manuscript, but without removing any tags if these have been used. Being able to refer to the original questions will be a great help to the editor when going over the author's changes. Second, the author should be asked not to erase any of the editor's marks on the manuscript and to use a different color from that used by the editor when making any additional changes. This will enable the editor to identify the changes at a glance, thus greatly speeding the final stage of the editing process. (The copy editor, in turn, should use a third color—and all three should use colors that will photocopy well.) Finally, any pages retyped by the author should be clipped to the original versions so that the editor will be sure to read them.

Assuming that the author has answered all questions satisfactorily, and that the illustrations, captions, and all other materials are in hand, the next step usually is to begin copyediting. At this time, too—perhaps even before, in the case of an art book or one that is unusually complex in other ways—a copy of the manuscript should go to the design department. In both instances, the editor should write background memos introducing the project to the copy editor and the designer and specifying the work to be done. Many houses have established release or transmittal forms for this purpose.

The memo to the copy editor should explain just how much leeway he has. Is every word sacred to the author (or the editor), or may the copy editor make minor changes in the text without arousing the wrath of either? Or—as sometimes happens—is the copy editor expected to rewrite as necessary to eliminate repetitions and clarify ambiguous phraseology? The editor also should warn the copy editor of any quirks or special preferences of the author that may deviate from established house style. Should British spellings be retained or changed? Does the author tend to use ellipses, brackets, and quotes incorrectly? Does the author have any favorite words or expressions that are overworked, which the editor hopes the copy editor will weed out? Does the author tend to allow participles to dangle? How much, if any, fact checking should the copy editor do?

The line between editing and copy editing, always blurred, has become even less distinct now that many firms are relying on in-house and free-lance copy editors to do more and more of the work editors once did. Even if the acquiring editor does all the editorial work on the manuscript, though, it is not usually a good idea to edit and copy edit simultaneously. It is difficult to do all the substantive things an editor is supposed to do and at the same time double-check spelling, grammar, and punctuation; style a manuscript for the printer; spot check facts; and perhaps do some rewriting. Almost inevitably, one function or the other—editing or copyediting—will suffer when the same person tries to perform both at the same time.

Ideally, the copy editor (and the proofreader as well) should be almost neurotically compulsive, with a fine eye for detail and a consuming passion for accuracy and consistency. Attention to detail must go hand in hand with good judgment, however. Correct punctuation is inferior to the text, which it is intended to illuminate, not to obscure. "Comma chasing" should not become an end in itself. For certain things, there is only one correct way; for others, there are alternatives that are equally, or almost equally, acceptable. In those cases, the editor or copy editor can make an arbitrary decision, sometimes based on the author's preference or the kind of manuscript involved. The important thing then is to stick with the decision—to be consistent in the treatment of that element throughout the manuscript.

Consistency, in fact, can be thought of as the watchword of copyediting. One of the copy editor's most important tasks is to make sure that a manuscript is consistent in styling—that is, in the use of punctuation, in the spellings of words where variants are permissible, in the placement and value of elements like headings and subheadings. But the goal is not consistency purely for its own sake. Consistency is not an arbitrary or aesthetic trait but an aid to communication; it can make the crucial difference between a clear and readable manuscript and one in which the author's meaning is clouded, confusing, and hard to decipher.

Probably because their work requires close attention to small details, copy editors frequently are less flexible than they should be. Some are even subject to fits of know-it-all arrogance (a disease that occasionally strikes editors, too). The most common and dangerous pitfall in copy-editing is for the copy editor to show off supposed "superiority" by making sarcastic or otherwise inappropriate comments on the manuscript. Instead of persuading authors to accept changes, such remarks are more likely to cause them to dig in their heels. Before you know it, the copy editor and the author have begun a major war, and the person caught in the middle is the editor. Thus, editors who want to save themselves grief are well advised to make sure that copy editors do their jobs without antagonizing authors.

Unfortunately, copy-editing skills often are not honored or rewarded, as they once were. Some firms and some editors, intent on crashing manuscripts through the production process, are more than content with a fast and necessarily light copy-editing job, regardless of what the manuscripts need. And if the copy editor asks too many questions or takes too much time on a manuscript, editors will become downright angry. Not surprisingly, the copy editors, sensing what is wanted in such instances, may well hold their comments to a minimum. In the end, no one is well served.

After a manuscript comes back from the copy editor, the editor always should check to see what has been done, or not done, before sending it on to the author. The editor may want to add some comments to offset those of the copy editor. In extreme cases, the editor may remove some of the copy editor's notes or otherwise repair the copyediting before presenting the manuscript to the author. As with the edited manuscript, and for the same reason, the author should be asked not to remove the copy editor's tags. The author should also be asked to refrain from making changes in the copyediting, particularly of recurring items. Chances are that the author would catch some but not all of the items, with the result that inconsistencies would creep into the text.

It is essential, of course, that the author see and approve every change that has been made by both editor and copy editor before the manuscript goes to the typesetter. Courts have upheld authors in cases where publishers neglected to gain the author's consent. Moreover, an extra word can be penciled in or deleted from a manuscript with no trouble at all, but when the book gets into galleys or pages, each minor change may cost several dollars—more, if redummying is required. Even worse, late changes may lead to the introduction of new mistakes when the typesetter resets lines.

Design and Production

The editor usually plays a role in planning the physical appearance of a book as well as its content, although degrees of editorial responsibility vary from company to company. In some cases, the design department is an appendage of production, with no real authority of its own; in other cases, the house art director is a powerful individual with a small kingdom of his own, who must be approached by editors on bended knee. Even in the latter case, however, the editor can greatly influence what is done simply by virtue of being the chief—and sometimes the only—source of information in the house about the book and the audience for which it is intended. Knowledge really is power—if exercised correctly.

When the manuscript is initially sent to production for design, the accompanying memo should list all the elements of the book, beginning with the title page, copyright page, table of contents, and any other front matter. The number of pages in the manuscript should be listed, and the designer's attention should be called to the existence and location of heads and subheads, illustrations, footnotes, and any other special features. If the book includes notes at the back, a bibliography, appendixes, or an index, these features also should be mentioned. (In due course, a separate memo to the indexer may also be in order.)

The editor must try to give the designer some sense of what he thinks the completed book should look like or the overall impression it should convey. This often can be done by referring to previously published books, whether of the editor's own house or another. Special problems also should be discussed: Is this a book for older people? In that case, the designer should be warned to pick a large and highly readable type face. Is the manuscript running long? The editor then may plead with the designer to figure out some way of cramming everything into a particular length so that the price of the book doesn't have to be raised to cover the extra paper costs. Is this a cookbook, a how-to book, a mystery, an experimental novel? The design should be different in each instance, and it is well for the editor to provide guidance. At the same time, the editor should beware of the dangers of overspecifying. Designers are artists, and they will be happier in their work and likely to do a better job if they are given some freedom to determine how general editorial goals are to be achieved visually.

These rules also apply to the design of jackets and paperback covers. Again, the editor should supply a memo describing any special elements that are important. The art director also will need complete copy for the front of the jacket or cover—title, subtitle, author's name, and any descriptive tag line, blurb, or quote—before beginning work on the design.

The chief problem in selecting jacket art in most companies is that too many people are involved and frequently no two of them will agree. Since the jacket is a prime tool in selling a book, the marketing department often has the final say in selecting the design. Even then, it will be helpful if the editor remembers such basics (which, in the heat of debate, may well be forgotten by others) as whether the design is striking enough to be noticed from six feet away in a crowded bookstore, whether the title lettering will still be legible when reproduced in postage-stamp-size ads, whether the colors of the jacket will translate well in black-and-white reproductions, and whether the jacket is likely to create a favorable impression when held up briefly before a camera during a TV interview.

Marketing

The editor, as chief in-house advocate for a book and principal source of information about it, is in an excellent position to influence the way in which it is marketed. And with the position goes the responsibility. Today, many books are not so much published as cast adrift. When a house is putting out two hundred or more titles a year, it can be very difficult for the people in the various marketing areas—sales, publicity, promotion, and advertising—to focus on more than a handful of them. Each editor must try (in competition to some extent with the other editors) to be sure that the marketing people give his books the attention they deserve.

The editor can influence the marketing department in a variety of ways, but first and probably foremost by oral reports at formal staff meetings and in informal contacts with key people. Conventional wisdom has it that word of mouth is the single most important factor in the sale of books after they are published, and it seems that it is just as important in selling books within the house *before* they are published.

The editor must be careful not to strain the limits of credibility.

Everyone in the business knows that not all manuscripts are equally good, and the editor who waxes enthusiastic about the merits of every manuscript will soon be treated like the boy who cried wolf too often—when a truly good manuscript does appear, this editor's praise for it may be ignored.

On the whole, it probably is better to undersell a book than oversell it—to be clear about its strengths and its salability but without raising unreasonable expectations. Obviously the editor should not keep silent when good things can be said about a book—things that will color the perceptions that marketing people have of it. These perceptions, in turn, will affect decisions on such important matters as printing quantities, advertising budgets, and the extent of promotional efforts.

The most important occasions when an editor's words may influence the marketing of a book are at the company's seasonal sales conference, when forthcoming titles are presented to the field sales force, and at the in-house presales conference (sometimes called the "preprint") that often precedes that meeting. The goal at both meetings is the same: to define as succinctly as possible what a particular book's sales points are. The editor's "brief" for the book should include a summary of its contents as well as a description of the intended audience. If there are competing titles in the field, the editor should be armed with evidence, including detailed comparisons, to prove that the new book is preferable. The main aim is to develop "sales handles"—short statements distilling the reasons for a book's existence that can be used by the sales representatives to persuade their customers to stock it.

In effect, the editor has to sell the sellers and, in doing so, give them the ammunition they need in order to present the book to the world at large. The editor must remember that the sales representative may have no more than thirty seconds to devote to each title during the course of a two- or three-hour call on a bookstore buyer. Thus, the editor who can reduce the reasons for buying a particular book to two or three short, punchy, memorable sentences or phrases is doing a great service for that book and its author.

When preparing for a sales conference, the editor often will find it helpful to return for inspiration to the original source—the author. Sometimes the editor will find a useful statement of the importance of the book in the author's original proposal or in the first or last chapter of the final manuscript. It also pays to check the publicity questionnaire, which most firms ask their authors to fill out, summarizing their books and explaining what is new and different about them. This material often makes excellent grist for the editor's mill.

The editor also helps out in the marketing of books by writing (or overseeing the writing of) catalog and jacket flap copy. These items cover much the same ground but from different points of view—the first being prepared with the needs of the company's sales reps and of booksellers in mind, the second aimed at the ultimate purchaser of the book. The catalog copy should describe the book and its key sales points, but without duplicating the pitch the editor plans to make at the sales conference. The flap copy must also describe the books, but in such a way as to entice the potential reader to buy the book. If well done, it also is likely to reappear in reviews, sometimes word for word, particularly in smaller newspapers that do not have regular reviewers. Because of the potentially wide dissemination of jacket copy, the job of writing or editing it is an important editorial function.

As the time nears for the book to be published, the editor must keep abreast of what other departments are doing—or not doing. If something is going wrong, the editor should try to put it right. With so many hands working on the project in so many different departments, the potential for mistakes is high. Just to list a few typical problems is to suggest their amazing diversity. For example: Have bound galleys been sent to friends of the author or of the house in the hope of obtaining advance quotes for use in advertising and promotion? Many editors take on this task to be sure that the letters sent to potential sources of quotes are as persuasive as possible. No doubt the subsidiary rights department will send galleys to the Book-of-the-Month Club and Literary Guild—but have they remembered that this book also is a candidate for the History Book Club, the Behavioral Science Book Club, the Music Book Society, or one of the other specialized clubs? It always pays for the editor to double-check.

Perhaps the company controls British rights, and the editor met eighteen months ago with a visiting British publisher who expressed interest in this title. The editor naturally wrote a memo at the time to the head of the foreign rights department, but since then the manager of this department and her top assistant have departed the firm. The new people should get a copy of the original memo as a reminder.

The publicity department probably will have sent galleys to *Publishers Weekly, Kirkus,* and *Library Journal,* whose early reviews are influential in the trade, but what about the magazine editor–friend of the author who promised a plug for the book if galleys were received early enough? It is wise never to assume that this sort of thing will be taken care of automatically, even in the best-run companies.

And now, getting closer to publication day, what about the autographing party that is supposed to take place at the Space Center in Huntsville, Alabama? Two hundred books are supposedly en route by truck, but forty-eight hours before the big event it turns out that no books are there and a very worried author is on the phone to the publisher. The person at the other end of the phone is, of course, the editor, who must then talk to the responsible departments about locating where in the distribution pipeline the missing shipment is, whether the original order can be moved to Huntsville in time, and, if not, whether it is possible to beat the deadline with a second shipment from a regional distributor or—horrible to contemplate because so costly—another shipment from the company's main warehouse, this time by air freight. All this will involve at least six telephone calls and several hours, during which time the editor will, of course, not actually be doing any editing.

*   *   *

And so it goes. At every step along the way, the editor has to be prepared to act as general coordinator, universal backstop, and constant nudge— all in the interest of ensuring that the book is published in the best possible manner. The entire process, from the inception of the idea to publication, requires a great deal of time and careful attention to the most minute details. The editor's responsibilities are so encompassing that it sometimes seems that the actual editing, in the sense of working on manuscripts, is just the tip of the iceberg of editorial duties.

Precisely because the job is so complex and demanding, however, the satisfactions in doing it well can be very great. When a book comes off press, the editor knows better than anyone else in the house how much effort went into the making of it, and he will take special pleasure in the finished work. And if the book is reviewed well and sells well, the editor's pride and joy will be exceeded only by the author's. These feelings are good ones, and it is principally because of them, not because of the pay (which is relatively low), that lines tend to form whenever editorial jobs open up. For all its daily difficulties, editing continues to be one of the most rewarding of professions.

CHAPTER FOUR

The Editor's Job
in Trade Publishing

ELISABETH SIFTON

Many years ago, when book publishing was a simpler and less competitive business than it is now, there were no editors as such. Publishers, aided by skeleton staffs, chose books they wanted to issue, delivered them to the typesetter, quickly printed and distributed them, and then looked for more. Writers sent their manuscripts to the publishers' offices and eventually received and corrected their proofs; thereafter the business of seeing these diverse scripts into bound-book form was fairly straightforward. Obviously there were people at each firm whose special competence was finance, production, proofreading, or sales, but there was hardly need for a specialist on books.

Even then, though, publishers had part-time or full-time employees called readers, whom they depended upon to judge the many manuscripts that flooded into their offices. These readers were often writers themselves, men and women of letters, novelists, critics, or scholars—people who were knowing about books, shrewd about writers, and enthusiastic about literature. Eventually they also became useful in helping the writers to get their work into its best final form. Simultaneously they were drawn into helping the publisher make the basic publishing decisions: how much money to spend to acquire what kinds of literary property.

Thus did the shape of a book editor's work evolve—borrowing freely from the fraternal role of a magazine or newspaper editor, in that one function is to decide what to print and to supervise the preparation of texts so that they suit the aims and standards of the publisher and the publication. Today, the editor in a trade-book publishing house seeks out writers and new books; negotiates to purchase the rights to books already written or to be written; monitors the progress of writers as their books are being completed—helping them in whatever way possible; makes the final decision as to whether each manuscript is acceptable for publication, suggesting revisions (whether large or small) if it could do

ELISABETH SIFTON is a vice president of Viking Penguin and publisher of Elisabeth Sifton Books.

with further improvement; supervises the manuscript's preparation for typesetting; acts as the author's principal advocate and representative within the firm, especially vis-à-vis the noneditorial colleagues whose support is essential to the success of the book; supervises (if she does not do it personally) the writing of blurbs, ads, jackets, and other descriptive material about the book; encourages and supports the author during the perilous moments when the book actually reaches the public—that is, when it is published.

It should be obvious that work of this kind must be undertaken by people who are sympathetic to writers and to books. But it is worth restating this basic prerequisite, for many pressures come to bear that cause the editor-author relationship to become or seem adversarial, and it is important that at heart it be quite the opposite. In essence, the editor must be the writer's best friend, constant reader, warm supporter, and loyal advocate.

Acquiring the Book

How does a trade editor go about finding authors? To begin with, a certain number will come along without the editor's lifting a finger. Every publishing house receives thousands of unsolicited manuscripts every year, and a cursory look through these will quickly reveal a small handful that are worth reading. Among these, some may be publishable but inappropriate for one reason or another; others may be possible candidates. Few published trade books originate in this so-called slush pile of unsolicited scripts, but still, there have been outstanding successes—Judith Guest's *Ordinary People* is a famous recent example—and the hope of finding gold in the dross encourages us all to continue the search.

Another source of manuscripts is the authors already published by the firm. Junior members of an editorial staff are frequently asked to join in looking after an already well established writer to whose work the company is committed. And a writer may have friends, students, relatives, and disciples to recommend to his publisher. This is one of the very best sources a publisher has: a happy author who advocates another writer whose work he admires. (Another version of this type of submission occurs when a writer who is unknown to the house admires a certain book the company has already published and thinks he might find a sympathetic reading for his own work, which, he believes, has a comparable or associated appeal.)

These sources are not part of some elitist and exclusionary network.

Personal enthusiasms and recommendations are woven into the very fabric of literary culture, and an editor should learn the weave; a quick scrutiny of publishers' lists will show that certain kinds of writers gravitate to certain companies, and clusters of associated writers may well end up under one imprint. But editors should be wary here: One should retain freedom of choice and maneuver and, while considering the most promising among recommended works, avoid being captured by cliques or overweening editorial views.

A third—and very important—source of writers and manuscripts is, of course, literary agents, whose job is to sell the work of their clients to publishers. Each publisher gets thousands of submissions from agents and must pick and choose among them.

A fourth source of books is other publishing houses. Every publishing company in the world collaborates with its rivals. Whether foreign, U.S., paperback, or hardcover, whether publishers of romances, westerns, avant-garde poetry, graphics, art books, or general books of fiction and nonfiction, these firms will buy and sell properties among themselves and will keep each other posted on new books. A British firm, for example, will look for a U.S. partner to share costs in producing a book to which it owns the world rights (and vice versa). And of course, the buying and selling of translation rights is still an important part of the publishing scene, although it is a perennial complaint that less and less of this is done. Similarly, paperback houses often look for hardcover publishers to take on the initial publication of a book they own or want to own; conversely, certain hardcover houses offer books to paperback firms whose collaboration (and available cash) they may need to acquire an expensive book or to assure its subsequent paperback publication. In all these transactions, the types of books submitted to a given house, among which an editor must choose, will be partly determined by the traditions and habits of the past, as well as by the present company's capabilities.

But no worthwhile editor will rely solely on passive modes of acquisition. One must go out and find books. Here the possibilities are limited only by the number of hours in the day. To begin with, one must treat all the sources I have mentioned actively instead of passively, and one must explore the potentialities that lie undiscovered but ready at hand. One must encourage published writers as to their future work— perhaps still undreamed of by the creators themselves. Here the editor will slowly learn the gentle art of timing, for it is folly, never mind rudeness, to push a writer to write something he does not want to write, to plan for a future book when he wants no plans at all—but equal folly to be indifferent to the future, deaf to the question that all writers in one way or another ask themselves all the time: What book will I write after *this* one?

Equally, one can't expect agents always to know which sort of book to show to which sort of editor: One must go out and talk to them oneself, find out who their clients are, describe one's interests, and ask them not only about their clients but for advice and counsel about books in general. It is imperative to let them know—to let anyone and everyone know—that one is always on the lookout for good books. (This brings up the vexed and delicate issue that people in the business call "raiding a list." It is unseemly and unprincipled to make energetic bids for books or authors under contract to another publishing firm; most good editors rightly believe that they publish not books but writers, that a long-standing partnership between a publisher and a writer is good for both parties. But it is certainly all right—indeed, it is generous and well mannered—to express enthusiasm for books published by a rival firm. If, in the future, an author becomes dissatisfied with his old publisher and wants a new one, and you believe you could make that author happy, *and* your enthusiasm is recollected, then you have simply proved that vigilant editors do everything they can to improve the publication of good books.)

The energetic editor will range beyond the easy marks—beyond the authors, agents, and companies with which her firm already does business. Good books can be found wherever good writing is found, and even the most fastidious editor will never forget that her central task is to read the written word omnivorously. In magazines and newspapers, in broadsheets, literary quarterlies, weekly and monthly glossies, in student publications, specialist organs, and learned journals—in all these places, book writers can be found. But one's search through the unending blizzard of periodicals must be discriminating: One can't go after writers who are unable to sustain the larger requirements of a book, or writers whose work one cannot publish well. The editor at a big trade house will not court a scholar whose monograph belongs with a university press, an editor of pulp westerns has a weak case with a writer of exquisitely wrought novellas, and a small regional publisher should not try to lure a writer whose first requirement is national or international distribution. On the other hand, it is silly to nurture preconceptions; talent crops up in unexpected forms and in unpromising circumstances.

No editor should forget *books* as a source for new publications, by which I mean not only untranslated masterpieces or an undiscovered glory that deserves republication in new form but also out-of-print books. The reissue of long-forgotten classics, or the republication in newly edited form of documents, fiction short and long, scholarship, journalism, poetry, and memoirs—this has been a regular part of literary culture for millennia.

But publishers agree that the central task is to find *un*published writing (although editors know all too well that a sadly large proportion of disgruntled writers are in fact unpublishable). Here the possibilities are virtually limitless. Students and teachers are one category: not only those at writing programs and courses, in creative-writing classes, or attending writers' conferences, but promising and gifted experts in other disciplines who are interested in writing for the general public. Diligent editors make a regular point of checking out these sources. Another category would be artists, public figures, politicians, athletes, activists, specialists, or eccentrics who are believed to have something to say. Certainly the public demand for "personality books" and autobiographies or memoirs is immense, and our culture seems to encourage any sentient person to believe he or she could write a book. Yet the technical requirements of book writing—every bit as demanding as those for painting a canvas, choreographing a ballet, or composing a string quartet—are often ignored, which is another reason why editors are useful, since in the end they may all but write the books these famous people put their names to. Still, one can find many wonderful good books in this category: There is *no* genre of book in which excellence cannot occur.

Yet the editor's enthusiasm should know bounds. After a while she may experience the slightly paranoid sense that everyone in the world either has just written a book or is about to complete one. It may be that one's cab driver, brother-in-law, piano teacher, or daughter's college professor have *all* written books they want one to publish. It is well at this point to remember that the world does not depend on books, that many of the greatest writers in the world never wrote books. Still, the fact is that in many informal and unexpected sources—at a party, at a child's school, at the dinner table, on a bus—one can find splendid book material that does oneself and the author proud.

Lastly, book editors should invent books. This is book editing in its most active mode—when an editor thinks up an idea for a book, figures out who would be a good author for it (if this is not intrinsic to the idea in the first place), and then persuades the writer to write it and the publishing company to publish it. The ideas can come from almost anywhere: from newspaper headlines, from a sense of public interest in some currently fashionable subject or concern, from other media (magazine articles, plays, television programs, lectures, performances of one sort or another, scientific experiments), or from hints buried in a writer's previous work that suggest excitement about a theme or subject to which he might devote full attention.

Making the Publishing Decision

Besides knowing where to find books or how to create them, an editor must know how to evaluate the various forms of books that arrive on her desk—often no more than mere hints of a hoped-for volume, sometimes a completed work.

The easiest situation to describe is nowadays the least frequent: the arrival of a full manuscript with the request that the editor read it and then recommend publication or not. When this pleasant circumstance arises, the editor is working with a known quantity.

Then what? A company decision will be made. What kind and how it is made depend on the structure and personality of the firm and on the editor in question. Paradoxically, the more likely it is that the firm wants the book, the more people will be involved in the decision to buy it.

Is the book already under contract? Or does the firm have an option on it? Has money been paid out? Or is the manuscript a brand-new surprise, a fresh possibility? What is the relation of this manuscript to the writer's other accomplishments? Is the author likely to write again, and what is his writing future likely to be? Does the book need expert outside evaluation? Is it so quirky or peculiar—either in the context of the firm's other books or in the context of the general culture—that it would be prudent to obtain more editorial readings? Is it ready for press or does it need line-by-line editing? Does it need structural reorganization? Does it have errors and flaws that the author could correct? that the author could but will not correct? that someone else could fix? Would elimination of its peculiarities also destroy the book's best features? Will the author abide by this editor's decisions? Will the book need a special sales effort, and in that case will the marketing people read it too? Or will its success depend upon sale through subsidiary markets—book clubs, magazines, paperback editions, foreign editions—in which case will the editor's colleagues in those fields read it? Will it earn the amount the author expects, wants, needs? Can the company afford a big, medium, or low risk, or none at all?

A good editor will ask most or all of these questions every time she recommends a book for publication or considers recommending one: Eventually, after years of doing this, the questions will become part of her "reading" of the book itself. Speculative rumination about how the book will fare, what other people might think about it, or how the book's qualities transcend or nullify these considerations is a kind of ground bass that supports and sets the key for an editor's evaluation.

Timing also plays into the business. A good editor will keep in mind the other books the company is publishing, for it is a waste of time to recommend a manuscript that is similar in subject, treatment, or purpose to one that is already on the list—unless repetition is wanted (as it is, in some cases) or there are other persuasive reasons to live with the juxtaposition.

Needless to say, general book knowledge is a vital ingredient in this part of the editorial task. One of the ways inexperienced young editors become old and wise is in championing books they find original but learn are old hat, books they find fashionable but discover are written in yesterday's mode, books they find compelling and yet, they are told, were better written by someone else years ago. This constant education should never cease, and it is one that draws editors and writers together, since together they face the immense burdens and the immense glories of the past, distant and immediate. Sometimes editors are quicker than writers to see that a given kind of book lacks the sharp cutting edge of originality. "There are certain books in a tradition which, after a while, everyone stops reading but no one can stop writing," Leslie Fiedler has written. "The less aware [the writer] is of these books, the more he is likely to submit to their pattern; and this is one of the best reasons for insisting that writers be educated."

The questions an editor asks herself or her colleagues about a book must be asked all the more urgently and answered all the more precisely if the situation is competitive—when the editor is only one of several, in competing companies, reading the manuscript at the same time. It used to be considered improper for a writer to send his work simultaneously to different publishers, but the sloth of slow-reading editors, the work load of even fast ones, and the advent of photocopying have changed all that; in truth it is probably more efficient and kinder to the writer to have these "multiple submissions."

Right away the editor must determine how the author, or the author's agent, will decide among his various suitors. In addition to the old questions, there are new ones: Will the author ask each publisher to make an offer and then take the best one? Or will each firm be given a chance to "improve" its offer once it sees what the other houses are willing to pay for the property? Is there a deadline for making an offer? How many rounds of bidding will there be? What, in short, are the rules of the game? Sometimes writers or their agents do not make these rules clear; the editor must insist that they do so before making any plans.

After the ground rules are established, the editor and her colleagues must judge the value of the book to the house and fix a price for it. No matter how the purchase is made—with a straightforward single offer or in repeated auctionlike bids—the editor must never forget the essential idea of what the book is and how it ought to be published, and of the writer and how he deserves to be treated, for this must govern what the publishing house does.

Matters become more complicated when a publishing house has to decide on a book without the manuscript in hand. An editor must develop diagnostic and prognostic skills, must learn to guess, on the basis of partial material, what the finished book will be like. For it is more and more true that writers come to publishers for financial as well as moral and editorial help *before* they start on a book. For writers who simply need time and money to do their work, the best source of income is still a readership, which is to say, a publisher. A publisher is an intermediary force between the public and the author, and the publisher's support gives some indication that a public exists for the writer's work and what that public is.

How is the editor to assess this as-yet unwritten work? Most editors insist on seeing a general scheme of the book as a whole and a sample of how it will be written. "Please show us an outline and sample chapters" is the well-known request. This sample material may be a long letter from author to editor or friend; a detailed, comprehensive chapter synopsis; or an uncompleted section, fully drafted, of the book to be. Editors should request or insist on textual material that is representative of the book and appropriate to the author's circumstance—material that is explicit enough to bind both author and publisher to a common understanding of what the book will be in the end.

The editor must also assess the likelihood that the author can pull it off—can in fact write the book and hand it in on time. And perforce the editor must do some business: How much money will the writer need? How much money is he likely to earn from its eventual sale?

Together with editorial and other colleagues, the editor will then decide whether the company wants to commission this unwritten work. Some editors want to sign up the kinds of books that are, at a given moment, doing well in the stores, that are popular with readers. Others want above all to support what is unknown and surprising and to avoid books that are à la mode (knowing that soon they will be passé). Both groups believe they can make money! The best publishers use both strategies or, even better, champion innovation in such a way as to suggest that it is either already successful or bound to be so tomorrow. Editorial equilibrium is continually reestablished and found anew on a balance between risk and prudence, between a desire to feed established tastes and interests in the reading public and to encourage the new, the uncertain, the innovative, the not yet proven.

Commissioning books is the trickiest of all editorial tasks: It calls for plain unvarnished skill in evaluating writers and books, but it also brings into play ineffable matters of spirit, culture, and commerce—an editor's wisdom, together with her knowledge of how to express her literary commitments in a businesslike way.

All the editorial work I have mentioned thus far adds up to only about half of what an editor actually does each day—and I should make it clear that the work is mostly negative; that is, an editor spends most of the time reading, reporting on, and then turning down books. Publishers pick only a tiny percentage of the thousands of manuscripts and proposals they receive. This work of evaluating books, whether negatively or positively, is the bread and butter in the editor's professional diet.

Editing the Manuscript

The other half of the editor's work is the spiritual nourishment in her business, the heart of it: By this I mean looking after the manuscripts and seeing them into bound-book form. Upon this effort the writers and their agents, let alone her employers, rightly measure much of an editor's value. Since this editorial work differs radically from one book to the next (and should), it is hard to describe it, and yet it is the part of the job that everyone most wants to grasp.

Let us begin with the task of reading the script. If the company did not buy the book until it was completed, then the editor knows what the book is like and knows whether changes will or can be made in the text. If the work was commissioned, then the editor has to read it against the expectations she (or, indeed, the writer) had of it at the beginning: Is the book up to scratch, is it what everyone imagined it would be, is it what the company can sell, or is it faulty in some way? All books, like people, have big mistakes in them, and even good books will reveal imperfections; sometimes one can live with these flaws, and other times one feels that the book won't work unless they can be fixed.

Let us suppose, for the sake of argument, that the manuscript seems just fine to the editor, that the author and everyone else is happy with it. What does the editor do then? Reads it again, nonetheless, and this time thinks about what the book is going to look like *as a book*. She thinks of the manuscript as a physical object and makes sure that in every mechanical sense it is ready to be given to the colleagues who will prepare it for the press. It must be legible, of course, but there is more to it than that. The editor should know exactly how long it is and should be sure that the parts, chapters, or any subdivisions make sense. She should have an idea of what sort of type design would be right and what kind of jacket would best suit the book and most enhance its commercial value; perhaps the author has wishes that should be taken into account here. The editor should be sure that all the needed illustrative material is there or know what has to be prepared and how (and who will pay for it); should circulate copies of the manuscript to her colleagues if that is called for; should predict likely legal problems—copyright, libel, invasion of privacy, and so on—and be ready to consult with attorneys if need be; should gauge how difficult or easy the copyediting, composition, and proofreading will be, in order to instruct her colleagues accordingly and estimate how long it will take to produce the book. The editor must know when the author is available for proofreading and whether he is likely to be slow or prompt.

The key here is to learn how to think sequentially and in anticipation of the steps that follow upon the first simple one of reading and accepting the manuscript for the house. A written work goes through a number of stages in its progress from manuscript to printed book, and it must be worked on by many different people—the managing editor, the copy editor, the production supervisor, the designer, the compositor, the proofreaders. It is the editor's job to make sure that all these people see the book and their work in regard to it clearly; that there are no ambiguities or uncertainties about what the end result is to be.

And then it is the editor's further task to see that this end—the physical object that is a bound book—is planned for and produced in a way that is suitable to the essential nature of the work. This is the deepest sort of commitment to the essence of the writer's vision and purpose—and thus does the editor represent the author's hopes and ambitions to the publishing house—but it is also sound business sense. One wants to avoid wasted motion, cancelled designs, ruined schedules, confusing instructions, and altered plans, for all these cost money; and one wants the book to come out looking most like itself, because that is the best way to sell it.

So in the first reading of the manuscript, the editor will keep all these matters well in mind. Even with the simplest text, the first reading must carry the weight of recognition of the book's future life; it is not a bad idea to have a kind of mental checklist of the details one will be coping with in the months to come and that one is going to have to handle shrewdly and efficiently if the book is to achieve its final, printed form. With each passing week, any problem will be more expensive and more cumbersome to resolve and will involve more and more people. It is easy to change a manuscript or a prospective schedule; it is still fairly easy to fix proofs, although much more expensive and now with greater pressure of time, since the publisher is by then committed to a production and selling schedule. It is hair-raisingly nasty to have to make major changes in a book when it is almost ready for press, when orders have already been placed for it in the stores, when catalogs and jackets have already been printed. Every editor keeps these harsh truths in mind from the start.

Going back to the first stage, let us suppose, again for the sake of argument, that the editor finds this script, which for the moment we shall imagine is a nonfiction work, flawed and wanting. What then? Maybe it is a simple matter of fixing a line, of changing, deleting, or adding single words or phrases. I think (some writers would disagree) that it is legitimate for the editor actually to change the manuscript if her intention is to correct simple error—a spelling or grammatical mistake, let us say. But these are minor flyspecks. If the "errors" are syntactical confusions or awkwardnesses that require rewriting to eliminate, factual inaccuracies the correction of which would affect the text in some way, illogicalities that demand rearrangement of sentences or phrases so that the argument is clear, or mixed metaphors or strained and implausible similes—then the editor can either point out the problem and request a change or actually indicate what the revision might be.

One of the things one has to learn is what is the best method of doing this for each author. Some authors hate the very idea of anyone else even marking their manuscripts; some are quite happy to entertain marginal queries; some are eager to have their prose improved; some only want to do this work collaboratively, with the editor and author hunched together over the manuscript and talking it out; others want to take home editorial memorandums that list the problems and brood over them in solitude. An editor must be ready, willing, and able to do the work whichever way the author wants—not only because that is courteous, but because it will bring the best results: the most conscientiously corrected script and the happiest writer.

In giving this close attention to the text, the editor should never propose or make changes that run counter to the writer's natural mode. It is a grand editorial ambition to expand and glorify the best aspects of a talent, but the editor should recognize a writer's natural limits and respect them. "Tenors, tenors," the great conductor Serge Koussevitzky is said to have implored the shrieking members of a choral group that was trying too hard, "do not give me more than you have!" Editors shouldn't ask writers for more than they have, and one important editorial skill is knowing what is the very best a writer can do and then getting him to write at that level as much as possible. "Not up to your usual standard," I have sometimes written in the margin of a given page— after all, maybe the writer was tired, angry, or despairing when writing that bit and will also recognize that it isn't up to snuff. So editors should read with a "nose," should sniff out the writer's essential rhythms and styles, and should make suggestions only when they are congruent with the evident intentions of the book.

I would like to add that the editor should also read the book and give advice to its writer on behalf of the eventual "general reader" who will pay money for it in the stores. Editors accumulate professional dope (literary wisdom) about how people read books, and they can help the writer by passing this knowledge along. Is the vocabulary plausible for the intended audience? Does the book presume more knowledge of a subject than any but a few experts possess? Is the reader asked to accept premises or ways of thinking that are hard to get used to, that need more explaining?

Now let us consider bigger editorial problems. What if the structure of the book is weak? What if the material in chapter 5 is needed before, and in order to understand, chapter 3? What if chapter 4 is cumbersome and repetitious? What if the book just stops and doesn't have a conclusion? What if the annotation is awkward and takes up too much space and thought on the page and would work better at the back of the book? What if there are dull and unconvincing passages that, being essential, need to be juiced up or, being inessential, could be cut? What if an argument should be recast in the interests of clarity, let alone persuasiveness? One can't cope with these larger issues by making squiggles in margins. They may be so momentous as to call into question whether the book is publishable. These macroeditorial matters should at least have been aired, therefore, even before the manuscript was officially accepted, and the editor should know whether the author is ready, willing, and able to change the script.

Sometimes, it is best to accept the manuscript and then broach these larger issues in the guise of making "mere copy-editorial queries"—if one thinks the writer is more likely to make changes or cuts when assured that the effect of these alterations will be minimal than when the result is promised to be life altering. It is impossible to generalize about this: One has to feel one's way and decide what is best anew each time. A book sets up its own magnetic field, and the iron filings will always pull around into a different pattern—one can't quite predict what the best way of editing a book might be. And a lot has to do with the personality of the editor vis-à-is the writer—though, like teachers or doctors, editors should behave a little differently with each book: pliant and agreeable, pleasantly coercive, impatiently dictatorial, demanding and fussy, meekly inquisitive, or soberly encouraging.

A sensitive, alert editor can do wonders to induce a good writer to make a fine book better, to make a poor book passable, and at the very least to make the process of being published easy and comprehensible for the author. Editors should never forget how lonely and difficult it is to write—it is an asocial, isolating, silent endeavor. When a writer has to see his work go out into the noisy, controversial, collaborative, cooperative social world—first of the publishing house, then of the booksellers, then of the critics and reviewers, and finally of the public at large—it can be terrifying, unsettling, disorienting. A tactful and efficient editor should make this ghastly process endurable and help the author face the dread moment when his book is read, when it is no longer a private composition but a public fact, when it is irretrievable.

Still, an editor edits not the writer but the book, and it is to the text of the book that the editor owes her primary allegiance; quite simply put, she is there to help make sure that there are no mistakes the author and publisher would be ashamed of when the book is published. But the author's name is on the book, not the editor's, and the author is the only one fully responsible for everything in it; an editor has no moral, ethical, or professional grounds for intervening except to advise as to likely improvements. The editor should honor the authority of the writer over his book.

It is often assumed that editing is very different when the text is fiction, that working on a novel is wholly unlike the job one does with, say, a cookbook, a biography, or a piece of investigative journalism. In some ways, surely, this is true. One might hazard the formula that the better a novel is, the less editorial work it requires, whereas the ratio is different with nonfiction: A major biography, for instance, even if it does not need much textual intervention, will require close attention, and the better and more ambitious it is, the more this is so. But learning how to read novels and to sympathize with novelists, to get the point of a work of fiction, is also no easy matter. Novelists need editors as *readers,* as encouragers. First-rank imaginative writers know exactly what they are doing and want only to be reassured that they are doing it as well as they can; less experienced novelists will be grateful for comments on technical aspects of their work. One wants them, for example, to avoid derivative or imitative patterns (unless they are writing genre fiction—a western or a mystery, say—where conventions and formulas are eagerly reused). They should attend to the coherence of the story, the resonance and power of the symbols, the expressivity of the dialogue, the effect of the point of view, and so forth. Should a character come in earlier? Does the climactic scene go on too long? Is the ending emotionally satisfactory, and are the tensions of the story resolved?

An editor watches these technical matters, but the writer needs the editor even more as a listener to his "voice"—not merely the prose style, but the book's tone, pitch, and timbre. If the editor senses this essential music, this unique way of seeing the world, this original way of thinking (novels are among other things a type of thought), then she will be able to help the writer more—and will forgive many other faults in the book. Insufficiently developed characters, a weakly modulated plot, a badly phased beginning—all these can be fixed, but only if the basic intelligence is there. And the faults are not worth fixing if it is lacking; an editor will doubt that the writer can revise or correct wisely—whether induced to do so by the editor or independently—if constancy and vigor of purpose have not made themselves known in the first place. This voice, or vision, is a technical quality but also a moral one, and it is unmistakable.

All these issues may well come up with a nonfiction book, too, but they are classically the concerns of the reader of novels. Publishers' memoirs are filled with fascinating stories about editorial advice that made a huge difference to some important novels—changing an ending, switching from third person to first, introducing a new character, cutting out a locale. Writers' memoirs are likewise loaded with horror stories about editors who thwarted, maimed, or poisoned the muse. These serve to remind us of what we have known all along: Making comments on other people's work is always fraught with danger.

Publishing the Book

An editor is on surer ground and may have a more confident stance when she comes to the end of her work, the book's actual publication. She must figure out how the publishing of the book can be both true to the text and commercially beneficent. Ideally, profit maximization and spiritual fidelity go hand in hand, but of course this can't always happen; instead, the editor has to make complicated little compromises to keep them in step, if not shoulder to shoulder.

Early on in a book's public life—the moment varies depending on the company's schedules and habits—and perhaps when the editor is the only one who has actually read the manuscript, she must also write about it; she must describe it honestly to her colleagues but make it sound enticing, present the book's main aspects and purpose, yet also put the best possible light on it (that is, hide or defend its weaknesses). This is not a critical task, but it requires critical acumen, understanding, sympathy, enthusiasm, and real thought. My impression is that even very talented and experienced editors find it gruesomely hard to do. One's affection for a book should show, but if one implausibly ascribes non-existent virtues to it, the book will be in big trouble. On the other hand, if with a lover's false modesty one gushes fondly and fails to make its real potential clear, it won't be published well. And if the author thinks what the editor has written is offensive or wrong, one has betrayed the soul-companionship one is theoretically there to assure.

The editor's written description is important because it sets the tone for everyone else's work on the book; it is also a sort of prompt sheet when the book goes on stage. Sales representatives will use it in some fashion when selling to their accounts; publicity people will crib from it when they talk to book-review editors or talk-show hosts; rights people will use it, recast, in their letters and "poop sheets." Shreds of it will even pop up in critical reviews a year hence! The editor will use it again when writing jacket copy and when or if helping to draft catalog blurbs, press releases, and so forth. As the manuscript is designed and typeset, proofed and reproofed, she will concoct all sorts of variations on this basic material—getting better and better at it, I hope, as publication day approaches.

The editor's collaborative tasks in the company are variations on this presentational theme. Publishing houses have procedures that encase the business in bureaucratic forms: data sheets, launch meetings, packaging briefs, sales conferences, and print-and-pricing meetings. When an editor attends, or attends to, these business arrangements, she is there to ensure that everybody understands what the book is and that the plans for it are plausible. Sometimes tremendous technical and logistical problems demand so much attention that the company, caught up in the challenge of solving them, may give short shrift to the book itself or in some odd way actually forget it. But publishing people should never forget that all their virtuoso work is derivative: If the book had not been written, they would be out of work; they are there to figure out how best to enhance the writer's initial labors—and the editor keeps them pointed in this direction, keeps the concerted effort on track, on schedule, and in focus. She sustains enthusiasm for even the most vexed, hexed, or risky project.

Simply being clearheaded helps. I mention efficiency because it is a technical requirement that editors know exactly at what stage of preparedness or finish each component part of the book is; the commonsense rule is to keep track of this *in writing*. No matter how much is done in person or on the telephone, the written record must show when the manuscript was received, for example, when it went into production, which pieces are not yet in place and when they are expected to be, and so on. Since an editor may be working on anywhere from, say, a dozen to thirty or forty books a year, not to mention several dozen longer-range projects, and it takes anywhere from eight to eighteen months to publish a book, the facts must be accessible on paper— otherwise the author and everyone else become nervous.

The more reassuring and organized the editor is, the more she has liberated herself and her colleagues for real work. Then she can help with "selling the book in the house," building up enthusiasm for it; help to prepare promotion material—press releases, the catalog blurb, the sales presentations; and keep up continual conversation with people inside and outside the company. Gabbing about books is an editorial must.

The editor will also send bound proofs and then finished books to people who might be disposed to comment on the author's work, review it, or promote it in some way—famous writers, experts, critics, or influential opinion makers; this must be done promptly, so that it will be of timely assistance to the marketing people, who need all the testimonial help they can get in the months before publication. The editor will write letters and memos, will pass judgment on the jacket design, and will help the sales and finance people decide how many books to print and at what price.

These last matters are not done by arbitrary calculation—certainly not in the 1980s, when the cost has risen for every component material and unit of labor, when book markets are dwindling, when it is harder and harder to publish books at a decent price. There are guesses, risks, and hopes embodied in the finance for each book on the list, just as there are built-in money factors that cannot be avoided. Suspicious writers, grouchy agents, and cynical readers allege that the publishers routinely grind out books at prices and quantities determined according to an avaricious and indifferent formula. Not only is this not true, but it would not be easy or profitable if it were. My own hunch is that it's more lustrous, more fun, and certainly better business if each book is done differently; after all, each book *is* unique and attracts its own readership. To maximize this readership—to increase sales—the editor will make each book's special allure and value clear, which means differentiating it from other books and its market from other markets. The final print-bind-and-price decisions, if done properly, will reflect this custom work.

An editor nevertheless can associate a new book with known earlier ones whose success seems comparable to what is hoped for the newcomer. But this is a slippery business. One can draw useful parallels with famous books: Booksellers and marketing people, who are notoriously conservative and cautious, always think in terms of last year's successes and failures, and editors must learn how to talk their language. But incessantly to describe new books in terms of old ones is to drain them of their unique juices and flavors, and it encourages derivative, copycat publishing. All too much of this goes on.

An editor will also help to decide what form the publication should take—not just whether the book will have a full-cloth binding or three-piece paper-over-board, but perhaps whether hardcover publication might be forgone in favor of trade paperback, for example, if it is within the competence of the house to do this; or whether a large illustrated format would be better than the plain text originally envisioned. Again, the editor should be a, if not the, decisive voice in such plans.

This is not to say that a naked book can't make its own way in this cruel world. It is simply that publishers are obliged to counter the odd, sometimes grotesque, deformations and inequities in the bookselling business and in our literary life—which means *paying attention to every detail* and being aware of the competitive nuances. Far too many books get published, and everyone in the book trade is flooded with verbiage and nonsense about uninteresting, unnecessary volumes, so writers need editors and publishers to help get their books *noticed,* not merely published in the sense of being made available in printed form. Careful editing, good design, the right format, a striking jacket, a sensible price, comprehensive review coverage, and loving care are all vital.

Given the intense competition for space in bookshops, and the tremendous diversity of book markets in the United States, the publisher will often feel the need to call on the author's help—in interviews, tours, book autographings, goodwill appearances, and so on—or, secondarily, for contacts, for ideas on how to promote, and for information on who or where the author's best public, noisiest fans, and most faithful supporters are. A publisher has no contractual or moral right to expect an author to do any of this—anything but write the book—and must not be disappointed if he does none of it. Yet if he not only is willing to help but turns out to be good at this work (only a very few writers are), that is cause for wild celebration.

Where is the editor in all this? Right in the middle. The editor advises the writer on how much to accede to the publisher's requests and the publisher on how much to ask for. The editor offers discreet counsel to both sides on what might work and what probably will not. She pushes, pushes, pushes on behalf of the book and protects the authors from all but the most necessary commercial pressures (unless of course they thrive on them, in which case she alters tactics). When a writer is geographically unavailable, or temperamentally disinclined, to help out in publication, then the editor is the surrogate. Again, and always in the middle, she forwards the author's or agent's requests (demands!) to the right people in the company and makes doubly certain that the author knows everything that is happening to the book, every kind of sale, publicity event, and review—setback or advance as it may be.

It should not be hard to keep up this running news commentary, because by publication date the editor has been with the writer for many months. After the editorial work was completed, she sent the author copy-editing queries and then proofs, double-checked to make sure he had time to read them and return them on schedule, perhaps even argued with him about his corrections—were they necessary or wise and, if extensive, worth the time and money required to make them? The editor may have shown the writer the jacket design and endured his comments about it and about the blurbs describing the book. (My experience is that authors are usually quite good at writing blurbs themselves—sometimes they insist on doing so—but that they are less trustworthy about jacket design. If they have friends or mates who are interested in designing the jacket, the publisher is usually in trouble.) The editor discussed with the author who should get early proofs or bound books—and why—gossiped about likely review coverage, and kept the author reassured when the book finally went to press. During the awful gap of several weeks after proofs were corrected and jackets prepared but before the book came in from the bindery—when there was nothing for the author to do but be anxious—the editor gave off signals that progress was being made even though there was no tangible evidence of this. (A wise publisher once counseled me to give a writer no more than one or two pieces of news in any one telephone call or letter—it was better to spread out the information and keep up a constant flow of short messages, which gave the right impression of unceasing labor on the writer's behalf.)

Although hardcover books are still given official publication days (a nice time to have a party—though a celebration does nothing for sales, it is nice for tempers), in fact there is no one moment of parturition and birth. The book arrives at the publisher's warehouse and then is shipped out, reaching bookstores at various times in the next few weeks. Simultaneously copies are sent to newspapers and magazines, with requests to observe the official publication date, but in fact reviews will precede and follow it. It would be better to say that each book has a publication season, and the editor must keep the author company during all of it. She must be there when the bad reviews come in or when none appear, when the unexpected front-page rave jolts the public into attention, when the advance sales are not followed by postpublication orders—or when the book proves to "have legs and just runs out of the stores." The editor must answer inquiries about the book and keep the author's spirits up. She must hear his complaints that *not enough is being done* and help him stay on balance when *too much is happening all at once.* All these tasks afford opportunities for encouraging the writer—among other things, to think about his next book.

Literary agents sometimes argue against the perpetuation of long-term relationships between writer and publisher; I think that was an argument born in a flush, easy time when publishing was lucrative, competition was less cautious than it had been before and is again now, and writers thought they could improve their lot by moving around. I find it hard to imagine that it doesn't help a writer to have a perennially supportive, discerning reader, strategically placed to advance his interests in a publishing house, a reader who keeps him company throughout his productive life. I don't see how that can inhibit or restrict anyone's livelihood. People are strangely diverse, and writers are as jumpy and uncertain as the rest of us; sometimes security and reassurance run counter to one's needs—but not often. An editor—in the early stages of composition, throughout the production time, and at publication— can afford a writer those essentials.

Whatever agents say or publishers do, the editor should be constant, faithful to the writer and to the books, cheerful about fashion and the general culture but not swayed by it, devoted to the written word and wary of schemes to make it obsolete. There have been writers for almost as long as there has been human history, and where there are writers there are readers. Editors can always find a place, mediating between the two.

CHAPTER FIVE

The Editor's Job in Professional/Scholarly Publishing

GLADYS S. TOPKIS

What Are Professional Books, and Who Publishes Them?

A professional book, strictly defined, is a work written by a practicing or teaching professional or scholar—for example, a research engineer, a psychotherapist, a professor of art history—and intended for the author's peers rather than for the general reader or for classroom use. The terms *scholarly* and *professional* are essentially interchangeable, except that in some houses *professional* is reserved for books in the commonly recognized professions such as education, medicine, law, and the physical sciences, whereas *scholarly* is applied to the whole range of academic disciplines. Such books differ from trade books most obviously in that their content is specialized and the audience for them is consequently both limited and predictable. They differ from textbooks in that most sales are made directly to the consumer, one copy at a time, rather than to school systems or college bookstores in bulk.

The specialized content and the inelastic market for the books govern every aspect of professional/scholarly publishing. For example, the most effective method of selling such books is by direct-mail promotion, targeted to carefully chosen lists of people who share the author's professional interests. The books are seldom carried in general bookstores, and the authors will almost never see their work advertised in a broad-circulation magazine or newspaper (although it is the rare author who will understand why and accept the reasoning).

Aside from professional associations, many of which issue books as well as journals, professional/scholarly books are produced by three

GLADYS S. TOPKIS is senior editor, Yale University Press.

categories of publishers: university presses, short-run or monograph houses, and the professional divisions of large general publishers. These days, few houses can afford to confine themselves to professional/ scholarly books, and even those that adhere most closely to the definition of professional publishing have changed the nature of their lists with the changing times to maximize profits—among other things, by publishing for a large professional audience rather than a small one (e.g., business management versus history), by looking for books with an interdisciplinary market (e.g., a book in criminal justice, which might conceivably sell to sociologists, criminologists, lawyers, policymakers, police administrators, and so on) rather than a narrowly focused one, or by favoring books that have the potential for bulk sale (e.g., a book endorsed or sponsored by a large foundation or a professional association, which might be willing to buy copies in quantity). Reference books of various types are indispensable staples on the lists of most successful professional/scholarly publishers.

As parts of educational institutions, university presses are legally regarded as nonprofit and are exempt from taxation. Most of them were originally established as outlets for the scholarly work of their institutions' own faculties and were subsidized to some extent by the universities themselves or by special endowment funds. The obligation to publish at least some worthwhile books with little or no commercial potential persists, but many university presses today—certainly the larger and more prestigious ones, such as Harvard, Yale, Chicago, Columbia, and California—are under pressure from their sponsoring institutions to be self-supporting. This means, in effect, that those presses must now draw their authors from a much wider circle—an international one, in fact— and that they must compete directly with commercial houses for salable books to support their small-market scholarly publications. The degree to which these "salable books" can be regarded as scholarly varies from press to press: Louisiana State University Press, for example, published a Pulitzer Prize–winning novel in 1980, *A Confederacy of Dunces*; Columbia University Press publishes a highly successful list of basic textbooks in social work; Harvard University Press has recently issued a cookbook. Most university presses publish no fiction, introductory textbooks, or how-to-do-it books. Many of the smaller university presses are still essentially regional, if not limited to their own faculties, and are still subsidized to some extent.

The prototype of short-run or monograph publishing, Praeger Special Studies, was established in the early 1960s by Frederick Praeger, who observed that although various branches of government and other institutions were willing to finance specialized research and the writing up of the results, few of these auspices took pains to see that the reports reached the hands of those to whom they were most relevant. Since the audience, like the writers, tended to be institutionally supported, there was little resistance to the relatively high prices that had to be charged for a book with, say, a 750-copy print run. To keep production costs down, the books were unjacketed, cover stamping was standardized, and in some cases the authors were even required to submit, or to pay for the preparation of, camera-ready copy—originally, typescripts with un-justified margins. Relatively little in-house editing was done on the manuscripts, and royalties were low or nonexistent.

Today the monograph publishers have also changed their focus some-what. New production techniques have improved the appearance of the books, and economic exigencies have forced these houses to raise their minimum print runs and to extend their lists to include upper-division textbooks and even occasional trade books. The leading monograph publishers—Westview Press, headed by Frederick Praeger; Praeger Special Studies, now owned by Holt, Rinehart & Winston; Sage; and Lexington Books, a subsidiary of D. C. Heath—compete with the university presses for high-quality dissertations and other serious nonfiction. Since the start-up costs are relatively low, there are dozens—perhaps even hundreds—of smaller monograph houses, most of them operated by former editors.

The third category (divisions of general publishers) is exemplified by Free Press, a subsidiary of Macmillan; Basic Books, a subsidiary of Harper & Row; and John Wiley, one of the few large independent publishers left. Founded in the days when most university presses were publishing only relatively esoteric scholarly work and before the mono-graph houses began to proliferate, these firms performed the important—and highly profitable—service of making new professional books and translations of European classics available to teachers, graduate students, researchers, clinicians, and others. In the process they had considerable impact on scholarship and teaching in this country, particularly in the social and behavioral sciences. Eventually acquired by large, diversified houses, they became, theoretically, their houses' professional divisions. Once again, change is evident; all three of the houses mentioned now publish textbooks, including books designed for introductory courses, and some trade books as well as their professional offerings.

As we have seen, the professional/scholarly publishers can no longer be so clearly distinguished from text and trade publishers on the basis of their lists. Nevertheless, publishers in this category continue to focus primarily on scholarly books, and the characteristics of those books determine the nature of the editor's job, even if he or she works occasionally on a book that is difficult to define as scholarly.

Acquisitions

Although the number of agents who represent professional/scholarly authors has been increasing, it is still small; the average professional book earns too little money to warrant an agent's time and effort. The source of most professional books, therefore, is the author ("over the transom"), a referral, or the editor.

THE AUTHOR

Except for academics caught in the familiar "publish or perish" bind, who are often obliged to sacrifice discrimination for speed, professional authors are chiefly interested in disseminating their work as widely as possible to the appropriate audience and in enhancing their professional prestige by association with a publisher whose backlist includes distinguished books in the same field. The reputation of the house, assuming it's a good one, will therefore attract a good many submissions. Some are directed to a specific editor who is known to the writer by name if not personally. A gratified author who takes the trouble to write an acknowledgment of the editor's contributions to his or her book can stimulate many submissions, by high-ranking members of the field as well as newcomers.

Most uninvited submissions are from people at the beginning of their careers, and a large number are doctoral dissertations. Relatively few dissertations are publishable by large commercial houses because graduate departments typically require a heavy emphasis on methodology, quantification rather than, say, imaginative speculation or policy recommendations, and research—which generally means an intensive focus on a small number of cases rather than a more broadly applicable survey—not to mention demonstrated facility in the use of the professional jargon. All of these characteristics limit the salability of the work. University presses tend to be slightly more hospitable to dissertations because they are less constricted by considerations of profits, but on the other hand they are committed to publishing books of lasting merit, which rules out the typical narrowly focused dissertation. Unless they have been heavily revised, then, most dissertations that achieve publication are issued by the monograph houses.

The chances for publication of fledgling writers, whether or not their work has the limitations of a dissertation, are undeniably rather slim. A manuscript by a much-published author or by a member of a distinguished faculty is likely to get more serious (and more prompt) consideration by a professional house than one by a young, previously unpublished writer, primarily because fellow professionals and librarians would be more likely to buy the prestigious writer's book. The assumption—which may or may not be warranted—is that his experience will enable, say, Daniel Bell to write a more interesting and more valid book on postindustrial capitalism than a newcomer to the field. Bell's book will almost certainly sell more copies. The prospects for the young writer are further dimmed by the fact that reviews in professional journals, which might alert colleagues to the novelty and significance of what the writer has to say, are notoriously tardy; it's not at all uncommon for such reviews to appear long after a book has gone out of print. Nor can the promotion and advertising techniques of most professional houses, which are aimed essentially at disseminating information rather than selling, be relied on to create an audience where one does not exist.

The response to the inevitable outcries of catch-22 is that professional journals are usually less elitist in their choices, and that a young writer with three or four published articles in good journals is considered to be in a different category from a novice. And there are occasional exceptions to the rule, some of them successful.

Although many trade houses now refuse to read unsolicited manuscripts, by and large professional houses still do, in part because a self-selection process is generally at work: It takes an unusual degree of self-confidence, or encouragement from mentors, for a previously unpublished author from an undistinguished school to submit his or her work to one of the great university presses, for example. Still, the most common source of published books is not the "slush pile" of unsolicited submissions but referrals.

REFERRALS

Previously published authors, prominent members of the author's discipline who are favorably disposed toward the house, and even the editor's colleagues in other houses are invaluable sources of publishable manuscripts. Some of the work referred, of course, falls into the novice category described above, but the endorsement of a prestigious member of the discipline or of a trusted adviser will certainly cause the editor to give the manuscript more attention than blind submission would.

Sometimes the referral process is formalized in a series editorship. That is, the editor locates a professional who is in a position to know about new developments in the discipline and about bright young comers and who has the persuasive ability and the zest to induce both senior authors and good new ones to write for the house. The series editor, who generally gets a small royalty percentage (called an override), is also expected to render a professional opinion on the manuscripts produced by the authors in that series. A series editor who is hard working, with good contacts and good judgment, is a valuable ally, especially for an acquisitions editor who is new to a discipline. But a series editor who uses the post to pay off old debts to former students and colleagues or one whose commitment to a special perspective makes him deaf or hostile to other approaches can seriously weaken the list.

Sources of referral also include persons employed in other departments of the editor's house. Most important are college travelers, if the house is a large commercial publisher with a college-text department. Since experience as a college rep is an accepted route to a job as a scholarly or textbook editor, many salespeople use part of their time on the road to sharpen (and demonstrate) their skills in locating publishable manuscripts. A textbook or trade editor with an author who has a professional manuscript that the editor's department or house cannot handle will often suggest that the writer contact a friend in another department or house.

THE EDITOR

It is a publishing truism that the best and most salable books usually originate with the editor. Editors "find" books in two ways: by literally searching in the most likely places for manuscripts in progress or under contemplation and by dreaming up the idea for a book and convincing the right person to produce it.

The most likely places to find a scholarly work are, obviously, universities, "think tanks," and other institutions that employ or sponsor scholars. Scholarly editors today spend a good deal of their time beating the academic bushes and attending meetings of professional associations. This is true even of university-press editors, who until recently had only to wait for their own faculties to deliver. Editors for monograph houses call Washington their second home, since many of the books they publish originate under the sponsorship of governmental or quasi-governmental organizations.

The professional editor also is on the lookout for information about sizable research grants, for many of them can lead to publishable books and sometimes to the big, high-ticket reference works that professional publishers love. An author with a large grant to survey the curricula of institutes of criminal justice across the country, for example, is in close touch with many leaders in the field and therefore is in an excellent position to put together a handbook on "crime and punishment," commissioning articles from the authors he or she meets in another context.

And finally, most editors find that it pays to keep an eye on the professional journals, and even on newspapers and consumer magazines, which frequently report on people who are doing interesting work or on "classics" that have been allowed to go out of print and might profitably be revived.

A serendipitous find of course brings a special kind of satisfaction, but every editor knows that there is no such thing as pure serendipity. The editor has to be on the spot, alert to all possibilities, and ready to pick up even mumbled or grunted clues to a publishable manuscript. A focus of admiration and envy at one commercial house was the editor who, while on a scouting trip to University X, picked up a casual reference to a multivolume encyclopedia being prepared by a group at University Y. He got on the telephone and then on a plane and within a few hours had nailed down an almost finished work of high quality, complete with a guarantee from a large corporation for the purchase of several thousand copies—at one hundred dollars a set. The editor himself—a seasoned pro—would define this accomplishment as a "lucky break," but the fact remains that he was on the scene, he was listening carefully, he recognized a good prospect when he heard about it, he acted immediately and decisively, and he was able to persuade the authors to accept his offer.

In their visits to campuses and other sites of potential authors, professional editors often find a warm reception. They have a great advantage over textbook editors in that the kinds of books they are paid to publish are generally the kinds the authors are most interested in writing, since scholarly books are the fruit of many years, perhaps a lifetime, of research and thinking about a subject. The editor who can convey genuine interest in the project that is closest to the writer's heart has at least made a friend and may well have found an author. The textbook editor, on the other hand, must frequently convince a reluctant prospect to write a text, generally using the crass argument of the money to be made.

By the same token, however, editors in professional houses are less likely than their colleagues in trade or text houses to initiate an idea and persuade the appropriate author to make a book of it. Nevertheless, there is considerable room for creativity in professional acquisitions. For example, an editor may suggest to a scholar immersed in basic research that he has the material and the data to write a useful book on the applications of his findings or the methodology he has used, without waiting to discover a second theory of relativity. The editor may think of ways in which an outstanding lecture can be expanded into a provocative book. If the editor takes the trouble to get to know potential authors as people, he or she will often find that the authors are knowledgeable about and interested in subjects other than the ones with which they are identified. Sometimes the editor can spot a broader potential in a manuscript that is unsuitable for the list as submitted. The most profitable use of the professional editor's creative energies is in finding a gap in the reference literature in a given area and persuading a scholar—more likely a group of scholars—to undertake to produce a handbook, encyclopedia, reader's guide, or some similar compendium that will, so the publisher hopes, be regarded as well worth the high price it will probably bear and will continue to sell for years.

It should be evident from what has been said so far that the output of any scholarly house is closely tied to the college curriculum, whether or not the house publishes textbooks. Academics are the chief source of manuscripts and the major buyers. It should also be evident that the acquisitions editor's chief resource is knowledge of a given discipline— the major trends, the big names and important centers of scholarship, who's doing what—along with a network of friends and acquaintances who can be counted on for advice and referrals. For these reasons scholarly editors, like textbook editors, are always assigned responsibility for a discipline—more often for a cluster of related disciplines, such as sociology and anthropology, or economics and political science. The editor need not be and probably is not a bona fide expert in those fields; most editors have a background in the humanities, and relatively few hold advanced degrees. But once a discipline is assigned, it is the editor's job to inform himself or herself, to keep abreast of developments, and, most important, to build up a network.

Among the essential qualifications of acquisitions editors, in fact, is network-building skill. That is, the editor must be able to assemble a group of contacts who are reliable sources of information about new directions in the discipline. The network must include a list of people who are qualified to advise about the publishability of a given manuscript—qualified not only in the sense that they know the field but also in their ability to provide more or less objective comments on the work in question, without permitting their evaluations to be colored too much by their own special approach to the subject. The ideal reviewer also has the ability to analyze what needs to be done to make a manuscript better and/or more salable. Such resources, carefully honed and expanded over time, are essential tools of the acquisitions editor's trade, and they are valued and guarded as a professional chef values and guards a favorite cleaver or saucepan. University-press editors often have a special advantage in their immediate access and collegial relationship to faculty members at their institutions.

The techniques involved in building a network of informants are very similar to those required in building a list; indeed, advisers and informants very often are sources of publishable manuscripts. The acquisitions editor also has to keep in touch with the field—by spending a good deal of time visiting university campuses, government agencies, and other places

where potential authors or informants congregate; by attending professional meetings; by constant perusal of the professional journals, college
catalogs, and bibliographies of new books; and by maintaining a mammoth
amount of correspondence. In these respects the job of the scholarly
editor is much like that of the textbook editor, and it is understandable
that many scholarly editors began their careers in textbook sales or
editorial departments.

The Publishing Decision

As is true of most editors, the scholarly editor proposes that the house
offer contracts for a book but is rarely empowered to make the final
decision. The editor assembles a dossier on each book being proposed,
similar in essence to the information other editors must provide to their
decision makers. In all university presses and most commercial scholarly
houses as well, the editor's opinion must be bolstered by at least one
favorable peer review, since few editors are qualified to pass judgment
on the work of a scholar. One of the editor's important functions, then,
is to solicit such reviews, drawing on the aforementioned network.

Because each editor in a professional house is assumed to be the
resident expert in a given discipline, full-staff editorial meetings are a
rarity, and hardly ever will anyone else in the house ask to see what the
author has submitted except for the table of contents or general rationale
for the book. Sales and marketing people generally have little or no say
in the scholarly publishing decision—an exception to the prevailing
practice in trade and textbook publishing. This of course puts an awesome
responsibility on the editors, who often know all too well that the
expertise the rest of the house is willing to grant them is a myth. The
advice of outside professionals is invaluable, but the editor must decide
what manuscripts are worth reviewing and endorsing.

In commercial houses the final decision may be made by one or two
people—perhaps the editor in chief and the president. University presses
have a board of advisers drawn from the senior faculty of the university
who are supposed to pass on the scholarly merits of each proposal,
without regard for financial considerations. Obviously peer review counts
heavily in these circumstances, whereas commercial houses must base
their decisions on the book's likely contribution to their "bottom line"
as well as—sometimes instead of—its advancement of the general state
of knowledge. (It bears repeating that even university presses, although
technically nonprofit, can no longer afford to ignore a book's potential
earnings: With a few exceptions, such presses need to earn enough on

each season's list to pay for producing the next season's list and to cover the inevitable inflationary rise in costs.)

Now that they are often competing with other types of publishing houses for manuscripts, most scholarly houses, even university presses, are willing to sign contracts on the basis of an incomplete manuscript, even a proposal, but at least at university presses it is understood that publication will not take place without one or two favorable reviews of the final manuscript. A contract based on a proposal or a preliminary draft therefore has little binding force on the publisher, although many authors will nevertheless derive a sense of security from a quasi-official piece of paper.

Time was when public, university, and specialized libraries, as well as such institutions as the military, could be depended upon for sufficient sales to support the publication of virtually any worthwhile book. In this respect as in at least some others, the "old days" were "good," and they are over, probably never to return. Now that library budgets have been brutally slashed, professional publishers can no longer take it for granted that a good book will make its way, and editors who acquire manuscripts for such houses have to look to other sources of prospective income.

Government and private agencies and institutions are sometimes willing to subsidize the publication of a book that, without such support, would have to be priced too high for the market. These sources, too, are increasingly hard to find, but professional editors and the management of scholarly houses spend a good deal of time exploring the possibilities (and filling out the endless forms most such institutions require). It should not need saying that a responsible house will not publish a book just because it comes equipped with a fat check from a sponsor—the book must be publishable on its own terms. Nor will most sponsoring institutions agree to support a book with enough commercial potential to make it on its own.

Backlist potential is a critically important factor in the decision to publish. Professional publishing is to certain kinds of trade publishing as long-term investment is to windfall profits; with little or no anticipated income from subsidiary rights and a limited market for each book within a given year, scholarly publishers count on the continuing sales of "old" books, some of them as old as twenty or thirty years. In most scholarly houses backlist sales account for as much as 70 percent of annual revenues.

A related consideration is the likelihood that the book, as a later paperback, will find its way into the college curriculum as a required or recommended text. This is often difficult to predict before publication; some books are so good or so important that courses are built around them, once people know they exist. Professional houses almost always do their own paperback editions, although there may be exceptions if the offer from a reprint house is sufficiently attractive. The other side of the backlist coin is that professional houses generally (but not always) avoid trendy or topical books.

Foreign sales are especially important to professional/scholarly publishers, in some cases producing as much as a third of the firm's income. Again, acquiring editors must bear this in mind, although they also publish some books that are not suitable for export.

Like all other editors, the scholarly editor also has to keep in mind the "flavor" of the house—the special kinds of books that the house seems to prefer and apparently knows best how to sell. An obvious clue is the sales history of the house's backlist. The scholarly editor will also pay particular attention to other books on the current or forthcoming list that form a logical grouping with the manuscript he or she is proposing, so that the costs of marketing the new book will be minimized by publicizing it with a number of related titles in a single direct-mail piece.

As should be clear, the sponsoring editor, even in the most bureaucratically structured house, has enormous control over the shape of the list. It is the acquisitions editor, empowered to decide which books to propose for contract and to reject manuscripts at will, who makes the initial and most critical decision about what is to be published.

In a university press, scholarly merit is the dominant criterion. If the house is a commercial enterprise, the editor must be convinced that the book will sell well. But even commercial professional houses have to put their money behind "books that matter" (to quote the motto of one such house)—books that have something new and important to say to someone who presumably is acquainted with the existing literature in the field. From this perspective, the job of a professional book editor may do less damage to one's youthful idealism than a similar job in trade or textbook publishing. But the editor in any house who forgets the imperative of the "bottom line" won't hold the job long. The trick is to find a good book that will also sell. These qualities, alas, are not inevitably linked, and the second is of course much harder to determine.

The Contract

Negotiating the contract for a professional book is generally a rather simple and straightforward matter. As compared with trade and textbook editors, professional editors face relatively little competition in bidding for manuscripts since there is only a handful of scholarly publishers.

Professional publishers are all dealing roughly the same set of figures—the size of the market, the optimal price, and the cost of manufacturing—so there tends to be little if any difference among them in the terms they can offer an author, and very little room for negotiation in any case. If there is competition for a title, the author is likely to base the choice on the prestige of the house and perhaps on his or her affinity for the editor. Sometimes an author to whom a very speedy decision and/or a quick publication is important will opt for a monograph house, but usually the greater prestige, higher royalty rates, and wider distribution that a general publisher or a major university press can offer are more appealing.

Again, because of the limited market and the absence of subsidiary income, professional publishers offer relatively low advances and frequently none at all. Whereas in trade publishing the size of the advance is usually a factor in competitive bidding for a manuscript and, so it is said, affects the amount of energy and money the house will put into promotion and advertising, in most cases the advance on a professional book, if any, is intended merely to ensure that the author is able to produce the book on schedule—that is, it is explicitly paid to cover typing expenses, the salary of a part-time research assistant, or permissions fees. It is not a sign of love or esteem or status, and it has no effect on the house's efforts to sell the book. Of course sometimes the authors have received government or university grants for researching and writing their books, and sometimes these grants include a subsidy for publication.

Editor-Author Relations

An important difference between the job of a scholarly editor and that of many trade editors is in the nature of the editor's relations with authors. Trade authors may develop a special fondness for their editors and even a loyalty to the house that has published their previous work, but the fact that many of them write primarily for money and employ agents to get them the best terms possible often means that each editor-author relationship is a one-time experience. Then, too, some trade authors never write more than one book.

Academics, on the other hand, are generally committed to a lifetime of writing and publishing; some are even required to do so as a condition of advancement or continued employment. Also, as has been mentioned, scholars constitute not only the authors but the primary buyers of professional/scholarly books, the critics on whose manuscript reports professional editors must depend, and a major source of referrals of manuscripts by others. The relationship between scholarly author and editor is therefore especially close and long lasting, and it is an important part of the editor's job to keep it that way. (In fact, at one commerical professional house editors are rated, at raise-giving time, on their ability to sustain good relationships with important authors.) A thoughtless or perfunctory rejection note, a seriously delayed response to an inquiry, or any other evidence of rudeness can have severe repercussions—especially when one recalls that scholars have a network of their own, more tightly organized than the editor's. Just as a happy author or correspondent may produce leads to publishable manuscripts by others, so an unhappy one may discourage his friends from sending the editor their work or even from adopting a textbook published by the house. Thus the editor, in appraising a manuscript, is also forming an opinion about the author's potential as writer or critic and filing it away for future reference.

If a project has been signed up on the basis of a proposal or a few sample chapters, it is the editor's job to beg, cajole, or threaten the author into delivering the final and complete work more or less when it is due, although scholarly houses have historically been relatively indulgent on this score. Once the draft of a manuscript under contract has been submitted, the acquiring editor has, at minimum, the responsibility of sending the author any professional reviews, making it clear that the author has the right to accept or ignore suggestions as he or she sees fit, but supplying persuasive support for those suggestions that seem especially worth heeding.

The fact that the typical scholarly book is not expected to earn much money means that the work load of scholarly editors is generally considerably heavier than that of their counterparts in other branches of publishing. Some houses have quotas requiring acquisitions editors to "bring in," say, forty or fifty projects a year or X dollars worth in estimated first-year sales.

One result of the heavy work load of scholarly editors is that those who do acquisitions are often discouraged from closely editing their manuscripts; the house may contend that such editors are paid more highly than copy editors because of their special ability to attract publishable manuscripts and that this scouting and weeding-out activity should occupy most of their time. On the other hand, some authors are disposed toward one house rather than another because they know that the editor with whom they have had primary contact, whom they presumably like and respect, is the one who will read and criticize the manuscripts. And some scholarly editors have experience and talent in manuscript editing, enjoy it, or feel uneasy about handing over a scholar's lifework to the questionably tender mercies of a junior editor in house or an unsupervised free lance. Responsible editors will at least read through the manuscript and indicate which, if any, of the outsiders' comments they endorse, adding whatever further suggestions and criticisms occur. And some acquiring editors do a large amount of the nitty-gritty on a manuscript—often on their own time.

As is true in any kind of house, the editor's responsibility to the author does not end when the book is turned over to production. The editor-author relationship often continues long after publication, since any scholarly author can be regarded as the potential source of one or three or six more publishable manuscripts. The editor's willingness to hear and deal with the author's complaints, requests, and needs can have an important professional payoff. For example, it is not unusual for an editor to be asked to recommend someone for a job opening on the basis of his or her wide acquaintance with people in the field. If an author or potential author lands a chair or a deanship as a result, in part, of the editor's suggestion or endorsement, his or her gratitude may be expressed in enormously useful ways. One such chairman makes it a point to have a cocktail party whenever a particular professional editor visits his campus, and attendance is virtually required of all members of the department. The inevitable result is that the editor gets the pick of the crop of manuscripts produced by that department. Maintaining good relations with one's network can also have a happy effect on the quality of the editor's life. An editor who has carefully tended his or her authors and other professionals will receive many invitations to social events, some of them pleasurable. And most important, the editor on a scouting trip will rarely have to spend a lonely evening in a gloomy motel if he or she has previously cultivated authors on the campus.

Thus far I've talked about the ways in which attention to their relationships with authors can further the professional goals of editors and perhaps enrich their social lives as well. It should also be said that scholarly editors have a special obligation to authors and would-be authors, over and above acknowledgment of the fact that they have demonstrated the courage, imagination, and sheer tenacity to produce a book-length manuscript—as the editor most likely has not. What a researcher, a teacher, or a practicing professional writes is in a sense a justification for the decision to follow scholarly pursuits rather than to seek a probably more lucrative career in, say, business or law—a demonstration that his or her life has been worthwhile. This is not to say that a trade or textbook writer doesn't or shouldn't feel intense pride of authorship, even a kind of parenthood; but in a society in which the intellectual career commands scant rewards in money or prestige, an editor's response to a scholarly manuscript can have an especially weighty effect on the author's self-esteem and sense of self.

The Editor and Other Staff

As kings or queens of their respective disciplinary domains, scholarly editors are in effect profit centers, with a great deal to say about the production and marketing of their books and considerable power in dealing with other departments. The trade-off is that their responsibilities are so clearly identified that their successes and failures are known to one and all.

Commercial scholarly houses are increasingly seeking to control costs by using free lances wherever possible, especially for copyediting and proofreading. University presses by and large still have manuscript editors and copy editors on staff, so that the sponsoring editors can feel reasonably confident that a book will be handled properly even if they haven't the time or inclination to edit it themselves. But whether or not the acquiring editor actually performs blue-pencil operations, he or she is responsible for the editing of the book and will oversee the work of the copy editor as much as possible. If problems arise in the course of editing, the acquiring editor is expected to resolve them.

As the recognized authorities on books in their disciplines, acquisitions editors are expected to recommend the optimal price for a book, when it should be published, and how it should look. The promotion and advertising departments will expect the acquisitions editor to supply the names of appropriate sources for jacket quotes, professional journals to which the books should be sent for review, and those in which an ad might yield results. The editor is generally consulted about the appropriate mailing lists to use and about which titles should be grouped together in a single mailing piece or ad.

If the house's marketing department includes a staff of sales representatives, as is true of most houses that publish textbooks and trade books (purely professional books, remember, are sold mainly by direct mail), it is usually the editor's job to present his or her part of the list at the semiannual sales conference. The editor represents the house at professional meetings where books are displayed. And finally, he or she is usually consulted about when to permit a book to go out of print, whether and when to sell reprint rights, and whether or when the house should do its own paperback or a revised edition.

Rewards and Penalties; Odds and Ends

Since one man's meat is another's *poisson*, readers will have to make their individual tallies of the pros and cons of professional publishing over trade or text. Here I will summarize some of the points made earlier, exposing those of my own prejudices that haven't been revealed before.

Editors who are themselves academics or would-be practitioners, who are drawn to ideas and men and women of ideas, and who don't enjoy the frenetic competiton that characterizes text and trade publishing will find the nature of a professional list and of the authors they deal with gratifying, by and large, and will feel less need to justify the way they spend their working lives than may be felt by, say, a Princeton Phi Beta Kappa obliged to edit low-level self-help manuals or the true confessions of performers. On the other hand, they may suffer more keenly from the inevitable tension between their personal quest for quality and the escalating fiscal demands of the house's management, whatever its nominal dedication to excellence. For editors who have chosen to make friends of their authors the tension becomes greater, for survival will oblige them to choose the interests of the house over those of the author in cases of conflict, which are also inevitable. Occasions may arise when the editor is simultaneously accused of cooptation by the house and of betrayal by an author. To deal with such situations demands a cool head and a tough hide, for not infrequently both charges are correct.

University-press editors are largely spared this problem, since they are expected to publish books of high merit; but, things being how they are, even the richest university press is often forced to reject high-quality, low-market manuscripts in favor of books that will contribute to the house's self-sufficiency. Then too, although the calm pleasures of membership in a remote academic community may be ample compensation for some, others will miss the excitement and glamor of big-city publishing, in which even professional publishers participate to some extent.

Distance from New York, Boston, and the West Coast centers of publishing—characteristic of many monograph houses as well as of most university presses—has other advantages and disadvantages, depending on one's point of view. Faculty and student spouses constitute a kind of captive labor pool; with few employment alternatives in the typical university town, they are often hired by publishers at exploitative salaries. Such houses thus tend to have overqualified staffs—a boon for the authors and for higher-ranking employees—but staffs that also tend to be unstable, for spouses generally follow when husband or wife decides to accept an offer from another institution. This tends to result in frequent turnover and relatively frequent opportunities for advancement. Then, too, such houses are likely to be willing to make arrangements for part-time work, flex-time, job sharing, and the like to accommodate the domestic responsibilities of exemplary workers.

The professional editor's control over the list and freedom from interference by other departments in the house are powerful attractions—

but they are, first of all, relative: The editor is generally not empowered to sign contracts, and his or her recommendations are always subject to review and reversal by management. Since the authors in a discipline tend to regard experienced editors in their field as virtually omnipotent, having to transmit the rejection of a project they have sponsored can cause scholarly editors an unusual degree of embarrassment and pain. Second, the flip side of power is of course responsibility. The editor is held immediately and directly accountable for the success or nonsuccess of his or her part of the list, even if the mailings didn't get out on time and the manufacturing department goofed; this is a weighty burden that some people would prefer to avoid.

It is difficult to find anything positive to say about the professional editor's work load, which is backbreaking, especially if the editor chooses or feels obliged to do a good deal of line editing on manuscripts. The job simply selects workaholics. On the other hand, the very size of the list means, in theory at least, that scholarly editors are allowed to choose one or two clunkers a season, if the balance of their lists is profitable or meritorious. Textbook editors, by contrast, can lose their jobs if the company loses its shirt on a single title. The risk factor per title is less in professional publishing in view of the lower advances and other controls on costs.

Professional editors are deeply involved in every aspect of the house's activity; in theory, therefore, their skills are more transferable than those of someone whose functions are more narrowly limited. In fact this is questionable. For one thing, acquisitions editors are so far advanced in the hierarchy that they probably can't afford or are unwilling to take a lower-level job in, say, marketing or some other aspect of publishing. Second, for reasons made clear throughout this chapter, the professional editor's job differs in many respects from that of the trade or text editor, perhaps most notably in that professional editors rarely operate in a highly competitive atmosphere. This tends to make them less attractive to trade or text houses—and there are increasingly few professional houses to which one can transfer. It is for this reason that a high percentage of the monograph houses that have sprung up in recent years have been started by former professional editors: These entrepreneurs are encouraged to do so by the fact that they have a wider range of skills and contacts than most other editors and are discouraged from seeking another job in an established house by the paucity of openings.

The growing diversity of the professional house's offerings, and hence of the individual editor's list, makes the editor's job more interesting; a relatively old dog *can* learn new tricks. But it can also produce frustrations. As professional editors are increasingly forced to publish textbooks and trade books, they will enter into competition, frequently unequal, with other houses. All textbooks, for example, are marketed in the same way, but the profesisonal editor is handicapped in competition with a full-time textbook editor in terms of the time and money that can be devoted to acquiring and producing the book. Yet the books are required to make a respectable showing in relation to books produced by editors who publish nothing else.

When the professional editor also publishes trade books, he or she faces the additional problem of convincing the advertising, publicity, and sales departments to give the book adequate treatment. If the trade department of a parent commerical house has a tradition of publishing serious nonfiction, the professional editor's task is not so difficult; but if there is a notable lack of fit between the conventional trade publications of the house and the trade books produced by the professional division, the latter will get short shrift.

As noted, almost all scholarly presses publish at least some books for the general reader, although the potential market for such books may be minute from the perspective of a commercial trade house. Until fairly recently it might have been said that the trade publications of such presses suffered from the typically small size of the house's sales staff. But the growing concentration of booksellers, while certainly ominous in other respects for the publisher of serious books, has the possibility of diminishing the liability that a tiny sales staff once represented: Since the large majority of trade books today are sold through a handful of chains and jobbers, even a single in-house representative can accomplish a great deal to gain national distribution for a book published by a scholarly house.

In sum, the cottage-industry aspect of publishing—personal attention to books and authors and the involvement of the whole staff in the whole list—is most likely to be preserved in a professional/scholarly house, where the contribution of each book to the success of the list over time is significant and where relations with authors must be continually nurtured. Among the various types of scholarly publishers, this aspect is most likely to be preserved in the university presses because of their relative freedom from financial pressures.

CHAPTER SIX

On Being a Literary Agent

ELAINE MARKSON

If you took a poll among your friends, I doubt that any of them would know a literary agent or want to be one. And yet it is a most wonderful profession: Next to his dog, you are the writer's best friend.

An agent nurtures and nourishes the writer. Actually selling an author's work is only one small part of the job. The good agent has an eye on every aspect of the publishing process and follows each author's work down the production trail to the bookstore. This means dealing not only with author and editor to keep that process smooth, but with publicity people, art departments, sales managers, subsidiary rights directors, foreign publishers, and newspaper and magazine editors, among others.

The agent is the negotiator for the author for all aspects of that author's work. That means making book publication and film deals, magazine and newspaper syndication sales, and taking care of permissions to reprint excerpts from an author's work in an anthology and/or magazine. For that pleasure, the agent receives a commission (10 to 15 percent, depending on agency regulations) of all monies earned. Most often, an agent will draw up a simple contract, outlining the duties of said agent and the term of contract, giving the agent exclusive right to sell, or attempt to sell, that writer's work. And attempt it is: Not everything an agent handles will result in a sale. That is why, for me, it is essential to take on only those projects for which I have tremendous enthusiasm and which, in fact, I believe I can sell.

A day in the life of *this* literary agent might offer you some insight into what the profession is like. I have hidden the warts and crises, although there is not a day without crisis, which can range from dire financial problems for an author to delayed publication of a book to late delivery of a manuscript to terrible jacket copy or artwork—and more. And for each author that crisis is a number-one priority.

And so, here's the scenario for my day:

8:30 A.M. Breakfast with an editor. This gives the agent a good opportunity to find out what kind of books that editor likes or is

ELAINE MARKSON is president of Elaine Markson Literary Agency, New York City.

searching for, in addition to digesting both breakfast and the latest gossip in that editor's publishing house or even in the industry at large. You need to start each day with a broad overview, and this is a good way to do it.

9:30 A.M. Conference with associates. This might be labeled a planning session. Here we discuss the disposition of manuscripts, deciding which editor seems right for each new manuscript. At the same time we also discuss the handling of first serial rights—that is, the sale of newspaper and magazine excerpt rights to books before publication—which can be crucial since it often serves as the introduction of the author to the reader and can also provide good publicity exposure for the book.

9:45 A.M. Phone calls to editors, both magazine and book, to discuss works in progress, new proposals, manuscripts, or problems. Periodic checks are made with editors to get decisions from them. A fast no is always preferable to a stalled project, as it gives the agent a chance to get the manuscript moving again. Often copies of the same manuscript are submitted to several editors at once, with each of them informed of the multiple submission. This can considerably shorten the time needed to sell the work, and it often gets the editorial adrenal glands working in competition, resulting in a higher purchase price than might have been the case under normal conditions. Such is not always the case, however, and the agent has to assess each property individually to decide which technique is best for that particular work. You can send a manuscript and tell the editor what your price tag is. If there's interest from that editor, a "ball park" figure is established. What happens next is called negotiation.

10:15 A.M. Contract negotiations. Agent and editor (after the offer has been made) must discuss all the complicated points of the contract. And this is where it is the duty of the agent to protect the writer to the utmost extent. Some of the questions an agent asks are, What is the advance to be paid? What are the royalties? How is the income from a paperback reprint sale split between author and publisher? What rights belong to the publisher and which to the author? What territories are involved—for instance, can the publisher sell the book in Great Britain as well as the United States? When is the book considered out of print and therefore available for the reversion of rights to the author?

Let us imagine a manuscript called *Destiny's Child*. The hypothetical publisher is Random House. The advance is $25,000, which is payable against future earnings of the book as sold by the publisher. Hardcover royalties are 10 percent, 12.5 percent, and 15 percent of the book's cover price, escalating in units of five thousand copies sold. The paperback split will be 50-50 between author and publisher up to $100,000 and 60-40 (60 percent to the author) thereafter. The author will also have approval of the paperback sale to another publisher. The publisher's exclusive sales territory is the United States, Canada, and the Philippines, with the rest of the world considered an open market. And so on. Some publisher's contracts are four pages of closely typewritten legal-size pages. Others may be as long as ten, fifteen, twenty, or even fifty pages. That seems reason enough for an author to engage a literary agent! All contracts have to be read, discussed, and negotiated anew with each book sold.

10:45 A.M. Meeting with British publisher. This is typical of any meeting with a foreign publisher. You must present your forthcoming books in a trenchant and lively fashion so that the publisher may want to buy one or more of them. It's important to provide an overall picture of your authors and their future works, even discussing works in progress. The foreign publisher could become more excited about a current book if given a sense of what looms in the future. At the same time it's sensible to get a clear picture of the foreign publishers with whom you deal and what kind of books each publishes. Most U.S. agents work with foreign agents in all languages. For example, I have representatives in France, the United Kingdom, Germany, Italy, Japan, Spain, the Netherlands, and the Scandinavian countries. (On these foreign sales an extra commission of 10 percent is paid to the agents who make them, and this comes off the total sale price.) Still, despite the activities of these foreign agents, most European publishers or their scouts and representatives visit the offices of every U.S. agent and subsidiary rights director in the business at least once or twice a year. Everyone wants to get that early look at the hot new property.

11:15 A.M. Meeting with author looking for new agent. Many published (and unpublished) authors make the rounds of several agents in order to find the situation that seems to promise the greatest likelihood of an ideal relationship. To prepare for the meeting you have to read the author's last book as well as any work under way. You discuss honestly your reactions to his or her writing and what you would hope to do for that author in the future. Sometimes you discover that the vibrations are not right, that you don't feel drawn to the person, or that the new work isn't interesting to you. Honesty, but tactful honesty, is the best policy in such cases.

11:45 A.M. Discussions with publicity director of a publishing house. This might involve the possibility of an author's tour to promote her new novel, where her books are being sent for review, or longer-range plans. You are communicating the author's ideas and requests at this time as well as your own, so that a prior discussion will have been held with the author to determine the genuine possibilities for promotion and publicity.

12:00 noon. Negotiations by telephone with Hollywood producer who wants to option a book. Many New York–based agents work in tandem with Hollywood agents, splitting commissions 50-50, to sell dramatic, TV, and motion-picture rights to each work; other New York agents work alone. To sell these rights, the agent needs to know the parameters of the deal and how to negotiate many subtle points that are quite different from book contracts. Often, an agent will work with a lawyer of the client's choosing on final negotiations, since these can be difficult contracts indeed. The producer at the other end of the line may, for example, be offering an option of $10,000 for one year to develop the book into a motion picture, with an eventual purchase price of $100,000 if the option is picked up. That is the easiest part of the negotiating process. Next you have to fret over sequels, remakes, TV series, net profits, and dozens of other equally ponderous, but absolutely necessary, clauses.

12:30 P.M. Lunch with editor. This is prime time and of prime importance. Lunch gives the agent a leisurely setting in which to discuss any ideas, proposals, or books that are current, to "introduce" clients to the editor, and to listen to the needs and desires of the publishing company. It's the time to match a writer with a publisher's project, to suggest ideas and get instant and direct feedback from the editor. An agent needs to know the likes and dislikes of all the editors with whom she deals, has to follow the best-seller charts, and, like a doctor, has to keep taking the pulse of the industry in order to get her writers working on projects that can be sold. This lunch also gives the agent the time to talk to the editor about those authors whose books are getting close to publication. The agent can get a good idea of publicity plans, print orders, and sales reaction and perhaps correct certain errors of omission prior to publication.

2:30 P.M. Meeting with the story editor of film company. This is very much like the meetings with foreign publishers, though the pitch has to be more of a hard sale and the books you're trying to sell must be those that, in your opinion, would make good films or television scripts. To do this, an agent needs to see endless movies and should also watch some television. In short, it's important to be up to date on what's going on in the media.

3:00 P.M. Return phone calls to editors, authors, Hollywood. On any given day, you may well be in the middle of an auction begun that morning. Let us say you've sent five Xerox copies of a first novel called *Breakaway* to five separate editors in five different publishing houses, asking that they make an offer before 5:00 P.M. Assuming there is interest, the offers will usually start coming in during the morning, and you must go back and forth via telephone all day until you have received the best offer. Conducting an auction requires coolness and honesty. You have to listen to the offers, relay new information back to all the bidders, hope that you get increased bids, and then assess the final situation, trying to make the best possible deal for the author. Sometimes you simply accept the best money offer; at other times you may specify that you reserve the right to base your decision on other factors as well—or to decline all offers if none is considered satisfactory. Auctions and/or multiple submissions continue to become more prevalent in the business. The difference between an auction and a multiple submission is largely a matter of formality—that is, the rules tend to be tighter in an auction.

3:30 P.M. Meeting with author to discuss new fiction idea. An agent can be very helpful in this early process when an author is beginning to develop a concept—pointing out pitfalls of plot and structure or adding to the existing story. It's an exciting time and can be very rewarding as you see the book through this stage. Sometimes a decision is made at this point to write the complete book and sell it in finished form—or to work up a good, dramatic plot outline and several chapters and to offer it on this partial basis. Selling a project on the basis of an outline is more common in the case of nonfiction ideas. A writer does not want to go through the expense of researching a complete biography, let's say, if indeed no publisher will want to publish it in the end. It can also happen, and sometimes does, that another author is already working on the same idea or subject—and it's obviously preferable to find this out early rather than when you have a complete manuscript.

4:15 P.M. Discussion with author about editor's suggestions for revision. It is often necessary for the agent to act as intermediary when author and editor become stalemated over editorial problems. And this happens more frequently than one would expect. New authors are on shaky ground and usually want to please, so that they may not have the courage of their own convictions. An agent, who knows the work from conception, can often help the writer to express his own feelings and to cope with the criticism of the editor.

4:45 P.M. Phone calls from the West Coast, from Chicago, from any place that's in an earlier time zone.

5:15 P.M. Drinks with magazine editor. This gives the agent an opportunity to discuss the nonfiction writers she represents and possible story assignments.

6:30 P.M. Home to the family—if you're lucky—to start dinner and to listen to your children.

7:30 P.M. Dinner—without, one hopes, telephone interruptions!

8:30 P.M. Read manuscripts and correspondence, dictate letters for the following day. Or go to a film screening, return home, and *then*

start reading manuscripts. Or go to late dinner with an editor, forei͓
publisher, or movie scout and then straggle home to dash off as much
work as possible. (All of this may explain the popularity of Perrier water
as the industry drink. How else could one maintain one's focus at 2
A.M.?)

There are several different kinds of agents in the business today. Some
are lawyer-agents who spend little or no time on writers' personal matters.
Some are connected with very large firms with offices in New York,
Hollywood, and abroad. There are middle-sized groups of, say, three or
four agents. And there are independent single agents who may work
with only an assistant or two. In any and all cases, their chief aim
should be to speak as the voice of their writers, to be their representative
to the industry, their lawyer, doctor, friend. Obviously, this business
would not exist without the presence of writers, and it is up to the
agent to continually remind those in powerful places that this is *the fact*
of life.

As my sample agent's schedule suggests, it's tough and demanding
but there is also much pleasure in the life of a literary agent. Quality
begins in the agent's office. It is up to you to search out that quality
and to press and impress upon publishers the necessity of maintaining
high standards even as they publish one *Princess Daisy* after another.
They have to make money, that is true. But sometimes they may forget
that quality outlasts the moment, and it is up to the dedicated agent
to remind them of that repeatedly.

An agent is in business to make money also, of course. You have to
assess your client list so that, although it may range from the most
literary avant garde to the most exciting nonfiction, it also includes
commercial novels. Agents like myself feel it is possible to have such a
range but also to maintain high standards. There's no excitement like
brilliant prose or interesting and cogent ideas, and being able to help
books with such qualities find their way step-by-step into print is what
makes an agent's job truly rewarding.

CHAPTER SEVEN

Publishing Contract: An introductory Overview to Publishing and the Law

JAMES FOX AND LINDA K. RAWSON

Our scheme for this introductory review of a publishing contract is to take you through the sequence of events from the author's first approach to a publisher to the reversion of rights to the author some time after a book is published. We will also discuss the contractual provisions and some other legal considerations that generally apply to the author-publisher relationship at each stage in that sequence.

The Deal

An author's first approach to a publisher, often made through a literary agent, may be a call or a letter to say that the author's next book is available. Let's say for our hypothetical case that the agent tells you, the editor, that the author wants $10,000. To know what "I want $10,000" means, you need to know about literary property rights and about how publishers generally make payments to authors.

The creator of a literary property, the author, owns all of the rights to that property (assuming it is wholly original) and can make one grant of all those rights or separate grants of each right. (From here on, our literary property will be referred to as "the work.") Determining what rights will be granted to the publisher is an important part of the negotiation of the deal.

A publisher obtains two kinds of rights: the right to publish editions of the work under its own imprints and the right to license other parties to exploit rights to the work, the latter commonly referred to as subrights. Subrights possibilities include first serial rights (publication in newspapers

JAMES FOX is assistant general counsel at Harper & Row, Publishers. LINDA K. RAWSON is assistant to the general counsel at the same firm.

and magazines prior to book publication); book-club and paperback rights; second serial rights (publication in newspapers and magazines after book publication); permission rights (publication of short sections of work in other books or in periodicals); British and foreign-language rights; motion-picture, television, radio, and live-stage dramatic adaptation rights; commercial rights (the right to use portions of the work as the basis for commercial products, such as renditions of characters on T-shirts); and recording rights, which include the right to authorize verbatim recordings of the work by any means, including electronic transmission, and storage and retrieval systems.

The author's compensation for sales of the publisher's editions is a royalty, generally expressed as a percentage of the publisher's suggested selling price or as a percentage of the amounts received by the publisher from such sales. The author's compensation from subrights is a percentage of the publisher's proceeds from each subrights license. How these proceeds are allocated or split is subject to negotiation.

Assume that in offering the work to you, the agent told you that the author is willing to grant your publisher U.S. hardcover book publication rights with a 10 percent royalty based on suggested retail price and to grant reprint, book-club, second serial, and permission rights, all on a 50-50 split. The author intends to retain all other rights.

Now that you know about rights and splits, how do you analyze the financial request? "The author wants $10,000" means that the author wants that sum as an advance, all of which would probably be paid prior to publication. After publication, royalties accruing to the author's account from sales and the author's share of subrights proceeds are held by the publisher until the total withheld equals the advance paid. Your concern is whether your publisher can reasonably expect to sell enough copies and receive enough money from subrights licenses to recoup an advance of $10,000 or, better, exceed it.

Your sales department estimates that about three thousand copies of the hardcover edition will be sold. You estimate that the suggested retail price will be $10. At a 10 percent royalty, this should generate $3,000 for the author's account. Your subrights department estimates that paperback rights will be licensed for a $5,000 advance and book-club rights for a $2,000 advance. Assuming a 50-50 split, these licenses will produce another $3,500 for the author's account. Since the estimated total of book royalties and subrights proceeds is only $6,500, the agent's request for a $10,000 advance appears high. You tell the agent you are interested in the book, but you offer $7,500 as an advance. The agent says that this is too low. You make a counteroffer: You will pay an advance of $8,500 if you also obtain first serial rights on a 90-10 split and translation rights on a 75-25 split.

Your subrights department prepared you with the information that the first serial rights might go for $1,000—on a 90-10 split that is $900 more for the author's account—and that translation rights might realize $2,000—on a 75-25 split that's $1,500 more for the author's account. This addition of $2,400 to the original $6,500 estimate gives you expected author's earnings of $8,900.

The agent replies that the author will grant these additional rights on the splits you've suggested, but holds out for a total advance of $9,000. This is close enough to your estimate, so you can make the deal: a $9,000 advance for U.S. book publication rights for a 10 percent royalty and a grant of first serial, second serial, book-club, reprint, and translation rights, subject to the above splits. (The revenues from second serial and permission rights are generally modest, so these sources have not been included in the calculations.)

The financial analysis of the deal described relates only to whether the author's advance will be earned out. It is not an analysis of the profitability of the publication of the book. In such an analysis, the unit cost of printing the book (paper, printing, binding, artwork, and so on) and expenses for advertising, overhead, shipping and warehousing, and sales would be considered along with the author's royalty advance and the royalty payments. The total of these expenditures is compared to the total of the publisher's estimated revenues from sales and subrights to determine whether the book will be profitable. Keep in mind that calculating the profitability of a project is quite different from calculating whether or not a royalty advance will be recouped. Even though the negotiation described between an agent and an editor applies to trade publishing, this analysis of rights and accountings applies to most publishing agreements.

The Contract—Do We Really Need All Those Words?

Your desk is covered with pieces of paper on which you made notes during your negotiations with the author's agent. You organize the notes and have the terms incorporated into your publisher's form agreement, a six-page document in small type. The agent gets the contract and immediately calls and asks, "Do we really need all these words?" In the same conversation, the agent suggests several riders that will add two more pages.

What are "all these words"? We are not going to go through a clause-by-clause analysis of a specific publishing contract, but will offer some generalities about publishing contracts; we will be more specific about some of these provisions at that point in the sequence of the publishing process where each is most applicable.

A contract is a written document that spells out the rights and obligations of each party. By signing a contract, each party agrees to be bound by its provisions. The simplest way to get through all the words in a publishing contract is to examine separately the obligations of the author and the obligations of the publisher.

The author's obligations include a grant of rights for a specified geographic territory and a specified period of time; a commitment to deliver a manuscript by a definite date; a specific description of that manuscript; and the author's representations about the work. The publisher's obligations include publication of the work by a certain date; payment of advances and accounting for royalties on a periodic basis; and protection of the published work by printing an appropriate copyright notice.

In preparing the contract, after you are sure these essential terms are covered, you should ask yourself whether any special provisions are important to the deal. Did you agree to an advertising budget or to give the author approval of the exploitation of any subrights or the jacket or of the advertising copy? Is there any unique commitment you want the author to make that is not provided for in your publisher's form contract? Is it important that the author be available for promotional appearances when the book is published? Have you asked the author not to write another book on the same subject for a period of time? If so, be sure these commitments are also included in the contract.

What we have been discussing is a license, a contract whereby the author, as the proprietor of the copyright to a work, grants to the publisher certain rights for a period of time, reserves others, and receives compensation for each right exercised by the publisher. There is a different kind of a contract that may be used on certain occasions. In a work-for-hire agreement, the person doing the writing acknowledges that it is being done under the direction and supervision of the publisher and that when completed, the publisher will be considered the author for copyright purposes and the owner of all rights to the copyright. Often, such work is done on a flat-fee basis. Under the Copyright Act, the kinds of works that can be considered works for hire are very specifically defined. They include specially ordered works such as translations, instructional texts, introductions, and graphic materials that supplement the underlying text. The most general guideline for determining whether a work-for-hire agreement is appropriate is to establish that the conceptual creation is the publisher's and that the author is simply fulfilling a very particular writing task under the direction and supervision of the publisher.

Manuscript Preparation and Acceptance

An author-publisher contract is often signed long before the work is written. Assume for our hypothetical case that the contract provides that the manuscript will be delivered three years after the contract is signed. How can you make sure that the manuscript, when delivered, will be the book you wanted to publish when you entered the contract?

The contract should state the length of the manuscript, generally expressed in the number of words, and it should include some details about the content. However, publishing contracts often include no more than a general reference to the topic of the work, such as "an untitled book of nonfiction about World War II." If you are willing to publish just about anything a well-known author might write, a vague description would be fine. However, if it is important that an author cover specific aspects of a subject in a particular way or if an outline prepared by an author was the basis for your interest in a project, it is advisable to attach a listing of those aspects or the outline. A more detailed description will serve as a guide to the author in fulfilling the author's obligation and will prove most helpful when you are considering the acceptability of the manuscript.

Many publishing contracts provide that the manuscript has to be satisfactory in content and form to the publisher. It does not matter that the author's agent, the author's mother, and the author's best friend, who happens to be an esteemed literary critic, think the manuscript is dandy. The author has agreed to meet the publisher's standards of what is acceptable and publishable. Such clauses should be considered in light of a recent court decision. It was held that an "acceptable to publisher" provision cannot be invoked in an arbitrary or capricious way and that if a publisher finds a manuscript unacceptable, it must enumerate its deficiencies and allow the author a reasonable opportunity to revise it. It is much easier to review manuscripts in accordance with the requisite good-faith standard if you are able to rely on a detailed description of the book, rather than on a vague reference to its subject matter. Hence, we reiterate our suggestion that it will prove helpful to add to a contract as much as possible about the content of the book.

Before you accept a manuscript, it is important to be sure that no revisions are required and that the author has performed all stipulated obligations (such as delivery of graphic materials or permissions), because acceptance means the author has completed performance and can rightfully expect that the manuscript will be published as accepted. After acceptance, it is customary not to make any changes without the author's approval, except for copyediting, and even copyediting changes often are contractually subject to the author's approval. If you are to have the right to take what the author has written and rework it, the contract should specifically give you that right.

Revisions

In addition to the author's obligation to deliver a manuscript, you may want to consider whether it is appropriate to include in a contract a commitment whereby the author agrees to provide revised copy for new editions of the work at some subsequent time. Such a provision has no place in a contract for a work of fiction, a biography, or another work that, when written, should be the author's definitive statement on a particular subject. However, where a work includes information that has a certain currency and is subject to change, such as medical and technical information, it may be appropriate to require in the contract that the author prepare revisions on a periodic basis.

   If the author has a contractual commitment to revise the manuscript, it is important to work out in advance what happens in the event that the author is unable or unwilling to revise at the time the publisher requests a revision. Some publishing contracts give the publisher the right, in such event, to arrange for the preparation of a revised edition by a reviser of the publisher's choice. Often, the amount paid to the reviser(s) and the credit given is determined by the publisher and deducted from the original author's royalties. How this is worked out is subject to negotiation.

Manuscript Review

After the manuscript has been accepted, there are certain legal issues that need to be considered before it is ready for publication. Does any material in the manuscript present a threat of lawsuits for invasion of privacy or libel? Does permission need to be obtained for material quoted from copyrighted sources? Is there any possibility that the application of information or instructions in the manuscript might cause damage when applied by the reader?

LIBEL

To introduce you to the law of libel, we quote from Robert D. Sack's book, *Libel, Slander, and Related Problems* (New York: Practising Law Institute, October 24, 1980): "Simple statements about the law of libel . . . should be made with caution. . . . Things are rarely simple."

Since any manuscript that presents libel issues will be turned over to your publisher's counsel for review, you may ask, why should I know anything about this area? First, authors may ask you questions as they prepare manuscripts and will expect you to provide guidance; second, you may be the person who determines whether a manuscript is to be reviewed by counsel. In addition, you may have to act as the liaison between the author and the lawyer who reviews the manuscript.

We present two general considerations before defining a libelous statement. First, not only individuals, but also corporations, partnerships, charitable organizations, and commercial products can be libeled. Second, individuals can maintain an action for libel only during their own lives; no such action can be brought posthumously.

A libelous statement can be defined in a generalized way as (1) an untruthful (2) statement (3) about an identifiable party (4) that is damaging to that party's reputation. The numbers in parentheses identify the elements of a libelous statement that we will discuss, in reverse order, to provide a sequence for you to use to identify potentially libelous material.

Certain kinds of statements traditionally have been found damaging to reputation: attributions of criminal conduct, statements that an individual is unfit for that individual's profession, and attributions of dishonesty. Statements that fall within these categories should be easy to identify. Another type of statement traditionally found libelous is one that causes individuals to suffer ridicule and contempt in their community. One test to determine whether a particular statement falls within this last category is to consider what your reaction might be if the statement were made about you: Might people avoid you or think of you as ridiculous? Or would people consider the statement good-natured ribbing? This test is not always reliable because you must also consider the unique circumstances of the community of the subject of the statement. To say that Mr. Brown, a stand-up comedian, is crude, lewd, and blasphemous is probably not damaging to his reputation because such traits are acceptable, if not expected, from many in that profession. To say that the Reverend Mr. Brown, a distinguished religious leader, is crude, lewd, and blasphemous would undoubtedly hold the cleric up to contempt in his community.

If you believe a statement is damaging to reputation, next consider whether readers will be able to identify the subject of the statement. The statement "A doctor in a major metropolitan hospital is known to have prescribed fourteen fatal doses of xychloroprene" certainly diminishes the reputation of a doctor, but assuming there is no other detail given about the doctor, the reader would not be able to identify the particular doctor referred to. However, look carefully for details that may lead to identification. This quote, harmless in itself, may appear on page 10; on page 42 there may be details that make it easy for the reader to identify the doctor discussed on page 10.

There may be no identification problem if a statement is made about a group so large that no member of the group can be identified. Consider the following possibilities. "Many department store clerks pilfer"; "many of the clerks at the Glutz department store (which employs six hundred people) pilfer"; "the clerks who work at the tie counter on the first floor of Glutz department store on Saturday afternoons pilfer." In the first two quotes, the groups are large, it is not stated that all clerks pilfer, and no particular clerk is identified. In the third example, the group is probably small; consequently, three or four clerks are probably identifiable and could maintain a libel action.

If you are concerned that a character in a work of fiction, described in a defamatory way, may be identifiable with a living person, a useful test is to list together all the details in the manuscript about that character (physical description, age, profession, marital status, residence, and so on), however scattered through the manuscript they may be. Then ask the author if those details, when presented together, could possibly lead to the identity of a living person. This test can also be useful in works of nonfiction where people are given fictitious names. In such books, simply using a fictitious name may not be sufficient to conceal identity.

After you have decided that a passage is damaging to reputation and identifies a living individual, consider whether the passage is fact or opinion. A statement of opinion may be defensible in libel action. Some statements are clearly statements of opinion: for instance, "It is not in the best interests of the United States to invade Tierra del Fuego." Others may be characterized as opinion if the factual basis for the opinion is presented and there is a rational nexus between those facts and the opinion expressed. This distinction is not easy to make, and questionable material should be reviewed by counsel.

If you are faced with a putative or nominally factual statement that is decidedly damaging to the reputation of an identifiable living individual, consider if the author can establish that the statement is true. Truth is a defense to a libel action. A conscientious effort should be undertaken to compile and review carefully with an author all the corroborating sources (such as notes from interviews, other published accounts, and court records) for statements of fact that are damaging to reputation and to make sure those sources are reputable and reliable, are readily available, and can substantiate such statements should a claim be made.

Where statements made about public officials and public figures have been the subject of libel actions, courts have held that such persons have to prove that an allegedly libelous statement was made with knowledge that it was false or with reckless disregard of whether it was true or false. Where statements about private figures involved in a matter of public interest have been the basis of a libel action, courts have held that the private figure must prove that an allegedly libelous statement was made with negligence. (This standard varies from state to state.)

The bottom line is: Exercise care in reviewing manuscripts and seek the advice of counsel about potentially troublesome material.

RIGHT OF PRIVACY

In addition to being alert to material that may be potentially libelous, you should also be sensitive to material that may infringe upon an individual's right of privacy. As in a libel action, only a living individual can maintain an invasion-of-privacy action. However, one cannot invade the privacy of corporations, partnerships, or charitable entities. This is only a right of individuals. An important similarity to libel is that the subject of the statement must be identifiable; all the tests for identity discussed in the libel section apply to determining whether a reasonable reader would find that material that presents a privacy problem is about an identifiable living individual.

The right of privacy is really three distinct rights. Living individuals are protected from (1) truthful, public revelation of embarrassing private facts; (2) publicity that places an individual in a false light; and (3) the use of an individual's name or likeness for purposes of trade. The phrase "the truthful, public revelation of embarrassing private facts" refers to the publication of information that most people would consider embarrassing, highly personal, and not of legitimate newsworthy concern to the public. Sometimes this aspect of privacy is described as the revelation of squeamish detail. Truth is not a defense here as it is in libel; the revelation of truthful but private details is prohibited. Obvious examples of such material include information about an individual's medical history or highly intimate aspects of marriages or other personal relationships. The test of whether a statement is actionable is whether a reasonable person would be shocked or outraged by the publication of the information.

The public official or public figure status of an individual is as important here as it is in libel. Court decisions have given such figures a lesser right to claim embarrassment than is allowed the nine-to-five accountant who minds her own business. When individuals who are private figures become part of a public event, such as a crime, hurricane, or other disaster, they may involuntarily relinquish some protection as information about them becomes newsworthy. In assessing whether information about such people can be published if it might be deemed private information, consider how such information is presented. If there is a sensational or morbid tone, the newsworthy defense may not apply.

False light is similar to libel and means giving a false impression of an individual that would be highly offensive to a reasonable person. What makes this different from libel is that the material need not be defamatory to be actionable. What individuals are protected from is the false attribution of characteristics, thoughts, or activities, even though flattering. A well-known case in this area involves a baseball player who was described in an unauthorized biography as having been an exemplary boy scout and an air force pilot. While the attribution of these accomplishments did not lessen the baseball player's reputation, both were untrue and he won the lawsuit. Another example involved the widow of a disaster victim who was described some time after her husband's death as being in a more pitiable, reduced state than was accurate. Truth is a defense to this aspect of privacy law because facts, if stated accurately, cannot create a false light.

By statute or by court decision, most states protect living individuals from having their names or likenesses used for purposes of trade without their written consent. The emphasis is on "for purposes of trade," and the primary aim of this right of privacy is to protect individuals from an unauthorized use of their names and likenesses for product endorsements. You may question what concerns this presents to book publishers. The connection is the issue as to whether use of photos on the cover or in the interior of a book falls within the statutory prohibition against use of a person's likeness for purposes of trade. Courts have ruled that the publication of photographs of public events does not infringe this right because, in participating in the public events, individuals are assumed to consent to press coverage of those events. Posed photographs, however, do present a problem, and photographers should be required before publication to provide written consents from the subjects of such photographs. Particular caution is in order with photographs that demonstrate medical procedures or that depict private activities (such as a group therapy session). Publisher's counsel should be consulted if you are uncertain about the form of release to use or about whether a particular photograph could pose a legal problem.

You should also review captions carefully, as they can distort the meaning of an otherwise innocent photograph. A photograph showing a group of people shouting slogans at a political rally in Central Park and simply identified as "Anti–Nuclear Arms Demonstrations in Central Park" would most likely not present a legal problem. The same photograph, captioned "Persons Demonstrating Mob Hysteric Schizophrenia," would present a legal problem, as individuals included in the photograph might contend that the ailment was attributed to them.

On the subject of releases, you may be able to avoid some libel and privacy problems with text by having authors obtain releases from people they interview. Such releases should provide that the subject of the interview agrees to the publication of information obtained during the interview and that the subject will not commence a libel or privacy suit based on publication of the interview. For certain books, you may find it helpful to have an author meet with counsel before the author starts interviewing people, in order to obtain an appropriate release form.

It is most important to keep careful records of your prepublication review and to obtain and have on file documents produced by an author in support of sensitive material. In the event a claim is made after publication, you will want to have such documentation readily available. And, as your own review may be at issue should there be litigation, you will want to have a good paper record of how thorough and conscientious the review has been.

PERMISSIONS
Manuscripts also have to be reviewed prior to publication to determine whether the author has used copyrighted material for which written permission must be obtained from the copyright proprietor. It is the author's responsibility to bring to the publisher's attention any portions of a manuscript that are excerpts from copyrighted sources. (Whether the author or the publisher is responsible for obtaining and paying for permission fees should be covered in the contract.) You will then have to determine if permission is necessary, or if the use is a fair use that does not require permission.

Fair use, a doctrine developed by the courts and incorporated into the 1976 Copyright Act as Section 107, puts certain limits on a copyright proprietor's right to control exclusively the use of material and allows certain uses of copyrighted material without permission. The four factors to be applied together in determining whether a particular use is fair, as set forth in Section 107 of the Copyright Act, are: (1) the purpose and character of the use, (2) the nature of the copyrighted work, (3) the amount and substantiality of the portion used in relation to the copyrighted work as a whole, and (4) the effect of the use upon the potential market for or value of the copyrighted work.

In light of these standards, it should be clear that while it might be fair use to include a short excerpt from a copyrighted book as part of a critical commentary, it would not be fair use to reproduce a substantial section of a work in an anthology where it would be reprinted for its own value and not for purpose of comment. Additionally, the shorter the source the author quotes from, the less the author may quote without permission.

If you are interested in knowing more about fair use, you should obtain a copy of the Congressional Committee Reports on the Copyright Revision Act of 1976 from Commerce Clearing House in Chicago. The reports contain a brief and enlightening review of the doctrine of fair use and of each of the four factors cited above.

PRODUCTS LIABILITY

In reviewing manuscripts, you should also be informed about an area of law known as products liability, which refers to the liability of a manufacturer for physical injuries and property damage that customers may suffer through the use of the manufacturer's product. This concept was recently applied to the editorial content of a book in an action where a publisher was held liable for the injuries suffered by two junior high school chemistry students while using the publisher's chemistry lab text. The court found that warnings in the book were insufficient.

The potential for this kind of liability should cause you to exercise care in editing books that contain information or advice that could cause injury. Such books include exercise books, diet books, cookbooks, and other instructional books. Be particularly cautious about books containing how-to projects for children. By browsing through a selection of diet, exercise, and instructional books, you will note that many of them include prominent warnings. For instance, diet books often have prominently placed in the introductory material a statement similar to the following: "You should consult your physician before starting any weight-loss program." Precautions often appear throughout the text of such books.

You might also want to consider having certain books reviewed or tested by experts. Authors are sometimes so close to their subject matter that they may oversimplify material or miss obvious inaccuracies. An expert with a fresh eye may be able to correct this.

Copyright

Copyright protection is obtained by printing an appropriate copyright notice in each copy of the work printed. The U.S. Copyright Act requires a notice to contain three elements: the word *Copyright* or the symbol

© (for Universal Copyright Convention protection it is essential that the © symbol appear), the name of the copyright proprietor, and the year the work was created. A proper notice would read as follows, "© 1982 by Osgood Spatsford." The Copyright Act does not prescribe where a notice should appear but only requires that it be placed in such manner and location as to give reasonable notice of copyright. Under the old Copyright Act, in effect until December 31, 1977, the notice had to appear on the title page or the verso of the title page, and most publishers continue to follow that rule.

In addition to printing a copyright notice in each copy of the publisher's edition of a work, the publisher also has a responsibility to protect the copyright by requiring purchasers of subsidiary rights to print the proper notice in copies of or portions of the work published by them. If an entire book is to be reprinted, it is appropriate to provide that the licensee will publish the notice exactly as it appears, in both form and placement, in the publisher's edition. Where the right to publish a portion of a work is granted, it is preferable to state in the license exactly what the contents of the notice should be and where it should appear.

Registration of a copyright with the U.S. Copyright Office is not a prerequisite for copyright protection in the United States. However, because registration is required to bring a copyright infringement suit, it is advisable to register the copyright promptly after publication. This is done by completing a TX form and submitting it, with a fee and two copies of the book on which copyright is claimed, to the Copyright Office in Washington, D.C. TX forms and helpful instructional materials about the completion of the TX form may be obtained from the Copyright Office. The Copyright Office will also answer some questions on the telephone.

The term of copyright available in the United States depends on whether a work was published before or after January 1, 1978, the effective date of the new Copyright Act. Table 7.1 sets forth how the duration of copyright is determined under the new act.

Publication

Most publishing contracts specify a time within which the publisher must publish an edition of a book, and the period usually begins to run from the date of acceptance of the manuscript. For this reason, it is important to keep records of the data on which a manuscript is accepted to make sure this commitment is met. The contract may also

TABLE 7.1 DETERMINATION OF DURATION OF COPYRIGHT

TYPE OF WORK	PERIOD OF PROTECTION
Works created after January 1, 1978	Life of the author plus 50 years (when there is more than one author, the date of death of the last surviving author is used to determine the duration of the term).
Works made for hire created after or published after January 1, 1978	75 years from publication or 100 years from creation, whichever expires first.
Works in their first term of copyright on January 1, 1978	Until the end of the 75th calendar year from first publication, provided a proper renewal is filed with the Copyright Office during the 28th year from first publication. (Under the old act, there were two terms of copyright of 28 years each, for a total term of 56 years. However, to obtain protection for the second term, a renewal application had to be filed with the Copyright Office. Renewal continues to be a requirement for works published before 1978.)
Works in their second term of copyright on January 1, 1978, because a proper renewal had been filed.	The end of the 75th calendar year from first publication.

require publication in a particular format, for example, a hardcover edition.

Other than these requirements, the details of publication (such as the quantity of the first printing, the design and presentation of the book, and advertising and promotional efforts) are left to the publisher's discretion, as these decisions fall within the publisher's area of expertise. Often publishers will consult with authors as a matter of courtesy about many of these details. However, if you have made a commitment on any of these matters (the most common is to agree that the author has the right to approve the jacket), be sure to include that commitment in the contract.

Accounting

Publishing agreements usually provide that accountings will be rendered on an annual or semiannual basis. These statements of account report the number of copies sold, the royalty rates at which those copies have sold, and any proceeds received from subrights during the applicable period.

Although the statements are prepared by an accounting department, most editors like to review them before they are sent out to authors. It is important to make sure that advances and other charges the author has agreed to apply to the account (such as permission or photography fees) are properly deducted. You will also want to make sure you understand your publisher's accountings so you can answer questions authors may have.

Subsidiary Rights

Having struck a hard bargain with the agent during the contract negotiations and obtained more subrights than originally offered, you should be armed with some information about how subrights are negotiated and what a subrights agreement should contain. Basically, a subrights agreement is a mirror image of the author-publisher contract; the difference is that the publisher stands in the position of author and makes commitments to the licensee similar to those commitments made by the author to the publisher. What follows is a summary of the terms of the publishing contract we have already discussed and how they should be considered when reviewing the subrights license.

1. Grant of Rights. The right granted should be very specifically defined. Look out for language that may expand on the right you specifically want to grant. For instance, if you want to license only the right to publish a reprint edition of the book for general distribution, the license should not include the right to sublicense that right or to publish book-club editions. If the right being granted is to publish an excerpt in a periodical, make sure the periodical publisher does not obtain the right to sublicense reprints of the excerpt.

2. Term. If you are granting the right to publish a work in its entirety, the term should be for a specific period of years, somewhere between five and ten years, and the rights granted should automatically revert at the end of that term. This reversion gives the publisher the right to negotiate a new license if the licensee is still interested in the work at the end of the initial term. If you are granting the right to publish a portion of the work in a periodical, the license should be specific about what portion will be published and in what issue it will be published.

3. Manuscript Delivery. Since subrights are usually licensed after a manuscript is accepted, the licensee should not be concerned about the problems of manuscript acceptability. The licensee should agree to publish the text exactly as printed by the licensor and should agree not to make any changes without the licensor's prior consent.

4. Representations, Warranties, and Indemnities. The licensee will most likely request the same kind of representations, warranties, and indemnities that the publisher obtained from the author, in effect an extension of these warranties and indemnities to the licensee. Because of this frequent requirement, the author contract should include a provision whereby the publisher may extend the author's warranties and indemnities to its licensees.

5. Publication. The license should provide the date or a time limit within which the licensee must publish and a provision for reversion of rights if the work is not published within the time agreed upon.

6. Payments. Payments made under a license are either in the form of royalties (if the license covers the right to reprint copies of the work and sell them over a period of time) or fees (more commonly the consideration where serialization and permission rights are granted). There should be a provision for periodic accountings if income from the license will take place over a period of time.

7. Copyright. As discussed above, it is crucial that each license include a provision whereby the licensee agrees to include in its edition or in portions published by it a copyright notice exactly as the copyright appears in the licensor's edition of the book.

What To Do in the Event a Claim Is Made

If after a book is published, you receive a letter either directly from a claimant or from a lawyer asserting that the book you have published infringes a copyright, libels someone, or invades a right of privacy, you should do two things immediately: get legal help and inform the author. Any legal claim, however frivolous it may appear to you, should immediately be brought to the attention of your publisher's counsel. Do not attempt to draft a response yourself without professional advice. You may say something that will serve you badly at a later time.

It is also important to bring a claim to the immediate attention of the author. In fact, the author's indemnification of the publisher may even be conditioned upon prompt receipt of information about any claim. You should also encourage the author not to try to respond to the claim before seeking legal advice. At the same time, ask the author to send you any information that may be relevant to the claim.

The allocation of the responsibility between the author and publisher in the event a claim is made is handled differently by every publisher. Lawsuits are very expensive, and the issue of how the expenses of such claims are to be allocated is of great concern to authors and publishers.

When we discussed the contents of the publishing contract, we stated that the author makes certain representations and warranties. Whether the author is responsible for the claim at all depends on whether it relates to a representation the author has made and what responsibility the indemnification provision imposes on the author in the event of a claim. The representations the author makes to the publisher include these: that no grant of rights has been made or will be made that conflicts with the grant of rights made to the publisher (that is, the book you are publishing is not subject to a prior grant of rights or some other contractual commitment), that the book is the original work of the author and has not been copied from another source (that is, that on publication the publisher will not be faced with an infringement claim), and that the book does not contain material that is libelous or constitutes an invasion of any of the rights of privacy.

Assume that a claim is made that a published book contains three chapters that are directly copied from another book. This claim would clearly relate to the author's representation of originality. Before discussing the author's responsibility for the claim, financial and otherwise, we should consider the potential outcome of any claim. There are three possibilities. The claimant may actually sue the publisher and the author, and there may be a court determination that the alleged infringement is not an infringement. In that event, there is no liability on the part of publisher or author to the claimant, but court costs and lawyers' fees have been incurred in defending the claim. The second possibility is that the claim will be settled. This means that the parties may examine the claim, determine that the claim has merit, and decide that the better course is to pay the claimant for use of the material. Or the claim might be settled because it makes better economic sense for the parties to avoid the expense of litigation. The third outcome is that a court could find that there was an infringement and that damages are owed to the claimant. The costs incurred in the respective claims would include (1) for successful defense, the counsel fees involved in that defense and court costs; (2) for a settlement, the cost of settlement and perhaps the counsel fees for negotiation of the settlement; and (3) for judgment, the cost of the damages awarded and, again, the counsel fees incurred. Whether the author is responsible for these amounts depends upon the indemnification provision in a specific publishing contract. Publishers handle these issues in as many ways as there are publishers. Your responsibility should be to become familiar with the warranty and indemnification provisions in your publisher's contract so you can fully and fairly advise an author about an author's responsibility for legal claims.

End of the Line—Reversion of Rights

Publishing agreements usually provide that the grant of rights is made for the full term of the copyright (under the new Copyright Act, the life of the author plus fifty years). You should be aware that the Copyright Act (in Section 203) provides that any grant of rights may be terminated thirty-five years from the date of the execution of that grant. The act allows a five-year period for such termination to take effect. This means a contract signed in 1980 could be terminated by the party that made the grant at any time between 2005 and 2010. (If the author is dead the author's rights of termination are owned and may be exercised by a widow or widower and by the author's children or grandchildren.)

In addition to this statutory right, authors often insist, and rightfully so, that contracts contain a provision whereby rights are to be reverted when a publisher stops exercising rights under the contract. The customary contractual provision requires the publisher to keep an edition of the book in print, either under its own imprint or under a license, and if the publisher fails to do so, the author has the right to demand that the book be reissued or to obtain a reversion of rights within an agreed-upon period of time.

If you receive a request for reversion, it is important to respond promptly. Usually, contracts allow the publisher a time within which to get the book back in print if it is out of print at the time a reversion request is received; the time begins to run when the request is received. If you want to reissue the book, you will want to use the allotted time period wisely.

Conclusion

Virtually every concept we have touched upon is the tip of an iceberg. There are entire books on many of these concepts, but our aim has been to give you a summary of issues you should be aware of. These subjects are complicated, but as you work with them you will gain more understanding of them.

PART TWO

Production

CHAPTER EIGHT

Book Production and Design

DOUGLAS KUBACH

The production process—converting an author's manuscript into a book—is central to the publishing process. Parameters of the production process (and answers to such fundamental questions as what the book will look like, how it will be made, or how much this will cost and how long it will take) are established by the author's intentions, as revealed by the form and content of the manuscript, and the publisher's intentions, as revealed by the plans for the book's sale and distribution. A plan for production must relate the exigencies of cost, the time pressures of scheduled deadlines, and the availability of efficient manufacturing processes and materials within these basic parameters.

Since most production tasks are performed by specialists, the primary job of people working in a production department is supervision; the process of producing a book typically involves coordinating the work of designers, illustrators, typesetters, printers, and binders with the work of authors, editors, and others involved in the publishing process. All of the production functions—planning, designing, estimating, scheduling, purchasing materials, and selecting and supervising suppliers— require a certain amount of technical knowledge that must be obtained through hands-on experience and the study of information that is too detailed to cover here except in summary fashion. Several more comprehensive sources for further study are cited later. I hope this chapter can be a starting place—an introduction to the business of book production and design.

Background

PRINTING
Traditionally, publishing has been synonomous with printing—creating multiple copies of a work for sale and distribution. This has already

DOUGLAS KUBACH is vice president and director of production and manufacturing at Westview Press.

begun to change in some fields, such as reference publishing, where other media than the printed page can offer advantages: Electronic data bases can be continuously updated and more easily searched through for specific information; microfiche or optical discs can hold massive collections of data in remarkably compact spaces; videotapes can contain images in motion along with static pictures, texts, and sound. But the primacy of the printed image for conveying ideas and information in an accessible form and as a permanent record of human thought is still very real.

Printing processes produce multiple copies of an image after converting the original image into a printing-image carrier; the printing-image carrier, or printing plate, can be inked, forming an ink image that can be transferred to paper to produce a printed image. Original images can be classified as (1) text, or reading matter composed of letters, words, and sentences; (2) line art, or illustrations composed of discrete lines, dots, and solid areas; (3) continuous-tone art, such as photographs, that contain a continuous range of tonal values; (4) multicolor art composed of two or more flat colors; and (5) full-color images, such as color photographs, that contain a full range of tones and colors. Each group presents unique reproduction problems, but all original images must be converted into printing-image carriers before they can be printed.

Printing-image carriers are the common denominator of printing; the major commercial printing methods use fundamentally different kinds of printing-image carriers:

1. Letterpress is a relief printing method: Printing images are raised in relief above nonprinting areas on the printing plate.
2. Gravure is an intaglio printing method: Printing images are embedded (etched or engraved) in the printing plate, below the surface, which is the nonprinting area.
3. Lithography is a planographic printing method: Printing images are carried on the same surface, or plane, as the nonprinting areas of the printing plate, but are made chemically distinct. The printing-image areas of the plate are made chemically receptive to a greasy ink, while nonprinting areas of the plate are chemically receptive to water and repel the ink. The printing plate is first dampened, then inked, and the ink adheres only to the ink-receptive image areas. Most commercial lithographic presses combine lithography with the offset principle: The inked image on the plate is transferred, or offset, to an intermediary surface—the blanket—then to the paper. The smooth rubber blanket improves printing quality on a variety of paper surfaces and lengthens plate life.
4. Screen printing is a porous printing method: Printing-image areas on

a porous screen fabric permit ink to pass through the screen onto the paper, while nonprinting areas on the screen block the ink.

Letterpress is the original printing method, but has been almost completely superseded in the book industry by offset lithography.[1] The reasons behind this are complex and relate to economic and technological factors. Simply explained, prepress costs for preparing original images and making plates for offset lithography are dramatically lower, and offset lithography can reproduce all kinds of images—including full-color images—on a wider variety of paper surfaces with superior results.

Offset lithography is often called photo-offset (or simply offset) because photographic techniques are essential to convert original images into printable images (see Figure 8.1). Conventional surface plates for offset are made by a photomechanical process. Original images are photographed using special films[2] to create negatives—images carried on a film base with reversed tonal values; light areas in the original become black and opaque on the film, dark areas become clear and transparent. The negatives, when placed over an unexposed printing plate, serve as masks to block light from nonprinting areas and admit light to printing-image areas on the plate. The plate is coated with a photosensitive emulsion that becomes ink-receptive after exposure to light. Unexposed areas blocked by the opaque, nonprinting areas on the negative mask are water-receptive after processing and do not carry ink on press. The prepress production of text and line images for printing simply involves the preparation of high-contrast images that can be photographed and converted into line negatives that can mask the plate material.[3]

Lithography is a discrete process in the sense that an area of a printing plate can be either ink-receptive or water-receptive but cannot be made ink- or water-receptive in continuously varying degrees. Therefore, continuous-tone images, such as photographs, cannot be printed until they are converted into line images containing only discrete areas that are either clear or opaque on a negative, ink- or water-receptive on a plate.[4] Halftones are line images made from continuous-tone images that create an illusion of a full range of tonal values through the use of closely spaced dots of varying sizes.[5] The eye does not perceive individual dots in the printed halftone, but rather an illusion of continuous tones created by the overall dot pattern (Figure 8.2). Finer halftones—halftones with smaller, more closely spaced dots—generally produce better illusions than coarser halftones, but the refinement of the paper surface and the printing equipment in use place constraints on how fine this can be.[6] For example, very fine dots printed at high speeds on rough-surfaced paper will spread and clump together, obscuring shadow details. All halftones are compromises that have less detail and a compressed tonal

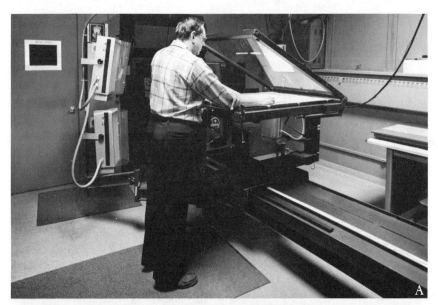

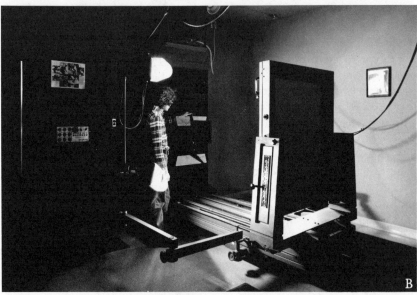

FIGURE 8.1 Image preparation, conversion, and transfer using photo-mechanical platemaking techniques and offset lithography: (a) placing camera-copy on the copy board of a camera; (b) setting the lens before exposing film; (c) stripping individual page negatives onto a platemaking flat—the platemaking mask—in correct imposition order (this is a 64-page form for sheetfed printing and will be one side of a press sheet); (d) exposing a plate in contact with the flat in a vacuum frame; (e)

developing the plate before printing; (f) the delivery end of a large-format sheetfed press (sheets are fed from a pile feeder and printed on both sides in one color, 128 pages per sheet, at a speed of 7,500 impressions per hour); (g) the delivery end of a quad folder delivering bundled 32-page signatures folded from press sheets, the step after sheetfed printing; (h) a half-size or narrow web press delivering 32-page signatures from rolls of paper in a single machine operation. (Photos courtesy the Maple-Vail Book Manufacturing Group)

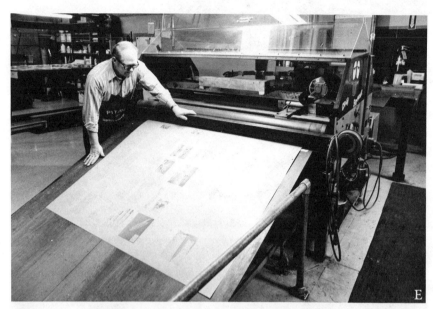

FIGURE 8.1, cont.

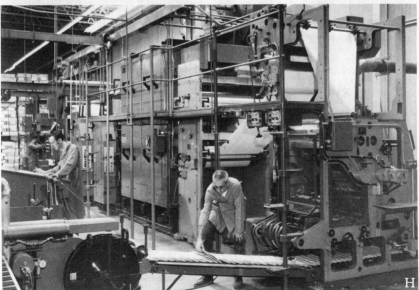

FIGURE 8.1, cont.

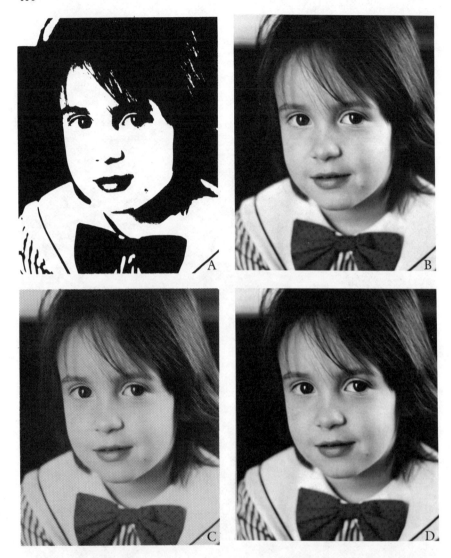

FIGURE 8.2 Line conversions: (a) high contrast; continuous-tone original reproduced without a halftone screen; (b) halftone, 133-line screen; (c) halftone, 85-line screen; (d) halftone, 150-line screen. Note that the fineness of the halftone dots must match press and paper characteristics for optimum reproduction. The 85-line screen, though clearly reproduced, is too coarse to capture fine details. The 150-line screen, usually used for printing on coated stock, is too fine to hold out on rough, uncoated paper. The 133-line screen seems the best compromise, and is the standard choice for uncoated stock.

range compared to the original image, but good reproduction is possible when the halftone contrast range and dot size match the potential of the press equipment and paper in use. The prepress preparation of continuous-tone images for printing simply involves creating halftone negatives, which can be combined with line negatives for text and line art before platemaking.[7]

The preparation of a text for printing could be as simple as writing a clean copy of the text on white paper with black ink, a high-contrast image that could be photographed to produce a platemaking negative. But most texts are converted into standard letterforms—printing types— to increase the legibility and readability of the printed text and to eliminate the need to decipher the individual and idiosyncratic charac- teristics of our handwriting. The shapes of our letters are artifacts from the past that underscore the conservative as well as the preservative nature of printing; not only are most common printing types based on designs in use in Europe in the fifteenth and sixteenth centuries, many of our capital letterforms are essentially unchanged from letterforms used in Athens before the fifth century B.C.[8] The history of type design and the evolution of standard letterforms can be seen as the interaction between the conservative pressure of readers—who depend on being able to discriminate easily recognizable letterforms—and the innovative pressure of designers and typographers who adapt letterforms to exploit changing mediums and production methods.[9] Although letterforms and type designs have changed quite slowly, there have been great technological changes—especially in this century—in the production of type.

Such technological changes have been tied to changes in platemaking and printing technology. Originally, printing types were cast in metal from hand-punched molds (matrixes); the letterforms sculpted and cast in relief on individual pieces of metal were assembled (composed) by hand, inked, and printed—the origin of letterpress.[10] The advent of steam-powered presses in the last century spurred the invention of machine methods for setting and casting type that eliminated laborious hand setting and kept pace with the stepped-up production of the powered printing presses. Since the fastest new presses used rotary printing cylinders instead of flat beds for holding type, printing plates had to be curved to wrap around the cylinders; thus various methods were developed for casting duplicate relief plates from type settings. When typesetting processes no longer were producing printing plates, but intermediary image carriers, their form could evolve to better fit this new purpose. Automatic typecasting machines used soft lead alloys with low melting points that were simpler to cast than the original type metals; the hardness and durability of the type metal were no longer an issue. Lead type could be easily cast in unlimited quantities and

F<small>IGURE</small> 8.3 Modern typesetting methods: (a) Each element in the manuscript is identified by the designer. Format codes for each element are assigned by the compositor based on the design specifications to control the typesetting parameters: typeface, size, line measure, indents, tabs, leading. (b) The manuscript is input on a keyboard with the format codes and stored on magnetic disc or tape. (c) First proofs—unpaged galleys—are produced by the typesetting device, and copies (typically made by xerography) are distributed to the author and proofreader; reference numbers enable lines to be quickly accessed for editing. (d) When proofs are returned, the original setting is corrected and a revised setting is produced on the typesetting device and made up into pages manually, on the

A

FIGURE 8.3, cont.

video display terminal (VDT) or in paste-up, or with the assistance of programs that determine page breaks and generate running heads and folios. Corrections at the later stages may be accomplished by stripping correction lines

B

Kubach / 20

is of course the first thing to consider in selecting the kind of type; and the number of pages to which the book will probably run is the determining factor as to what size of type is possible. The width and length of the type page are then to be proportioned to the paper page, which in turn also helps to determine the size of the type. All these considerations are interlocking.

The important characteristics of a typeface that affect design are (1) the set width of the letters; (2) the proportions of the letters (the relationship of the x-height, capitals, ascenders, and descenders to the type body and point size; (3) the shading and color of the strokes (the proportion of thick and thin lines); and (4) the use of serifs--ending cross-strokes--which affect the overall weight and color of the type on a page. These characteristics have practical ramifications in addition to their aesthetic effect on the page.

The set widths of various type faces vary considerably; the selection of a text type face will largely determine the setting length of a book, a major factor in production cost. Within a single typeface, set width is a strict function of point size--although it is variable in digital typography.

The preference for light or medium weights of type over heavier weights and darker colors is largely subjective but should be considered in the context of the choice of paper, interline spacing (leading), the closeness of setting (the range of normal interword and interletter spacing), and the margins around the type page (the blank areas between the type page or image area and the trim edges). Type faces with bold strokes (for example, the Modern designs derived from the types of Bodoni) may need wider margins, more leading, and whiter shades of paper to contrast with their black color; a bold, heavy face that is set very tightly may be hard to read for lack of sufficient contrast and balance. Generally, lighter types may be set larger and tighter, with less leading, than darker faces; a face with long ascenders and descenders may be set tighter and with less leading than a similar face with short ascenders and descenders since the long ascenders and descenders result in a background of apparent white space

C

The important characteristics of a typeface that affect design are the set width of the letters; the proportions of the letters (the relatinship of the x-height, capitals, ascenders, and descenders to the type body and point size; the shading and color of the strokes (the proportion of thick and thin lines); and the use of serifs—ending cross-strokes—that affect the overall weight and color of the type on a page. These characteristics have practical ramifications in addition to their aesthetic effect on the page.

The set widths of various typefaces vary considerably; the selection of a text typeface will largely determine the setting length of a book, a major factor in production cost. Within a single typeface, set width is a strict function of point size—although it is variable in digital typography.

The preference for light or medium weights of type over heavier weights and darker colors is largely subjective but should be considered in the context of the choice of paper, interline spacing (leading), the closeness of setting (the range of normal interword and interletter spacing), and the margins around the type page (the blank areas between the type page or image area and the trim edges). Type faces with bold strokes (for example, the Modern designs derived from the types of Bodoni) may need wider margins, more leading, and whiter shades of paper to contrast with their black color; a bold, heavy face that is set very tightly may be hard toread for lack of sufficient contrast and balance. Generally, lighter types may be set larger and tighter, with less leading, than darker types; a face with long ascenders and descenders may be set tighter and with less leading than a similar face with short ascenders and descenders, since the long ascenders and descenders result in a background of apparent white space inside the type page.

Typefaces without serifs (sans serif) have a clean, modern look, but the evenness of line and lack of contrast within letters may detract from readibility when the type is set in large blocks. Traditionally, serif faces are used for text settings because they are perceived to be easier to read, but this perception may be the result of reader expectation and is entirely subjective. Some faces (for example, Optima) combine the clean lines of a sans serif face with shadings of thick and thin lines that add contrast and color to a page.

The type page should be placed on the book page so that there are sufficient margins to accommodate binding and trimming allowances while maintaining a proportional balance between the type and the margins, the color and the white space. Each spread of facing pages should be a coherent unit. For reasons of economy the ample margins that were standard in the past have disappeared, but attractive layouts are still possible within the more economical frames of today.

The perceived center of a page is higher than its true center; this is perhaps because our eye falls first at the top of a page of text to find its beginning in the upper left corner. A type page with a slightly larger margin below than above appears more balanced than one exactly centered on the page.

The body of text is usually perceived by the reader as a unit; space around the text, including runningheads and folios, as marginal space. The placement of the type page in relation to the book page depth is determined by the head margin—the distance from the top trim edge to the uppermost element on the page, usually the ascenders at the top of the runninghead or the top of the folios. The placement of the type area in relation to the page width is determined by the gutter margin—the distance from the inside edge of the book (the binding edge) to the inside of the type page. The first consideration in determining the gutter margin is the effect of binding. Sufficient space must be left between facing type pages to accommodate the grind-off of the folds during perfect binding, stitches through the sides of the folds during side-sewing, or the holes for mechanical devices such as plastic combs or metal rings. A special consideration for library books with an anticipated long life is enough additional space to accommodate rebindings, which usually consume at least one-eighth inch of gutter space each time.

Traditionally the gutter margin is the smallest margin bordering the type page, followed in size by the head margin, the outside margin, then the food margin this configuration brings the facing pages of a spread together so that they are perceived as a unit, facilitating jumps from the foot of one page to the top of the next; it also balances the page at its perceived center. Some modern book designers have broken with this tradition and positioned the type page so that there is a constant, ample margin at the left edge of the teft, identical on both verso and recto pages, with the view that this placement increases the readability of the text by helping our eye find the beginning of each line at the left edge A layout such as this based on asymmetrical relationships can be dynamic and beautiful, but it probably requires a keener eye for proportion and balance to be as successful as more traditional but more static layouts.

D

134 DOUGLAS KUBACH

factor as to what size of type is possible. The width and length of the type page are then to be proportioned to the paper page, which in turn also helps to determine the size of the type. All these considerations are interlocking.[14]

The important characteristics of a typeface that affect design are the set width of the letters; the proportions of the letters (the relationship of the x-height, capitals, ascenders, and descenders to the type body and point size); the shading and color of the strokes (the proportion of thick and thin lines); and the use of serifs—ending cross-strokes—that affect the overall weight and color of the type on a page. These characteristics have practical ramifications in addition to their aesthetic effect on the page.

The set widths of various typefaces vary considerably; the selection of a text typeface will largely determine the setting length of a book, a major factor in production cost. Within a single typeface, set width is a strict function of point size—although it is variable in digital typography.

The preference for light or medium weights of type over heavier weights and darker colors is largely subjective but should be considered in the context of the choice of paper, interline spacing (leading), the closeness of setting (the range of normal interword and interletter spacing), and the margins around the type page (the blank areas between the type page or image area and the trim edges). Type faces with bold strokes (for example, the Modern designs derived from the types of Bodoni) may need wider margins, more leading, and whiter shades of paper to contrast with their black color; a bold, heavy face that is set very tightly may be hard to read for lack of sufficient contrast and balance. Generally, lighter types may be set larger and tighter, with less leading, than darker types; a face with long ascenders and descenders may be set tighter and with less leading than a similar face with short ascenders and descenders, since the long ascenders and descenders result in a background of apparent white space inside the type page.

Typefaces without serifs (sans serif) have a clean, modern look, but the evenness of line and lack of contrast within letters may detract from readability when the type is set in large blocks. Traditionally, serif faces are used for text settings because they are perceived to be easier to read, but this perception may be the result of reader expectation and is entirely subjective. Some faces (for example, Optima) combine the clean lines of a sans serif face with shadings of thick and thin lines that add contrast and color to a page.

The type page should be placed on the book page so that there are sufficient margins to accommodate binding and trimming allowances

Figure 8.3, cont.

onto reproduction proofs in paste-up or by completely resetting pages. (e) At the final stages, all repro (camera-copy) must be carefully checked to ensure that the type images will have a consistent color and weight throughout the book. These examples illustrate the extremes of poor quality that can easily occur if image quality is not carefully controlled during exposure and processing; examples were all taken from the same book. (f) A simplified diagram showing the major components of a computerized typesetting system: The VDT/keyboard for inputting and editing; the main CPU and tape drives for storage, manipulation, and processing; the output device for final imaging. (The output device shown is an APS Micro-5 CRT typesetter; the detail shows the cathode-ray tube and

E

FIGURE 8.3, cont.

lens system where the type images are formed.) Not shown are alternative off-line input devices, such as optical scanners, disc translators/readers, modems, etc., which enable the compositor to capture the author's original keystrokes and eliminate rekeying the text. Texts which enter the typesetting computer through alternative input devices must still be formatted, edited, and processed before type images can be formed by the output device.

F

melted down after platemaking for reuse. The development of offset lithography and photographic platemaking techniques in this century allowed an even more radical change in the production of type: When relief type images were no longer necessary for platemaking, typesetting systems evolved to produce high-contrast type images carried on paper or film especially suited to photographic platemaking.

The various ways of producing type are distinguished by different methods for generating type forms or images from a master form or image, the type matrix.

1. Metal typography uses a recessed, or intaglio, matrix to cast relief images in metal. Foundry types are cast with hard metal alloys, assembled by hand into lines and pages of type, and inked for letterpress. Machine-set metal types are mechanically assembled and cast with soft lead alloys, then used to impress molds to create duplicate relief plates or inked to produce a master impression that can be photographically reproduced.

2. Impact typography uses a relief matrix to strike an impression of each character onto paper through an ink or carbon ribbon. Typewriters, a common example, are generally quite limited in the number of characters and styles of type they can set and in the amount of control an operator has over the position of images. Strike-on composers are more sophisticated and can produce high-quality type images. Most computer line printers are strike-on devices but vary widely in the quality of their output.

3. Photographic typography uses film matrixes—master images of each character carried on film—to expose photosensitive materials. The typesetting mechanism, controlled by a digital computer, mechanically locates the right matrix for each character in succession, properly positions and focuses the image on the film, then exposes the material to light. Photographic type can be of the highest quality for reproduction; it can be enlarged in size without appreciable loss of resolution and successfully carried through many stages of photomechanical transfer and manipulation.

4. Digital typography uses a digital matrix—a character-matrix program stored in a digital computer—that contains instructions for duplicating a unique pattern of horizontal or vertical lines to construct each character with the electronic beam of a cathode-ray tube (CRT) or with a laser light that exposes photographic film.[11] Digital typesetters can surpass all others for speed and flexibility. Digital images are characterized by a rough profile when viewed under magnification, the result of the pattern of lines that constructs each type character.

Photographic and digital typography are the most common today, since both can combine high-quality type images especially suited for photographic prepress production with the speed, flexibility, and efficient text-editing capabilities of digital computers (Figure 8.3).

PAPER

A book is a set of printed leaves of paper fastened together along one edge (the spine or backbone) and bound into a cover or a case. Each leaf of paper contains two pages, front (recto) and back (verso). The set of leaves that comprise a book is usually formed by folding large printed sheets of paper into sections (signatures) and then gathering the folded sections in sequence (folded sections are called signatures from the old practice of placing an initial at the foot of the first page of each section to identify its place in the book). Signatures can be made in any multiple of four pages, but commonly contain eight, sixteen, or thirty-two pages created by folding press sheets with simple right-angled folds. The number and sequence of folds determines where pages must be printed on the press sheet in order to be properly placed within the signature after folding; this arrangement of pages is the imposition of the sheet.

The best imposition for a given book will fold the greatest number of pages into the least number of signatures in a single machine operation from a full press sheet, subject to limitations imposed by the trim size of the book, the weight of the paper, and the size of the press equipment that is available. Sheetfed presses print on individual sheets of paper the size of the press form; web presses print on a continuous web of paper fed from a roll that is slit, chopped, and folded into signatures at the delivery end of the press. Web presses can be more cost-effective for long press runs since they are faster and deliver folded signatures directly from paper rolls in a single machine operation. Sheetfed presses are more accurate, usually produce higher-quality impressions, and are more cost-effective for short press runs.

Paper is the major material component of a book; as the carrier of print its surface affects how printed images are perceived and how faithfully they can be reproduced; its longevity largely determines their life. Papers are made from bonded fibers. The highest-quality papers have rag content, a percentage of cotton or linen fibers. Most book papers in the United States (with the exception of handmade papers) are made exclusively with cellulose fibers derived from wood pulp. Hardwoods provide short fibers that give papers bulk and body; softwoods provide longer fibers that give papers strength. Most papers are made from a mixture of hardwood and softwood fibers, along with sizings to prepare the surface for printing, pigments that enhance the brightness and opacity of the surface, dyes that control shade and color, and coatings that refine the finished surface. Strong, caustic chemicals are used to separate individual fibers from wood chips by dissolving the natural adhesives (lignins) in the wood that bond fibers together. Acidic residues left in the fibers after processing will react with light, heat, moisture, and other environmental agents to create acids that eventually destroy papers. Papers that have an alkaline composition will last much longer than acidic papers.

Handmade papers have been made the same way for hundreds of years. A wire mesh stretched on a wood frame (the mold) is dipped into a mixture of fibers and water called furnish. The frame is lifted from the furnish and shaken to intermesh the fibers and give the sheet more strength. The mold holding the sheet of wet fibers (the water leaf) is pressed (couched) onto a sheet of felt. The water leaf adheres to the felt, freeing the mold to make another sheet. The felt helps to remove excess moisture from the couched sheets. Machine-made papers are made on huge machines (fourdriniers) that utilize a continuous wire-screen web instead of a wire frame and create a continuous web of paper instead of individual sheets. The furnish, made up of approximately 99.5 percent water and .5 percent fibers, sizings, pigments, and opacifiers, is pumped onto the moving wire screen. The speed of the moving wire screen, the flow rate of the furnish onto the screen, and the density of the furnish determine the paper's basis weight. Smooth iron rollers (calendars) control surface finish and bulk (thickness) by compressing and polishing the fibers. Coatings to further refine the surface can be applied at the end of the fourdrinier or on separate coating machines.

Paper weight is measured by basis weight (or grams per square meter in countries that use the metric system). A paper's basis weight is the weight of one ream (five hundred sheets) of that paper in the basis size, which differs for different kinds of papers (there are different basis sizes for book papers, cover papers, writing papers, index, or newsprint, for example). Basis weight is a convention that offers a standard for relating the weights of various papers independent of sheet size, roll size, or quantity. The basis size for book paper is 25 inches by 38 inches. Therefore five hundred sheets of 50-pound book paper measuring 25 inches by 38 inches will weigh 50 pounds; one thousand sheets will weigh 100 pounds. Since paper is purchased by weight, basis weight is an important factor for controlling paper cost, and distribution costs as well, since these are directly related to book weight.

Paper bulk can be increased by either increasing basis weight or controlling surface finish. Smoother papers can more faithfully carry fine details, such as halftone dots; they can also be useful for controlling the thickness of very long books in order to keep the thickness (or bulk) of the book within the limitations of binding equipment. In constrast, rougher papers are useful for lending bulk to short books. Most grades of paper are made in a series of basis weights and a variety of finishes.

For example, most book papers are made in basis weights of 45 pounds to 60 pounds; a 50-pound book paper may be made in a range of surface finishes from antique or rough (ca. 360 pages per inch—ppi) to smooth (ca. 576 ppi)— the same paper made in a 60-pound basis would bulk between 296 and 490 ppi.

The smoothest uncoated surface is actually very rough when compared to coated surfaces under magnification. Surface coatings fill in the gaps between individual fibers on the paper surface and provide a smooth, level surface that is able to carry the finest printed details. Coatings also help to keep ink on the surface of the paper and limit ink absorption into fibers; when more ink stays on the surface, printed images have more contrast and a richer color.

The moving wire screen of the fourdrinier aligns paper fibers parallel to the line of movement; this creates a grain in the finished paper running parallel to the length of a roll. Grain direction has two major effects on paper: Paper folds more easily along the grain, and paper expands and contracts in reaction to environmental changes in temperature and humidity perpendicular to its grain (paper fibers expand and contract more in diameter than in length). All books should be made with the grain of text papers, cover papers, and endpapers parallel to the spine, or binding edge. If a book is bound against the grain, the paper will be prevented from expanding and contracting along the length of the spine by the binding, and it may warp or buckle. Cross-grain pages will be noticeably stiffer, will not turn as easily, and will not lie as flat. Grain direction most always be specified when ordering sheeted papers; it is indicated by an underscore beneath the dimension parallel to the grain. A sheet that has its grain direction parallel to its shorter dimension is a short-grain sheet. For example, a sheet with dimensions specified as 29 by 41 has a grain parallel to the 41-inch direction; a sheet with dimensions specified as 57 by 41 has a grain parallel to the 41-inch direction and is short-grain. The grain direction is usually specified last for emphasis and to avoid confusion when communicating paper specifications orally.

BINDING

Most books are either casebound or paperbound (Figure 8.4).[12] Casebound or hardcover books are fastened into a case by means of a folded endsheet glued to the inside of the case and reinforced along the hinge. Paperbound or softcover books are glued along the back into a simple cover, flush-cut with the edges of the text (Figure 8.5).

Smyth sewing is the standard for binding casebound books and high-quality paperbacks. Threads are stitched through the backs of folded signatures, through the center of each fold. The principal advantage of

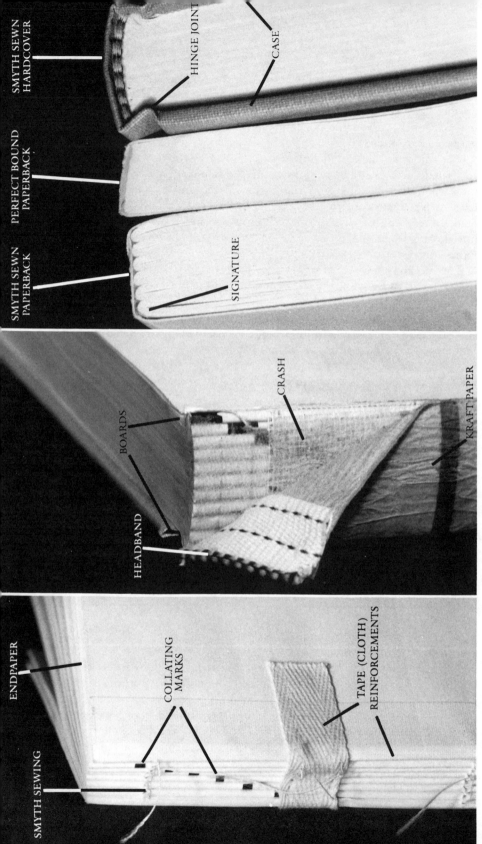

FIGURE 8.4 Examples of common binding styles showing the parts of a book.

FIGURE 8.5 Modern bookbinding methods: (a) The gathering station, the first stage of a high-speed binding line. Each pocket on the gathering line holds a folded section of the book. This gathering line is collating two-up signatures. (b) Smyth sewing machines with automatic in-feed; each signature of a book is sewed together one at a time. (c) The delivery end of a high-speed automated binding line consisting of a gathering machine, endpaper tipping device, adhesive binder, rounder-backer-gluer,

crash-and-paper attachment stations, splitter (for two-up signatures), trimmer, casing-in machine, and building-in machine. Bound books are being delivered by conveyor from the building-in machine, ready for inspection, packing, and distribution. (d) Applying jackets to bound books by hand before packing and shipping; many bindery operations are still labor-intensive. The conveyor is sending cartoned books to the shipping dock. (Photos courtesy the Maple-Vail Book Manufacturing Group) smyth sewing is that it allows a book to open easily and lie flat. Side-sewing is widely used for binding children's books, reference books, and other books requiring strong bindings. Thread is sewn through the side of each signature from front to back. A side-sewn book is very rigid and resists opening. Oversewing is the principal method employed by library binders; it is patterned after a form of hand sewing called overcast stitching and allows for great strength combined with flexibility.

Perfect binding is the principal method of paperback binding; it is widely used for economical casebindings. The folds of gathered signatures are ground off and coated with adhesives; individual leaves are glued directly to the cover or lining. Perfect binding can be as strong as sewn binding and has been greatly improved in the last decade with advances in adhesive composition and technology. Notch binding (also called burst or em-lock binding) is a variation of perfect binding; notches are cut through the backs of folded and gathered signatures and glue is forced up into the notches to secure each page. Unlike perfect binding, the folds are not completely ground off and signatures remain intact.

Small booklets and pamphlets are usually bound with wire staples. Saddle-stitching wires staples through the center of a folded signature; side-stitching wires staples through the sides and is sometimes used to reinforce perfect bindings.

Mechanical bindings hold leaves of paper together with the help of mechanical devices placed through holes drilled through the sides of the pages along the binding edge. Common examples are loose-leaf ring binders, spiral wire, and plastic comb bindings. The advantage of a mechanical binding is that it allows each page to lie completely flat when the book is opened—a very practical feature for cookbooks and instruction manuals. The advantage of a loose-leaf ring binder is that it is the only binding that allows easy removal and replacement of pages to update a volume.

THE PRODUCTION PROCESS

The basic stages of the production process follow in outline form; this example is based on a typical production sequence and is not meant to be definitive, but rather to be illustrative of how the production of a book might be organized in the context of the publishing process as a whole. Note that the actual times for each stage of the process vary widely and that different publishers may organize their production in different ways.

    A. Manuscript proposal and evaluation:
        1. An acquisitions editor presents a proposal for publishing

an author's manuscript, forecasts potential sales, and suggests print/bind quantities.

2. Production estimates plant and manufacturing costs.

3. Management computes the potential profit or loss of the venture and approves, rejects, or modifies the proposal.

B. Manuscript preparation and design:

1. Production advises the author on technical details of manuscript preparation: the preparation of charts, tables, maps, graphs, drawings, and photographs; typing specifications; and coding electronic manuscripts for transmission to typesetting computers.

2. Editorial, Production, and Marketing agree on the details of the book plan: trim size, optimal length, print/bind quantities, preliminary retail prices, and projected publication date.

3. Production issues a preliminary schedule that balances marketing priorities against the complexity of production.

4. Production estimates the book length and designs the text.

5. Editorial, Production, and Marketing approve the text design for editorial coherence and accuracy, technical feasability and cost, and aesthetic suitability to the book's content and market.

6. Production supervises the coding of design elements and prepares final typesetting specifications.

7. Production requests bids for typesetting and art-preparation services.

8. Marketing reforecasts potential sales and revises print/bind quantities.

9. Production prepares revised cost estimates based on the length estimate, revised print/bind quantities, and actual typesetting bids.

10. Production chooses suppliers and orders typesetting and art preparation.

11. Production revises the schedule.

C. Image preparation (note that the production of book components printed separately from the text, such as covers, jackets, or inserts, follows a parallel course to the production of the text):

1. The typesetter (compositor) inputs and processes the manuscript and prepares first proofs (unpaged galleys or rough page proofs).

2. Editorial reviews the proofs and coordinates proofreading with the author.

3. Production and Editorial approve the final art.

4. Production prepares a dummy layout and/or paging instructions and releases corrected proofs and final art for paging.

5. The typesetter corrects the setting and prepares second proofs (usually pages).

6. Editorial reviews the proofs and coordinates proof-reading and indexing with the author.

7. Production checks the proofs for adherence to specifications, designs the index, and adjusts the page layout to efficiently utilize press forms.

8. Production requests bids for paper, printing, and binding and prepares revised cost estimates based on actual bids.

9. Marketing sets final print/bind quantities and retail prices.

10. Management computes potential profit or loss and approves or modifies final print/bind quantities and retail prices.

11. The typesetter completes final corrections and prepares final reproduction proofs.

12. Editorial approves final reproduction proofs for accuracy and completeness.

13. Production approves final reproduction proofs for image quality.

14. Production chooses suppliers, purchases materials, places manufacturing orders, and releases final reproduction proofs and art for platemaking.

15. Production revises the schedule.

D. Image conversion (platemaking):

1. The printer prepares final film negatives from reproduction proofs and art, then assembles (strips) individual negatives into platemaking masks (flats) in accordance with the binder's imposition and the size of the press form.

2. The printer makes contact proofs of the flats (blues, silverprints, van dykes, Dylux proofs, Warren proofs), folds and trims the proofs to final size, and checks image quality and imposition.

3. Editorial checks the proofs for completeness and accuracy.

4. Production checks the proofs for image quality, ac-

curacy of layout and registration, and correctness of imposition.

5. Production approves proofs and releases flats for plate-making.

6. The printer exposes printing plates in contact with flats.

E. Image transfer (presswork):

1. The printer completes the presswork.

2. Production approves a set of printed sheets.

3. The printer delivers printed sheets to the bindery.

F. Binding:

1. The binder folds printed sheets into signatures and adds tips, wraps, and inserts as required.

2. For a casebound or hardcover edition (in this example a traditional smyth-sewn edition) the binder glues end-sheets to the outside signatures; gathers and sews the signatures together; smashes and compresses the folds along the spine; trims the pages at the top (head), front, and bottom (foot); glues, rounds, and lines the back; makes and decorates cases; glues the book blocks into their cases; and then builds-in the joint along the hinges of the case. Production approves a sample case, then a bound book.

3. For a paperbound or softcover edition (in this example the common perfect-bound paperback) the binder gathers the signatures into sets, mills off the folds along the spine to prepare the pages for adhesion, applies glue down the back, applies covers, and then trims each book at top, front and foot. Production approves a bound book.

G. Distribution: The binder counts, wraps, and packs books according to specifications; then ships or stores books in coordination with marketing or sales requirements.

H. Accounting:

1. Production compares all invoices for services and materials against bids and purchase orders, resolves discrepancies with suppliers, and approves charges for payment.

2. Production prepares final edition costs.

3. Management values finished inventory and accounts for the cost of sales, unsalable inventory, and profit or loss.

Typography and Design

The procedure for setting a manuscript into type begins with identifying each design element in the manuscript and then defining setting specifications. Format specifications are input with the manuscript to control basic setting parameters: typeface, size, line measure, margins, indents, tabs, minimum and maximum interword spaces, leading or interline space, and page-placement instructions. Corrections are easier to accomplish before a setting is made up into pages, so a complete reading is usually done in unpaged (galley) form. Since the end results of photographic and digital typesetting are high-contrast type images suitable for photographic platemaking, the quality of the setting must be carefully controlled to ensure that all type images are consistent in color and weight. The most common quality problem associated with photographic and digital typesetting is a variation in image density and exposure, the result of poor control over type processing or the use of poor-quality photographic papers.

The importance of strict quality control during type processing cannot be overemphasized; a traditional letterpress printer had much more control over maintaining an even, balanced color than the offset lithographer, who is dependent on receiving a consistent image from the typesetter in order to produce a comparable result. Since we have moved away from printing three-dimensional type to photographically reproducing type images, this primary responsibility for controlling type color from page to page within a book has shifted toward the producers of the original type image—typesetters—who must accept this responsibility. Type design is another factor—many type designs that were originally designed for letterpress, which fattens and spreads an image with the pressure of impression, appear weak or broken when not properly exposed and developed during photographic manipulation.

Typefaces are identified by family name (such as Baskerville or Garamond) and are frequently adaptations of historical types (Figure 8.6). Different designs based on the same historical model may have the same name but vary noticeably in style, proportion, and weight. It is virtually impossible to mix types set on different systems without observing this difference.

A font of type is a set of characters in a given typeface, size, and weight (Figure 8.7). A font usually contains upper- and lower-case letters, small capitals, marks of punctuation and reference, numerals and fractions, accents and special characters, ligatures (joined characters), and other common symbols, made from a unique set of matrixes. Type families usually contain fonts in a range of related sizes and weights. Typefaces

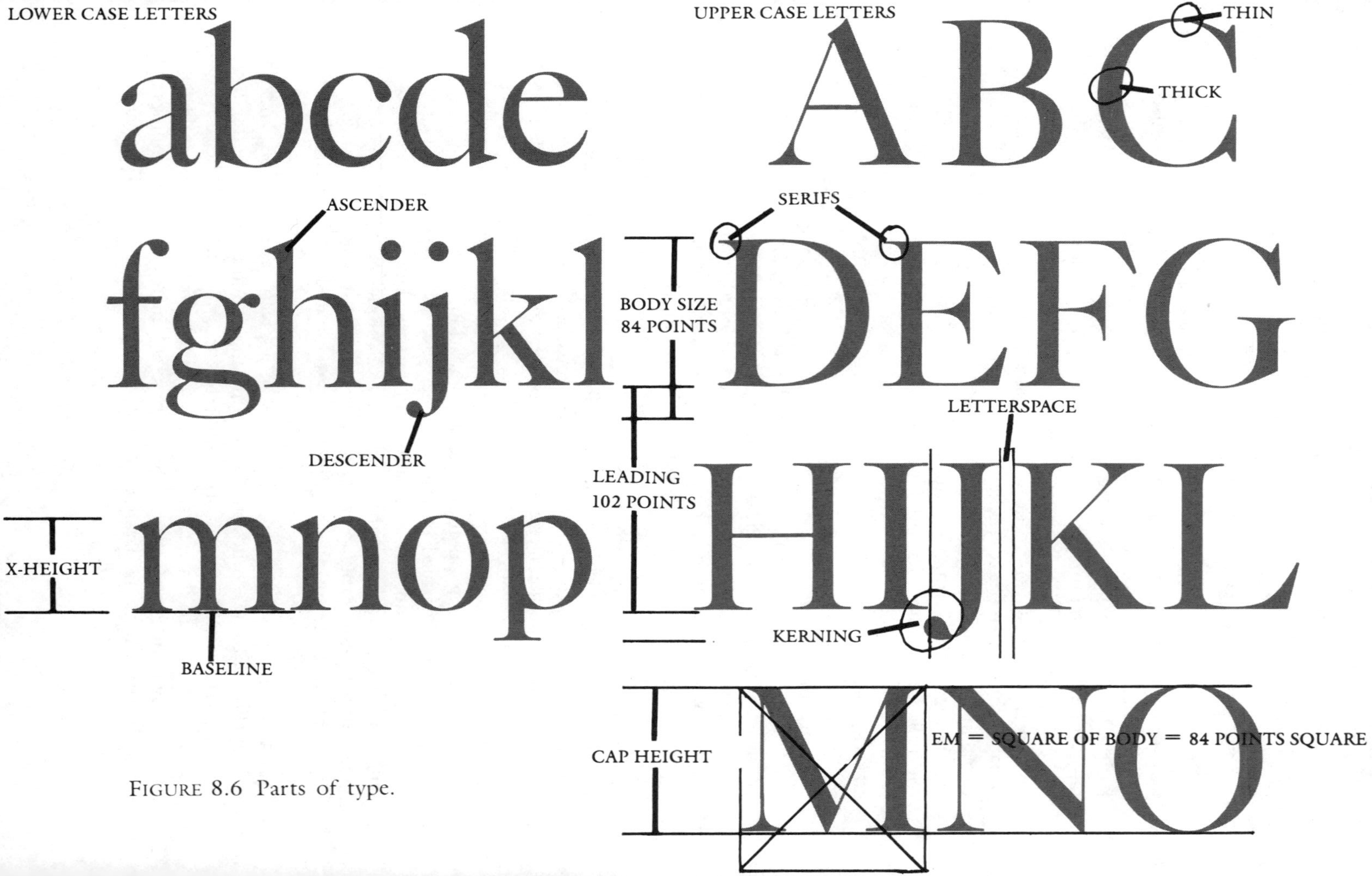

UPPER CASE LETTERS

ABCG

THIN
THICK

DEFG

SERIFS
BODY SIZE
84 POINTS

HIJKL

LETTERSPACE

LEADING
102 POINTS

KERNING

MNO

EM = SQUARE OF BODY = 84 POINTS SQUARE

CAP HEIGHT

LOWER CASE LETTERS

abcde

ASCENDER

fghijkl

DESCENDER

mnop

X-HEIGHT

BASELINE

FIGURE 8.6 Parts of type.

for book settings usually contain roman, italic, bold, and bold italic fonts, among others.

In the American Point system, the basic units for the linear measurement of type size are the point and the pica. A pica is approximately one-sixth of an inch,[13] and twelve points equal one pica. Specifications pertaining to a typeset page are measured in points and picas; areas outside of typeset areas (such as margins and page dimensions) are measured in inches (since we measure paper in inches).

Type size is specified by point size, which should not be confused with actual or apparent size, as measured in points. Point size is not a measure of the height of a type image, but a measurement of the full body of the characters in a font, including the length of strokes that fall above and below the baseline (ascenders and descenders). Actual or apparent size will depend upon the visual proportions of the font design, specifically the relation of the height of lower-case letters (the x-height) to the height of capital letters, ascenders, and descenders. For example, a ten-point typeface with a proportionally large x-height will appear to be larger than another ten-point face with a smaller x-height, although each is set on the same size body (Figure 8.8).

The em is a variable measure of area relative to point size—the square of the body size of a typeface (a ten-point em is ten points square, a nine-point em, nine points square, and so on). Proportional spacings such as interword spaces and character widths are easily defined in ems and proportions of ems.

The only criteria for typographical design are that the text be readable and the result balanced and pleasing to the eye. There are no rigid rules. A sensible approach toward designing texts would be a study of models that are attractive and effective with a view toward understanding how different type styles, sizes, and weights can be arranged on a page for a harmonious effect. The master book designer Bruce Rogers advised,

> You think of the *book,* the size and shape of the book, before you consider type or anything else. What kind of a volume should it be? In what particular form and in what face of type would *you* like to read it? The type and format should be governed by your conception of the character of the subject matter. . . . The character of the text to be printed is of course the first thing to consider in selecting the kind of type; and the number of pages to which the book will probably run is the determining factor as to what size of type is possible. The width and length of the type page are then to be proportioned to the paper page, which in turn also helps to determine the size of the type. All these considerations are interlocking.[14]

The important characteristics of a typeface that affect design are the

ROMAN

ABCDEFGHIJKLMNOPQRSTUVWXYZ ÆŒ ÅĄÇÐĘŁØ
abcdefghijklmnopqrstuvwxyz ffffifflfifl æœ åąçđęłøß
ABCDEFGHIJKLMNOPQRSTUVWXYZ
& ÆŒÅĄÇÐĘŁØ 1234567890 1234567890
.,:;'"!?-()[]----£$$*†‡§||¶¡¿«»ÉÈÊĚĔĖĒÈÈ éèêěĕēëè

ITALIC

abcdefghijklmnopqrstuvwxyz ffffifflfifl æœ åąçđęłøß & ÆŒ
ABCDEFGHIJKLMNOPQRSTUVWXYZ ÅĄÇÐĘŁØ
1234567890 1234567890 .,:;'"!?()[]£$$ ÉÈÊĚĔĖĒÈÈ éèêěĕēëè

BOLD

abcdefghijklmnopqrstuvwxyz ffffifflfifl æœ åąçđęłøß
ABCDEFGHIJKLMNOPQRSTUVWXYZ & ÆŒ
1234567890 1234567890 .,:;'"!?()[]¡¿«»-—£$$
ÅĄÇÐĘŁØ ÉÈÊĚĔĖĒÈÈ éèêěĕēëè

BOLD ITALIC ***abcdefghijklmnopqrstuvwxyz ffffifflfifl åçøß***
ABCDEFGHIJKLMNOPQRSTUVWXYZ & ÅÇØ
1234567890 .,:;'"!?() ÉÈÊ èèê

PI CHARACTERS

$+ - \times = < > \pm \cdot // ' \% °® © ||$

FIGURE 8.7 A series of four fonts in the Baskerville family: roman, italic, bold, and bold italic, with a pi font of special characters that can be used with each. This is a setting of the complete series in ten point.

The history of type design and the evolution of standard letterforms can be seen as the interaction between the conservative pressure of readers—who depend on discriminating easily recognizable letterforms—and the innovative pressure of designers and typographers who adapt letterforms to exploit changing mediums and production methods. [GARAMOND]

OLD STYLE (RENAISSANCE)

The history of type design and the evolution of standard letterforms can be seen as the interaction between the conservative pressure of readers—who depend on discriminating easily recognizable letterforms—and the innovative pressure of designers and typographers who adapt letterforms to exploit changing mediums and production methods. [BASKERVILLE]

TRANSITIONAL (BAROQUE)

The history of type design and the evolution of standard letterforms can be seen as the interaction between the conservative pressure of readers—who depend on discriminating easily recognizable letterforms—and the innovative pressure of designers and typographers who adapt letterforms to exploit changing mediums and production methods. [TIMES ROMAN]

MODERN (CLASSICAL)

The history of type design and the evolution of standard letterforms can be seen as the interaction between the conservative pressure of readers—who depend on discriminating easily recognizable letterforms—and the innovative pressure of designers and typographers who adapt letterforms to exploit changing mediums and production methods. [ITC GARAMOND]

CONTEMPORARY

The history of type design and the evolution of standard letterforms can be seen as the interaction between the conservative pressure of readers—who depend on discriminating easily recognizable letterforms—and the innovative pressure of designers and typographers who adapt letterforms to exploit changing mediums and production methods. [HELVETICA]

SANS SERIF

FIGURE 8.8 Examples of the same copy set in various fonts, all ten point in size, which illustrate how apparent size is related to the proportions of the x-height of the font to the body. The old style fonts are very small on their body and appear small in size. The contemporary fonts are very large on their body and appear to be larger.

set width of the letters; the proportions of the letters (the relationship of the x-height, capitals, ascenders, and descenders to the type body and point size); the shading and color of the strokes (the proportion of thick and thin lines); and the use of serifs—ending cross-strokes—that affect the overall weight and color of the type on a page. These characteristics have practical ramifications in addition to their aesthetic effect on the page.

The set widths of various typefaces vary considerably; the selection of a text typeface will largely determine the setting length of a book, a major factor in production cost. Within a single typeface, set width is a strict function of point size—although it is variable in digital typography.

The preference for light or medium weights of type over heavier weights and darker colors is largely subjective but should be considered in the context of the choice of paper, interline spacing (leading), the closeness of setting (the range of normal interword and interletter spacing), and the margins around the type page (the blank areas between the type page or image area and the trim edges). Type faces with bold strokes (for example, the Modern designs derived from the types of Bodoni) may need wider margins, more leading, and whiter shades of paper to contrast with their black color; a bold, heavy face that is set very tightly may be hard to read for lack of sufficient contrast and balance. Generally, lighter types may be set larger and tighter, with less leading, than darker types; a face with long ascenders and descenders may be set tighter and with less leading than a similar face with short ascenders and descenders, since the long ascenders and descenders result in a background of apparent white space inside the type page.

Typefaces without serifs (sans serif) have a clean, modern look, but the evenness of line and lack of contrast within letters may detract from readability when the type is set in large blocks. Traditionally, serif faces are used for text settings because they are perceived to be easier to read, but this perception may be the result of reader expectation and is entirely subjective. Some faces (for example, Optima) combine the clean lines of a sans serif face with shadings of thick and thin lines that add contrast and color to a page.

The type page should be placed on the book page so that there are sufficient margins to accommodate binding and trimming allowances while maintaining a proportional balance between the type and the margins, the color and the white space. Each spread of facing pages should be a coherent unit. For reasons of economy the ample margins that were standard in the past have disappeared, but attractive layouts are still possible within the more economical frames of today.

The perceived center of a page is higher than its true center; this is perhaps because our eye falls first at the top of a page of text to find its beginning in the upper left corner. A type page with a slightly larger margin below than above appears more balanced than one exactly centered on the page.

The body of text is usually perceived by the reader as a unit; space around the text, including runningheads and folios, as marginal space. The placement of the type page in relation to the book page depth is determined by the head margin—the distance from the top trim edge to the uppermost element on the page, usually the ascenders at the top of the runninghead or the top of the folios. The placement of the type area in relation to the page width is determined by the gutter margin— the distance from the inside edge of the book (the binding edge) to the inside of the type page. The first consideration in determining the gutter margin is the effect of binding. Sufficient space must be left between facing type pages to accommodate the grind-off of the folds during perfect binding, stitches through the sides of the folds during side-sewing, or the holes for mechanical devices such as plastic combs or metal rings. A special consideration for library books with an anticipated long life is enough additional space to accommodate rebindings, which usually consume at least one-eighth inch of gutter space each time.

Traditionally the gutter margin is the smallest margin bordering the type page, followed in size by the head margin, the outside margin, then the foot margin;[15] this configuration brings the facing pages of a spread together so that they are perceived as a unit, facilitating jumps from the foot of one page to the top of the next; it also balances the page at its perceived center. Some modern book designers have broken with this tradition and positioned the type page so that there is a constant, ample margin at the left edge of the text, identical on both verso and recto pages, with the view that this placement increases the readability of the text by helping our eye find the beginning of each line at the left edge.[16] A layout such as this based on asymmetrical relationships can be dynamic and beautiful, but probably requires a keener eye for proportion and balance to be as successful as more traditional but more static layouts.

The various elements in a design must have sufficient contrast for legibility—for example, a reader should be able to easily tell the difference between settings of text, references, notes, and extracted materials and between chapter headings and various levels of subheadings within chapters. Typographical contrast can be obtained by varying type size, style, arrangement, and/or setting style. Elegance in design results from the use of only the degree of contrast necessary for the purpose while maintaining a unity of appearance. Usually three to five sizes and one or two type families are sufficient for designing even the most complex texts.[17]

A book's length affects most components of its cost. Adjustments to typographical specifications can change the setting length of a manuscript by as much as 30 percent. The first step of estimating length is the character count, an analysis of the physical length of the manuscript, accomplished by multiplying the average number of characters per line of manuscript by the number of lines in the manuscript. All punctuation marks, numerals, miscellaneous symbols, and linear spaces between words are counted as characters, along with upper- and lower-case letters. A separate count is compiled for each element that will receive distinctive design treatment—footnotes, extracted material, and so on. A separate count compiled for each chapter will be more accurate and more useful for adjusting length. The number of occurrences of each element that will be separated from the text by space during page make-up must be counted so that the extra space around each occurrence can be incorporated into the length estimate.

The number of characters per line of manuscript is easily determined if each page has been typed in a single font. Fixed-space typewriter fonts have a fixed width that is the same for each character—either ten (pica style) or twelve (elite style) characters per inch—so that one need only to multiply the average line length (in inches) by the number of characters per inch (either ten or twelve) to determine the average number of characters per line of manuscript. When a manuscript is typed in several fonts, with varying line lengths, with variably spaced fonts (such as type fonts, increasingly available on most word processors and personal computers), or with variable spaces between words (necessary to have justified lines—lines of equal length), the character count of the manuscript is much more complicated.

With the character count in hand, the designer plans the layout of the type page and the size, style, and arrangement of each element in the manuscript, then writes complete specifications to instruct the compositor setting the manuscript. Visual layouts of sample pages are necessary for complicated designs. Specifications for each element should define (1) the point size of type; (2) the leading; (3) minimum, maximum, and optimum interword spacing, as appropriate; (4) line length or measure; (5) the set width, if different than the point size, in digital typography; (6) the name of the type face; (7) the style of the setting (justified, centered, ragged right, and so on); (8) the spacing above and below elements, as appropriate; and (9) any special paging considerations, such as limitations on the division of elements and the identification of spaces that are fixed and those that are variable during page make-up. For example, typical instructions for defining a text setting might be:

10/12 × 27 Times Roman (10 point Times Roman set with 2 points of extra leading—12 points interline space from the baseline of one line to the baseline of the next—on a 27-pica line). For setting a displayed subheading, the instructions might be: *18/24 Times Roman Bold c/lc × 18max, each line centered × 27, 36pts space above and 24pts space below to text* (18 point Times Roman Bold, 24 points interline space from baseline to baseline, set with initial capitals, each line a maximum of 18 picas long and centered on the 27-pica measure, each occurrence spaced from the text by 36 points above the first line and 24 points below the last line, measured from baseline to baseline).

Controlling Purchases and Costs

Production costs are either fixed (plant or compilation) costs or edition (manufacturing) costs. Plant costs are one-time expenses and are independent of the number of books that are made. They include design, editing, production supervision, typesetting and proofreading (including alterations, corrections, and page make-up), illustration, photography, art preparation, and all camera, film, and stripping operations that prepare final platemaking films and image carriers. Plant costs are distinguished from operating costs (overhead expenses) in that they are specifically allocated to individual projects and are compiled as part of the monetary valuation of the final product; as such they can be carried as an asset until a book is sold, at which point the cost of that sale is expensed. Often general administrative and supervisory expenses—including production supervision expenses and all editorial costs—are not allocated to specific projects but are considered operating costs and are expensed as they are incurred. Platemaking costs are included with plant costs only if the plates can be saved for subsequent reprintings (this is not the case for conventional offset plates, but is true for Cameron Belt plates, for example). Plant costs can be amortized over the original printing (in this way only by increasing the size of the edition or by reducing the total costs can the per-book plant costs be lowered), the usual practice; or over a fixed term, such as three or five years.

Manufacturing costs—paper, printing, and binding—can be broken down into set-up costs, material costs, and running costs. Set-up costs are fixed and independent of the number of books that are made; they include manufacturing supervision and time spent preparing a machine to perform a task, as opposed to the time a machine takes to actually perform the task (running time). Some material costs are fixed when materials are purchased in very large lots for use on many different editions (such as standard papers, inks, adhesives, and so on). Other material costs are variable, when materials are purchased in small lots for a single edition (such as special inks, special papers or cover materials, and so on). Fixed set-up costs are incurred for each reprinting; these can be spread over more units to lower per-book costs by ganging (grouping together) the manufacture of several standardized products or by increasing the quantity of any one order. Set-up costs can also be reduced by using assembly-line systems that can combine several operations, so that a single set-up can replace several. Examples of this are the web press, which combines sheeting, presswork, and folding operations; and modern casebinding lines, which combine all of the steps from gathering signatures to packaging finished books in a single operation. Material costs can be lowered by substituting different, cheaper materials or by purchasing in bulk. Running costs—functions of machine output capacity and the manufacturer's hourly rates (including salaries, overhead, equipment depreciation, and so on) are usually beyond a publisher's control.

Generally, most costs can be controlled by competitive bidding, which usually ensures that a particular job will be matched with the supplier who is best suited to complete it at that particular time. The use of standard trim sizes is probably more important than any other single factor for controlling production costs, since it ensures that there will be standard papers economically available for reprints or small editions and a wide selection of possible suppliers with compatible equipment configurations.

The complete set of design specifications with the character count of the manuscript can be used to request competitive bids for composition services. It can be more efficient to send a compositor preliminary specifications and a duplicate manuscript and let the compositor compile the character count and length estimate as part of preparing a bid. If a manuscript contains poor copy, such as photostats, an unusual amount of handwritten corrections, or complex settings such as foreign languages and mathematical equations, the compositor must see a copy of the manuscript in order to prepare an accurate cost estimate.

Composition estimates should be broken down to include prices for setting the main text, tables, front matter, and index pages; for alterations made in proof; and for extra sets of proofs. Since compositors differ in the way they prepare their quotations, total costs should be compiled to reflect a true comparison of competing bids: For example, one compositor may include extra sets of proofs in the base price, and another may separate keyboarding costs from page make-up costs. In some cases where heavy corrections in proof seem inevitable, a low cost for alterations may be critical. Request a time schedule with each bid, since this may be the deciding factor in choosing between very similar bids.

The experience of working with a compositor over a period of time will prove the reliability of that company's quotations, length estimates, and work schedules, as well as the helpfulness of the staff. These intangible factors are often more important than price over the long term. Much can be judged about prospective new suppliers by carefully reviewing samples of books and reproduction proofs they have set.[18] Look at the spacing between letters and words: Is it proportional and balanced, or are there awkward and uneven letter combinations, very loose or very tight lines that are not pleasing and that are hard to read? Look at the density and color of the printed text and repro: Has this factor been controlled throughout the job? Are correction patches visible because of variations in color and weight? Is the repro properly exposed and developed, or will it cause problems for the printer, and delays and extra expenses in prepress preparation? Check the compositor's reputation for accuracy and service with other publishers.

Composition orders should outline exactly what is expected of the compositor and should include (1) specifications for setting with any design layouts; (2) the number and form of any proofs required, and the final product—repro or film; (3) the proposed schedule, including the estimated length of time that proofs will be held for reading by author and editor; and (4) your understanding of the price. Ask the compositor to acknowledge receipt of the order and to confirm your understanding of the schedule and the price.

A printer should be furnished with the following information in order to prepare an accurate estimate: (1) the number of book pages; (2) the size of the trimmed pages of the book; (3) the print run; (4) the prepress image preparation that will be required, whether you will supply repro or film, and what kinds of illustrations will be photographed; (5) the number and position of bleed images that will extend to the very edges of the trimmed pages after binding—these must be printed to extend past the trim edge and require a slightly larger sheet of paper if they fall at the outside of a press form; (6) the number of ink colors that will be used; (7) the type of paper that will be used, and who will supply it; (8) the proposed schedule and special delivery requirements; and (9) the number and kinds of proofs that will be necessary.

Request a breakdown of costs so that any price changes due to material increases or specification changes can be isolated. Printing estimates will include charges for prepress preparation (including camera work, film, stripping, and proofing); platemaking; paper; makeready and presswork. The best printer for a particular job will be able to match their machine configuration with your job requirements; much of the variation in pricing between printers as revealed by competitive bids will be due to differences in equipment capabilities and press formats. Usually a few printers will emerge as being the most competitive for a particular configuration; the choice between them is then narrowed from price to questions of reliability, service, and printing quality.

The complete camera copy for the text and all of the illustrations should be sent to the printer with a detailed order; specifications should clearly indicate proofing requirements (blueprints and other contact proofs are routinely made from flats to check platemaking films before plate-making and printing; proofing a job on press is considerably more expensive and inconvenient and should be reserved for the very special and important jobs that demand this attention), paper specifications, the print run, the proposed schedule, your understanding of the price, and delivery or finishing requirements. Ask the printer to acknowledge receipt of your order and copy and confirm your understanding of the schedule and the price.

Most book manufacturers control printing and binding under one roof; there are obvious advantages, especially in scheduling and quality control, in letting a single supplier produce the book from printing through distribution. But in many cases there are advantages to using small, specialized printers, who may not have complete binding capability, so binding must be ordered and controlled separately. In either case, binding costs should be broken out from presswork costs for control. To prepare an accurate estimate, a bindery should have the following information: (1) the number of book pages and their imposition; (2) the trim size; (3) whether the binder will work with flat or folded sheets; (4) the kind of paper used; (5) the method of binding desired (such as smyth-sewn casebound, perfect paperback, and so on); (6) the kind of materials that will be used (particularly important in casebinding—grade of cover material, binders board, and so on); (7) the extent of case decoration; and (8) the kind of packaging (bulk in cartons, individually wrapped into mailing cartons) and distribution. A bindery's quality can be judged from its sample books. Remember that the quality of a binding is about half the quality of binding materials and half the binding process and quality of workmanship. Mismatched materials and processes can be disastrous, so binders should always be consulted when planning difficult or unusual projects—very large books, odd sizes, or whenever strength is a very important factor. Some markets have rigid requirements that affect binding specifications, of which the binder should be aware— elementary school textbooks must meet National Association of School Textbook Administrators (NASTA) specifications; library bindings must meet standards promulgated by the Library Binding Institute.

As a final note, production people must control many details, particularly specifications, and be meticulous in following up on orders, checking proofs, and comparing progress against schedules. Obviously this is important because errors can not only increase a publisher's costs and directly impair profits but can result in poorly made books that are not accepted in the marketplace. The business of production must be approached systematically when attempted on even a moderate scale. Although many jobs have to be specialized because of their technical nature, a broad, general knowledge of the historical development of manufacturing processes and the business of publishing as a whole is necessary to make well-informed production decisions and to responsibly organize procedures and schedules.

The greatest impact on production in the next decade and beyond is sure to come from the proliferation of computer technology, soon to spread to the smallest offices and businesses. Computers not only help to systematically control specifications, schedules, and costs but are changing many production tasks. Authors are more frequently submitting electronic manuscripts prepared on their personal computers instead of typescripts. Many of the functions now performed by production people— such as identifying and coding design elements and format specifications, as well as the more fundamental task of creating the actual data base for composition—are shifting to authors and editors. If this shift is not to create a more difficult task for all involved, clear standards that authors can use for preparing electronic manuscripts must be established. Some publishing houses have already created their own standards; some industry groups (notably the AAP) are working to create industry-wide standards that may benefit compositors and the smaller publishers as well.[19] Although producing simple texts via a word processor–to–compositor interface using standard formats is already a reality, it may be several years before complex texts can be efficiently composed in this manner. Undoubtedly the computer has changed the way production people, as well as editors and authors, conceive of their jobs.

Notes

1. The principal exception to this is the Cameron Belt press, primarily used for manufacturing mass-market paperbacks and some trade titles. It is a high-speed web press with in-line binding that produces finished books from rolls of paper in a single machine operation. The Cameron uses flexible plastic relief plates that are only suitable for reproducing text and line images. Since Cameron plates are made by a photomechanical process from film negatives, the prepress procedure for preparing text and line images is the same as for offset lithography. The rest of this discussion will be limited to offset lithography. See Victor Strauss, *The Printing Industry* (Washington, D.C.: The Printing Industries of America, 1967) for a comprehensive discussion of other printing processes.

2. Lithographic films are most sensitive to black and red, least sensitive to light blue (called nonrepro blue since it will not be reproduced). See *Pocket Pal: A Graphic Arts Production Handbook* (New York: International Paper Co., 1974) for a clear explication of graphic-arts photographic techniques.

3. Direct camera plates made without intermediary films or image carriers by an electrostatic process, directly from original repro, are widely used in the quick-printing industry and are replacing conventional offset plates in some short-run applications. Direct-to-plate digital typesetting/laser technology is established in the newspaper industry and may begin to replace photomechanical platemaking in the future if its cost dramatically decreases.

4. Collotype (a planographic process) and gravure are examples of printing methods that *can* print continuous-tone images by applying continuously varying amounts of ink to paper. Letterpress and screen printing, however, are discrete printing processes, like offset lithography.

5. Halftones are usually made by photographing the original continuous-tone image through a finely ruled glass or film screen placed between the lens and the film in a camera. The crossed rules of the halftone screen focus light reflected from the original image into dots on the film. The size of each dot is a function of the size of the spaces between the rules in the screen and the amount of light reflected from the original image. The halftone negative must be made to final size as it cannot be enlarged or reduced without altering the dot pattern and thus the quality of the printed image. A recent development is a digital conversion process that involves scanning the original image with a laser light. The tones in the original image modulate the laser in a pattern that can be stored as digital codes in a computer, which can later control digital typesetting devices or exposing lasers to generate the halftone image. The final result will be indistinguishable from a halftone made by photographic conversion; the main advantage of a digital halftone is its ability to be integrated with texts in computer systems or transmitted over great distances (as are the Associated Press Laserphotos reproduced in many newspapers).

6. Generally, screens with 85–100 lines per inch are suitable for medium-quality reproduction, as in newspapers or quick printing; 100–150 lines per inch for good-quality reproduction on uncoated paper; 150–200 lines per inch for best-quality reproduction on smooth, coated surfaces.

7. Image assembly operations—stripping—combine line, halftone, and combination images by taping individual negatives to a heavy, opaque paper (goldenrod) the exact size of a press form. Windows are cut behind image areas to create the platemaking mask (called the flat). Stripping must be very precise if registration and image placement is to be exact. This is especially difficult in multicolor printing where several flats must be closely registered to each other to create the plates for each press form. Color printing is too complex to cover in detail in this limited space. Generally, multicolor printing involves successively printing different inks. In preparing images for multicolor printing, a different flat and plate are prepared for each different ink on each press form. A special form of multicolor printing, four-color process reproduction, creates an illusion of the full spectrum of colors using only four inks: magenta (process red), cyan (process blue), yellow, and black. Since the originals are usually continuous-tone images, such as color photographs, they must be separated into four halftones. The principles of color reproduction are based on a theory of color perception; for more information on color theory, separations, and printing see Miles Southworth, *Pocket Guide to Color Reproduction: Communication and Control* (Livonia, N.Y.: Graphic Arts Publishing Co., 1979).

8. The definitive study of the history and evolution of printing types remains Daniel Berkeley Updike, *Printing Types: Their History, Forms, and Use*, 2 vols. (Cambridge: Harvard University Press, 1937; reprinted by Dover Publications, New York, in 1980). Updike has

called his work "A Study in Survivals," noting the conservative, preservative aspect of type design. A more general treatise on the development of standard letterforms from early models and the early development of printing types modeled on calligraphic hands is Frederic W. Goudy, *The Alphabet and Elements of Lettering* (Berkeley: The University of California Press, 1952; reprinted by Dover Publications, New York, in 1963).

9. An exciting and stimulating analysis of the historical relationships between type designs and production technologies, especially with emphasis on the ramifications of digital technology, can be found in Charles Bigelow and Donald Day, "Digital Typography," *Scientific American* 249, no. 2 (August 1983), pp. 106–119. This is a very clear explication of the development of the new typesetting technology and its potential impact on the design of our standard letterforms.

10. Note that originally printing was synonomous with setting metal type—modern printing began with the invention and development of movable metal type. Hand setting metal types is essentially a printing-plate assembly process.

11. Laser typesetters are different from laser textsetters, which use an electrostatic process to fuse digital images on the drum of a copying machine that can produce copies of the image by a xerographic process. The main reason why laser textsetters cannot be classified as true typesetters at present is the low resolution and poor quality of their digital images—although the future will perhaps not make this distinction.

12. Edith Diehl correctly argues that commercial machine-binding technology produces not a truly "casebound" book but a "cased" book. A truly bound book is securely sewn into its case; " . . . the so-called commercial binders do not 'bind' books in the technical sense of the word, but 'case' them. The 'casing' of the commercial binder serves [only] as a temporary protection to the text of a book. . . . " Her classic work covers the history and practice of traditional bookbinding methods in great detail; it is informative to note the evolution of traditional techniques as adapted and altered by machine production. See Edith Diehl, *Bookbinding: Its Background and Technique* (New York: Rinehart & Co, 1946, in two volumes; reprinted and bound in one volume by Dover Publications, New York, 1980).

13. The American Point System is based on an equivalence with the metric system so that 83 picas equal exactly 35 centimeters; a close approximation of 6 picas is .996 inch.

14. *Paragraphs on Printing Elicited from Bruce Rogers in Talks with James Hendrickson on the Functions of the Book Designer* (New York: William E. Rudge's Sons, 1943; reprinted by Dover Publications, New York, 1979), pp. 14, 49.

15. Again, Bruce Rogers:

> The proportioning of margins is a most vexing problem. It is generally agreed (except by some of the ultra-modern designers) that the inner margin should be the smallest, the top larger than the inner, the outer still larger, and the bottom widest of all. Formulas have been devised by printers and writers on printing: that, starting with the inner margin there should be an increase of twenty per cent all round; or that the outer and lower margins should be double the width of the inner and top ones; and several other pronouncements of the kind. Such rules may be taken as starting points; but so much depends upon the size and shape of your type page, and the kind of book you are making, that any rule is far from being universally applicable. The margins of a scientific or text book, those of a novel, and those of a luxurious edition would all vary in proportion as well as in size. The proportions of margins in a slim book of verse would probably be most unsuitable for a folio volume.

Paragraphs on Printing, p. 105.

16. Jan Tschichold (surely one of the "ultra-modern" designers mentioned by Bruce Rogers above) was perhaps the first to explicitly formulate this concept; cf. Ruari McLean, *Jan Tschichold: Typographer* (Boston: David R. Godine, 1975).

17. Stanley Rice has developed a practical system for planning simple text settings that takes advantage of variations and contrasts possible within a single family of type; cf. *Book Design*, 2 vols. (New York: R. R. Bowker, 1978). His system is particularly applicable since it is based on digital typesetting and can be used in conjunction with computer programs to simplify design tasks. His contribution to the organization and management of type design and type production is clear, and his system has found favor among many designers as it gives a framework within which to work. Actual results, though perhaps acceptable, ultimately fail (with this or any other strictly applied system) without a well-developed sensibility in the eye of the designer.

18. A good impression of various compositor's work can also be gleaned from examining their type sample books, which can reveal the extent of their commitment and attitude toward book setting. For a model sample book illustrating the highest standards of book typography, see Hugh Williamson, comp., *Photocomposition at the Alden Press, Oxford: A Printer's Type-Specimen Book* (Oxford: The Alden Press, 1981).

19. It must be recognized that the preparation of electronic manuscripts for typesetting is a collaboration between the author, publisher, and typesetter, each sharing and assuming responsibilities that were previously clearly defined, but need to be clearly stated and understood anew by each party. For example, who actually corrects the electronic data base after editing? Who incorporates format codes into the manuscript? A critical factor, since clear standards are not available, is the testing of a few of the author's pages early on in the publishing process, to identify problems before production is well under way.

PART THREE
Marketing

CHAPTER NINE

Marketing Trade Books

CAROLE SINCLAIR

Marketing

It is the responsibility of the marketing department to plan and execute the selling strategy for all products in a publishing company. This includes not only new books, but new authors, new imprints, and new lines of books, plus the company's active backlist books.

A marketing department is a team of people (the number depending on the size of the company), all having different functions, who work together to create a favorable climate for a product. Figure 9.1 shows the structure of a typical marketing department and how it fits into the corporate structure.

THE MARKETING DEPARTMENT

Heading the department is the *marketing director,* who is responsible for directing the marketing staff and coordinating all marketing functions, both within the department and with other departments in the company.

The job descriptions of the managers and marketing personnel, as defined by the Association of American Publishers, are as follows:

Market Research Manager: responsible for studying the market to keep abreast of what is selling, to identify where potential for development of new products exists, to identify new markets, and to provide data for the development of new products

Sales Manager: supervises the activities of the sales force, provides sales tools for the sales force, participates in the establishment of policies related to the sales force, and prepares sales-forecast budgets

Advertising Manager: responsible for promoting all products of the company through advertising campaigns aimed at both the trade and consumers and for developing and meeting advertising budgets

Sales Promotion Manager: responsible for creating and distributing pro-

CAROLE SINCLAIR is the publisher and editorial director of *Sylvia Porter's Personal Finance Magazine;* she was formerly promotion director, Doubleday Publishing Company.

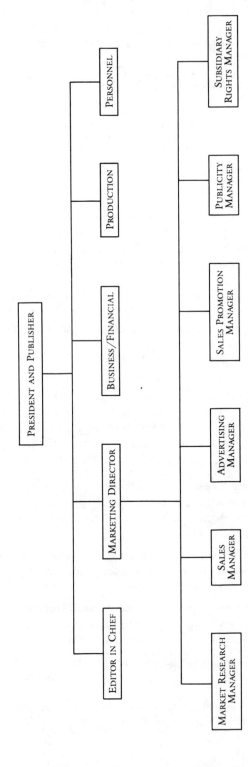

FIGURE 9.1 Marketing department.

motional material, including direct-mail brochures, sales ads, point-of-purchase (bookstore) displays, exhibit displays, and other visual materials

Publicity Manager: responsible for generating broad awareness and interest in the company's products in all targeted markets through effective use of the media and through developing good relations with all appropriate segments of the marketplace

Subsidiary Rights Manager: responsible for marketing the company's products to those people interested in licensing the subsidiary rights (paperback reprint, film, book club, translation, newspaper and magazine serialization, and so on)

All of these marketing components are closely interrelated, and the department operates most successfully when they work together as a team. You may find, though, that the person specializing in advertising, for instance, will say that marketing centers about advertising, with everything else being support activity. The sales promotion manager sometimes feels the same way about sales promotion, the publicist about publicity, and the sales director about sales. In truth, however, the strength or domination of one area over another generally depends on the expertise and strength of the person in charge of it. So at some companies publicity is the core, at others sales, and so on.

DEVELOPING A MARKETING PLAN

For each book, the marketing department develops a marketing plan, which consists of every element required to package and position the book. Crucial to this plan are elements actually decided on by other departments (editorial, art, production, and financial) in consultation with marketing: title and subtitle, jacket treatment (including design and flap copy), price and first print quantity, and publication date. The marketing department is directly responsible for determining special discounts and/or terms offered as part of the sales package, advertising (trade, consumer, and cooperative), sales promotion aids (including selling aids for sales representatives and material for booksellers), and publicity efforts, including press releases; radio, TV, and print exposure; feature and review coverage; and use of the author for interviews, personal appearances, or special events.

Lee Simmons, president of Franklin Spier, the book advertising agency, told me this about the marketing plan:

Our concern in developing a marketing strategy is positioning. Positioning simply means establishing a product, in this case a book, within an overall category in such a way that potential buyers discern a distinct personality—an individual style—that sets it apart from the competition. If the position staked out for a book is a successful one, the book differences are discerned as unique product advantages by a large enough percentage of buyers in a category to make the product profitable. It is important to recognize in any positioning strategy the fact that no product can or should try to garner a 100% share of market, and that establishing a strong and distinctive position for a book will always alienate a certain percentage of total potential buyers as well as attract a certain percentage. In other words, it is okay to turn off even 90% of all potential book buyers, if 10% are strongly motivated to buy, provided that a 10% share of market makes the product profitable.

In developing the marketing plan and strategy, it is important first to determine whether there is a natural audience or market for the book, as well as any secondary markets. The purpose of the plan then is to be able to reach these markets in the most cost-effective way during the launch of the book, during any follow-up marketing, and when the book becomes a part of the company's backlist (usually a year after publication).

Work on the plan usually begins as soon as the book is signed up, although rough plans may well be a part of the very first sessions where the decision on whether or not to publish the book is made. Prepublication planning sessions are subsequently held with each of the operating departments, including business and sales, as well as editorial.

It is at this preplanning stage that the sales department sets a tentative advance—that is, the number of books it wants to have placed in the stores at the time the book is published. There will also be an estimate made of the total first year's sale, and this will be considered in setting the size of the first printing.

The budget for the book is also established at this stage. A typical marketing budget at a general trade publishing house is equal to 20 percent of the company's net sales dollars. Roughly half of that goes to maintain the cost of the sales operation, and the other half goes for the total promotion effort. Within the promotion budget, about 75 percent is usually allotted for advertising of all kinds—trade, consumer, and cooperative—with the bulk of it going to consumer advertising. The other 25 percent of the promotion budget in any given year is most probably divided equally between publicity (including the cost of galleys, review copies, press releases, and author-related tours and events) and sales promotion.

Although the overall promotion budget might be an across-the-board percentage of net sales on all books for any given year, the budget per book varies widely. Every book has a certain amount of overhead (general operating expenses of the company, such as staff, office space, and

TABLE 9.1 SAMPLE BOOK BUDGET
_____

Cover price of book: $10.00
Number of copies printed: 20,000
$10.00 × 20,000: $200,000 gross income
Less 46% discount: $108,000 net
$108,000 net income × 20% for marketing support: $21,600
$21,600 × 50%: $10,800 for sales costs

This leaves $10,800 for the promotion budget, which would be
   allocated as follows:
      $1,500 Trade advertising
      $7,000 Consumer advertising
      $1,000 Sales promotion
      $1,300 Miscellaneous publicity
_____

supplies) charged against it, and most books receive basic publicity support in the form of press releases and review copies. Beyond that, individual campaigns are tailored to what is considered to be the marketing potential for each book. Obviously, the books perceived to have the largest potential for sales usually get the largest budgets. Table 9.1 is a sample of what a typical book promotion budget would look like.

Once the planning stage is done, marketing people sit down to work out specific details of the promotion for each book. Managers from each area of marketing meet together to closely coordinate all efforts. This is essential in putting together a successful campaign for a book: Copywriting must support the advertising approach, advertising must support author appearances, publicity must generate reviews for use by advertising, promotion must provide sales with selling materials, and so on.

Everyone in the marketing department is concerned with one thing on every book—finding the sales handle. The handle is a one-sentence, one-phrase, or even one-word description of why somebody should buy the particular book, of what it offers, and of its potential benefit to the reader. The first sale made on a book is in-house—that is, the editor selling it to the other departments, including sales and promotion. The second sale is made when the sales people sell it to various accounts— retail and wholesale, trade, school, library, academic. And the final sale is made by the account to the ultimate consumer. Each sale involves identifying the handle and using it effectively in the material that is prepared for the audience you are trying to reach.

Developing Promotional Materials

The actual promotion of a book begins with the preparation of catalog copy. The copywriter tries to reduce everything there is to say about a book to five hundred to eight hundred words of descriptive copy. This copy in the new-publications announcement catalog tries to sell the bookseller as well as the reviewer on the product.

Jacket-flap copy has to do a different kind of selling job—to move the book out of the bookstore or library into the hands of a reader. This copy, which is usually about five hundred to eight hundred words long, again has to contain the handle—the reason the ultimate consumer should buy the book.

Next comes development of point-of-purchase materials—such things as special selling kits, window streamers, window stickers, and special gimmicks like aprons, pop-ups, or buttons, whatever is applicable. There is sometimes no room on most of this material for a handle or a sales pitch, so it must be visually striking. It is usually graphic impact that counts, as well as maybe one or two words of very carefully selected copy. The advertising department develops trade advertising aimed at the publisher's customers, as well as consumer advertising aimed at the ultimate consumer. The handle here becomes the headline in many cases.

Finally, just before publication date, the publicity staff gets to work. As soon as finished books are ready, they are sent out to reviewers and other media people with a press release, which again has to have a handle. The press release is selling copy also, but slightly different from catalog and flap copy in that it is aimed at a potential reviewer, feature writer, or interviewer. The first paragraph should contain a description of what the book is about and why it would be of interest to that reviewer or feature writer. If you're lucky, all you have to do is mention a famous author's name. If you're not that lucky, it's a bit more difficult.

Last, if the author of a book is going on tour, a fact sheet about the author is prepared. This sheet is used to convince a radio or TV show to interview the author, and it also includes ten to twenty suggestions on what to talk about with the author if he is booked on the show. Again you need a handle, but this handle is directed at the potential interviewer.

All of the people working on the promotion of a book frequently share ideas, so the flap copywriter may come up with a handle the publicist can use, or the publicist might come up with a handle that the advertising manager could use. There must be constant coordination of their efforts.

Advertising

The advertising department also works on development of the handle for each book, allots a portion of the available advertising money to it, and then develops the campaign. The advertising manager works with the company's advertising agency to develop a strategy for each campaign; the department's traffic coordinator then handles all the paperwork of getting the rough sketch and copy from the agency to the manager and other interested persons (such as the book's editor), gets the material back to the agency for revision, and then gets approval for the final ad.

It would be misleading to talk only in terms of campaigns, since so few of them are done. Most books receive only one or two announcement ads, and some only what are called list ads. Since budgets are based on overall sales expectations, the bulk of the budgets is allotted for books with broad appeal. These can be books by established authors, celebrities, or newsworthy persons; gimmick books, such as diet and sex and money how-to titles; occasionally a first novel by an author the publishers believe deserves wide exposure to reach what they hope is a large audience for his or her work.

In advertising, you start with a plan. Part of that plan involves positioning your book. Does it have a natural market? If so, is there a best medium through which to reach that natural market? Does it have a secondary market? What are the most cost-effective ways of reaching that secondary market? Can you afford this at all?

In developing advertising for a particular book, you should find out everything you can that bears on your book. You will be helped in this by the media department of your advertising agency, whose responsibility it is to be experts in media selection. It is up to you, however, to let your agency know the audience at which your book is aimed. You can expect that the copywriters and artists working on preparation of your ads at the agency will have read all or part of every book that will receive a major campaign. Those books that will simply appear as one of many in a list ad usually aren't read at the agency, though, and you shouldn't insist that they be. Remember that all aspects of the marketing plan must fit together. You can't price and package a book for one market and then advertise it for another.

There are essentially three types of advertising in general publishing. The first is trade advertising, which is aimed at booksellers and librarians. Then there is consumer advertising, which is print, radio, and TV advertising that the publisher pays for to reach the consumer directly.

Finally, there is cooperative advertising, which the publisher and bookseller pay for jointly.

TRADE ADVERTISING

Trade advertising is most commonly run in *Publishers Weekly, Library Journal,* the *New York Times Book Review* (also for consumers), *Choice, Booklist,* and *American Bookseller.* The purpose of this advertising is to convince the bookseller or librarian that he or she needs your book, that your book is important, that your book will sell, and that the publisher will be promoting the title and consequently creating consumer demand for it.

The basic elements in a trade ad are, of course, the title, author, publication date, and price. Inclusion of an author photo is a good idea if the author is a celebrity or has a track record of good sales, or if he or she is currently in the news or generally visible. Second, a trade ad should contain a brief description of what the book will do for the customer. If it's fiction, will it have special appeal to World War II buffs, gothic readers, spy buffs, and so forth? If it's nonfiction, will it improve one's health, body, mind, or sex life, increase one's ability to earn money, or fill some other pressing need? The point is to promise the customer something.

The trade ad also should list all promotion plans. Will the author travel around the country? Will he or she make network TV appearances or radio appearances? Will there be big publisher ads in print, radio, or TV? Will there be special in-store display material? Is there any special feature from the sales department such as extra discount or deferred billing?

CONSUMER ADVERTISING

The purpose of consumer advertising obviously is to let consumers know that your book exists and to convince them that they need it. The consumer ad must build demand and, if possible, offer a benefit. This could be a new book by an author the reader has previously enjoyed, a cure for something, a good escape, or perhaps a gift item for a particular holiday. Whatever the handle is, it should be featured in the headline. Chances are, if you don't get consumers there, you'll never get them to read the rest of the ad. Radio and TV for the consumer have similar objectives.

COOPERATIVE ADVERTISING

Cooperative advertising not only sells the book, it has the additional purpose of selling the store. In other words, even if the ad features a known author or a terrific new diet title, it will always have as an equally important goal selling the book at the bookstore that is cooperating in the ad. The cooperative ad may feature only one title, or talk about an author appearance in a store, but it must also try to build traffic so that the browsing customer buys not only the book in the ad but perhaps five or six others. Some stores have a fixed line of copy that they run on every ad, promising, for example, good and friendly service, special orders, a particularly good paperback selection, or a strong juvenile department. Such cooperative ads have the benefit of repetition.

Most hardbound publishers offer their accounts cooperative advertising. An example of the typical arrangement would be that the publisher offers accounts an amount equal to 5 percent of the previous year's net sales of that publisher's books. This money can be used to advertise any of that publisher's titles, new or old, hardbound or paperback. Invoices for these ads are submitted to the publisher, and the publisher pays 75 percent of the cost. So, if an account had net sales with the company of $10,000, its allowance would be $500. Then, if it ran a newspaper ad that cost $100, the publisher would pay $75, and deduct that amount from the overall allowance of $500, leaving $425 for other ads. Most cooperative policies are some variation on this theme.

WHY ADVERTISE AND FOR WHOM?

The reasons for advertising a book vary. Some of the more important ones are (1) to attract large numbers of potential readers; (2) to develop an author; (3) to attract a large subsidiary rights sale; (4) to convince the people to whom the large subsidiary rights sale has already been made that the publisher is behind the book; (5) to please the author; (6) to support an author on a modest project because a big project is coming; and (7) to advertise the publishing house—that is, to attract good authors, agents, and subsidiary rights sales to the publishing house.

What is a good ad? A good ad is an ad you ran for a book that sold. A great ad is one you ran for a book that got on the best-seller list. Conversely, a bad ad is an ad you ran for a book that didn't sell. Another way to look at it is that a good ad is one the author, agent, and editor liked. A terrific ad is one they all loved. A terrible ad is one they all hated.

This approach isn't as cynical as it may seem. One advertises not only to sell books, but for what is known as author ego. A happy author means you have a happy editor and a happy agent. There are, of course, financial constraints that limit this kind of practice.

Then, of course, your ad must please your sales force, the booksellers, and the consumers. You'll probably find that your sales department likes an ad with what they consider to be hard-sell copy. Booksellers tend to like ads with lots of good quotes from reviewers. Consumers generally react to ads with headlines that are in some way sensational or eye-catching. Such an ad could feature a famous author's name, possibly a famous author's photograph, or one line of copy describing something important about the book—its benefit or promise.

Whatever the reason for advertising, it is important to remember that the advertising *must* support the rest of the marketing plan for the title.

SCHEDULING THE AD CAMPAIGN

An advertising campaign for a trade book usually starts with an announcement in *Publishers Weekly* to alert booksellers that the publisher is behind a particular book. This may run from three to six months before publication date—at the same time that the sales representatives are out selling the book. The hope is that one reinforces the other.

On publication date announcement advertising is done in anywhere from three to twenty markets. New York, Los Angeles, and Chicago are the big markets; in fact, more than 50 percent of most books sold are sold in these three markets. Announcement ads ideally contain good advance quotes or some striking piece of information about why the consumer should be buying the particular book.

Reviews tend to break on publication date or within the weeks immediately following publication date, so big review ads are generally scheduled for three to four weeks after publication. If things are going well, then it's time to start running small reminder ads. There's very little room in these ads so you have to get one major idea across, possibly one sensational quote.

The fourth round of advertising—the stage that you've been aiming for—is the best-seller ad. The best thing you can say about any book is that it is a best-seller. Once you can put that in your headline—and you can't do that until it actually is a best-seller somewhere—you generate a whole new market: those people who read best-sellers, but little else.

Publishers prefer print advertising over radio and TV because innumerable research projects have shown that the hard-core, hardbound book-buying audience is moved most by print, and in fact spends little time listening to the radio or watching television. Even more important to remember is that only a small percentage of the population buys more than five books a year, so all advertising efforts are aimed at a very special audience.

THE AD

Great ideas are simple. That can't be stressed enough. Even if a major nonfiction book has five or six wonderful things going for it, a good copywriter or art director will single out one and develop it fully. In this way, the consumer will be reminded over and over again about the book's handle. This is particularly important for the small number of big books that have broad-based initial campaigns with big ads in print, radio, and TV, followed up with small print reminder ads and perhaps a ten-second slide with voice-over on TV. There must be one idea to carry through and to reduce for these small ads.

Book advertising for major hardcover fiction and nonfiction is usually filled with quotes. Research shows that serious book buyers want endorsements or recommendations from people they respect—reviewers, commentators, well-known people in various fields.

Nonfiction is easier to advertise than fiction because you are selling a specific idea, benefit, or approach. In fiction, you must sell the author either on the basis of his or her previous track record, on high literary quality as supported by quotes, or possibly through an unusual plot. This is difficult. With category fiction such as gothics, romantic suspense, or science fiction, you are reaching a buff market, and what you really need to get across is that the title is an outstanding one within the particular genre that the consumer is already interested in reading.

It's important to stay competitive within the market area. A person interested in building a garage, for instance, will go to his local bookstore and buy the best-designed, best-displayed, best-priced package available on building a garage. There is an occasional exception, such as *Sylvia Porter's Money Book,* a book we published when I was at Doubleday. There was no other book quite like it at the time. Here we had an established author with wide exposure and an incredibly comprehensive book at a good price. We did extensive advertising for this book because the author went on tour and also because there was a good coupon market for it—that is, it was the kind of book that attracted a number of people to order it by mail. And all our efforts in marketing the book paid off: It did become a best-seller.

An important thing to remember with basic books like *Sylvia Porter's Money Book* is that they have a long shelf life—sometimes two years, sometimes twenty—whereas most trade books have a shelf life of ninety days, and you have to make a big impact during those ninety days or the cause is lost.

Trade advertising is always a gamble. First of all, most trade books lose money before earning subsidiary rights income. One in perhaps twenty-five or thirty first novels or first general nonfiction books even breaks even. The big success is rare indeed. There are books like *Jaws* by Peter Benchley, a first novel that sold millions of copies, but this kind of success is definitely the exception to the rule.

In advertising first novels, or even second or third novels by promising writers, you can usually allot a list-type announcement ad in the *New York Times Book Review* or in another likely publication, such as a

Houston newspaper for a Houston author. Many of these books receive no advertising at all, largely because their distribution is not large enough. Others, however, might advance 7,500 to 10,000 copies, and then advertising can really make a difference. If you can develop a campaign that stirs up a little interest, perhaps backed by some author appearances, you can sometimes get a book off the ground. A distribution of anything less than 7,500 copies on a national basis renders much of your advertising pointless, in that even if the ads create some demand there are not enough books available in the stores. But with good initial distribution and some good ads, you can get something started.

SELECTING AN ADVERTISING AGENCY

In selecting an agency, match your needs with the agency's capabilities. Don't choose a big flashy agency if you don't intend to do big flashy things. There are smaller agencies that do specialize in book advertising, and these may be your best bet for most routine projects. You can always take on a second or third agency to handle special or unusual projects that might come along once or twice a year for your publishing house, although that's not really practical, because the agencies only make decent money on the big campaigns and would not want to bother with doing only list ads.

Book advertising is different from advertising for many, if not most, other consumer products. When I was at Doubleday, we published 700 titles a year. That's 700 different products, each with a different audience. At Lever Brothers, there may be 10 or 15 new products a year—soap, toothpaste, shaving cream, and so on. Lever Brothers can develop advertising campaigns to be tested in key markets, refined, and then run on a national basis for anywhere from three months to several years. Book advertising tends to be a one-shot business. During any four-month period at Doubleday, we introduced about 250 new books. Of these, about 150 were mentioned early in list ads, generally broken down by category, aimed at specific markets. The other 100 consisted of those that got one or two individual ads (most of them—about 75 books) and the handful that got expensive campaigns over several months.

There are only four or five ad agencies that specialize in book advertising in New York, and most publishers are better off using these because nonbook agencies are not staffed to deal with the harassment of several hundred new products a year.

Sales Promotion

The *Sales Promotion Handbook* (Chicago: Dartnell Corporation, 1979) defines sales promotion as "those activities that supplement both personal selling and advertising, coordinate them, and help to make them effective, such as displays, shows, and expositions, demonstrations, and other non-recurrent selling efforts not in the ordinary routine. Sales promotions bring people to the retail store."

Trade sales promotion is split into two areas: materials produced to help the sales representatives get the books into the bookstore and materials produced to help the bookstores get books out of the stores to the ultimate consumer. The first category includes all selling aids, such as title information kits, individual sales kits for big titles, photo composites, order forms, and catalogs.

TITLE INFORMATION KIT

The title information (TI) kit contains fact sheets for each title. The TI sheet is a one- to two-page summary of everything the sales representative needs for a quick sell: author, title, subtitle, price, pagination, format, publication month, keynote description, selling handle, useful information about the author, the direct competition, and the general market. Sales representatives use TIs in conjunction with announcement catalogs and order forms when making presentations to their accounts.

ANNOUNCEMENT CATALOGS

Announcement catalogs are published two or three times a year, depending on the company's publishing span. They feature the new publications for that season, but also often provide a listing of some of the company's leading backlist titles. The catalog gives all the essential information about a title, as well as descriptive copy, and sometimes features the book's jacket. The catalog is an essential selling tool, especially when an account does not have time to sit down with the salesperson to go over all titles. In those cases, the representative might highlight three or four titles on the list and then leave the catalog marked up for the particular account, or star titles the sales representative feels this specific account might sell very well. In addition to regular trade catalogs, there are specialized catalogs featuring categories like books on religion or books for college adoption. New publication catalogs are often mailed to reviewers and feature writers, as well as to all active sales accounts.

ORDER FORMS

The order form is the most important of all selling aids. The sales order form for new publications is usually arranged by month of publication and lists all titles to be published in that particular month, along with author and price. There are also backlist order forms, which list all books already published and on the publisher's active backlist. These are usually available in alphabetical listings by title, by author, and by category. Sales representatives use these forms for taking inventory in particular accounts and for recommending orders by category to their accounts. When a salesperson is unable to see a buyer, he or she frequently leaves an order form, or mails one to a prospective account, with suggested quantities of particular titles. Occasionally, there is a special promotion order form, on which special discounts or shipping terms are offered.

SPECIAL SALES KITS

Another selling aid prepared for the sales force is the special sales kit. These kits are put together for key titles to pull them out of the list and emphasize them. They generally contain a photograph of the author, copies of reviews, prints of material from inside the book, possibly a table of contents, articles written for newspapers and magazines by the author, and just about anything else that will give the salespeople an aid in representing a particular book.

BOOKSELLER MAILINGS

Occasionally, mailings are sent to booksellers on key titles. These mailings usually go out three months before publication time, to coincide with the representative's call. Since it is generally accepted that booksellers throw out much of the material they receive through the mail, these mailings aren't sent out very often.

Now let's turn to materials that are prepared to help the bookseller move books out of the bookstore.

PREPACKS

Prepacks are counter displays that generally hold from ten to twenty copies. It is hoped when a publisher produces a prepack that it will be placed by the cash register at the checkout counter in the bookstore. This is obviously a high-traffic area, and prepacked books must be suitable for impulse buying. Since competition for this space next to the cash register is intense, the prepack must be attractive and attention drawing, and the book you intend to prepack must be a potentially fast-moving item. If a prepacked item doesn't move fast, booksellers will simply unpack it and put the books on the shelf, instead of by the cash register.

A variation on the prepack is the L-shaped counter cart, on which you simply stack books. This is generally used for large-format hardbound bestsellers.

SLIT CARDS

A slit card is attached to the top of a book to draw attention to a particular feature—for instance, a sensational review or a photograph of a well-known author. The problem with slit cards is that they're really only suitable for books placed on the top shelf in bookstores. They don't fit on a regular lower shelf. So unless you expect to get this kind of key, face-out exposure in the bookstore, you are wasting money to prepare these at all.

WINDOW STREAMERS AND STICKERS

You've undoubtedly seen window streamers and stickers for many big books. They generally carry a headline reading something like See the Movie, Read the Book or As Featured on TV or, in the case of a long-awaited book, simply the title and We Have It. Occasionally, if you've had a celebrity endorsement for a book in a TV commerical, you can take a still from the commercial and use it, tying your advertising spot in with your sales promotion material.

POINT-OF-PURCHASE POSTER

These posters are particularly useful at autographing parties or when you have a coupon or advance order form that you want to give away. It is very difficult to get bookstore space for these posters unless the announcement they make is significant. Posters are occasionally used in window displays, but again, it's difficult to get a window display for a single title. Most booksellers put best-sellers or other key drawing items in their windows.

BOOK JACKET

The book jacket is the best point-of-purchase item you can provide. Alex Gotfryd, Doubleday art director and one of the best in the business as well as a well-known photographer, has the following guidelines for good jackets:

- keep them simple and direct
- sell the best feature—the author's name, the title, or art spot
- try to use type that will work as a logo or art element and that can be reduced well and used in black and white, since most ads are printed in black and white
- stay away from committee decisions on jackets
- make it striking—the jacket is the best point-of-purchase seller you have

STATEMENT ENCLOSURES

Statement enclosures are usually three by five inches and fit into a no. 6 envelope, the kind that most department stores use to send out their monthly billings. Statement enclosures can be simple one-sheet flyers or elaborate eight-fold, full-color brochures. Space in monthly mailings is tightly controlled by booksellers, and in order to get a statement enclosure placed, you must be able to persuade the bookseller that he will make money on the mailing. Most requests for these come from specialty accounts, such as religious or how-to booksellers, but occasionally they are also done for the general trade, if a book comes along that has broad-based appeal.

OTHER MATERIALS
There are hundreds of variations on sales promotion materials—bookmarks, mobiles—the possibilities are endless. One of my favorites is a cocktail napkin that I prepared for *Scoring,* by Dan Greenburg, when I was at Doubleday. I was sitting around trying to think of a way to reach the singles market in New York, and it occurred to me that singles bars would be the place, and I didn't have any idea of how to go about getting a book displayed in a singles bar.

So I designed a cocktail napkin and hired a young female disc jockey to dress up in an old prom dress and call on the twenty major singles bars in New York. I also hired a photographer to follow her around and take photographs of her going into singles bars and giving the owners a copy of *Scoring* and a hundred or so cocktail napkins advertising the book. The whole promotion cost about two hundred dollars and was extremely effective. The day after the promotion we sent photographs to the press and got fairly wide pickup, including the *New York Times, Daily News,* and the *Village Voice.*

EXHIBITS AND TRADE SHOWS
These exhibits are an important part of a publisher's sales promotion support program. There are three main annual conventions: the American Booksellers Association (ABA), the American Library Association (ALA), and the Christian Booksellers Association (CBA). Each of these exhibits is attended by key people involved in these areas. The purpose of the ABA is to give every trade publisher a chance to exhibit its upcoming fall list, as well as selected backlist, to all booksellers, both retail and wholesale; new authors are also introduced, already published authors are reintroduced, and special events are held. The ALA convention is similar to the ABA, except that it is aimed at the institutional market, and the CBA convention is focused on books of religious and inspirational interest for Christian booksellers.

For these and other trade conventions, the sales promotion department must design the overall booth; pick the location on the floor; select materials to be displayed; consult with sales on special programs, series, or titles they are pushing; and coordinate author appearances.

SALES CONTESTS
Sales promotion must develop and handle sales contests for either the sales representatives or booksellers. In each case a gimmick must be

developed, simple rules must be set, and the contest must be administered. And, of course, good graphic materials must be developed to announce the contest and to stimulate participation.

COPYWRITING

In some houses, sales promotion handles the writing of jacket, flap, and back copy for a book, as well as copy for the catalog.

One thing to remember about the writing of copy in the publishing industry is that the product about which you are writing is, in fact, writing. You will almost always find that the author has written extended descriptions of his or her book that you can draw on for flap copy, sales letters, ads, and so on. Chances are the author has been describing the book for the agent, the editor, and others and will frequently have come up with many pithy phrases that you can use in various copy assignments.

Ned Parkhouse, copy chief at Doubleday, told me:

> Remember when you're writing advertising copy that you're talking to the customer, not to yourself. What you say is not meant as a display of your own brilliance, but as a means of reaching a potential buyer of a book.
>
> In writing jacket copy for a novel, don't tell the story. Talk about the story but don't give it away. Tell what kind of novel it is and what the reader is likely to find in it. I know this isn't possible sometimes, but when the effort is made, the results are usually successful and certainly better than merely summarizing the story.
>
> Don't try to sell a book (most of them, anyway) by writing what is known as "selling copy." Sell the book by describing it in as appealing a way as possible.

A sales promotion piece is good if it attracts immediate attention and compels retailers or consumers to buy what you're selling. It is particularly effective if it can tie into a campaign they have already seen, such as a TV or radio ad, so it serves as a reminder. Color is important. It must stand out in a bookstore, which is generally full of color. As with all promotion, simplicity is the key. Don't try to go with more than one idea or one graphic element. The point is to grab buyers, not confuse them.

In summary, successful marketing consists of developing a strategy for the positioning of your product and the effective execution of this selling strategy.

CHAPTER TEN

Trade-Book Publicity

ESTHER MARGOLIS

Publicists are a lot like matchmakers. Instead of trying to bring a husband and wife together, they're trying to make another kind of connection—between the book and the media contact. Their success and satisfaction come from kindling the interest of newspaper reporters, gossip columnists, book reviewers, TV or radio producers, magazine editors, or any other persons who have access to a communications outlet, which means access to the public. However a publicist manages to interest a contact—whether in conversation over lunch, cocktails, or dinner; over the phone; or by letter, mailgram, or carrier pigeon—his or her part in the marketing process is quite clear and important: A publicist's function is to make the book known through all available media sources *without* paying for the time or space devoted to the book. Without question, this is the least expensive marketing support in launching a new book, author, or publishing program, and it can be the most potent.

As Oscar Dystel, who was chief executive officer of Bantam Books for twenty-five years, affirmed in the Bowker Memorial Lecture in November 1980: "Intelligent publicity has leverage beyond price. Handled with style and grace, respectful of facts—and not of a company's exaggerated hopes for a book—it can make a major contribution to publishing success, perhaps more effectively than any other promotional activity."

What distinguishes the publicist from other kinds of promoters is that other specialists usually *buy* their access to the consumer. The direct response specialist buys space or rents lists, produces brochures, flyers, or coupon ads, uses the mails or media; the advertising manager buys time or space for commercials or paid ads. Publicists, though, have to woo their messengers with words, written or spoken, and hope that these messengers will use their media to pass the words on to potential consumers.

To be an effective book publicist, it will help you to know the peculiar

ESTHER MARGOLIS is president and publisher of Newmarket Press. She was formerly a senior vice president at Bantam Books, in charge of promotions, advertising, publicity, and public relations.

place publicity has had in the industry and how book promotion has changed. Although publicists have always had an active role in entertainment, business, government, and politics, they are Johnny-come-latelies (more accurately, Janie-come-latelies) in book publishing. Until the 1970s, publicity was rarely considered very important in most publishing houses. No wonder, then, that it became an ideal job for women. Publicity drew on so-called traditional feminine talents—talking, nurturing, and working hard—and it was a natural route of progress for the editor's or the publisher's female secretary.

Originally, the publicist's main tasks were to establish and maintain contact with reviewers, organize publication parties, send out catalog data and review copies, schedule book-and-author luncheon talks, and occasionally arrange an author interview for a newspaper's book page or a guest spot on a local radio or TV program. Her salary was low, but the work was exciting, stimulating, even glamorous. The results of her efforts were not often directly traceable in book sales, and since publicity budgets were small, especially in comparison to advertising and promotion, the area remained largely undervalued and unrecognized.

Fortunately, the accomplishments of publicists as part of successful book marketing became greater and greater, and by the end of the 1970s, many heads of publicity departments had become officers of their companies. A number were promoted to run promotion, advertising, rights, and marketing operations as well, and others left staff jobs to start independent publicity businesses. With success recognized, a growing number of men entered the field, too.

The change in attitude toward publicity and the recognition of its value came about largely as a result of some striking success stories, an almost revolutionary growth in media opportunities, and the emergence of "big money" in relation to the book business, both through the buying and selling of publishing companies by conglomerates and through the buying and selling of authors and book rights. The 1970s were the decade when the publishing industry went public, in both the financial and the publicity sense. Whereas in previous decades publishing news was the province of *Publishers Weekly,* the newspaper book page, or the *Authors Guild Newsletter,* now book deals, mergers, management changes, author disputes—in fact the whole business of publishing—made Gene Shalit's broadcasts and Liz Smith's columns and became the subject of stories in all sections of the *New York Times* as well as the *Wall Street Journal.*

Successes like Jacqueline Susann's *Valley of the Dolls,* Erich Segal's *Love Story,* Arthur Hailey's *Hotel,* Dr. David Reuben's *Everything You Always Wanted to Know About Sex,* William Peter Blatty's *The Exorcist,* Judith Krantz's *Scruples,* and Dr. Kenneth Cooper's *Aerobics*—all of these books were the first major successes by these authors—demonstrated that hard-hitting publicity could help sell books like the proverbial hotcake and establish an author's celebrity or authority, probably for his or her lifetime.

During the 1970s, more media attention was lavished on books and authors than ever before, not just because there was more to publicize but also because the media had expanded so remarkably. The decade also brought the return of the gossip columnist, in the press and on television; the rise of the all-talk radio show; longer local and national TV news shows; the introduction and success of the TV newsmagazine format, like "60 Minutes"; and the proliferation of local, network, and nationally syndicated TV talk shows, like "Donahue," and "Good Morning America," the last of which became a rival of the once-formidable "Today" show. The recovery of the magazine business, which had been in a painful slump in the 1960s, and the emergence of many new specialized mass-market magazines, like *Self, Money, Ms,* and *Working Woman* aided the publicity cause immeasurably, as did the increase in feature and "soft news" sections of newspapers. These so-called off-the-book-page outlets, combined with the more traditional book-review and publishing-news outlets, provided more opportunities for publicists to promote books than ever before.

Today, no one questions the ability of publicity to sell books. Book-sellers and publishers have been sensitized to its powers and can no longer afford to ignore it as part of their marketing strategy. They've seen how the TV adaptations of *Rich Man, Poor Man, Roots,* and *Shogun* drove up book sales by hundreds of thousands of copies and how a public TV series on economics by Milton and Rose Friedman made a best-seller out of *Free to Choose.* They witnessed how a rave review by John Leonard in the *New York Times* transformed Maxine Hong Kingston's *The Woman Warrior* into a hardcover best-seller and helped it achieve a high-priced paperback sale. (Leonard's review did not accomplish this feat directly or instantaneously. Its power lay in its influence on others— an influence the good publicist exploits by relaying the reviews to other media and booksellers.)

The publishers and booksellers also know that the success of *The Complete Scarsdale Medical Diet,* which sold over 800,000 hardcover copies in its first year and another million or so in paperback a year later, was triggered initially by a single *New York Times* syndicated newspaper story on the diet. (Two years later, when Jean Harris was accused of killing the book's author, Dr. Herman Tarnower, and one of the most sensational trials of the century followed, the paperback returned to the bestseller list and sold a million more copies. A morbid break if there ever was one, but it is the publicist's responsibility to respond to events, as well as create them, and the Rawson and Bantam publicity departments were kept pretty busy responding to press queries about the book's history and record.)

They marveled at the success of Judith Guest's first novel, *Ordinary People*, which became known at first through the story of its discovery. The media were enchanted by the news (relayed by Viking's publicity department) that the book had been an over-the-transom submission, that it was receiving strong word of mouth in the trade, that it had generated a hot paperback auction (culminating in a high six-figure sale), and that eventually Robert Redford had acquired the movie rights. The book became a celebrity without an extensive author tour.

The point is that skilled book publicists can be very effective in initiating and generating coverage for books, and publicity skills can be learned. They take time and experience to develop and are best learned through apprenticeships, although workshops and courses in the techniques can be helpful. Typing and general office skills are usually required for entry-level jobs; some journalism or other communications background is extremely helpful.

There are essentially five basic guidelines for doing effective book publicity:

1. Know the media (*whom* are you selling to?).
2. Know the book and/or author and/or publishing program (*what* are you selling?).
3. Develop a strategy; plan a campaign (*how* will you sell it?).
4. Execute your plan, but stay flexible! (Be prepared for amendments, changes, modifications; remember the adage "the best laid plans. . . ."— it applies!)
5. Communicate and evaluate (keep colleagues and the trade continuously informed of the results of your campaign—they affect everybody's planning!).

Know the Media

Some of the best publicists are "media junkies." They read—or more likely, skim—all the dailies published in their city, as well as many out-of-town papers. They read the news weeklies, the biweeklies, the "trades," and a host of monthly general and special-interest magazines. They study by-lines and editorial mastheads and subscribe to public relations (PR) newsletters that report on media personnel and prospects. They flip TV channels incessantly and tune in to the most unlikely radio talk shows, just to check them out so that they can talk knowledgeably to the shows' producers.

Publicists know that in order to service the media they must know the character, circulation, style, audience, deadlines, and needs of the media and that they can jeopardize their credibility—and their access— if they find themselves pitching an author interview about a book on a World War II battleship to the producer of a daytime program for housewives. (Nora Ephron tells the story about her interview segment on a local Midwest TV show. She soon realized that the host had mistaken her collection of essays about women, entitled *Crazy Salad,* for a book about lettuce. "It was a farm-news show, and it was me and a cattle rancher and a catfish farmer, and we were all supposed to make wonderful conversation together, and it was just insane," Ms. Ephron recalled in a April 5, 1976, *Time* magazine article called "Flogging It.") With skilled planning and communications, a publicist should be able to ensure that a TV host knows what subject is supposed to be discussed with what guest. But things do go wrong with even the most experienced planners. The only thing to do is "chalk it up."

For most book publicists, knowing the book-review media is even more important than knowing the off-the-book-page or radio-TV media. Book reviews are one of the most potent ways for a book to win recognition and sales. And the book editor, remember, is employed to cover books; he can be a natural ally. About forty thousand new trade books are published annually, so it's no easy task for the publicist to make his or her company's books stand out from the pack and catch a book editor's attention—another reason to know the contact's taste, style, and interests.

Don't expect to know everything all the time. The most important thing to know is *where* to find what you need *when* you need it. To identify the media, numerous reference publications are available, such as *Literary Market Place, Editor and Publisher, Ayer's Directory of Publications, Television Contacts,* and *Radio Contacts.* (An annotated listing of these and other reference guides to media is carried in *Literary Market Place.*) Other valuable sources are your house's local sales representatives, booksellers, your publicity colleagues, and press agents in other media and product fields. Be an active participant in trade groups like the Publishers' Publicity Association or Women in Communications. Attend meetings. Don't be timid about asking for help or trading information.

Know the Book

Many times it's the publicist, not the author or editor, who first talks about a book to a reviewer, reporter, or producer. You should know what you're talking about. If you don't—which happens, too—be honest enough to admit it. Your reputation for credibility and reliability may be tested at these times, but, in the long run, your company is better served by your maintaining an honest relationship with your contact than by exaggerating the claim for a book. Here are some pointers:

1. Review the author's questionnaire. It will give you essential biographical data, background on the writing of the book, and useful contacts and associations.

2. Read the manuscript, or parts of it, as early as possible. Usually the manuscript will be in the house about nine months before it is published. Sometimes the editor may share parts of it even before that. Begin to think about what types of book review media are most likely to respond. The book editors of *Cosmopolitan* magazine and the *New Republic* are likely to have different interests!

3. Interview the book's editor—surely the book's first, best advocate. Find out why he or she acquired the book, what it is about, what are its best (and most vulnerable) points, what are its special features, its principal market, and so on. The editor usually prepares a title information form when the property is first acquired. Review this carefully.

4. If possible, talk directly to the author—if not face-to-face, then in writing or by phone. Usually, he or she will suggest possible publicity avenues and furnish names of experts, fans, and favorably inclined reviewers. Listen as though you were the editor of a newspaper or the producer of a talk show. Is there a story here? Does this person make a good interview subject? How can you generate publicity about the author and the book?

Develop a Strategy: Plan a Campaign

Once you have some sense of the book and the right media for it, examine your budget and develop your strategy. Some books are best built through reviews. In this instance, pay prime attention to assembling your review lists, to writing letters and postcards and making personal calls to the reviewers, and also to the packaging and delivery of reviewers' copies. Reviewers are inundated with review copies; devise a way to make your book stand out. This aspect of publicity should never be underestimated; good reviews—even in apparently obscure media—can yield tremendous benefits.

The clue to some campaigns may be in the book's subject matter. The book may reveal some never-before-reported information, which could suggest giving an advance copy of the book or manuscript exclusively to the *Los Angeles Times,* the *Ladies Home Journal,* or Jack

Anderson. This strategy often works well for the memoirs of political or show-business figures or for nonfiction works based on new research, but it should be closely coordinated with the subsidiary rights department, who may be building a parallel strategy regarding serial rights. For example, portions of the second Woodward-Bernstein book, *The Final Days,* broke exclusively in *Newsweek,* sold by subsidiary rights; bits and pieces of the Albert Goldman biography of *Elvis,* on the other hand, were "leaked" to eager gossip columnists by publicity.

Other books may be best introduced by putting the spotlight on the author. A publicity tour may be suitable if the author is an effective personality. It might be ideal for a new cookbook, a science book, a book on finance, or psychological self-help. Talk shows love experts as guests. It's much more difficult—but not impossible—to arrange radio-TV and feature interviews for novelists who are not celebrities; it can be done if you work with the author to develop a factual theme or provocative issue for discussion. Many of Jacqueline Susann's initial *Valley of the Dolls* publicity appearances were booked on the basis that she would discuss the growing incidence of pill popping and drug overdosing in show business; for years, the interviews of Western historical novelist Louis L'Amour were secured on the basis of his knowledge of the American West, not on his novels. Once he became one of the best-selling authors of all time, however, his celebrity was established, and one could generate publicity interest in him as a writer as well as a Western historian.

For music columnist Lisa Robinson's first novel, *Walk on Glass,* Newmarket Press had to take an unusual risk. Coverage was discouraged from rock and music media, where the author was a cherished celebrity, in favor of the more traditional book media, where she was an unknown. Newmarket wanted the Robinson book perceived as an insider's novel about a woman's struggle to survive in show business, *not* as a rock music exposé. The legend was that rock books did not *sell* in hardcover. To counter that, we wanted Lisa's interviews to be assigned by the book editors, not the music editors, because we believed this strategy would get us reviews as well as the more serious hardcover book purchaser. It worked, and more than ten thousand copies of *Walk on Glass* were sold in hardcover.

Sometimes a book can be publicized around a special event created for the sole purpose of spotlighting the book or the publisher or publishing program. For example, in order to guarantee a publicity advantage for the paperback release of Garson Kanin's *Tracy and Hepburn,* Bantam created and sponsored a Tracy-Hepburn Film Festival as a fund raiser for the Lincoln Center Library for Performing Arts. The Literary Guild staged a star-studded dinner dance at the elegant Four Seasons restaurant to celebrate its fiftieth anniversary. Harry Abrams launched its beautifully illustrated book on *Faeries* with a late-night "illustrated event" at the Old Custom House in lower New York, complete with chamber music and costumed characters recreating scenes from the book. In 1973, Time-Life Books introduced its twenty-seven-volume Old West series to the media and booksellers at a barbecue and shoot-out staged at the Universal Pictures lot during the American Booksellers Association convention, which was held in Los Angeles that year. And, at the 1980 ABA convention in Atlanta, Jove actually produced a real wedding, between two booksellers, to publicize its new Second Chance at Love paperback series of romances.

Still another strategy may be devised on the basis of the publisher's campaign or the publishing news surrounding a book. For example, Bantam's 1.2-million-copy paperback release of Thomas Harris's *Black Sunday* was publicized with a campaign that spotlighted the book's cover packaging, deliberately designed to echo the hugely successful *Jaws* image; and the press was always attentive to the stories surrounding the "instant publishing" procedures pioneered by Bantam with the Warren Commission Report in 1964, which was issued eighty hours after receipt of the manuscript. Other Bantam "extras"—*The Pentagon Papers*, William Stevenson's *90 Minutes at Entebbe*, and *The White House Transcripts* among them—were projects that could be highly publicized because of *how* they were published as well as what they contained.

The paperback release of *Future Shock* received major coverage in the press and on television not only because of its hardcover success and Alvin Toffler's dynamic media and lecture appearances but also because of the attention paid to Bantam's Selectacolor campaign. The book was packaged in six different-colored covers, which demonstrated Toffler's thesis of "overchoice" and at the same time introduced an entirely new concept in book packaging. Although Toffler could not do another appearance on NBC's "Today" show (he'd already done one when the book appeared in hardcover), the Selectacolor cover campaign did!

Another effective technique to build excitement is to sample portions of the book or manuscript—even the entire work—in advance of publication. Again, you must be selective in choosing the book and the target previewers. When Frederick Forsythe's first novel, *Day of the Jackal*, was acquired by Viking in 1970 and soon after by Bantam for paperback, the two publicity departments devised a plan to circulate over twenty-five hundred free advance paperback reading copies of the book, months before hardcover publication. We wanted word of Forsythe's unique, compelling story to spread like brushfire. Since this could be helped along by people who are sociable and good talkers, we built what we affectionately called a "big mouth" list, featuring media people, opinion makers, restaurateurs, producers, buyers, publicists, wholesalers, relatives, politicians, stewardesses, and other types of book enthusiasts. By publication date, the book had become one of the most talked-about new novels of the year.

Eight years and many successful sampling campaigns later, the quality of Hank Searles's exciting *Jaws 2* novel, based on characters in Peter Benchley's *Jaws,* inspired an unusual variation of the technique. Although the novel had been commissioned as a promotional tie-in for release with the film in June 1978, Bantam executives were so impressed with Searles's manuscript that we convinced Universal Pictures to allow the book to be published three months *before* the film's release, so that an extensive publicity effort could be made independently of the film. A startling new strategy was devised. In order to generate word of mouth, 25,000 advance reading copies were distributed to sales and publicity lists and to respondents to a *New York Times Book Review* ad—the first time a *free* book offer had been made to the general public. In fact, the ad itself was publicized, resulting in *its* appearance on the "Today" show. Also, the first chapter of the book was so compelling that it was placed in the back of 1,100,000 copies of other Bantam titles and sent on what we called a Chapter One tour; that is, the chapter was published in thirty-eight newspapers two weeks before the book went on sale, on an exclusive-in-your-city basis. The results were tremendous: *Jaws 2* became a best-seller ten weeks *before* the film opened. In fact, the book's success became such a marketing advantage for the movie that the technique of advance publication for books based on original scripts has become one of the strategies now commonly considered in early campaign planning.

Review-copy mailings, author tours, sampling, press releases, event planning—they are all merely techniques employed to trigger media attention. And not to be forgotten in the execution are the support materials. Press kits, releases, tip sheets, sample question-and-answer materials, photos, film clips, pitch letters, invitations—these items represent your communication to the media and are well worth the investment of time, imagination, and budget. When you're planning your support material, try to put yourself in the place of the recipient. If that recipient is a newspaper or magazine book editor who gets bushel basketsful of mail, ask yourself how you can make your mailing stand out. Keep alert to new mailing and communication devices; examine promotion and direct-mail-production trade publications for tips; query your media contacts about what does and doesn't work for them. The tried-and-true techniques are always good ones, but don't let them become routine, and don't be afraid to experiment with new strategies when they seem appropriate to the assignment.

Execute Your Plan, But Stay Flexible

The important guideline is to stay alert to the reaction your campaign is producing and to keep in close touch with the promotion and sales departments. Suppose after talking to an author you thought at first that he or she would make a poor interview, and you booked the author only a few programs in his or her hometown, yet the local sales representative reports that the book sold out after the interview, and the producer wants to do a repeat. Obviously something is working. Check it out yourself and recommend a change in the strategy accordingly.

Suppose you're promoting a mystery novel, and you send review copies to your usual list of mystery reviewers. Then, seemingly out of the blue, the *New York Times Book Review* features the mystery on its front page, treating it as general fiction, not just a category mystery. (This actually occurred with Ross Macdonald's *The Goodbye Look*.) Seize the opportunity; circulate review copies and talk up the book to general fiction reviewers as well.

Suppose you've planned to schedule a round of author interviews later in the year for a particular book, but a pertinent news story breaks that could enable you to generate coverage for the book earlier than you planned. For example, in 1975 Bantam had planned an extensive tour for the authors of *Helter Skelter*, but the schedule was accelerated as a result of the assassination attempt on President Ford's life in San Fransisco. The Vince Bugliosi–Curt Gentry book carried a lot of information about the two relatively unknown women who had zoomed onto the front pages, since they were part of the Charles Manson gang. Bantam immediately issued a press release quoting from the book, citing page references, and offering to schedule telephone interviews with Bugliosi or Gentry. As a result, *Helter Skelter* figured in a lot of the press coverage about that news story.

Suppose you're getting only modest results from booking a tour for a relatively unknown but articulate author on a somewhat specialized subject. You know he'd be a fascinating interview, but you have to convince the media, and it's taking longer than you expected. More and more good reviews are appearing, but the press kits were distributed weeks earlier, and you need time to circulate the new reviews. Talk to your sales director and the author. Consider delaying the tour until a better approach to the media can be developed. This happened to good result with Newmarket's first title, *A Glorious Way to Die*. This unusual book about the kamikaze mission that doomed the world's biggest battleship at the end of World War II told the story for the first time from both Japanese and U.S. points of view. Although the author, Russell

Spurr, was a professional communicator (ABC's network radio corre-spondent for China and host of his own talk show in Hong Kong), he was unknown to U.S. media. Initially, bookings were slow in developing. Originally scheduled for early October 1981, the tour was postponed until November/December to allow time for the reviews (which ultimately compared the book to *A Night to Remember* and *A Bridge Too Far* and featured it on the front page of the *Washington Post*'s *Book World* supplement) to be promoted and to offer interviewers the benefit of a "hook" to make the subject matter more timely. In this instance, the "hook" was Veterans Day (November 11) and the fortieth anniversary of Pearl Harbor (December 7). As a result of the change in schedule a very successful eleven-city tour was booked, well worth the six-week postponement.

Remember, books take time to build audiences, especially if they are by new or lesser-known authors. Don't be discouraged if your initial strategy does not appear to be working immediately, but don't be unrealistic either. Sometimes you just have to cut your losses and go on to the next assignment.

Communicate and Evaluate

Publicity breaks need to be promoted and communicated if they are going to be effective sales producers. A major book story in the *Chicago Tribune* may look good in somebody's scrapbook, but if there are no books in the Chicago-area stores, it will have a deflating effect on everyone involved. It is essential for publicists to stay in close touch with the sales operation and to circulate the publicity to the trade publications and other media contacts. Realizing the importance of this connection, the American Booksellers Association conceived its weekly newsletter, *ABA Newswire,* in 1974 to relay breaking publicity and media news to booksellers, so that they could take advantage of publicity at the point of sale.

The B. Dalton bookstore chain produces a valuable Merchandise Bulletin that is mailed weekly to its store managers to keep them up to the minute on publicity breaks as well as on other sales, promotion, and merchandising matters. Taking the process one step farther, in 1981 Waldenbooks installed a computerized system in its stores that allows store managers to read a tape every morning, programmed during the night, telling them which books are being featured on that morning's TV shows and in the next Sunday's *New York Times Book Review* or which author is promoting a book in their city that day.

After the entire campaign is completed, it is important to make time for an internal wrap-up memo. Publicity, when it hits, generally happens fast; to the nonprofessional, it appears as though the reviews, the column breaks, the author interviews happened with barely a snap of the fingers. One good break in Detroit on Monday can be forgotten by Friday if similar breaks occurred in Cleveland and Pittsburgh.

A publicity wrap-up on the campaign helps the sales and marketing people stay in touch with the total effort, evaluate results, and plan future marketing strategies.

The Key to It All

For many years, I did an exercise at publishing workshops to demonstrate the role of promotion and publicity in the book-marketing process. I asked students to write down the title of a book they'd read during the previous year—one they'd chosen at leisure, not one required for school or business. Then I asked them to consider why they had chosen to read that particular book—that is, what had stimulated them to buy or borrow it. I then told them I thought it likely that they had responded to one (or a combination) of nine stimuli. The first is an author interview or lecture (e.g., John Irving interviewed by Dick Cavett, or Jerzy Kosinski lecturing at a university series, may have triggered an interest in reading their works). Second is a news or feature story on a particular event or issue (e.g., the Mt. St. Helens eruption may have stimulated interest in books on volcanoes). Third is a book excerpt (e.g., sections of Alvin Toffler's or Gail Sheehy's new book may have appeared in *Omni, Redbook,* or in one of the airlines magazines and intrigued the reader enough to want to read the entire work), and fourth is a movie or TV presentation (e.g., a viewer was impressed by the TV presentation of *War and Remembrance* or *The Autobiography of Miss Jane Pittman,* or by feature films like *Gandhi, One Flew Over the Cuckoo's Nest, Ragtime,* or *The French Lieutenant's Woman* and wanted to read the literary works from which they were derived).

Advertising is the fifth stimulus (a particular print ad or radio or TV commercial caught a person's attention, perhaps reminding him or her that the new book by a favorite author was now in the bookstores or that a respected book critic had a new favorite). The sixth is direct mail (a flyer or phone call from an association, book club, or political group directed attention to a book on a favorite subject, like bridge, bird-watching, China, colonial history, art collecting, or politics), and the seventh is a book review. Eighth is book browsing (a person browsing in a book outlet became intrigued by a jacket or cover or merchandising display, picked up the book, read the flap or cover copy, leafed through the pages, and made the purchase). Word of mouth is the ninth stimulus (somebody known and respected—a relative, teacher, friend, or colleague—said "Read it, you'll like it").

The last point—word of mouth—is *always* the most common reason given for reading a particular book. But how does word of mouth start? How does it roll out from the book's first advocate, the editor, to the browser in a bookshop in a Midwestern shopping mall? It generally moves in ever-widening circles—from within the publishing house itself, to the publishing trade, to the other media, to special-interest groups, and ultimately, to the individual consumer. How is it done? Essentially, through communication, through a combination of all or some of the previously mentioned stimuli, through an accumulation of incidents triggered as early as two and three years before a book hits the marketplace—and the publicist's role is one of the most essential in this process. That's why effective publicists must be skilled communicators, clear conveyors of ideas and information. They should be convincing, reliable, and credible; should have imagination and a sense of humor; should care about details and deadlines; and should be willing to work late and at odd hours. And they should believe in luck—and not be afraid to take advantage of it when it strikes!

CHAPTER ELEVEN

Trade Sales

ALLAN LANG

Not much has changed during the last fifty years in the selling of trade books. At a time when nearly every other industry uses marketing tools to test packaging, retail price, and advertising strategy and content before launching a product into national distribution, trade publishers continue to determine publication primarily on the basis of the quality of the manuscript and its cost. Unlike products that remain relatively the same for long periods of time (and therefore justify a large initial expenditure of marketing moneys), most trade books have short life spans. More to the point, each new book is unique and requires a special selling effort to both the booksellers and the ultimate consumers.

Today there are more than 40,000 titles published every year, and an additional 500,000 backlist titles are still in print. Add to this the fact that we are not a nation of book readers (a recent Gallup study revealed that less than 10 percent of the adult U.S. population regularly buys books and less than 18 percent of the population is currently reading *any* book, whether borrowed or bought), and you will begin to understand why selling books is a difficult and frustrating business for publishers and booksellers alike.

Two additional factors contribute to the problem: Books are sold to bookstores on a 100 percent returnable basis (which means that all unsold books can be returned to the publisher for full credit), and book publishers honor orders from the general public. Just try to buy a car directly from General Motors or a television set from RCA; you cannot, but you can order books from just about every book publisher.

Still, nearly half of all publishers' sales of books are made to bookstores. There are approximately ten thousand independent bookstores that carry best-sellers, cookbooks, Bibles, and a small selection of backlist titles; fewer than two thousand of these stores regularly buy and stock newly published hardcover books. Another two thousand stores are owned and operated by national chains such as B. Dalton, Walden, Brentano's, Classics, and Coles. Strong regional chains such as Kroch's & Brentano's

ALLAN LANG is president of International Book Marketing, New York City.

in Chicago and Gateway in the Southeast account for an additional two hundred stores. Finally, there are three thousand college bookstores.

Of these more than fourteen thousand bookstores, only about three thousand are important enough to warrant regular calls by publishers' sales representatives. The outlets for new trade books break down as follows:

	Total	*Called on by* *Sales Representative*
Independent bookstores	10,000	2,500
College bookstores	3,000	500
Chain bookstores	2,200	200

Because of the buying policies of the book chains, publishers do not send sales representatives to call on each one of the chain bookstores, which represent more than 30 percent of the total trade bookstores sales for most publishers, but they do make every effort to see that these stores stock new titles by selling their lists to the home buying offices on regular cycles.

Even with more than three thousand key bookstores to call on, most publishers find that fewer than one thousand will actually order the average book prior to publication. Additional printings of a book will be undertaken by the publisher only if it is actually selling in the stores; otherwise, it will be abandoned. In most cases, then, selling the first printing is the publisher's only marketing effort.

With more than five thousand active accounts and an average of three thousand to five thousand backlist titles, a publisher alone could not effectively process orders for all the books in the warehouse. Wholesalers help publishers to meet the needs of the book market. They buy new titles in quantity and then reorder from the publisher, according to the rate of sale, as often as needed. Unlike publishers, whose one warehouse (which is usually separate from the main office) must service the entire country, wholesalers receive, process, and ship orders within the same building and rely on their own trucks and regional warehouses to cut shipping time. It's not surprising, then, that most bookstores tend to order from wholesalers rather than placing their reorders with publishers, since delivery time is usually much shorter. There are three major national wholesalers: The largest, Baker & Taylor, handles nearly 75 percent of the wholesale library trade; Ingram concentrates on supplying trade bookstores; and Bro-Dart, after focusing on the library market for the last twenty years, has begun to expand into the trade bookstore business as well.

Selling the List

Now, let's consider how publishers sell their books to the book trade. New titles are announced and cataloged on a seasonal basis. For example, a publisher will generally announce a Fall/Winter (August–February) list and a Spring/Summer (March–June) list. The books to be published in the Fall/Winter season are actually scheduled during the prior spring, presented to the sales representative at a sales conference in May, announced to the book trade at the annual American Booksellers Association (ABA) convention in June, sold by the sales representatives to the book buyers in June and July, and finally shipped to the bookstores four to six weeks ahead of the official publication day. Spring/Summer titles are scheduled during the fall, presented to the sales representatives in December, and then sold to the bookstores in January and February. Of course, there are variations for individual houses in the number of lists they publish and the months covered.

Generally, publishers try to schedule their strongest titles for the fall months, since more than 75 percent of the total bookstore business occurs between September and Christmas. But, of course, publishers want to have "lead" titles on every list in order to attract the attention of the book trade to the entire list and to make it necessary for most bookstores to order these titles in advance of publication.

One of the most important moments in the life of a book is the publisher's sales conference, where editors and management gather with sales representatives from all over the country to present the forthcoming list of titles. It is here that publishers do all they can to give the representative the information and "sales handles" that will be needed to sell the books to the buyers in each store. Prior to the conference, the publisher sets an estimated print order for each book, which represents management's best guess regarding potential sales. The information used to determine this figure includes the advance paid to the author, readings of the book by senior marketing people, sales of book-club and paperback reprint rights, advance reviews, and, of course, projected sales for the first year of publication.

Sales representatives will often provide constructive feedback following the house's presentation of its list. Such aspects as the book's title, jacket, and print order are frequently subject to the reactions of the sales representative. After all the discussions, final sales quotas are given to the representatives for each title, representing the number of copies they are expected to sell to their accounts prior to publication date. The grand sum of all the representatives' quotas for each title is called the advance—that is, the number of copies the publisher expects to place in bookstores prior to the official publication date. The print order (or first printing) for the title is usually 15–20 percent greater than the advance, so that the publisher will have enough copies on hand for review and publicity purposes and to fill library orders and early reorders.

At the conference, the representatives are given sales kits containing jackets or jacket proofs, sample illustrations and text, and other pertinent information such as reviews for previous books, which will be used for sales presentations. There will also be discussions at the conference about current titles—how to obtain reorders for them and how to improve backlist sales.

Once the sales conference is over, the representatives return to their individual territories. Although they report either to regional managers (in large companies) or directly to the sales manager, representatives work from day to day on their own. Sales calls are scheduled in advance, and routes are planned to minimize travel time and maximize the number of calls made each day. Some stores will be seen only twice a year, others as often as every four to six weeks. As a rule, however, most stores are visited only three to four times a year. Generally, a representative is expected to sell three to five accounts every working day, depending on the size of the publisher, the size of the account, and the amount of travel time needed to cover the territory. Table 11.1 shows an example of a typical three-month itinerary of a representative for a publisher with approximately one hundred new titles per season and an active backlist. Three to five calls are scheduled for each day, except for such variations as attendance at the ABA convention and visits to wholesaler accounts (the latter require at least a half-day and often a full day to check stock and back orders in addition to selling the new titles).

The representative carefully studies the sales kit and other material brought back from the sales conference before setting out on his initial trip to the bookstores. Since he usually has only half a minute or so to present each new title, the representative must develop a "sales handle" that will clearly explain the book, its audience, and its potential sale— all in an incredibly short time. Paradoxically, the longer the representative has to explain the reasons for a book's existence, the less likely the buyer may be to want to order it. Most buyers have keen memories for past sales; they know their customers and thus can estimate the sales potential for just about any title on any subject once the representative has made a presentation. And sometimes, to the disappointment of the publishers and the representative, the buyer will blurt out a quick no in response to a title in the catalog before the representative has a chance to say one word.

The sales presentation by the representative to the buyer—for which there is no known substitute—requires that the book's title and jacket be as effective as possible in conveying just what it is all about. The title and jacket are, in fact, the most important marketing tools the publisher has. The title must clearly describe the book, and the jacket should enhance the title and add an element of design that can be remembered easily and can be used in ads to increase the visual impact. Because of the limits on advertising budgets for each book, the jacket is seen by more potential consumers than any other element during the life of the book.

Today, nonfiction outsells fiction by more than twelve to one. It's not surprising, then, that it is very difficult for the representative to sell any novels, particularly first novels, except for those by authors with proven track records. Occasionally publishers will have enough confidence in a novel that does not fit the success formula and decide (for various reasons) to back it with extra publicity and advertising. In such cases, most booksellers will support the publisher by purchasing more than the two or three copies that would usually be ordered prior to publication.

It's even more difficult for the representative to sell poetry and short stories, even by well-known authors. Most publishers find that they advance fewer than two thousand copies of collections of poems and short stories in bookstores before publication.

The main function of the sales representative is to present the publisher's new titles in bookstores prior to publication. Although some stores will want more copies of certain titles than anticipated and others may not want to order any, representatives are expected to even out these hills and valleys so that at the end of the season the accounts are carrying a well-rounded selection of all of the titles on the seasonal list. Of course, representatives will also allow time to check back stock and current titles when they call on their accounts.

The commission representative, an independent book salesperson who is used by small publishers and by medium-sized publishers in sparsely populated bookstore areas, usually will just "highlight" the list, selecting those titles that can be sold easily. Commission representatives must sell lists from several publishers and travel to many small accounts in order to make their efforts worthwhile.

The average publisher's representative will regularly call on 150 to 200 accounts. Most of the visits will be made from home, with a few overnight trips. Representatives are expected to keep accurate records of their calls and of the number of new and backlist books sold. Usually orders are mailed to the sales department or computer processing center every day or two. When representatives receive information about an author tour, a new printing, or virtually any other positive news about a book, they are expected to use the information to increase orders

TABLE 11.1 SUMMER TRIP OF ALLAN LANG

June		
	5–9	ABA—Washington, D.C.
	10	Cosmo, Elizabeth, New Jersey (Wholesaler)
	11	Bookazine, New York City (Wholesaler)
	14	NJ: Morristown (2), Passaic (1)
	15	NJ: Hackensack (2), Paramus (1), Bloomfield (1)
	16	NJ: New Brunswick (3)
	17	NY: Sayville (1), Bellport (1), Setauket (1)
	18	NY: White Plains (3), Scarsdale (2)
	22	NY: Briarcliffe Manor (2), Bronxville (1)
	23	NY: New Canaan (2), Bedford Hills (1), Mt. Kisco (2)
	24	CT: Washington Depot (1), Woodbury (1), Waterbury (1)
	25	Bookazine (W), New York office
	28	PA: Wilkes-Barre (2), Bethlehem (1)
	29	PA: Norristown (2), King of Prussia (1)
	30	PA: Kennett Square (1), West Chester (2), Paoli (1)
	31	PA: Reading (2), Pottstown (1), Media (1)
July		
	2	PA: Yardley (1), Newtown (1), New Hope (1)
	5	Holiday
	6	NJ: Cranbury (1), Red Bank (2)
	7	CT: Middletown (1), Wallingford (2)
	8	Cosmo, Elizabeth, N.J. (W)
	9	Bookazine (W), New York office
	12	NY: Albany (3)
	13	NY: Glen Falls (1), Saratoga Falls (1), Schenectady (1)
	14	NY: Utica (2), Ithaca (2)
	15	NY: Ithaca (2)
	16	NY: Birmingham (2)
	19	PA: York (3)
	20	PA: State College (4)
	21	PA: Harrisburg (3)
	22	PA: Lancaster (3)
	23	Bookazine (W), New York office
	26	MA: Williamstown (3)
	27	VT: Bennington (1), Brattleboro (2)
	28	MA: Amherst (3), South Hadley (2)
	29	MA: Northampton (3), Holyoke (1)
	30	CT: Storrs (2)

TABLE 11.1, cont.

August

2	NJ: Atlantic City (2), Haddonfield (1)
3	NJ: Cherry Hill (1), Morristown (1)
4	NJ: Jenkintown (2)
5	Cosmo, Elizabeth, N.J. (W)
6	Bookazine (W), New York office
9	Vacation
10	Vacation
11	Vacation
12	Vacation

Note: Numbers in parentheses indicate number of accounts in a town; (W) indicates wholesaler.

already taken and sometimes actually to resell the title in order to increase the advance.

Although the trade sales representative carries around jackets, tables of contents, sample illustrations, and author information to share with booksellers, there is usually little else the publisher offers the retailer to help sell the book. Major authors and obvious best-sellers come with tours and ad budgets to support their requested advance figures, but most titles are published with fewer than five thousand copies in the stores on publication date and correspondingly smaller advertising and publicity budgets.

Selling in the Future

Some basic problems have hampered retail book sales. Many people in bookselling, and publishing in general for that matter, come to their endeavor because of their love for books, rather than viewing their chosen vocation as a business. ABA records indicate that most privately owned bookstores make no profit at all and that owners work an average of over sixty hours a week. Booksellers would argue that too many books are being published today and that publishers do not offer enough incentives such as additional discounts, more advertising support for local stores, and faster service for reorders. Of course, the answers would seem to lie somewhere between the concerns of the publisher and the bookseller. Needless to say, both want to increase sales to consumers, but the fact is that the actual number of books sold from year to year has remained relatively constant—it is the inflationary increases in retail prices that account for the rise in sales income in the last few years. Book sales depend on discretionary income and on leisure time; discretionary income has been eroded by inflation, and much leisure time is now taken up by watching television.

No doubt books will continue to be published in the traditional ways for many years to come. But publishers will have to streamline the selling and distribution process by publishing fewer titles, will have to develop major distributors that will function for many publishers, and will have to support the bookstores with incentives to order and sell larger numbers of new books.

CHAPTER TWELVE

Marketing Scholarly and Professional Books

PEARL BOWMAN AND NANCY ESSIG

The vocabulary of scholarly copy is more restrained than that of commercial publishing. Seldom can we make use of "pulsating," "scintillating," "sex-maddened," or other juicy adjectives. But there are always "trenchant," "searching," "well-documented."
—Dorothy Sutherland, *A Marketing Handbook for Scholarly Publishers*[1]

It wouldn't be scholarly and professional publishing without a citation from an authority, so how better to begin considering the marketing of scholarly books than with a quote from one of the best university-press promotion people? The marketing of books that warrant such restrained adjectives as "trenchant" and "well-documented" differs from selling trade books in approach as well as in vocabulary. Scholarly marketing means focusing on specific audiences and specific ways to reach them, generally with a limited budget that demands both care and ingenuity in managing.

Success in selling scholarly books depends on being willing to undertake the effort of planning, projecting, testing, measuring; applying the lessons learned; and then revising and replanning. Scholarly publishers seldom know the elation of bestsellerdom; disposing of unexpectedly large profits is not a frequent problem. But a healthy backlist and a reasonable return on investment in new titles are within reach.

Responsibilities of the Marketing Department

In many if not most publishing houses, marketing opinions are used in making the initial publishing decision. Once the decision is taken, the marketing department sets or recommends print run and list price

PEARL BOWMAN is a New York marketing consultant and representative for scholarly publishers; NANCY ESSIG is assistant director/marketing manager, Johns Hopkins University Press.

on the basis of sales projections (themselves usually based on how well and where similar books have sold) and current marketing information.

Whether or not it participates in the decision to publish, the marketing department is responsible for assessing the sales potential of each title and deciding how best to reach its audiences. First, information must be gathered from the author, the editor, reports of the manuscript readers, and, yes, the manuscript itself. It is impossible to overemphasize the value of the author's assistance. As a scholar or professional, he is writing for an audience of peers and knows what journals they read, what professional associations they join, whose opinions will influence them. Ask the author to share that information (and hound him if he doesn't). The marketing questionnaire (Figure 12.1 is an example) is a typical way of eliciting it.

Equally useful to the marketer is the sponsoring editor's description of the book (which may be called a Product Profile, a New Book Fact Sheet, an Editor's Tip Sheet, or some similar name—see Figure 12.2), and whatever descriptive material the editor has prepared for the decision-making body.

The markets for most scholarly books include libraries, wholesalers and independent bookstores, universities and other institutions, and individual scholars, professionals, and researchers (see Figure 12.3). The trick is to pinpoint the specific audiences for a particular book. Publishing is a specialized business, and a house learns proficiency in marketing certain types of books. Scholarly marketing offers a special challenge in that it may require knowledge of many different marketing possibilities. In a single selling season a scholarly publisher may have one or two books that are believed to have greater than usual bookstore potential, a few books with college-adoption potential, some high-level scholarly monographs, a general reference volume, and perhaps a few books with possibilities for subsidiary rights, book-club, or special sales.

The marketing and editorial staff must first decide what each book's major marketing thrust will be. (This is sometimes called positioning the book.) Is it primarily for the trade? Will there be text adoption? Should it get exceptional publicity treatment—press releases and press kits? Where should review copies go? What about space advertising? How many libraries and what types might be expected to buy it? Once the general decisions are made, the marketing plan proceeds.

Certain tasks must be performed in every marketing department. In a small house, two very busy people (or even one infinitely harried soul!) may have responsibility for all of them; a publisher with a large list and sales base may have publicity and advertising managers, a direct-mail manager, a sales manager, and an exhibits manager as well as the

Marketing Department

THE JOHNS HOPKINS UNIVERSITY PRESS

Baltimore, Maryland 21218

Telephone: (301) 338-7850

MARKETING QUESTIONNAIRE

At your earliest convenience, please complete this questionnaire and return it to the Marketing Department. The information you provide is extremely helpful to us in promoting and selling your book.

DATE:

TITLE OF BOOK:

YOUR NAME AS IT WILL APPEAR ON TITLE PAGE:

HOME ADDRESS AND TELEPHONE NUMBER:

OFFICE ADDRESS AND TELEPHONE NUMBER:

TITLES OF PREVIOUS BOOKS (including publisher, date and sales figures if available). Please indicate any which have been serialized or book club selections.

HAVE YOU BEEN ASSOCIATED WITH ANY MAGAZINES OR JOURNALS AS EDITOR OR CONTRIBUTOR? Please give titles and dates of recent articles.

HAVE ANY SECTIONS OF THIS BOOK APPEARED IN PERIODICALS?

COMPETING BOOKS:

FIGURE 12.1

PLEASE LIST ANY PROMINENT PEOPLE (scholars, government officials, authors) WHO MIGHT GIVE US A COMMENT TO USE IN PROMOTION. Indicate with an asterisk beside the name any you know personally and please include addresses if you have them.

NAMES AND ADDRESSES OF ANY ORGANIZATIONS OR ASSOCIATIONS OF WHICH YOU ARE A MEMBER OR WHICH YOU FEEL WILL HAVE A SPECIAL INTEREST IN YOUR BOOK, WHOSE MEMBERSHIP LISTS MIGHT BE AVAILABLE FOR DIRECT MAIL USE AND/OR AT WHOSE MEETINGS WE MIGHT EXHIBIT.

AWARDS FOR WHICH YOU FEEL YOUR BOOK MAY BE ELIGIBLE:

TEXTBOOK POSSIBILITIES (Please give us the names of individuals teaching courses for which your book might be used).

REVIEW MEDIA. Copies of your book will be sent to appropriate newspapers, magazines and scholarly journals. Please list any professional periodicals, college papers or alumni magazines that should receive information on your book. Suggestions about British and European publications will also be helpful.

FIGURE 12.1, cont.

NAMES AND ADDRESSES OF BOOKSTORES WHERE YOU ARE KNOWN PERSONALLY:

WHICH DO YOU FEEL ARE THE THREE OR FOUR MOST APPROPRIATE JOURNALS IN WHICH TO ADVERTISE YOUR BOOK?

PLEASE LIST LOCALITIES WHERE YOU HAVE LIVED SO THAT LOCAL PUBLICITY CAN BE ARRANGED.

ARE YOU WILLING TO DO RADIO, TV AND PRESS INTERVIEWS IF THE OPPORTUNITY ARISES?

INDIVIDUAL BOOK BUYERS. Can you supply us with a list of individuals who would be particularly interested in buying your book?

PLEASE GIVE A CONCISE DESCRIPTION OF YOUR BOOK, INCLUDING IMPORTANT POINTS TO EMPHASIZE IN PROMOTION (about 200 words). How does it differ from other books in the field? Does it present new information? Is it controversial or especially timely?

FIGURE 12.1, cont.

192

PLEASE LIST ANY SPEAKING ENGAGEMENTS PLANNED FOR THE NEXT 18 MONTHS, INCLUDING DATE
AND PLACE WHEN POSSIBLE.

PLEASE WRITE A BRIEF BIOGRAPHY OF YOURSELF AS YOU WOULD LIKE IT TO APPEAR ON THE BOOK
JACKET. (about 50 words).

IMPORTANT. PLEASE SEND A RECENT PHOTOGRAPH OF YOURSELF. A clear snapshot will suffice.
Photographs are not always used on book jackets but are often needed for publicity
purposes. If one is not available now, please indicate when we may expect to receive it.

FIGURE 12.1, cont.

PRODUCT PROFILE

TITLE AND SUBTITLE:

     Final_____

   Tentative_____

AUTHOR(S) OR EDITOR(S):_____

_____

   Title and   _____
   Affiliation   _____

SUBJECT CATEGORY:_____ SERIES:_____

HOW SPECIALIZED?_____Narrow _____Average _____General Interest

THE MARKET: _____Scholars   RECOMMENDED EDITION:_____

          _____Grad Students   SUBSIDY?_____

          _____Undergrads   PAPERBACK?_____

          _____Course Use?   MARKET RESTRICTIONS_____

          _____Special purchase   _____
              (foundation, government
              agency, society, etc.)   _____

COMPETITION:_____

FORMAT ("Standard," oversize, special binding, etc.)_____

ILLUSTRATIONS?_____ SUITABLE FOR PROMOTIONAL USE?_____

SERIALIZATION?_____ WHICH MAGAZINES?_____

PROMOTIONAL "HANDLE" (Timely, controversial, eminent author, etc.):

CAPSULE DESCRIPTION OF BOOK:

FIGURE 12.2

marketing director and backup staff. But certain essential tasks must be performed, whatever the number and titles of the persons who do them.

Promotion is a term that covers a variety of activities, principally direct mail and advertising. Direct mail means the planning and execution of efforts to sell books directly to individuals and libraries by mail. In some cases this involves mailing several thousand copies of a large subject brochure; in others, a few hundred individualized letters on a single book. The promotion department also is responsible for the planning,

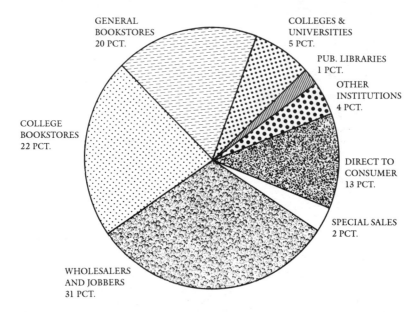

GENERAL BOOKSTORES 20 PCT.

COLLEGES & UNIVERSITIES 5 PCT.

PUB. LIBRARIES 1 PCT.

OTHER INSTITUTIONS 4 PCT.

COLLEGE BOOKSTORES 22 PCT.

DIRECT TO CONSUMER 13 PCT.

SPECIAL SALES 2 PCT.

WHOLESALERS AND JOBBERS 31 PCT.

FIGURE 12.3 Estimated market distribution of books published by university presses. Reproduced by permission from Association of American Publishers 1979 Industry Statistics Report.

writing, and production of annual, seasonal, and special catalogs and price lists and for the planning, budgeting, and preparation of trade, major-media, and journal advertisements. A large scholarly publisher may run three hundred or more advertisements a year in publications ranging from the *New York Times Book Review* to the *James Joyce Quarterly*. Larger publishers may employ writers who work on general copy of all kinds or who specialize in publicity or direct mail. They may have an art department that designs everything from jackets to order forms. Smaller houses may require each marketing-department member to write and design or may use free-lance help.

Choosing and shipping books for display at scholarly and professional meetings and staffing the exhibits, sometimes in concert with other publishers, are the tasks of exhibits personnel. Publicists undertake a combination of efforts to call books to the attention of book reviewers, reporters, radio and television interviewers, and other influential people.

Marketing also, of course, includes trade sales (getting books into general bookstores), special sales (selling books in bulk to nontraditional outlets), and foreign sales. Not all books require all types of marketing efforts. For a book with genuine trade potential, bookstore sales efforts backed by heavy advertising and publicity will be paramount; direct mail and exhibits may well be ignored. (In scholarly publishing, general bookstore sales rarely account for more than 20 percent of the total, and in many cases far less.) On the other hand, a high-priced, specialized technical book will be sold almost exclusively by direct mail, not by sales representation to bookstores.

Scholarly presses commonly devote 14 to 20 percent of their annual net income to marketing efforts. Unlike trade publishers, they give direct mail the largest share of the marketing budget—30 to 40 percent. Space advertising, which accounts for 75 percent of the trade promotion budget, amounts to only about 20 percent of the scholarly outlay.

Marketing plans are usually prepared on a seasonal basis, for the fall and spring lists, even in houses that do not have seasonal sales meetings. A marketing plan must be devised for each new book as well as overall plans for direct mail, exhibits, and space advertising. Figure 12.4 shows a marketing planning sheet typical of those used by scholarly publishers for individual titles. Managers in charge of the various functions put down their specific plans, noting whether the book is to be promoted jointly with other titles or alone. The plans are reviewed and revised at regularly scheduled marketing meetings and also in consultation with editors. The final plan is then typed and distributed and becomes a permanent record—most useful when another book of the same sort comes along and in keeping the author informed about what exactly has been done for the book.

CATALOGS

Like trade publishers, most scholarly houses prepare two seasonal catalogs a year, and some issue annual listings of their books in print. The seasonal catalog, sent mainly to bookstores and libraries, is viewed as a sales representative's tool. Trade sales representatives like catalogs with pictures of the books or authors and vivid descriptive phrases and with the most salable books up front. Librarians like catalogs that are arranged by subject and fully annotated or, better yet, separate catalogs for each discipline. Heads of houses like catalogs that reflect their particular image of the house. Editors like catalogs that give preferential treatment to their books. Pleasing everyone is not possible, but a compromise must be reached, and sensible, economical, yet attractive, catalogs must be produced, on time.

In many houses the preparation of the catalog is the first step in the seasonal marketing effort. Gathering the information, getting photos and jackets, establishing prices, writing copy, and assembling it all gets everyone in gear for the greater efforts to come. Although trade publishers often relegate books with relatively low print runs to the bottom of the

```
MARKETING PLANS

AUTHOR:                                                      DATE:

TITLE:

SERIES:

COMPARABLE PREVIOUS TITLES:
   (With date of publication, number of pages, price, total sales and quantity left
   in stock, 1st/2nd/3rd year sales)


AUDIENCES:
_____

Bookstore potential:
   (enough to justify trade discount?)

Special sales potential:

Book Club potential:

Direct mail:



Advertising:



Exhibits:

Estimated number of review copies needed:

Special publicity activities:


Special foreign sales potential:

Dates to meet: (academic meetings, trade sales opportunities, course book deadlines)

Other comments:

Final Budget:
```

FIGURE 12.4

marketing heap, scholarly publishers try to give the maximum promotional effort to every book on the list.

PUBLICITY

Sometimes called the art of getting something for nothing, publicity plays an important role in the selling of scholarly books. Although tip sheets, author tours, and TV appearances are rarely warranted for scholarly books, a careful publicity program can greatly enhance a serious book's chances.

R. R. Bowker, through its major bibliographies, performs a great service to publishers as well as to bookstores, libraries, and the rest of the book universe by its publications such as *Forthcoming Books, Books in Print, Subject Guide, American Book Publishing Record,* and *Paperbound Books in Print.* Information for each new book is supplied to Bowker by the publisher about six months before publication, in the form of an Advance Book Information (ABI) sheet. It's important to get the information for the ABIs on time. Being in all the right lists at the right times greatly improves a book's chance to be recommended to readers and buyers. Many publishers duplicate the ABI sheet and send it to major wholesalers and sales representatives as well.

A few review media—especially *Publishers Weekly, Library Journal,* the Kirkus Service, *Choice,* and the *New York Times Book Review*—want to see proofs of new books as soon as they are available. Trade publishers routinely bind up galleys for these and other advance readers. Scholarly publishers who have a book with real trade potential should order at least four extra sets of galleys for this purpose. If jacket testimonials are to be solicited, more galleys may be needed.

Press releases can serve as the basis for news or feature stories in the media and may also arouse the interest of potential reviewers. A press release should tell its story in a straightforward way, in a style that is often called the "inverted pyramid" because the most important facts appear at the beginning with less important or background information at the end. The story can then be cut from the bottom without the loss of critical information. A release intended solely to arouse reviewer interest can be a bit more provocative, but blatant puffery should be avoided. Releases may be sent out before the book is ready, with the book, or even later, depending on circumstances and strategy (see Figure 12.5).

Review possibilities for scholarly books number in the thousands. Every discipline has specialized journals that run reviews, and many subdisciplines have their own journals as well. Some general journals also occasionally review a scholarly book. Where to send each book is

198

Yale Book News

Yale University Press   For more information, please contact
92A Yale Station   Sarah F. Clark, *Publicist*   203-432-4979
New Haven, Ct. 06520   Marianne McKeon, *Publicity Assistant*   203-436-3263   May 16, 1982

FOR RELEASE AUGUST 15, 1983

NEW BOOK NAMES WHITE COLLAR CRIMINALS

Thirty-five years ago Edwin Sutherland wrote an exposé of the
criminal activity that existed in seventy of America's largest corporations.
The term he used to describe this activity -- "white-collar crime" --
became a part of our language as the book became an instant classic.

Until now, however, Sutherland's work has been known to the public
only in an expurgated version published in 1949. Sutherland's original
publisher, fearing legal repercussions, demanded that he remove the
names and other identifying descriptions of the guilty corporations
and officials. After agonizing debate, Sutherland agreed.

Now Sutherland's original study -- in all its colorful detail, and
with the names and case studies of offenders restored -- is at last
available to readers in WHITE COLLAR CRIME: THE UNCUT VERSION,
to be published by Yale University Press August 17, 1983.

This new edition of Sutherland's classic work reveals that two companies
stood at the top of the list in total number of convictions for white-collar
crime -- Armour and Co. and Swift and Co; these were followed by
General Motors, Sears and Roebuck, and Montgomery Ward. Other
corporate culprits named for the first time include movie companies
(Loew's, Paramount, and Warner Brothers) as well as General Electric,
Ford, and American Tobacco.

FIGURE 12.5

In an introduction to the new version of WHITE COLLAR CRIME, sociologists Gilbert Geis and Colin Goff note that Sutherland was the first to show that such corporate offenses as paying wages below the permissible limits, unsafe working conditions, and illegal union-breaking tactics had more severe consequences than the street crimes that preoccupied the public at the time. By emphasizing that dangerous criminal activity could be found among middle and upper class populations, Sutherland challenged the practice of employing class-related explanations to interpret criminal behavior. In so doing, he revolutionized the field of criminology.

FIGURE 12.5, cont.

Yale Book News

Yale University Press
92A Yale Station
New Haven, Ct. 06520

For more information, please contact
Sarah F. Clark, *Publicist*
Marianne McKeon, *Publicity Assistant*

203-432-4979
203-436-3263

Advance Praise For

WHITE COLLAR CRIME
The Uncut Version
by Edwin H. Sutherland

To be published by Yale University Press August 17, 1983

"When first issued in 1949, *White Collar Crime,* Sutherland's seminal work, temporarily shifted academic and public focus from crime in the streets to crime in the suites, sending tremors through corporate boardrooms. Prior to publication of the first edition, Sutherland agreed, under pressure from his university and his publisher, to expurgate his exposé by removing the corporate names, thus leaving a volume of misdeeds in crime without the culprits and criminals. Now that corporate crime has become a documented tradition of widespread scope, Sutherland's proper-name data can be released to fill out this remarkable and courageous work of criminological scholarship."

—**Ralph Nader**

"*White Collar Crime* is the most significant book ever published in American criminology. This edition provides data and details about corporation crimes never before made public. The Introduction alone makes the book worth its price. I worked closely with Sutherland for three years, but I learned much more about him from the Introduction than I learned from personal association. Geis and Goff have painted a revealing intellectual portrait of Sutherland and have nicely documented the history of research on white-collar crime. It, like the book it introduces, is bound to become a classic."

—**Donald R. Cressey**

"*White Collar Crime* will be enormously useful to social scientists focusing on the criminal careers of particular U.S.A. corporations and to those drawing comparisons between the crimes of U.S.A. corporations and their counterparts in Europe and Asia. With names of corporations restored, this new edition is much more readable than the emasculated 1949 edition. The late E. H. Sutherland would be pleased by the news that his original version at last is appearing in published form."

—**Karl Schuessler**

FIGURE 12.5, cont.

a matter worthy of thought and research. Judicious use of review copies is one of the key promotional efforts for scholarly books.

The major library reviewing media are *Library Journal* (*LJ*) *Choice* (aimed at academic libraries), and the *ALA Booklist*. The *Publishers Weekly* forecasts are of course read throughout the trade. The most important general review media are the major newspapers and magazines, most of which have book pages and book-review columns. Several newspapers have separate weekly book-review sections as well.

Literary Market Place (*LMP*)[2] lists important newspaper and magazine reviewers as well as radio and TV people. *Ayer Directory of Publications* and *Standard Rate & Data,* a master directory much used in advertising, also provide extensive information on the general media. *Bacon's Publicity Checker,* Gebbie's *Directory, Editor & Publisher,* and the *Standard Periodicals Directory* are other sources. All are regularly revised, mostly on an annual basis.

For specialized and scholarly journals, the most extensive source is *Ulrich's International Periodicals Directory.* Its 2,212 pages list thousands of publications over the world, classified by subject matter as well as by geographic location. The entries indicate circulation and whether or not book reviews are included. The *Ad Guide,* published by the Association of American University Presses (AAUP), gives comprehensive information on some twenty-five hundred scholarly periodicals and is very useful for both publicity and advertising purposes. The last edition was published in 1979–1980, and unfortunately the AAUP has no current plans to revise it.

How many copies of a scholarly book should be sent out for review? There is no pat answer. Some disciplines have only a few possible sources; others have dozens. Authors and editors who know the field can help to identify the most worthwhile. It is often a mistake to set a ceiling on the number of review copies or to refuse requests for review copies from lesser-known journals. A review copy is one of the cheapest promotion devices—the book and postage cost far less than a space ad or the fee for showing a book at an exhibit. A good review, even in a limited-circulation journal, can really sell books.

If the resources are available, by all means computerize your review lists. Be sure, though, that you can make corrections rapidly; some journals change book review editors annually, and sending a book to last year's editor can be an expensive mistake. (Most experts advise addressing the copy to a specific person rather than "editor" or "book reviewer," to prevent the book from being lost or stolen or from sitting around in a receiving room for weeks awaiting the proper recipient.) Plan to send the books out as far ahead of publication as possible—six weeks is minimal, eight is better. Each copy should be accompanied by a slip giving the date of publication and the price.

The scholarly publisher faced with a potential best-seller may be pardoned a moment of panic. Publicity in a trade-book context is so very different. However, the names of capable publicity consultants may be found in *LMP,* in the "wanted" columns of *PW,* and by asking around. For a reasonable fee a consultant will provide press releases and review lists and will even arrange author tours and TV appearances. Wise scholarly publishers know their limitations and get outside help when appropriate.

SPACE ADVERTISING

An ongoing debate in scholarly publishing concerns the efficacy of space ads, since sales can seldom be traced directly to such ads. But space ads in scholarly and specialized journals can also serve the purposes of promoting the house image, pleasing the author, reinforcing direct mail, calling attention to the publisher's exhibit at scholarly meetings, and supporting journals important to the house. The last should not be underestimated. Journals need advertising dollars to survive. The loss of a vehicle for important articles and reviews (and a source of authors for future books) is very damaging to all.

Many journals are published quarterly and have deadlines two or more months prior to publication. Prices for space vary depending on circulation. Some will "pub set" from copy and a rough layout supplied by the publisher, whereas others want a finished mechanical.

Most advertising agencies are not interested in the relatively small business of scholarly publishers since they are paid on a commission basis. The traffic, writing, and design of ads will have to be handled in-house or by free lances. Make sure your ads look professional. Try to cultivate a "house style" by using the same combination of type faces and a distinctive colophon. Use photos of the book or author wherever possible. Agitate for photogenic jackets!

Try to make sure each new book gets exposure in at least the major journal of the discipline. Use list ads where you have several books, but allow enough room to get in a good description. Consider placing seasonal list ads in *Choice, LJ,* and *PW* if you have the budget. Do up a seasonal schedule of ads and send out insertion orders early on. When the tear sheets come in, circulate them in-house and send them to the authors. Everybody will love you!

Some publishers use coupon ads with success; others disdain them. Take a careful look through the journal or magazine before you specify a coupon ad to make sure it won't look out of place. Cooperative ads are mainly used in conjunction with bookstores for potential best-sellers, so probably needn't concern you.

EXHIBITS

Exhibiting books at scholarly and professional meetings provides a good opportunity—sometimes the only one—for potential buyers to get their hands on the books, peruse them, and sometimes even sit down at the exhibit booth and read them. Although few exhibits pay their way in direct sales, they can be effective marketing tools. Scholars who frequent the exhibit halls may subsequently order the books they find there, assign them for course use, or tell their university libraries about them.

The annual exhibits directory of the Association of American Publishers currently lists more than two hundred international, national, state, and regional meetings of associations where publishers are invited to exhibit books. Included are book-trade, library, and academic meetings—everything from the Frankfurt International Book Fair to the Florida Association for Media in Education.

A publisher with a substantial list in a particular field may want to rent his own booth to display his full line of appropriate titles. The costs of doing so plus preparing and sending materials and books, not to mention people to staff the booth, will be high, depending on the type of meeting, the amount of space rented, and the distance the staff must travel. If this method isn't affordable or the number of appropriate titles is limited, the publisher can send a selection of books for a combined exhibit for a per-title fee. The American University Press Services, a subsidiary of the Association of American University Presses, makes a very extensive schedule of exhibits available to its members in this way. The Association of American Publishers has recently inaugurated a similar service for its members. Other commercial services include the Conference Book Service, Combined Book Exhibit, and the Book Examination Center. Addresses for these and others can be found in *Literary Market Place.*

COLLEGE ADOPTIONS

Few scholarly publishers attempt to compete with commercial houses in the basic text market, but scholarly publishers have been successful with texts for more specialized and higher-level courses and with books intended as supplementary rather than required reading.

When a scholarly house does have a book that could be used as a required text, it must generally resort to direct mail rather than the army of field representatives used by textbook houses to build up an examination-copy list. Lists of instructors teaching appropriate courses can be obtained from the Educational Directory or the College Marketing

Group (see the Bibliography at the end of this chapter). The mailing piece can be quite simple and inexpensive, but it should carefully explain the purpose and plan of the text, identify the courses for which it is intended, and give the price. The instructor should be told to write on departmental letterhead for an examination copy, specifying the name and expected enrollment of the course and when it will be offered.

Traditionally examination copies have been sent without charge. In recent years there have been some changes. Some scholarly publishers send paperbacks free but send hardcover copies only "on approval," generally with a thirty-day invoice advising that the charge will be canceled if ten or more copies of the book are ordered. As the prices of paperbacks edge ever upward, even some commercial publishers ask a nominal sum for paperbacks, and many will send expensive paperbacks only on approval.

Figure 12.6 shows a mailer for a new elementary German text prepared in-house. It was typed on an electric typewriter, with display type picked up from photocopies of the book's front matter. The piece was mailed to 1,529 senior and junior college teachers of German. Total cost of the mailing: $530. Requests received: 75. Possible adoption potential: 1,000–2,000 copies per year. Actual adoptions: too early to tell.

In order to track replies, some publishers insert a form in the book, asking the professor's evaluation; others send such a form separately a few weeks after the book.

Direct Mail

A few years back, a publishing executive addressing a direct-mail seminar recalled her early experiences as college promotion manager in a commercial house. As part of her training, she accompanied one of the college travelers on his rounds. He took her to the post office on campus, then located next to the bookstore, and suggested she spend some time simply watching. What she, appalled, saw was a steady stream of faculty come in, pick up their mail, and head for the row of wastebaskets, where they proceeded to dump all third-class mail, unopened. The lesson she learned and remembered was that the relationship between the direct-mail marketer and the audience is a tenuous and fragile one at best!

Direct mail is a multibillion-dollar industry. Most of us get piles of what some persist in calling junk mail—with garish colors, screaming headlines, and exhortations to "act now or else." How do scholarly publishers fit into this hard-sell, high-powered industry?

Scholarly publishers in fact pioneered the use of direct mail for books,

Deutsch-Lernen macht Spaß!

Rosalie M. Russell

A dynamic new approach to learning
German ... for the college classroom ... for adult education ...
for home study

Here are all the necessary tools to
learn to communicate in German -- and
to continue learning the German language
long after the course is completed.

Rosalie Russell's text proceeds from the premise that adult second-language
learners need to modify normal English language behaviour to accommodate
the patterns of the native speaker. Her book allows the student to understand
how the native speaker behaves in everyday situations and how language is
used in those situations.

The dialogues in DEUTSCH-LERNEN MACHT SPASS give typical conversations and
useful daily expressions, providing the words and structures needed for
special situations. Students learn basic patterns and can respond in familiar
situations -- shopping, travelling, family situations, visiting a doctor,
watching television, education, the theatre and the like.

Each of the 20 chapters in the text includes exercises, a dialogue, a reading
piece, pronunciation exercises and grammar. Lexical items, idioms and
structures are introduced in context. The book also includes a vocabulary,
list of verbs and an index. The text is printed in two colors.

Also available is taped material for private study and computer disks to provide
a private tutor.

ROSALIE RUSSELL received her tertiary education in Canada and the United
States. Since 1970 she has taught language and literature at the tertiary
level in both the U.S. and Australia. Of German parents, Dr. Russell is
totally bilingual.

DEUTSCH-LERNEN MACHT SPASS - 461 pages softcover ISBN 0 7022 1639 9 $24.50

Examination copy policy

Please send your request on departmental letterhead, indicating course name,
expected enrollment and date. If the book is adopted and ordered through
the bookstore, usual discount will apply.

FIGURE 12.6 Mailer.

more by necessity than choice. For books with limited and specialized
audiences, small print runs, and the prospect of few bookstore sales,
direct mail is the most potent medium available. The highly specialized,
pinpointed academic mailing lists that are now taken for granted were
first developed by university presses.

In the selling of books by mail, two concepts are of key importance: focus and market segmentation. *Focus* refers to the mailing offer itself. Is it directed to a discernible, discrete audience—not just everyone out there who is interested in books but specific admirers of Henry James or those with a special interest in medieval architecture? If the mailing is for a number of books, does it have an inherent logic as a group?

Market segmentation refers to the availability of lists suitable to match the focus of the mailing. Even though an astonishing number of segmented lists are available, there are still offerings for which no suitable list can be found. Some years back, a diligent search for a list of Spanish-speaking electrical engineers in the United States ended in failure. A more recent search for a list of coaches and trainers of women athletes, as well as for serious women athletes themselves, was only partially successful.

Direct mail differs from other types of marketing in that it combines advertising and selling in one package (you make the pitch and close the sale all at the same time, in print); it provides built-in feedback (the results can be measured directly); it adds value to a product, perhaps with a special discount or a bonus for buyers; and it is action-oriented to encourage impulse sales (since there is no salesman to break down the customer's inertia, the piece must anticipate and overcome sales resistance).

Direct mail is a field full of experts and rules, many of them contradictory. Successful direct-mail users remain flexible and pragmatic—if something works, fly with it—if not, back to square one.

The major elements to be considered are planning, budgeting, the mailing lists, the offer and terms of sale, the format, the copy and artwork, the mailing process, and the method of tracking the returns.

PLANNING

Plan your seasonal mailing programs in advance, taking into account the budget and the total number of books to be promoted. First decide whether any book warrants a separate promotion, for instance, a major work with a price high enough to make direct mail feasible. Group the remaining books by subject areas, adding recent backlist titles in each area that could use another "push."

Most of your mailing pieces will promote a focused group of books to a carefully segmented audience. Alas for "orphans of the storm"—books that stand alone with no other newly published titles for the same market and little backlist either. Such books must be either promoted separately or allowed to "find their own market." Wise publishers cultivate a list with strength in certain areas and decline books that don't fit, even if they are desirable for other reasons.

Count on needing at least six weeks to produce a direct-mail campaign.

Attempting to push one through more quickly may cause you to make serious errors in strategy, list choice, and the handling of details.

BUDGETING

The basic expenditures for direct mail include list rental, design, type-setting, paper, printing, addressing, postage, and mailing and reply envelopes and order card, if they are used. Here are some rough figures on costs as of 1983. Although these costs will change and will vary from region to region, they are included to provide some general guidance.

- List rental: about $50 per 1,000 names.
- Typesetting: $50–$75 per page for a 6-by-9-inch to 8½-by-11-inch page, depending on the number of typefaces used and the amount of type to be set. This is for cold type or computer type; linotype costs more.
- Design: $200–$500 for an average brochure, depending on size and artist.
- Printing: 15,000 copies of an 11-by-17-inch self-mailer printed in black on colored 60-pound stock, with 3 veloxes (prescreened photos), recently cost $575. Another printer in the same city quoted $1,100 for the same piece, which suggests the importance of getting estimates before ordering printing.

    An 8½-by-11-inch letter printed on one side only in black ink costs about $30 per 1,000.

    A no. 10 mailing envelope costs $22 per 1,000. (Larger sizes cost more, of course.) A no. 6½ reply envelope costs $18 per 1,000.
- Postage: Publishers registered at the post office as not-for-profit orga-nizations pay a bulk rate of 5.4 cents per piece up to 2 ounces in weight. Others pay the commercial bulk rate of 10.8 cents. Bulk rate requires presorting and banding and is subject to other regulations. Check with your local postmaster for details.
- Lettershop: for a self-mailer, affixing labels, sorting, and mailing, about $30 per 1,000. For a letter or brochure, about $60 per 1,000.

Thus, it will cost about $3,600 to produce and mail 15,000 copies of a simple self-mailer at the nonprofit rate and $4,500 at the commercial rate. Add envelopes, letter, and order card and the cost goes up by $75–$100 per thousand.

Clearly, direct mail is hardly inexpensive, and it is important to get the most out of every dollar spent. How do you project the response to a mail campaign? The best guideline is past performance of a similar promotion to a similar audience. It's easy enough to make a prediction if your flyer offers only one book, but for a multiple offer, some guesswork is necessary. A general rule of thumb is that where the offering is for 10 books, the average order will be for 1.8 books. Some people will order all 10, but many will order only 1. So average the prices out and use that figure, remembering to deduct any discount you may be offering. When you have a dollar amount for the average order, project total income by percentages. Start with a response of one-half of a percent (75 orders of the 15,000 mailed). Work your way up to 2 percent. You should "break even" at no more than nine-tenths of a percent—that is, pay the costs of the mailing, the books themselves, and order fulfillment. If your break-even point is much higher, the mailing will probably lose money. In direct-mail circles a 2 percent response is considered excellent, and more is exceptional. Don't count on a high response unless past experience indicates that it is possible.

The Lists

One of the sad facts of life in direct mail is that a great mailing to the wrong list will fall flat, while a mediocre effort to the right list can pull very well. Your job is to find the right lists and then to maximize the return with the right offer. There are several types of lists.

COMPILED. A list that has been put together from directories, membership rosters, or similar sources is referred to as a compiled list. Usually it is a large list that can be manipulated by computer to reach the most effective segment for a particular need. The key things to know about such a list are how it was compiled, what sources were used, and how recently the list was updated.

RESPONSE. Response lists are made up from the names of people who have previously bought books by mail, joined book clubs, subscribed to magazines, and so forth. Key factors: What did they buy? How closely does it relate to the books you are offering? How recent is the list?

HOUSE. This is a list of your own customers. Key factors: Are you in a position to use the list at least twice a year, to keep it up to date, to add new names as they come in, and to rent it or exchange it for the lists of other houses to get greater mileage?

PROSPECT. Prospect lists include people who have asked to be on your list but who are not currently your customers. Key factors are recency and the possibility of converting them to buyers.

Publishers claim that their own house lists usually outpull any others they use. Others claim that response lists pull best if they are carefully chosen for a particular offering. Both the Educational Directory and the College Marketing Group rent book-buyer lists as well as highly detailed compiled lists of academics. Many scholarly journals and associations will also rent their subscriber or membership lists. Response lists tend to be too large for many highly specialized mailings, and one must use a segmented compiled list.

In choosing a list, first determine the entire universe for an offering, then narrow it down to the core market and include as much of the secondary market as you can afford. If a list is very large, test a sample. If this pulls, take the rest of the list. A mailing of 2,000 is usually considered the minimal size to test a large list. As an example, take the case of a book on genetics. One academic list supplier offers a total of some 21,000 teachers of biology at the college level and 19,500 individuals who have bought scholarly books on biology, for a total "universe" of some 40,000. A breakdown of the first list reveals 2,500 academics in genetics, and of the second, 2,200 book buyers. There are, in addition, libraries and members of scholarly societies that may also be considered part of the "universe." Choice of specific lists would depend on the marketing assessment of the book's potential. How wide is the appeal of the book beyond those specifically in the field of genetics? Is it primarily intended for classroom use or as a library reference volume? Would it make sense to test 2,000 each from the large lists and see how they respond?

There are many good sources for mailing lists. The Educational Directory, owned by the Association of American University Presses, has the names of thousands of academics in all disciplines, both in broad categories and with fine breakdowns. It also acts as broker for a range of scholarly journals and associations. The College Marketing Group has similar lists and breakdowns. Both offer lists of book buyers by subject as well as lists of college and public libraries. R. R. Bowker Company is also well known for its lists of libraries and bookstores, and the Gale Research Company has a variety of useful lists. The Special Libraries Association has lists of libraries in its specialized fields. Market Data Retrieval offers extensive lists of teachers, librarians, and educational specialists at K–12 schools.

The "bible" for locating sources of membership lists is Gale's *En-cyclopedia of Associations,* a huge book with detailed listings of 14,500 active associations. Many are willing to rent their membership lists. Many publish journals and newsletters and will rent these subscriber lists as well.

When you are seeking lists in untried or unfamiliar fields, a useful source is Standard Rate and Data Service's (SRDS) *Direct Mail Rates & Data,* a quarterly subscription service with information on fifty thousand lists. If you need more help a list broker can probably guide you to appropriate lists. The broker's commission is paid by the list owner, not by you. A section on list brokers is found in *LMP.*

The Offer

Given the same book and the same market, the structure of the offer can have a considerable effect on the results. Direct mail is an action-oriented selling medium. Don't prepare something that looks like a page in a catalog or a space ad in a scholarly journal with a coupon added. Think about ways to overcome human inertia, the great enemy of the direct marketer.

Consider special offers—discounts, bonuses, free sample issues (for subscriptions), or a "free trial offer." By now, the 20 percent mail-order discount is quite common in scholarly circles. Try a graduated discount— the higher the order, the larger the discount. Or offer a free book or some other valuable premium.

Giving the reader a deadline for responding also helps to overcome inertia, but be sure to allow enough time. If you are mailing in January, you may want to allow until the end of April or even May, given the vagaries of the postal service and all the other things that can cause delays.

Spell out the terms of sale clearly: cash or check required with order, credit cards, billing for institutions only (with purchase order number supplied by the customer), sales tax due, postage and handling charges, and so on. Allow sufficient space for the customer to write in his full name and address. Make the order form easy to use and the type large enough to read. Lead the customer step-by-step. It's a good idea to show the order forms to your fulfillment people *before* the piece is printed, so that they can identify any problems in advance.

If you are selling a set or series, offer a very attractive deal to encourage standing orders. It's nice to know you have a certain number of advance sales in the pocket. Offer a special discount, or the final volume free, to buyers of the complete set.

Devising offers challenges creativity and distinguishes the clever from the ordinary. If you should come up with a really successful new proposition, you'll soon find your colleagues elsewhere following suit, thus paying you the highest form of flattery.

Format

The two common formats for direct mail are the "classic" package and the self-mailer. Most experts say that the classic, a package of a brochure, letter, order form, and reply envelope, outpulls the self-mailer. It also costs a good deal more.

Why the preference for the classic package? Because it allows the mailer to establish the most important factor of all in direct mail, the personal touch. The model for direct mail is a letter on a letterhead, reproduced from typewriter type, headed by a salutation, signed by a name, and in the form of a personal exhortation. Do the recipients read this stuff? Test after test shows that they do. Use a nom de plume in signing your letters and soon letters and telephone calls to that name will start arriving.

This personal touch, the "you" approach, is the bedrock of most successful direct marketers. When writing direct-mail copy, get into the "you" mode. Put yourself in the place of customers and tell them what they want to know: what your offer will do for them. The discount, bonus, or whatever is known as a "benefit"—but so is the book itself, if its features are presented properly!

Lead with your best benefit, your most potent fact (also called the hook). You have perhaps ten seconds to engage your reader—remember that ever-beckoning trash basket! The classic formula for a sales letter is "tell 'em what you are going to tell 'em, tell 'em, and then tell 'em what you told 'em." If you don't believe it, read some successful sales letters, such as the ones the Kiplinger organization sends out. Notice how benefit oriented they are. See how they lead off with strength and then build benefit upon benefit until the close, urging the reader to act today. Don't forget in closing to ask for the order. You'd be surprised how many direct-mail offerings fail to do this.

If you cannot afford a classic package and must use self-mailers, don't despair. Clever direct mailers find ways to incorporate "sales letters" in self-mailers and in catalogs too.

THE COPY

The sales letter is the style most frequently identified with direct mail. The other style is brochure copy, which more closely resembles copy for a catalog, jacket flap, or space ad. The sales letter is the hardest form of copywriting to master; even the most talented writer will make many false starts before hitting his stride.

Don't be afraid to write strong, benefit-oriented copy. Don't worry about soft-sell, hard-sell, or whatever. In talking to specialists, you are addressing people who know their fields better than you ever will. Librarians, scholars, and professionals respond best to factual presentations, so roll out the facts. Use quotes, samples, tables of contents, and credentials of the author, and express it all with force and confidence. Truth is the best marketing device of all, so don't make unsupportable claims. If you say a book is the first to put forth a certain view, someone will come along to tell you it was done before in 1879 by a German philosopher you never heard of.

The American National Standards Institute (ANSI) has drafted the following checklist for book advertising. It is useful to bear this in mind whenever you write copy.

CHECKLIST FOR ADVERTISING BOOKS BY DIRECT MAIL

1. author(s) (and/or editor, compiler)
2. title
3. subtitle, if any
4. list price
5. publication (or availability) date—for older books, copyright date
6. paging and/or number of volumes, if more than one
7. edition (number, trade versus text, hardcover versus paper)
8. identification of publisher
9. ISBN (International Standard Book Number)
10. dates when prepublication price available, if any
11. Library of Congress catalog card number
12. special physical features (such as large-size print; unbound accompanying material; preprocessed books; or special bindings, with a list of the type of binding standard used for those books for which this is a particularly important feature)
13. series identification (name and number)
14. translation information (original title and language, original copyright date, translator)
15. description of contents of book
16. conference information if any (place and date of meeting, sponsors)
17. pertinent information on authors
18. size (if unusual), number and type of graphic features (if significant), index (if any)
19. prior publication record: source and date of the original material (such as a previously published book, a periodical issue, a technical report, a hearing)

TESTING AND TRACKING

Large commercial mailers test everything—lists, offers, copy, formats, even colors of ink. A true test means pitting one thing against another, with all other factors held constant; keeping careful track of the results; and then acting on them. Scholarly publishers can seldom afford the outlay necessary to do these things. In our world, testing often means trying one list one year and another the next. A number of different ways of coding mailings may be used to track returns. If the mailing label will be returned as part of the order device, a code may be imprinted on the label. The coupon itself may be coded with numbers or letters. You can use "Suite PDQ" or some such in the mailing address.

Whether you test or simply mail and see what happens, you should keep careful records of returns. Chart the day-to-day response by list, by book, and by dollars. Check the total sales of each book included in the mailing to see if you have stimulated an "echo affect," which means simply that in addition to the directly attributable responses, direct mail also produces sales that come in via wholesalers, library jobbers, bookstores, and in other ways as well. "Echo" is an integral component of direct mail and should be considered in any evaluation.

Library Promotion

Since libraries constitute such a large portion of the audience for scholarly books, it is important to think of their needs when planning all promotions. Many university presses routinely send libraries monthly promotions on new books consisting of a separate letter for each book, giving a rather full factual description of the book. Sometimes a discount is offered, too. Librarians like the format of these mailings because each sheet can be distributed to the library's acquisition expert in the appropriate field.

Another type of promotion that librarians like is the so-called card deck—a packet of three-by-five-inch cards, each giving a brief description of a book, all mailed together with a covering letter and an order form. Sometimes the card is itself a return device with a built-in order form. Scientific, technical, and professional publishers in particular often make use of card decks.

Librarians also give high marks to subject-arranged catalogs or, better yet, separate subject catalogs. They like discount offers and will respond to special deals. The buying habits and needs of libraries are as diverse and puzzling as those of publishers themselves. Many can and do prepay orders, while others must solicit bids from several jobbers before they can order an inexpensive paperback. Most libraries have a staff of subject specialists doing acquisitions. As library acquisitions budgets shrink, faculty recommendations become increasingly important. It doesn't hurt to put a little reminder to this effect in your promotion to scholars.

Sales Efforts

SELLING TO THE TRADE

Isn't selling scholarly books to the trade a contradiction in terms? Like so much else in publishing, the answer is yes and no. Yes, the presentation of scholarly monographs and technical treatises by a sales representative to trade bookstores is not only unnecessary but futile. But there are a few titles on the lists of most scholarly publishers that will be purchased for the trade sections of university bookstores and the shelves of general stores.

How to sell this small but very noticeable portion of the list? Combined efforts are most cost effective for many publishers. Sometimes several presses share the expenses of a representative or group of representatives, as is done by Harvard, Yale, Princeton, and the Massachusetts Institute of Technology (MIT). Sometimes one publisher provides such service to others on a fee basis. Columbia, for example, covers the country for ten other publishers. Johns Hopkins and Indiana provide trade-sales representation in the East and Midwest, respectively, for each other and five other presses. Most smaller scholarly and professional publishers use commission representatives who sell the list in return for a percentage of the sales income produced. Commission representatives will usually be selling the books in the front of the catalog rather than the entire list of a scholarly publisher.

Scholarly publishers are often ambivalent about making efforts to obtain trade sales but usually decide they are worth the effort. The key is to find the most cost-effective sales-representation arrangement for your particular list (for instance, do you need intensive representation in your own locale but only a skimming of major university bookstores and general accounts in other territories?). Once identified, the arrangement can be facilitated by providing catalogs, order forms, and other sales aids in timely fashion. Realize, too, that if you wish to deal with trade bookstores, you must offer trade discounts or at least an agency plan that allows larger discounts than usual on short-discount titles.

SPECIAL SALES

Special sales means selling an individual title in bulk (anywhere from ten copies to thousands) at a discount to nontraditional book outlets, which will then resell the books or give them as premiums to customers or members. Selling a cookbook to a chain of shops that sell gourmet food is a special sale to a nontraditional book outlet. Selling a regional guide to a local bank to offer as a deposit inducement to customers is a special sale. Selling a title to an association to resell to its members is a special sale.

In the direct-mail section we discussed selling by mail to members of a professional association by renting the membership list and mailing to each name on it. That's good marketing, but it is even better, and much less expensive, to sell a quantity of books at a discount to the association itself, which in turn promotes them to its members at no additional cost to the publisher. You can see why publishers are excited about special sales these days.

FOREIGN SALES

The types of books published by scholarly and professional publishers travel well. Foreign markets can account for 20 percent or more of the unit sales of a scholarly publisher. This is in part because the scholars and professionals for whom the books are written are likely to be able to read English.

The process of selling and promoting to foreign markets can be bewildering to the novice, or to the old hand at domestic marketing, for that matter. If you have ever guiltily slipped an unanswered inquiry from an unknown Pakistani book dealer into the wastebasket, you are not alone. The barriers of language, currency, customs, collections, and just plain lack of knowledge of another part of the world can seem truly insurmountable, but that's why God created specialists. You need enough knowledge and sense to select the right specialist or specialists to market your books in foreign territories and the interest and perseverance to keep in touch with them.

Unless you represent a publisher of very high dollar volume books, such as a scientific and technical publisher, it is unlikely that you will be able to devote time to gathering the expertise to assess and keep up with changes in the varied foreign markets yourself. The solution is to learn enough to select others to handle your books and then to support their efforts by providing effective promotional materials for their markets and to monitor their activities to determine whether they are indeed resulting in increased sales of your books.

There are several ways to handle foreign sales. A U.S. firm can be hired as your export representative to sell your books in all or some of the foreign territories they cover. Feffer & Simons and Kaiman & Polon are the two largest; their addresses and others are listed in *LMP*. They do the selling and take the credit risks and you do the fulfillment of individual orders received from them.

Some very large publishers (Prentice-Hall, Harper & Row, and Oxford University Press come to mind) have offices in various parts of the world and are willing to act as agents for other publishers. Sometimes they will stock books in the individual territories; sometimes they will send all orders to the United States to be filled.

Another option is to select individual local sales agents in each of several territories. Some local agents buy books from the U.S. publisher to resell; others hold stock on consignment and pay only as they sell the books; others forward orders to the United States for fulfillment.

Some university presses form consortia to provide a financial base for sales and promotion efforts that no one press could afford on its own. Many university presses have such group arrangements covering the United Kingdom and Europe. Edirep sells university-press books in Latin America, and a combination of half a dozen of the largest U.S. university presses has recently opened a sales office in Japan. East West Export Books, based at the University of Hawaii Press, was one of the earliest such efforts and has been successfully selling books throughout Asia since 1965.

Whatever arrangement is chosen, it is important to gain a thorough knowledge of what efforts the agent will make on your behalf and to supply the information and materials to aid those efforts. "Keep in touch" should be printed in large type on every foreign sales representation contract. The farther away the agent, the more important is close communication. Do your part, then don't hesitate to insist that the agent do his or hers. Most agents represent many publishers; the squeaky-wheel principle definitely applies here.

*   *   *

It seems appropriate to conclude this chapter with a brief word on marketing scholarly books as a career choice. For many years, too many scholarly publishers seemed to regard their promotion people as necessary evils. One of the present writers recalls a very intellectual editor reading one of her sales letters years ago and commenting, "You do this rather well, don't you? What would one call it—*suasion,* I suppose, after the Greek, you know?" He thought he was delivering flattery! Now some editors complain that the pendulum has swung too far in the other direction, making marketing considerations supreme and "the bottom line" the only measure of worth.

The truth is that scholarly publishing must have a competent staff in both editing and marketing if it is to survive. We must not lower our standards of quality while competing for the ever-scarcer book dollar, but compete successfully we must! Those of us who have chosen careers in scholarly marketing sometimes feel that we have had the best of both worlds—the chance to come in close contact with the brilliant minds and ideas of scholars and the chance to deal in the "real world" of the marketplace. We know that the fad books and "blockbusters" that hog the space in bookstores and the media today will soon be forgotten, whereas the obscure monograph we labor to make known may eventually stimulate a whole new direction in scholarship and a better and more secure world for all of us.

Notes

1. Published by American University Press Services, 1971, for member presses.
2. Information on this and other publications cited is presented in the Bibliography at the end of this chapter.

Bibliography

Ad Guide: Advertiser's Guide to Scholarly Periodicals. New York: American University Press Services, 1979–1980.

Ayer Directory of Publications. Bala Cynwyd, Pa.: Ayer Press, annual.

Bacon's Publicity Checker. Chicago: Bacon Publishing Co., annual.

Bodian, Nat. *Book Marketing Handbook.* New York: R. R. Bowker, 1980.

Editor and Publisher International Yearbook. New York: Editor and Publisher, annual.

Encyclopedia of Associations. Detroit: Gale Research Company, annual.

Gebbie's Directory. New Paltz, N.Y.: Gebbie's Press, 1980.

Levin, Howard. *Evaluation of Book Promotion Devices.* Glen Cove, Ill.: Text Fiche Press, 1979.

1983 Exhibits Directory. New York: Association of American Publishers, 1984.

SRDS Business Publication Rates & Data. Skokie, Ill.: Standard Rate and Data Service, monthly.

SRDS Direct Mail Lists & Data. Skokie, Ill.: Standard Rate and Data Service, quarterly.

Standard Periodicals Directory. New York: Oxbridge Communications, 1982.

Stone, Bob. *Successful Direct Marketing Methods.* 2d ed. Chicago: Crain Books, 1979.

R. R. Bowker Co. is the publisher of *American Book Publishing Record* (subscription), *Books in Print* (annual), *Forthcoming Books* (quarterly), *Library Journal* (subscription), *Literary Market Place* (annual), *Magazines for Libraries* (edited by Bill Katz and Linda Stenberg Katz, 4th ed., 1982), *Paperbound Books in Print* (annual), *Publishers' Trade List Annual* (annual), *Publishers Weekly* (subscription), *Subject Guide to Books in Print* (annual), and *Ulrich's International Periodicals Directory* (annual).

Mailing lists are available from: College Marketing Group, 50 Cross St., Winchester, Mass., 01890 (academic mailing lists); The Educational Directory, 1 Park Avenue, New York, N.Y., 10016 (academic mailing lists); and Market Data Retrieval, Ketchum Place, Westport, Conn., 06880 (educational mailing lists).

CHAPTER THIRTEEN

Subsidiary Rights

MILDRED MARMUR

Subsidiary rights may be defined as those rights acquired by a publisher along with the basic (primary) right to publish and sell a work in volume form. The author and publisher share the income from the licensing of such rights in varying proportions.

The major subsidiary rights (and potentially the most lucrative) cover the following general areas: book club; reprint; first serial; dramatic, including motion picture, television, and stage; and foreign, including British. When the author is represented by a literary agent, the first serial, foreign, and dramatic rights are usually retained by the agent. The publisher almost always controls book-club and paperback rights. In this chapter we will proceed on the assumption that the publisher controls all rights.

Book-club rights are those licensed to clubs to enable them to offer their members the publisher's book. Clubs such as Book-of-the-Month Club, the Literary Guild, History Book Club, Macmillan Book Clubs, Preferred Choice Bookplan, and Reader's Subscription each offer their members up to 175 books a month (many titles being offered more than once). The publisher's share of income from the licensing of these rights is usually 50 percent.[1]

Rights licensed to publishing houses for other editions (usually either paperback or cheap hardcover) of the work are called reprint rights. Paperback reprints—mass-market (rack-size) and/or trade editions (usually the same size as the hardcover)—are generally published a year after the original publication. The publisher's share of these rights is usually 50 percent.

First serial (prepublication) rights are those licensed to periodicals (magazines and newspapers) prior to publication in book form. Though the selections tend to be abridged, occasionally a book will be run in its entirety. (The *New Yorker*, for example, frequently runs complete books over the course of a few issues.) The publisher's share of these rights can vary from 10 percent to 25 percent.

MILDRED MARMUR is president and publisher of Charles Scribner's Sons and was formerly vice president, director of subsidiary rights, adult trade division, Random House.

Motion picture, television, and dramatic rights are the rights licensed for adaptation of the book into dramatic form for airing or screening in the various media. The publisher's share of these rights is usually 10 percent. Foreign rights are those licensed to foreign-language and British book and periodical publishers to be translated and published in other countries throughout the world. The publisher's share of these rights varies from 10 to 50 percent.

Depending on the basic contract with the publisher and the rights involved, the author will have either no approval on any of these licenses, consultation rights, or (usually in the area of paperback and motion-picture rights) formal approval.

How Major Rights Work

BOOK CLUBS

The two major book clubs, Book-of-the-Month-Club and Literary Guild, each make about fifteen offerings a year in the form of advance brochures mailed to their members describing their various selections. The fifteen "cycles" cover every calendar month, with the nonmonthly brochures carrying such designations as Winter, Midsummer, Special Fall, and so on. One or two lead titles will be offered as the main, or dual main, selection(s) and fully described in the brochure sent to the club member. The selection(s) will be automatically shipped unless the member returns an enclosed card stipulating that no book (or another book) is desired. This is called negative option, in that the member need do nothing to receive the current selection(s).

From the book publisher's point of view, it is very valuable to have one's book selected as a main choice by either of the two major clubs. For one thing, the money guaranteed against royalties for a main selection can vary from $50,000 (Literary Guild usual minimum for a single selection) to $85,000 (Book-of-the-Month Club current minimum for a single selection) to high six figures if both clubs want the same book and are willing to bid against each other for a selection. This bidding process is usually accomplished by telephone over a period of one or two days. The bids are made to the rights director, who informs each club in turn of the size of the other's current bid; the book usually goes to the final top bidder.

The Book-of-the-Month Club operates specialized clubs: the Cooking and Crafts Club, the Dolphin Book Club for sailboat owners, the Fortune Book Club (business), the Quality Paperback Book Club, and the Book-of-the-Month/Science. The Literary Guild is the flagship club of the

Doubleday Book Clubs, which also includes these specialized clubs: Doubleday Book Club, Fireside Theatre, International Collectors Library, Military Book Club, Mystery Guild, and Science Fiction Book Club. If a book in question can be successfully offered by more than one associate club, the book will be that much more desirable to the main club. Even if the book is not one of the lucky fifty a year (calculating thirty cycles between the two clubs and allowing for each of them to offer a number of dual selections each year) to be a main selection of the Literary Guild or of the Book-of-the-Month Club, it is still very desirable for the book to be taken as an alternate selection. The money for alternate selections can vary from $1,500 for a book that is appealing but not predictable as a success to over $100,000 for surefire winners that, for one reason or another, can't be selections. For instance, the publisher might be rushing the book out because of its timeliness and not be able to wait for the club's usual four-to-five month selection schedule, or the book may be too politically explosive or overtly sexual in content to be shipped automatically to members.

Alternate club choice of a book is useful to the publisher because it may help convince bookstore personnel, faced with an overwhelming number of titles to order from each publisher's list, that the book has already been singled out because of its potential commercial appeal. It can have the same effect on the paperback editors, who are faced with the problem of evaluating hundreds of books for reprint in limited time.

The actual submission to book clubs is the simplest of all the five major subsidiary rights areas. Along with Book-of-the-Month Club and Literary Guild and their associated clubs, there are a number of other, more specialized clubs, with varying and different spheres of interest. Table 13.1 shows what a checklist might look like for submissions of two or three different books.

After the submission of the manuscript or galleys, the rights department follows up with news likely to inspire faster acceptance of a book, such as the establishment of a substantial printing quantity (twenty-five thousand copies or more), advance quotes, news of motion-picture options or sales. As soon as any one club has checked in with an offer, one alerts all other clubs to whom the book was submitted and sets a reasonable time period for their bids (no more than a week and sometimes as little as a day or two, depending on how long the book has been with the club and how long it takes to read it). One can expect a reaction on a short book fairly rapidly, but obviously more time is needed for a family saga totaling six hundred galley pages. One can usually combine book-club use by Book-of-the-Month Club and some of the other clubs, but Book-of-the-Month Club and Literary Guild

TABLE 13.1 CHECKLIST OF BOOK CLUB SUBMISSIONS

Send fiction to:
    Book-of-the-Month-Club
    The Literary Guild
    Macmillan Book Clubs
    Preferred Choice Bookplan
    Reader's Digest Condensed Books
    Readers' Subscription

Send special interest nonfiction to:
    Book-of-the-Month Club
    The Literary Guild
    Conservative Book Club
    History Book Club
    Macmillan Book Clubs
    McGraw-Hill Book Clubs
    Preferred Choice Bookplan
    Reader's Digest
    Readers' Subscription

Send cooking, crafts, beauty, and other specialty books to:
    Book-of-the-Month Club
    The Literary Guild
    Better Homes & Gardens Book Club
    Macmillan Book Clubs
    Outdoor Life Book Club

virtually never offer the same book, and Literary Guild almost never shares with another club.

It is usually at the stage of book-club submissions that the rights department submits manuscripts or galleys to Reader's Digest Condensed Books. Not to be confused with the magazine (which acquires first or second periodical rights), Condensed Books offers by direct-mail volumes containing four or five condensations of popular fiction and nonfiction. The condensations appear only in these volumes (not in *Reader's Digest* magazine).

Condensed Books (CB) is virtually in a class by itself in terms of subsidiary rights. It has no competitors who approach the amount of money CB pays for condensed-book use. CB advance payments can range from $20,000 for a first novel that the editors feel would be of interest to their mail-order subscribers to $50,000 or higher for a new work by an author who has been successfully received by subscribers before. There are further royalty moneys payable after distribution to the subscribers, who numbered about 1.5 million in 1984.

Although there is no identified major competitor in the form of a condensed-book operation, the Condensed Book editors do maintain at times that certain book-club use and certain magazine use (usually the women's interest magazines) overlap to some degree with the CB operation. So, in negotiating with CB one does sometimes have to make a choice between a periodical license and/or a book-club license. Sometimes adjusting the timing of the various release dates and offerings will allow all parties desirous of using the material to be able to do so.

REPRINT RIGHTS

Currently about eleven paperback houses acquire mass-market and, in many cases, trade reprint rights from hardcover publishers for paperback publication: Avon, Ballantine/Fawcett, Bantam, Berkley/Jove/Ace/Playboy, Dell, New American Library, Penguin, Pinnacle, Pocket Books, and Warner/Popular Library. Some trade paperback houses are: Anchor Books (Doubleday), Beacon Press, Columbia University Press, Contemporary Books, Harvard University Press, Holt (Owl), McGraw-Hill, Northpoint Press, W. W. Norton & Company, Princeton University Press, Oxford University Press, Schocken Books, Harper (Torch Books), University of Chicago Press, E. P. Dutton (Obelisk), and Wilshire Book Company.

Most of these houses are eclectic enough that one can submit many different types of books (in manuscript, galley, or finished form) to each, again with as much selling information as is available (print quantity, movie news, book-club adoption, and so on). If a book appeals to a paperback publisher, he or she may telephone the rights director (except for the initial submission by mail or messenger, most subsequent contact is made by telephone) and try to acquire it on a preemptive basis, precluding other bids. If the rights director is unwilling to close out a book, the paperback publisher might agree to participate in an auction for the paperback rights. In this case the rights person will set a "closing date" for bids to be made, again usually by telephone.

A generally accepted method in the industry for closing dates is for the seller (technically, the licenser) to take bids from different paperback editors in "rounds" (see Table 13.2). Thus, in the first round, one might have increasing bids from seven reprinters, with the licenser telling each new reprinter how many people are bidding and what the current high bid is. When round one has been completed, the licenser goes on to round two, and now the order followed is that the lowest bidder in round one bids (or passes) first, while the highest bidder bids or passes last. By the end of round two, there may be four bidders left and by round three or four there may be two, who would then bid against each other until one bidder decides to go no further.

The procedure just described could be termed an open auction since the book would go to the top bidder. Another auction approach is to give one paperback publisher a "topping privilege." This usually involves one paperback house early on offering a minimum guaranteed bid against royalties for a book, in return for the unilateral right to acquire the book at the end of the auction by bidding either a preagreed percentage based on the highest outside bid (traditionally 10 percent higher than the top bid but sometimes a different percentage) or a specified sum of money (which could be anything from $10,000 over the highest outside bid to $25,000 or $50,000).

Thus a reprinter might offer a $25,000 guaranteed bid (usually called a floor bid) in return for a 10 percent topping privilege. During the course of the auction the floor bidder is usually not required to bid in rounds, so once the $25,000 minimum bid has been announced and other houses have made increasing offers over it, the floor bidder simply waits to bid against the final remaining outside bidder. The usual procedure, when there is a floor bid with a topping privilege, is for the licenser to inform the remaining outside bidder that he or she may voluntarily increase the final bid before it is submitted to the floor bidder. Thus, if the outside bid, established at auction, were $80,000, and the topping privilege were preagreed at 10 percent, the outside bidder would have the choice of leaving the $80,000 so the floor bidder would have to decide about taking the book at $88,000 or of increasing the bid to $90,000, in the hopes that such a jump would surpass the floor bidder's own budget. The advantage of topping from the paperback publisher's point of view is that he or she retains the unilateral right to take the book, without the possibility of anyone bidding again; the advantage to the publisher is that bidding is started at an agreed-upon price that will never go lower. It should be noted, though, that other reprint houses may sometimes feel inhibited from bidding because of the topping privilege.

There are many cases where a book is sold to the floor bidder without any higher competitive bids from other houses. There are also many situations where books are sold to the previous paperback publisher of the author without an auction. In such situations the paperback house and the hardcover house negotiate on a unilateral basis until the parties mutually arrive at a price that seems acceptable in terms of the author's previous track record and the current value of the book because of outside circumstances (motion-picture sale, book-club selection, and so on).

There are also cases where licenses are made without auction and not

TABLE 13.2 PAPERBACK AUCTION

Rounds	Bid	Royalties
Round One		
Bidder A	$ 5,000	Mass-market: 10%. Trade: 7½%.
Bidder B	$ 6,500	Mass-market: 10%. Trade: 6% to 20,000 copies; 7½% thereafter. Note: Bidder B has offered a reduced trade-paperback royalty for the first 20,000 copies in order to help amortize more rapidly the setting-up expenses of preparing the book for publication.
Bidder C	$ 9,000	Mass-market: 8% to 100,000 copies; 10% thereafter. Trade: 7½% to 50,000 copies; 10% thereafter. Note: Bidder C is offering 2% less on mass-market for the first 100,000 copies for the same reason, namely, to help amortize early set-up expenses. Bidder C is also making the trade-paperback bid more acceptable by offering 2½% more, or 10%, after 50,000 copies are sold, calculating that at that point early expenses will have been amortized and that such a possibility will be of appeal to the licenser.
Bidder D	$13,000	Mass-market: 10%. Trade: 7½% to 50,000 copies; 10% thereafter.
Bidder E	$18,000	Mass-market: 10%. Trade: 7½% to 50,000 copies; 10% thereafter.
Bidder F	$20,500	Mass-market: 8% to 100,000 copies; 10% thereafter. Trade: 7½% to 150,000 copies; 10% thereafter.
Bidder G	$25,000	Mass-market: 10%. Trade: 7½% to 50,000 copies; 10% thereafter.

Round Two

Bidder A	$27,500	Bidding same royalties as in round one.
Bidder B		Out of auction as predetermined ceiling was $17,500. This company felt that $17,500 was just about the amount of money the book could earn in its first three years and therefore did not want to bid anymore.
Bidder C		Out of auction as predetermined ceiling was $15,000.
Bidder D	$30,000	Same royalties as before.
Bidder E		Out of auction as predetermined ceiling was $20,000.
Bidder F	$32,500	Agrees, since this is a competitive situation, to meet the same royalties as bidder D and therefore to improve the royalties bid in round one.
Bidder G		Out of auction as predetermined ceiling was $30,000.

Round Three

Bidder A	$35,000	Bidder A also agrees, since this is a competition, to meet the most attractive royalties that have been offered so far.
Bidder D		Out of auction as predetermined ceiling was $35,000.
Bidder F		Out of auction as predetermined ceiling was $35,000.

Bidder A therefore buys the book for $35,000, with a mass-market royalty of 10% and a trade royalty of 7½% to 50,000 copies and 10% thereafter.

to option holders. Sometimes one paperback editor will telephone the rights director shortly after he or she has received galleys or manuscripts (rarely as late as a finished book) to make a "preemptive" bid. Industry understanding of the term *preemptive* is that the hardcover house is being given a take-it-or-leave-it offer that has to be accepted, usually immediately, without the offer being relayed to the other houses. Obviously, if the money is so substantial that the publishing house and the author do not wish to risk getting less elsewhere, it may very well be accepted. On the other hand, occasionally the hardcover publisher will feel that the first person's enthusiasm will be echoed elsewhere and, usually after consultation with the author, the house may decide to take a chance on a later auction that might bring in even more income.

Another situation where only one publisher will be shown a book, without that publisher's being the option holder, can occur because of specific circumstances: Sometimes the editor who bought the author's last book at another house has moved to a new paperback house and is keenly interested in the author; sometimes a paperback house has a specific line (child care, masculine adventure, or religion) that makes it logical to try that house to be assured of the best possible publication and marketing approach.

First Serial

Let us suppose that one's upcoming season's list includes a new novel by a major literary writer and a nonfiction book about the Washington political scene. Both manuscripts have been delivered to the subsidiary rights department—which can number from one person with or without a secretary to a group of ten people or more. The first step is to read and evaluate the books in order to decide where to submit them.

A literary novel might be sent to the *Atlantic Monthly, Family Circle, Harper's, Ladies Home Journal, McCall's,* the *New Yorker, Playboy, Redbook,* and *Vogue.* A less serious novel—a light romance or a family saga, for example—would not be sent to the *Atlantic, Harper's,* or the *New Yorker.* A novel of primarily male interest—one without a strong female character with which the reader can identify—would probably not be of interest to a women's magazine. In other words, knowledge of the fiction market, gained by reading the book and reading as many magazines as possible to see what kind of fiction they are currently printing, is important in successful periodical placement.

This is equally true in the licensing of nonfiction to magazines. The hypothetical nonfiction book about the Washington political scene might be logically submitted to some of the same periodicals mentioned above: the *Atlantic Monthly, Harper's,* the *New Yorker,* and *Playboy.* But it could also be sent to some of the Washington-based magazines and, assuming the content was of major national or international importance, to *Time* and *Newsweek*. *Time*, for example, ran sections of Henry Kissinger's two books and Alexander Haig's book *Caveat* before the volumes were officially published. *People* magazine, another Time-Life publication, buys many celebrity biographies and autobiographies.

It is also very important to know how long the magazine's lead time is—that is, the time it takes from acquisition of material to appearance in the issue. For monthly magazines, lead time can be as much as six months or longer. Weekly periodicals require less lead time, but they still may need two or three months in order to get material together to be edited for both content and space requirements and set in type.

Subsidiary rights in all areas involves a continuous process of decision making. In handling periodical rights, the first principal decision one must make is whether to make an exclusive submission to a single periodical in the hope that it will elicit a very high offer, thereby precluding other people from being shown the book. Or should one submit simultaneously to several periodicals to establish a general market price? First serial guarantees can range from a low of under $1,000 to over $100,000. The second major decision—if more than one magazine makes an offer and if the moneys offered are not too different—is to determine which of the two (or more) magazines would be better in terms of publicity and advance promotion for the book. One magazine might offer less money but more prestige—or vice versa. Obviously, the author should be consulted if the decision would make a substantial difference to his or her pocket, but one should also take into account not only the money but the influence that particular periodical sale would have on the other subsidiary rights. A factor that should be borne in mind is that periodical licenses are almost invariably for a flat fee and not guaranteed against royalties.

MOTION-PICTURE, DRAMATIC, AND TELEVISION RIGHTS

In recent years there has been a trend away from the "majors"—Warner, Fox, Universal, MGM/United Artists, Columbia, and so on—in movies and television as initial acquirers of rights for their media. Currently, independent producers vie with these majors in trying to acquire a book (which they more often than not call a property), frequently on an option basis with a prearranged price for a later total purchase, for appearance on either television or theatrical screen or both. The rights department will find that very soon after a novel is delivered to the publisher, the phones will buzz with calls from people from (usually) New York and California, wanting to consider the book. Since the publisher's share of these rights is likely to be no more than 10 percent on the rare occasion that the publisher controls them, there may not be much immediate economic incentive. However, news of a movie or TV miniseries[2] sale will greatly enhance the value of the book to prospective book-club or paperback-reprint buyers. The number of people to be dealt with in the movies and TV is ever increasing and, unless one has had years of work in the field, it is very difficult to separate out the potential buyers from the browsers. Furthermore, with the contractual complications of movie, TV, and now videocassette rights multiplying all the time, some publishers find that it is more practical for them to retain one of the many established West Coast movie agencies to handle such rights for them.

In theory stage rights also come under this category. Although it is occasionally possible to arrange such a license, these are few and far between.

FOREIGN RIGHTS

The languages that most publishers deal with on a continuing basis are English (United Kingdom, Australia, and other British Commonwealth countries), German (Austria, Germany, and Switzerland), Portuguese (Brazil and Portugal), and Spanish (Argentina, Mexico, Spain, and all of Latin America except Brazil). Countries not covered by these languages, but dealt with regularly, are Denmark, Finland, France, Italy, Japan, the Netherlands, Norway, and Sweden. Some rights departments work directly, publisher to publisher, in each country. They feel that they can learn enough about the overseas marketplace by reading publishers' catalogs, by looking at overseas best-seller lists, and by making occasional overseas visits. Other publishers feel that their income from foreign rights does not justify this much effort, and they prefer to share their percentages with overseas agents who will represent them in different countries. In this latter case, the U.S.-based publisher will send advance lists of forthcoming books to the coagents. These lists indicate which books are going to be handled by the publisher and which will be handled by U.S. or British literary agents. If the author is extremely well known, and if his or her previous books have been successful in overseas markets, foreign publishers will clamor to obtain first access to rights in their countries. *Ragtime* by E. L. Doctorow and *Sophie's Choice* by William Stryon were rapidly acquired by publishers over the globe during the time of their U.S. publication.

Some foreign publishers have found that it is useful to appoint representatives in New York to scout for future titles from the various publishers. These scouts will often represent more than one publisher, although they usually represent only one publisher per country. Thus the same person will report to one house in Italy, one in France, and one each in Sweden, Germany, and Great Britain and try to relay back to each of the home offices just what seems to be appropriate for the respective lists. An effective scout must therefore know not only the U.S. book scene but the specific requirements and tastes of each different European publishing house (there are relatively few scouts for the Orient or for South America in the United States).

Additional Rights

These five areas provide the major income and publicity benefits for a publisher. Some other areas that a rights department handles or could handle are:

1. Second serial/periodical rights: licensing to newspapers and magazines after book publication (income from these is usually relatively modest and primarily serves as extra publicity for the book)
2. Hardcover reprint rights: the right to reprint hardcover editions of the book, primarily for library use, usually for a modest advance ($100 to $1,000) against royalties
3. Cassette rights: licensing the right to transcribe books on tape or records to be sold or rented to people who want to "read" as they drive, cook, or knit or to visually handicapped people
4. Licensing rights: licensing the right to manufacture articles connected with books—for instance, licensing illustrations from a book to a wallpaper company for reproduction as wallpaper art (the needlework launching of items based on *Paddington Bear* is one example)

To sum up, if something from a book can be adapted into another form or medium, there is the possibility of a subsidiary rights license. The areas touched on in this chapter are those areas most frequently negotiated. But the challenge of subsidiary rights, and the fun, is in thinking about new areas to explore and about old (backlist) titles to "recycle." Of course, the major part of one's daily work involves current titles and the more usual areas of negotiation. But the alert rights department worker—whether department head or newly arrived entry-level assistant—can expand the rights horizon substantially by thinking creatively about reuse of backlist books and/or new and different ways to exploit all books.

Notes

1. The percentages cited in this section, which are negotiated separately for each publishing agreement, are averages based upon my publishing experience.

2. A one-time appearance on TV is less meaningful, since it is difficult to coordinate paperback release with the changing TV schedules.

PART FOUR

The Channels of Marketing

CHAPTER FOURTEEN

Personal Bookshops

RICHARD H. NOYES

There is no such thing as a typical independent personal U.S. bookstore. There are large stores, very small "Mom and Pop" operations, and everything in between. Many have simple low-cost fixtures, with book jackets supplying the decoration. At the other extreme, there is the elegance of stores like Rizzoli and Scribners in New York City. Most general bookstores carry adult trade, juvenile, professional, and a smattering of scientific, technical, and perhaps medical books. Most also have trade and mass-market paperbacks, which now account for as much as 40–50 percent of a store's gross sales, as opposed to 10–20 percent not so many years ago. Rarely are textbooks stocked, as they have a much more limited market and are sold at short discount by the publisher (that is, 20 percent rather than the usual 40 percent). The majority of personal bookstores will special order in-print books for their customers. Despite the increased costs involved they realize that it stimulates repeat business and builds considerable customer loyalty.

U.S. bookstores vary in many ways, but we also have a number of things in common. We operate with a predetermined retail price instead of the net pricing system found in a number of other countries. There is no acceptable way to mark up prices except with specially imported, out-of-print, and secondhand books. So, the secret for survival is quite simple, although it's hardly easy: All expenses must be controlled rigorously. Rents can't be decreased, and utilities and many other expenses are fixed. Salaries are about the only significant expense that can be adjusted. Historically, bookstores have paid their staffs poorly; often they have relied on those who had outside income.

Until only a few years ago bookstores paid about 1.5 percent of sales for postal charges on incoming shipments of books from the publishers. But because of marked increases in postal rates (350 percent since 1970), these charges now amount to 3.5 percent or more. When a respectable net profit for a store is a modest 3 or 4 percent, one can imagine how a tripling of this one cost factor has hurt all retail booksellers. Add to this the marked increases in the retail prices of books in the last few

RICHARD H. NOYES owns The Chinook Bookshop, Colorado Springs, Colorado.

years and the fact that many consumers have come to view books as a discretionary purchase that must be weighed against the staples in their budgets: The result is that although dollar sales have grown considerably since 1974, the increase in unit sales has been modest.

A recent survey has established that about half of the independent trade bookstores today have net profits of less than 1 percent of sales, and thus are not profitable when judged by reasonable standards of financial performance. Obviously this is a troubled time for books in this country, yet retail bookselling is experiencing the greatest surge of growth and vitality since World War II. In 1970 there were about three hundred retail stores whose primary business was bookselling. Today the tally is closer to eight thousand, with much of the growth in the chains.

The most apparent change in bookselling in this country in the last decade of course has been the meteoric nationwide growth of chain bookstores. The recognized giants—B. Dalton Bookseller and Walden-books—have hundreds of stores, located in nearly every large shopping center. We have seen the trend toward giantism as it has affected book publishing, with independent companies being swallowed up by con-glomerates. Now many of us who are independent booksellers are becoming concerned that the privately owned and operated bookshop may become a relic of the past.

In 1972, there was only one chain with more than one hundred branches, and the four largest chains accounted for 11.6 percent of all trade book sales. If B. Dalton's and Waldenbooks' long-term predictions were correct, they shared over 50 percent of all general-interest bookstore sales by 1983.

There is no question that the chains have created many more customers for books by opening stores in high-traffic, expensive locations that did not have bookstores, and their bright, new advertising and merchandising methods have shaken the cobwebs from the minds of many an old-fashioned bookseller. No doubt the traditional bookstore will continue to benefit from this enlarged reading public. But I can't help wondering about the role of the individual in the giant book-chain operations. Overall, are the managers and employees of these branch stores more knowledgeable and professional? Are they better paid or rewarded in other less tangible but important ways? Do they really care personally about their particular branch store and the quality of service they provide their customers?

Will they (I quote from the objectives of the American Booksellers Association—ABA) "recognize and respond to their unique educative and cultural responsibilities which they owe to their communities"? Will they also "promote high standards of professional competence, conduct, and ethics, and combat unfair trade practices by all legal means"? Or is it more likely ultimately that their individualism and imagination will be frustrated and submerged?

The fact is that for some happy reason the chains have not prevented budding independent booksellers from opening new stores, particularly in smaller towns. More independent stores started up in the 1970s than in the twenty years before. The optimists in our ranks believe that by offering full personal service and a well-maintained inventory of variety and depth, geared to local tastes, the independent bookstore will be able to survive.

The Book Inventory

Because of the enormous increase in the number of books published in recent years and the greater expansion of subject matter now covered, the retail bookseller understandably often feels somewhat overwhelmed. Most stores can stock from five thousand to ten thousand titles out of the tens of thousands available, and this overabundance is bound to have some interesting ramifications. One likely trend is toward more small stores specializing in certain subject areas such as children's books, science fiction, or health books.

The most significant technological advance in bookselling in a hundred years, of course, is the development of the computer and its related facilities, particularly in the area of bookstore inventory control. The chains and the very largest independent stores are now plugged in, and the possibilities for the future are fascinating. Manual control of inventory is still preferable for the small- and middle-sized store, but the day will come when a public system is available, affordable, and capable of giving full information on a daily basis.

Selecting a new season's books for the store as much as six months before publication can be one of the bookseller's most pleasant and challenging functions. Most booksellers rely heavily on publishers' representatives for their advice and additional information during the two or more annual visits they make to the stores. The number of copies planned for the first printing, the advertising moneys to be expended, author tours, and other special promotion plans—this information is valuable. The buyer bases the decision on various other factors as well, such as an author's previous track record, possible particular local interest, and the representative's personal recommendation.

Certain subject areas like new fiction (of course as yet unread by the buyer) can be a real test for us. As one bookseller said, "It's like playing blindman's bluff." Years ago, I ordered no copies of a first novel with a southern setting about which the representative really knew nothing. Yes, I was later proven just a wee bit wrong; the book was Harper Lee's *To Kill a Mockingbird*.

The general public probably assumes that a larger bookstore regularly orders new titles in quantities of fifty to one hundred or more, but that's far from the case. Ones to threes are quite respectable quantities for titles that often have first printings of from five thousand to ten thousand copies. Of course, we order larger quantities for the few obvious best-sellers, but frugality in the initial order is generally good advice. It is far better for both bookseller and publisher if a store samples titles widely, rather than ordering fewer in great depth. And since bookstores pay the freight on returns to publishers, excessive returns must be avoided with the increased postal rates.

Returns are an aspect of bookstore operation that is unique in retailing. Most publishers (the manufacturer) and wholesalers offer books to retailers on a returnable basis. The policies vary considerably, but a typical one would permit a store to return excess stock of a title (in salable condition) any time after four months beyond publication but not later than one year. About half of the publishers require permission in advance, with the bookseller supplying the original quantity ordered, invoice number, date, and the discount noted for each title. The store then receives credit for future purchases at its invoiced discount. At our own store, Chinook, our returns in the past several years have been running from 10 to 13 percent of the year's purchases, which is just about right. If they were higher we'd be overordering; if lower, we'd probably be understocked or not sampling widely enough. Some stores opt to put some or all of their unsold books, marked down, on their sale table rather than return them (it saves the freight and handling). But generally I believe it is preferable to return on a predetermined regular basis. Nothing is as unsalable at almost any price as most year-old hardbound fiction, and a bookstore must not build up dead stock. Some publishers have seen the wisdom of loosening up their returns policies to encourage booksellers to keep titles in stock longer and to effect better representation of their backstock, but as it is today, most new fiction rarely has a shelf life of more than four to five months.

Traditionally, bookstores in this country have ordered their new and backstock hardbound books directly from each publisher, whereas the book wholesalers serviced libraries as their major market. Among the benefits of direct ordering for the store were higher discounts and seasonal backstock offers, and it was particularly practical for those bookstores doing a heavy special-order business. Only in the last few years have wholesalers become a significant source of supply for bookstores nationwide. New ordering programs like the microfiche system originated by the Ingram Book Company have assured booksellers of a title's availability, and the ease of telephone ordering by title code number has cut down delivery time on the more popular titles to about five days on average.

A large wholesaler can inventory many more titles than the average bookstore, and such a single source of supply for at least a large number of their needs has been the dream of booksellers for generations. Currently about 40 percent of bookstore purchases are from wholesalers; this percentage probably will increase in coming years. Most stores will continue to do their seasonal new title hardbound and trade paperback ordering direct, but the majority will probably divide their reorders between wholesalers and publishers. Certainly all of us are eager to have a healthy wholesale scene regionally and nationally, if for no other purpose than the quick supply of fast-moving titles. As anyone in the industry is well aware, Phil Donahue, Gene Shalit, and others can "sell" thousands of copies of a title by noon of the day it has been featured on their morning shows.

Advertising

Bookstores usually turn to newspapers for their advertising efforts, either to promote a particular book or line of books on a cooperative basis with the publisher (whereby they are generally reimbursed 75 percent of the cost) or with institutional ads promoting the store, its services, and its inventory, which of course they pay for themselves. Often ads will be slotted into the book section, or sometimes an appropriate title ad will be placed in related sections like business, sports, or cooking.

Budget limitations and the target audience determine the choice of media: everything from the Yellow Pages, to local magazines, performing arts programs, direct mail, and—increasingly in recent years—radio, which is much more affordable than TV. There is a lot of truth to the old adage that word of mouth is the best advertising of all; too often bookstores seem to forget that first-class service, the quality and quantity of their inventory, their window displays, staff demeanor, and the like will spread the word to the community, either good or bad. For many years a famous bookstore on the West Coast did no formal advertising. Its owner believed that his store's competence and its huge inventory did the advertising: "that's where I put my money." But most booksellers find that more is needed, particularly in the case of a new store that has to establish an image for itself.

Most stores allocate from 1 to 2 percent of gross sales for regular advertising expense and prepare a plan for the year in advance. As the majority of independent bookstores gross only in the range of $100,000 to $150,000 a year, this means a budget of about $2,000 for advertising, which can buy very little. The energetic bookseller can double his money by using publisher cooperative funds, but this involves a lot of time and paperwork, which is much more affordable for the very large store and the chains. As a result, the primary financial burden for promoting a book remains with the publisher.

Bookstores have always enjoyed considerable free advertising and promotion in the media simply because their product is books, not pencils, and books are news. Many booksellers have reviewed books in newspapers and on the radio, at no expense to them except time, establishing themselves as personalities and, of course, plugging their stores as well. The possibilities of free promotion are endless, particularly for the bookseller who is active in public life. Over the years the Chinook has garnered thousands of dollars worth of free attention in the media; no other kind of retailing is so fortunate in this respect.

Distribution Problems

The words "book distribution" conjure up all sorts of feelings in the retail bookseller—most of them unpleasant. Despite the endless debate over the years, the pattern of book distribution remains as chaotic as ever. Perhaps electronic data processing will supply the answer one day, but in the meantime we remain hobbled by antiquated shipping and delivery procedures, and the age-old problems seem to grow more exhausting every day. I'm convinced that "service" is the magic word for the successful independent bookseller in the future—full personal service. And a bookseller who is to give good service obviously must receive the same from his source of supply. In my own store, one of our key services is our complete special-ordering program—literally thousands of books a year for individual customers. A recent study we made revealed that our average order direct to a publisher now takes six days longer to arrive in our receiving room than it did only a few years ago—and that additional time was mostly taken up by publisher's processing and was not the fault of the postal system. Moreover, only 6 percent of the time did we receive full information on books not shipped.

All too often we receive notice with a carton of books that the shipment is incomplete and that "the original invoice when it arrives will explain." In the case of one well-known publisher, the invoice arrival time lag is still another week to ten days. In many cases, the packing list does not indicate the discount or even the retail price. If publishers regularly fail to explain the status of titles not shipped, what can we tell our customers?

Last year the Chinook ordered books from more than five hundred U.S. publishers, and almost every one had different policies, terms, and forms. Most of them billed us for the insurance charges on their shipments to us as well as postal costs; many also billed us for what they term "handling charges" on each shipment. I cannot understand why we should pay what is their proper cost of doing business, not ours. I would guess that it takes about four months for most publishers to give us credit for books we have returned to them, but of course we are expected to pay our bills in full each month.

In most cases when problems arise the bookseller is increasingly frustrated with his inability to communicate with publishers. Years ago we could telephone or write to a person (a human being) in a publishing house and expect to receive an answer or at least the assurance that something would be done. In recent years, since the advent of the computer, our efforts often seem futile. The list of bookseller complaints about publisher distribution is a long one. Perhaps the most frustrating thing is that they seem to us to be in-house problems—problems that the publisher should be able to control.

Booksellers and Bookselling

What are the basics of good retail bookselling? Here's one opinion. Good booksellers are professionals and handle themselves accordingly. They take their job seriously, find bookselling an absorbing and challenging vocation, and quite in accord with their avocation, which is usually the world of books and reading. As professionals they need never "scrape and bow" to the customer; they are not clerks in a dime store. At the same time, professionals know enough to recognize that they don't know it all and that arrogance will never win or influence anybody. When staff members (and I insist they should never be called clerks or salespeople) take their jobs seriously they exude this professionalism somehow, in a subtle way, and customers invariably respond with interest and respect. Professional booksellers have their own literary preferences and judgments, of course, and many of their customers seek their advice and rely on their judgment. But when the tastes of their customers differ, the situation must be handled with cheerful tact. If someone comes in and asks what you think of giving *The Prophet* to a girl who is graduating from Stanford, with highest honors in English Literature, you don't have to collapse in literary indignation and mirth. A touch of humility is always a charming quality—and can be totally disarming when coupled with competence.

The good bookseller is also an actor to a significant degree—a role player, a semichameleon of sorts who can't quite resist responding differently and appropriately to each person he deals with during the day. It is gamesmanship to be sure, but it's honest, creative, and valid. And it should be fun; that's one of the rewards of the retail book business. For example, I really enjoy getting through to that high school girl who hates books, me, and particularly her teacher who assigned her those three paperbacks to read over Christmas vacation. I want to have her leave the store smiling and maybe with a glimmer of a feeling that she may actually enjoy one of these titles. Or there's the hard-hat guy who came in for an auto repair manual, who distrusts anyone with longish hair and presumed intelligence, and of course feels out of place surrounded by all these books. It's not that difficult to make him feel comfortable; if I succeed he'll come back to us when the family needs a cookbook, a dictionary, or a calorie counter or whatever.

It's the simple sales that aren't much fun actually—the customers who know exactly what they want, whether they want it wrapped or sent, and don't ask questions or demand much time. These sales are a godsend during rush hours, but if that were all there were to bookselling, you could count me out.

Robert Hale, one of New England's most respected booksellers, described the job this way in his lecture on the history of bookselling given at the ABA Bookseller's School, 1972–1980:

> When a clerk in a shoe store sells a pair of shoes, the customer has acquired protection for his feet. When the clerk in a hardware store sells an extension cord, he has provided a plastic product to serve a single purpose—to conduct energy from one place to another. These are tangibles. The bookseller's product is tangible. It is physical in that it can be held, wrapped, carried about, but only the package of the product is finite. The bookseller's real product is boundless, beyond measure, infinite.
>
> When I sell someone a copy of *Out of Africa,* I'm not selling a few ounces of paper, I am passing on the glory of unspoiled Kenya, people and animals living free. I am introducing the reader to Farah and Kamante, whom they will never forget, and to Isak Dinesen, the Baroness Blixen, who is going to open whole new worlds for them. They will become a part of their experience and enrich their existence.
>
> Booksellers are magicians. As did Houdini, we open locks, we release

chains. As with Saroyan, we exchange illusions for dreams and surrealism for reality.

The American Booksellers Association was formed in 1900 particularly to address booksellers' problems of discounting, distribution, and pricing—much the same problems that exist today (though it is interesting that antitrust laws now largely forbid us as an organization to discuss them publicly or privately).

Member stores receive a full battery of publications, including the all-important *Book Buyers Handbook,* which lists complete information and terms for hundreds of publishers and distributors; the weekly "Newswire," which lists forthcoming author tour schedules, radio and television interviews, and book reviews; the hardbound and paperback *Basic Book Lists;* and the *Manual on Bookselling,* which covers every aspect of opening and maintaining a bookstore. In addition the ABA publishes a monthly magazine for booksellers, conducts seminars around the country, supports regional organizations, and several times a year offers three- to five-day in-depth bookseller schools for the prospective and the experienced booksellers.

New bookstores, sufficiently capitalized and under capitalized, are opening at a surprising rate in all parts of the country, operated by people young and old, experienced and raw, some of whom have taken the time to do a proper job of market research. A lot of preparatory work is absolutely necessary to assume a reasonable chance of success. Despite the aids of the ABA, the best background of all is several years of experience working in a successful store.

We are told that one out of thirteen Americans buys books and that a community of at least twenty-five thousand is necessary to support a bookstore. Equally as important are the demographics of income and education levels, the age and life-styles of the people, future growth potential, and of course the competitive scene. I have been convinced that an initial investment of at least $50,000 is required for almost any new store anywhere (others believe the figure now should be closer to $100,000). But many stores today are opening on far less.

So what are the personal qualities basic to bookselling? For a start, here is one bookseller's list of criteria for selecting new sales staff members:

1. A strong literary background—the best you can afford. Yet we've found that degrees don't really mean that much. Bookselling should be a constant state of learning. The person who continues to grow is my dish of tea.

2. Extensive bookselling experience would be nice, but this is probably the least important criterion. We'd rather have a basically bright person

whom we can train—in our way. It always surprises us how quickly a good new staff member learns the field.

3. We try to find someone who is logical and direct, with a good memory, someone who is not averse to picky detail work—there is plenty of it.

4. We look for a person who complements our staff as it is at that moment. A variety of ages, races, types, backgrounds, and interests is highly desirable.

5. In a store that is not totally departmentalized, the staff is very much a team and must work together. We avoid the prima donna or the lone wolf; however, we certainly do draw on the individual talents and interests of the staff. For example, we have a Bible expert who knows no peer, and we use that expertise whenever possible.

6. Old-fashioned common sense is another vital ingredient. We can tolerate almost any idiosyncracy if the staff member has a high degree of common sense, joined with a basic thoughtfulness and a sensitivity to, and a sincere interest in, people.

7. Of course, anyone we hire to sell books must have a truly deep affection for books and reading, and we want him or her to have a very personal pride in our bookshop. We feel very lucky that we have a staff that feels proud and possessive about "their" store.

8. Call it self-motivation—we try to find the individual who will do more than the average adequate job and who has the energy for it.

Bookselling is hard work, make no mistake. Particularly when the store is small it involves long hours and rare vacations and a lot of routine chores far less glamorous than the general public realizes. The successful bookseller not only must know how to buy and sell books but also all the many intricacies of maintaining a retail business. Even when your store turns a profit the prospects for wealth are slim. Why in the world then do so many intelligent people open bookstores every year?

The owner-manager (and most are both) of an independent bookstore is his own person; success or failure is largely in his own hands. He or she no doubt is an addicted reader; somehow bookselling became the special province in the world of books. On a daily basis the bookseller meets and discusses books (ideas) with the most interesting people in the community. What a pleasure it is putting books and people together.

Most booksellers consider themselves unique in the world of retailing. At best, we truly are an unusual group. We tend to be articulate, intelligent, sensitive people, whose job, if we are to be successful, requires us to be comfortable in the world of arts and letters and also expert in day-to-day retail commerce. Bookstores are allied with schools and libraries in promoting the reading habit. Good booksellers are guides, counselors, and friends to their customers and communities; they truly respect their merchandise and believe a vital part of their function is to improve the human condition.

Personal bookselling has always been a little different; certainly we have not been representative of industry in the usual sense. It has always appealed to people of intelligence with a strong feeling of individuality. Perhaps it's because of these people and the reservoir of their talents that a healthy environment for invention and innovation will continue in bookselling in our country.

The most heartening development in recent years is the appearance of a new type of professionalism in our ranks, and it is long overdue. It is all well and good to admire the uniqueness of bookselling, but it is folly to ignore the proven practices of retail management and merchandising. Only those stores that recognize the need for better business management will survive in the years to come. With new attitudes and methods of operating, and a genuinely competitive marketplace, the smaller independent bookstore will have a reasonable chance to prosper in the future.

The audience for books will continue to increase; there is no other form of communication more flexible and capable of responding quickly to change in our society. Bookstores too will grow in number and competence, and this country one day will have adequate retail book resources in every community of any size.

CHAPTER FIFTEEN

Bookstore Chains

ELIOT LEONARD

One of the most important developments in the trade-book industry over the past two decades has been the growth of the retail bookstore chains. Two companies that evolved in the mid-1960s, B. Dalton and Waldenbooks, have far outdistanced the others in sales volume and number of branches. Together they now have over fifteen hundred branches, and each expects to add sixty to ninety stores annually. B. Dalton, owned by the Dayton Hudson Corporation, is based in Minneapolis. Walden's parent is K-Mart Corporation; it is headquartered in Stamford, Connecticut. Both owners are retail conglomerates.

There are about ten other national and regional bookstore chains with twenty to seventy branches each. They include established firms like Doubleday nationally and Kroch's & Brentano's (Chicago) and Barnes & Noble (New York) regionally. There are two large religious bookstore chains, Zondervan and Cokesbury. And in the past six years, a large and fast-growing discount chain has come on the scene: Crown Books. It is establishing itself as a major factor and competitor in bookselling. Crown has already opened over one hundred stores in Washington, D.C., Los Angeles, San Francisco, San Diego, and other cities. Evidently Crown's goal is to blanket the big, established book markets of the country with branches. There are also dozens of other book chains of all kinds and sizes, most with fewer than ten units.

Today, bookstore chains have about 4,000 branches across the country. It is estimated that in 1984, the total volume of the twelve largest chains was about $1 billion in about 2,000 stores. The two giants, Walden and Dalton, produced about 75 percent of this volume, equal to about 20 percent of the national trade-book sales in bookstores. These two companies achieved about the same volume, although Walden had about 150 more stores than Dalton.

Many factors account for the development and expansion of the book chains. The growth of large regional shopping centers was a major element in the expansion of all kinds of specialty retail chains from one or two regions to national distribution. Dayton Department Store Management

---

ELIOT LEONARD was formerly senior vice president of B. Dalton Bookseller, Minneapolis.

in Minneapolis saw the need for a national chain of general bookstores and started opening B. Dalton stores in the big malls in 1966. Shortly before this, Walden had started its chain. Originally the company had hundreds of leased book and rental departments in department stores all over the country, but it gradually released these units as the chain of bookstores throve.

The general acceptance of self-service and self-selection was of major importance in shedding the carriage-trade image that had been characteristic of bookselling and in inviting more and more people to cross the thresholds of the book emporiums. The explosion of the paperback industry helped to alert more people to books. Another factor in the growth of the chains was the apparent downgrading of the book departments in department stores in the 1960s and 1970s. Their managements looked for higher sales per square foot and return on investment comparable to other departments of the store. When it was not produced, book departments were condensed and/or moved to upstairs areas where customer traffic was much smaller. Fewer potential customers and reduced inventories to attain higher turnover led to a cycle of lower and lower volume.

The larger the chain, the more likely it is to have a range of store sizes, with inventory tailored to each location. In the smaller chains, most of which are privately owned with all branches within a single city or region, the stores are usually more uniform in inventory selection and image. Some of the smaller chains are owned by book and magazine wholesalers and sell mainly those two categories. And some medium and small chains have so many sidelines that books constitute only 30–70 percent of the inventory and sales. Social and commercial stationery, greeting cards, and miscellaneous gift lines compose the nonbook inventory. Almost every general bookstore in the country, even the largest, sells at least one sideline during the year, such as calendars, magazines, and bookmarks and bookplates.

Up to now, the two leading chains have concentrated their stores in the large regional shopping centers, with 80 percent or more of their branches in these malls. Some units of other chains are also in these same centers, many of which have two or three bookstores. Most of the traffic is brought in by the department stores located in the centers, but bookstores are among the specialty-store leaders in attracting shoppers. It is difficult for an independent bookstore operator to locate in these malls because the developers understandably prefer the virtually guaranteed rent that will be paid over the term of the lease by the successful large-chain booksellers.

Not many new regional malls are being built today, so the chains are looking for more locations in other kinds of business areas. Dalton and

Walden are now opening many units in community or neighborhood centers, in downtown central business districts, on high-traffic city arteries, and in other areas where large numbers of potential customers can park and shop conveniently. The major chains know how to analyze the demographics of areas to determine how good a market each would be for books and how to open the right-size store with the right inventory. Both Walden and Dalton have a very good record of successful stores: It is estimated that 90–95 percent of all their stores are profitable.

Although the two leaders have opened stores as small as 1,500 square feet with volumes under $300,000 a year, most of their attention is focused on locations with a potential volume of $400,000 and up. Some branches are as large as 10,000 or even 25,000 square feet and achieve sales of $2 million and more. On the average, the leading chains seek markets of seventy-five thousand or more people, of above-average education and income, with a high percentage in the 20–50 age bracket. There are exceptions where chains have opened stores in much smaller markets, but these have an educated and very high income clientele.

The cost of retail space has increased so much in recent years that the average size of chain branches has been reduced steadily. To keep up their high return on investment, the large chains attempt to use space more efficiently. They look for sales of at least $125 per square foot in the first year of a store's operation, and $200 to $300 per square foot in three to six years. It is estimated that the average sales of all leading chains, including new and mature stores, is now in the range of $150 to $175 per square foot.

The large retail companies differ in the way in which they are controlled and managed and in their operating and merchandising philosophies. But one element is common to most chains: They are engaged in mass merchandising. They are in business to make books available to as many people as possible and to make a reasonable profit. The chains attempt to offer a large selection of general books, although some emphasize certain departments and categories over others. Hardbound books are stocked in most chains, but because of the rising cost of books in recent years, paperbounds are increasing in their share of space used, titles stocked, and dollar sales. Today, most leading chains sell more softbound than hardbound books, and in some companies even the dollar volume of paperback sales is higher.

Of the two major chains, Walden seems to emphasize paperbacks and bargain books in most of its branches, with a smaller selection of new and basic hardbound titles. Dalton emphasizes a wide selection of all kinds of new and backstock titles, with bargain books a smaller segment of inventory than Walden's in most stores. Recently, Walden has been stocking more titles, with the average store having between 12,000 and

20,000, while Dalton claims an average of 2,000 or 3,000 more titles in similar-size stores, with over 30,000 in very large stores. It is assumed that Dalton plans an inventory turnover of about three times a year, whereas Walden aims for a little faster turnover. It is estimated that Dalton achieves a volume of about seventy-five thousand dollars more per average branch annually. It also has many more stores of over six thousand square feet, some with two or three floors of books in the downtown areas of large cities.

Stores of other leading chains also vary in size, volume, and merchandise mix. Each promotes the uniqueness the chain feels serves its market and clientele best and most profitably. Most of the smaller chains stock more sidelines than Dalton and Walden, which have gradually dropped those lines although they continue to stock calendars and magazines in most branches.

One reason for B. Dalton's ability to maintain a wide selection profitably is its well-organized central buying system, almost totally controlled by computer. All inventory needs are divided by departments and categories among thirty or more buyers, who watch individual titles and store sales results to reorder books, using past history and experience to buy new titles in categories for which they are responsible. The main departments are hardbound books, mass-market paperbacks, trade paperbacks, bargain books, and children's books. Category breakdown on the computers for reorder purposes varies by department, with over one hundred in the hardback and paperback areas to about a dozen in the juvenile department. Subject breakdown in the stores for display purposes differs from branch to branch, mainly according to space and inventory. A small store may have only seventy-five to one hundred categories in all, but a very large store might have two or three times as many. As Walden has been developing its computer and buying systems recently, many of its procedures are now comparable to Dalton's, but are tailored for Walden's individual needs. Both companies have ongoing programs for refining their buying systems according to results and personnel available.

Up-to-date sales history is accumulated at least weekly, and daily if necessary, on computer printouts showing each store's stock condition on the fastest-selling titles. Monthly or less frequently, printouts are produced showing basic stock movement, nonmoving titles, and any other important information the Dalton and Walden buyers want to review. Reorders are placed using this most recent and past history. Periodic transaction studies are made of sales, titles, and subjects related to shoppers' buying habits and in-store traffic patterns. Dalton uses these for placement of subjects, scheduling of personnel, determining business hours, merchandise mix, and so on. These kinds of studies are needed because of the huge size of the chains, in volume and number of units;

because the top management making decisions is often hundreds of miles away; and because of the high turnover of store management and staff. The owner-manager of an independent bookstore has the advantage of being on the scene, knowing what is happening at all times, and being able to make instant changes in procedures, policies, and merchandising.

Publishing people state that Dalton is one of the best-organized companies in retail bookselling. Its computer controls and informational output in merchandising, operating, and accounting areas have been prime factors in the company's high return on sales, thought to be at or near the top of all the leading chains. The computer programs are continually being refined for more efficient output and uses in all areas of the company.

Walden has recently installed a sophisticated "point of sale" system in all stores. As a sale is made, the title is captured by the cash register computer. Reorder requests from stores are also keyed into the register daily. Each night the branches are polled, and sales and ordering information is collected for review by buyers the next morning. Walden and Dalton assign authority and responsibility to the store managers for buying—from local wholesalers or the nearest source—regional books, books by local authors, emergency copies of any title, and any stock customers want that is not provided by the central buyers.

The central buyers of both chains tell the branches where each title should be displayed in the stores, specifying the titles to be promoted in the best impulse locations. All personnel are reviewed at least once a year to ensure high motivation and productivity.

All leading chains and especially the two majors plan for and need high return on investment. Where the independent bookseller is often satisfied with a reasonable profit on sales at the end of the year, the big companies must satisfy their officers, stockholders, and other investors. Expense control is of very high priority. Economies of scale are sought at all times in all areas of the operation, which is one reason for so much standardization, uniformity, and centralization. Most direction in personnel, merchandising, and general operations comes from headquarters. Walden and Dalton have regional managers in the field, each supervising ten to twenty stores, checking that the branches are following management direction, and recommending changes to improve weak points. The regional managers visit each branch three to six times per year on the average, with preprinted checklists to audit financial and operational results.

Because payroll is the largest operating expense, is highly controllable, and has a tremendous effect on profit, it is watched on almost a daily basis. The big companies cut payroll to the bone during some periods of the year, an action that has led to the charge that their employees are indifferent, have little knowledge of books and the stock in the stores, and offer little service. To some extent this is true, although many branches do provide service equal to local competition. The chains' policy of using many part-timers, coupled with fairly high employee turnover in some units, tends to reduce staff efficiency. The store managers are responsible for calling in help for peak sales periods. Admittedly, having the large selection and convenient shopping conditions are the main services the chains aim to provide. The sales results seem to prove that this image goal works.

The independent booksellers complain about the advantages of the chains, especially the better buying terms and high advertising allowances the publishers give the big-quantity book buyers. The small booksellers claim that the terms favor big stores and chains well beyond the economies publishers gain when selling to them versus their smaller customers. For example, a small bookseller might order from 5 to 50 books from some publishers and receive a 40–42 percent discount, whereas chains and other large booksellers could combine 100 to 500 books on an order to the same resource and earn a 43–46 percent discount or more. And there is also a complaint that there are additional, unpublished special terms for the big fellows. These allegations have not been proved, but the American Booksellers Association (ABA) and some of its member stores have been assembling factual evidence for possible legal action against some publishers.

At the 1982 ABA convention, there was a great deal of discussion about a suit brought by the Northern California Booksellers Association (NCBA) against Avon Books concerning unlawful discriminatory practices in favor of the large chains. The board of the ABA voted against offering financial support but later passed a resolution applauding the NCBA action. It also stated its intention to continue to try to persuade publishers to change their pricing policies and to help correct industry abuses. There has not yet been a resolution to the suit.

No doubt chains put competitive pressure on the independent book-sellers. We have heard that some small stores have gone out of business, and other booksellers say they cannot compete with the big inventories, heavy advertising and promotion, and huge investment money behind the chains. But we have also heard that many have been holding their own with nearby chains and have become better merchandisers and managers in the process of adjustment. And according to reports, more small bookshops open each year than close. It is obvious that an in-depth survey needs to be made to get a true picture of the situation and status of small stores, the real effect of big-store competition, and how it is contested.

In the competitive struggle for customers and sales, both kinds of bookstores have their advantages and disadvantages. Along with electronic automation, the chains have centralized with quantity buying, professional merchandising and operating direction, efficient market research, good locations with large stores, heavy promotional budgets, tight expense controls, and available backup financing. The majors have the resources to stock their branches with as wide and deep a selection of books as is needed, while trying to offer some services. On the other hand, the smaller independent stores have the managing owner on site, with the entrepreneurial spirit, feeling, and intuition that have made many such stores very successful and profitable. The owner is available to supervise, teach, and motivate employees on the spot, to alter procedures, and to make other changes immediately in merchandising and operations. On average, there is more personal selling and customer service and less employee turnover, which helps create an image of book knowledge and of interest in the customer. This image is also helped by the fact that small-store people are always dealing with authors and titles rather than with International Standard Book Number (ISBN) and other machine numbers when working with the inventory. The salespeople gain more merchandise knowledge, which makes it easier for them to discuss books with customers and even allows them more time to spend with potential customers. In the chains, staff more often tends to be tied up with the duties of checking, receiving, displaying, and returning that turn their attention away from customers at times.

A major problem of the chains is personnel. In large companies with hundreds of branches and ten or more employees per unit, communications from headquarters and field management sometimes break down. The policies, routines, and philosophy of top management are sometimes not followed or are misunderstood. Some employees might not be fully motivated, and with direction coming from hundreds of miles away, they sometimes hedge on effort. The key to good branch-store management is the store manager. Many are excellent supervisors, but others are average or just adequate. Most have trained quickly and risen through the ranks of the fast-growing major chains, becoming managers in one to three years, and have not attained the knack of teaching and effective supervision, especially with the comparatively heavy turnover of employees.

A great advantage of the chains and all large-volume booksellers is that they have the attention of the publishers. There is fairly constant communication between the publishers and their big accounts concerning the movement of new titles, promotional activities, and the potential size of the chains' orders of upcoming titles. Publishers' representatives often call on the major chains first with new books to get a feel of the titles' salability to store buyers, and they might also make more calls on the big fellows during the year, whereas many small bookshops must dig out title information on their own from circulars, periodicals, reviews, catalogs, and other media. But it should be stated that many booksellers say that the latter system of buying is preferable for them.

It is said by some that when the big chains talk, the publishers listen, even though many of them are nervous about the growth and influence of the two majors. But it must also be stated that most publishers are delighted with the volume and business the chains, discounters, and other big accounts give them. There is complaint in the industry that the chains stock only the blockbuster titles that will be heavily promoted, paying no attention to works by new authors and likely slow movers. This charge is true to some extent, just as small independent booksellers operate with different merchandising goals. But a close comparison of many chain branches with their local competition will show a much larger selection of titles in the chains. And there have been cases where the chain buyers have discovered "sleepers" by new authors on a publisher's list and started the titles on the way to best-seller sales.

The growth of the bookstore chains has been a boon to most publishers. Hundreds of new branches were opened between 1966 and 1984, selling books to millions of book readers and buyers. Walden and Dalton especially opened stores in many areas of the country where no large selections were offered before, and the inviting stores and merchandise displays practically pulled strolling shoppers into the stores from the malls and sidewalks. Though some people, both inside and outside the book industry, decry the promotion and merchandising of books like supermarket items, such techniques do put more books into the hands of more people and create more book buyers for the independents as well as the chains. Browsing bookstores has become more exciting to more people, and this development has meant that small stores have adopted some ideas for displaying books from the chains.

It is the leading chains that do most of the newspaper and other media advertising of books, earning the bulk of the cooperative-advertising money available from publishers because of their quantity buying of titles. No doubt most promotional time and money are spent with the chains, and on the top 5–10 percent of the new titles, but the people brought into the stores for these hyped titles are potential buyers for all the other books. Mass-marketing techniques are commercial, but they build volume and profit in the book business as in other specialty merchandise chains.

Those publishers who are worried about the expansion of the chains feel that they themselves might be dominated by the big companies in the future and wonder whether in a few years, when the two majors may have an even larger share of the national trade-book volume, they will be dictating what should be published. Will fewer and fewer scholarly and esoteric titles be published and stocked? Will books in the future be sold like cookies and candy, pots and pans? Will standardization eliminate the risk-taking characteristics of the retail book trade, with stores stocking only best-sellers and the hyped, expected blockbusters? Some retailers say that there are too many books published anyway. Chain buyers claim that they do stock many of the slow movers and very often have the best selection in town of many categories. They affirm that they concentrate on what the customers want and that standardization makes them more efficient and allows them to stock more of the serious literature.

Another concern of publishers is the pressure exerted by the chains and other large accounts for higher discounts, increasing in recent years with the rapid growth of discount booksellers and the increasing cost of transportation and other costs of doing business. Most of the established chains have generally held their selling prices to the suggested prices of publishers. But now that Crown Books has grown to be a major chain, with great influence in the marketplace, the other leading chains and all bookstores in competition with discounters are rethinking their pricing policies. Crown sells national best-selling hardbounds at 35 percent off, paperbounds at 25 percent off, and other recent and basic books at 10–25 percent off the list prices. But a large segment of the inventory in Crown and other discount stores includes reprints, publishers' remainders, and special buys that might be available at the identical prices in other bookstores that wish to stock them. These so-called bargain books have been reduced in price by the original publishers or have been created in cheaper format and carry full trade discounts to all bookstores. They help create a price-saving image for the stores.

Dalton and others are now experimenting with selective price cutting in competitive shopping areas, attempting to retain their customer traffic. Dalton, for example, periodically promotes a few of the national best-sellers at 40 percent off, along with a special buy of miscellaneous books at very low clearance prices. So far it appears that some volume is built with this kind of competitive promotion, but it is too early to tell the effect on annual gross margin and profit. To build a great deal of incremental traffic requires an image that *all* books in the store are discounted, which needs continual promotion of price savings. Many conventional booksellers feel that some of the glow will fade from the discounters when more bookstores promote more bargain books, including some loss leaders among best-sellers once in a while.

Industry publications and the business press have spread the word about the growth and expansion of the discounters, and many of the conventional-price booksellers, especially the independents, are in a state of panic. Some are becoming too conservative, cutting inventories and services rather than seeking ways to merchandise and manage their stores more efficiently. No doubt some small and marginal bookstores will go out of business when they lose a portion of their customers to the low-margin booksellers. The major chains are in a better position to combat the potential loss of sales because of their larger stores, wider selection of titles, and ability to pinpoint their big advertising budgets in the highly competitive areas. But it looks as though discounting is here to stay. More and more such stores and small chains have sprung up in the past couple of years. Dalton has recently announced the formation of a subsidiary company to create a chain of discount stores, Pickwick Discount Books. Branches have been opened in Columbus, Ohio, and Denver, Colorado, with plans to open dozens more in other cities in the next five years.

The policy of selling most titles at publishers' list prices might be coming to an end for more and more stores, and discounting could become prevalent, as it did in the record business some years ago. This does not bode well for the smaller bookstores, but it is difficult to see how any of the chains and other big stores can refrain from following this course. Low-margin bookselling will inevitably have an effect on the depth and spread of titles in many stores and on the stores' buying habits, their sources of supply, and customer service. Both independent bookstores and the chains will probably bring pressure on publishers for more discounts and better buying terms.

The increase in book prices in recent years has been one cause of price cutting. High prices make it worthwhile for people to drive five or ten miles to save on the purchase of one, two, or more books. The independent bookseller and others who can't compete on price will have to adjust to more specialization, more sidelines, more basic stock, more customer service, and any other action that will help them retain traffic, customers, and volume.

Thus far very few discount stores are in large regional-type shopping centers, usually because of the high rental costs. With the future growth plans of Walden, Dalton, Crown, and other chains already announced, there will be a great demand for bookstore space in all types of shopping areas. Most future stores will be in secondary-type locations like community and neighborhood "strip" centers, usually located in densely populated residential areas, with medium to high income, on the main streets with good automobile traffic. We will also see more branches of the chains in free-standing locations with parking around them, in large office complexes, and in other specialized market and shopping areas.

The 1960s and 1970s were a period of fairly easy growth for the chains. There were many primary and secondary book markets untapped by large complete bookstores. In general, the chains opened their medium- and large-size stores in primary markets of over 100,000 people within a fifteen-mile radius, containing many professional and managerial people with medium to high incomes and above-average education. Demographics for locating smaller branches in the secondary locations were usually about the same except that there might be only 50,000 to 100,000 people in a smaller area. As the chains checked out the new centers being built, they discovered high potential book markets served by stores with sparse book selections. Some were mainly paperback stores with magazines and/or other sidelines, carrying a few hardbound best-sellers and reference books. Some specialized in one or two categories with a small selection of other books. New branch after branch of the expanding chains proved that a larger market was available, as they displayed more complete general-book inventories and quickly doubled and tripled the book business in the area. It was also a period when deteriorating downtown shopping areas of the cities were being deserted for the new shopping centers, with their tremendous one-stop merchandise selections. The major book chains fit into this setting nicely, with a visually merchandised, impulse product that could be conveniently browsed by the thousands of mall shoppers.

But it is going to be tougher for the chains to grow in the 1980s. With fewer large book markets left untapped, bookstores will be smaller in size and opened in smaller markets with lower volume and profit potential per branch. More and more paperbacks will be sold, bringing down the dollar volume in the average store. It is also questionable whether the trend to discounting will create more readers and book buyers. What is certain is that profit margins will be lower in the future, and that only extraordinary sales gains will sustain or increase the current rate. If there is a reduction of return on investment, the major chains may think twice about expanding as fast as in the past. Expense control will be even more important, which could mean less customer service and reduced inventory selection. This might be advantageous to the independent bookseller in the future.

As the majors add hundreds more units, managing them could become unwieldy, and ways will be sought to alleviate the situation. There could be more authority and responsibility placed in the stores or at least within regions. There could be more buying from local wholesalers, to get needed books faster than headquarters' buyers can provide them. Current chain policy is to combine as many store orders as possible to get the best discounts from the publishers, but this will have to be weighed against the possibility of better stock turnover and lower inventory investment when buying locally, even at a lower discount.

The swiftly increasing cost of transportation will also have to be considered in the chain buying policies. Overstocks and returns to publishers are very costly, and many chains have been noted for their aggressive buying and heavy returns. Buyers might have to become more conservative. Walden has recently announced the opening of a warehouse and distribution center to stock and ship 5,000 to 7,000 titles to about three hundred of its stores in the Northeast. It expects in this way to reduce transportation costs and time and also in-store inventory. The company plans more of these centers in the future to serve branches all over the country. Some booksellers believe that the extra handling and warehouse expense could offset the advantages planned.

The chains have added a new dimension to bookselling over the past two decades, and if the problems indicated here can be overcome, the future can be bright for them. The leading chains are in a better position to sway with the blows of discounting; the increasing costs of labor, space, and transportation; and even the competition of other forms of communications emerging from the electronic revolution. The big challenge to all booksellers is to motivate more people to read and buy books. Here again the two major chains will probably lead the way. Perhaps this goal will be reached when there is more market research about who reads and why, and about what they want to read. The answers will help all booksellers.

CHAPTER SIXTEEN

The Library Market

DORIS BASS

The R. R. Bowker Company, a primary reference source for the book industry, lists 22,494 bookselling outlets in the United States. The same source indicated that there are more than four and a half times that number of libraries, broken down as follows:

- 9,335 public libraries
- 1,500 government, federal, and armed-forces libraries
- 1,865 college and university libraries
- over 10,966 business, technical, and other special libraries
- approximately 16,500 public high-school libraries and 50,086 elementary-school libraries
- 3,000 private nonreligious school libraries plus an additional number of parochial school libraries

Book budgets run the gamut: About 3,000 public libraries spend under $1,000 a year for books; about 800 public libraries spend over $50,000; and over 100 spend over $200,000. In excess of 600 university libraries spend more than $100,000 annually.

According to a Knowledge Industry Publications study, in 1976 domestic library acquisition accounted for 30 percent of all trade books published, 70 percent of all children's books, 18 percent of all professional books, and 27 percent of all books published by university presses. It is no wonder that publishers tend to believe that libraries can make winners out of losers, not just because of their number, but because libraries, not bookstores, are the primary audience for certain kinds of books. Scholarly works, first novels, poetry, beautiful children's books, and books of interest to small audiences might never see the light of day were it not for anticipated purchase by libraries. Libraries permit publishers to be public spirited without going into the red, and almost always encourage the publishing of books that enhance both knowledge and the arts. Another way in which libraries can spell the difference between profit and loss is in the relative importance of backlist books

---

DORIS BASS is director of school and college sales and marketing manager of young readers books at Bantam Books.

in their acquisitions. If one considers books over a year old and across the board in subject areas, it is probable that libraries would rank first among backlist customers for hardcover publishers.

Even though libraries outnumber booksellers by over 4.5 to 1, the overall apparatus of trade publishing, from scheduling through distribution, is geared toward retailers. Bookstores purchase in advance of publication, and, not surprisingly, Christmas is their major season. Publishers devote most of their energies, therefore, toward producing strong fall lists and developing marketing strategies that will generate sales for books before they are even printed. Libraries, on the other hand, operate under totally different conditions: They generally use public funds and are thus accountable for the materials in their collections; unlike jobbers and retailers, they cannot return books that do not move or do not live up to the publishers' descriptions; and they most often need to purchase smaller quantities of a much larger number of titles (including backlist titles, which make up a basic part of their collections) than do bookstores.

The development of systematic approaches to meeting these conditions requires a constant flow of information in a unique time frame. In a 1974 survey conducted by a task force of the Association of American Publishers and the American Library Association, 25 percent of the sixty-one publishers who responded said that libraries accounted for 70 percent of their total volume but only 11 percent of their total marketing budget. Whatever the amount of money spent, the target is to overcome the dichotomy that exists between the way books are published and the way libraries traditionally approach the acquisition of new books.

Marketing to Libraries

Children's book editors were among the first to realize that attempting to reach librarians through the normal sales and marketing channels was ineffective. Shortly after World War II, separate departments for library promotion were started by several hardcover publishers of children's books. Then in the 1960s, during the halcyon days of massive federal funding for school and public libraries, library promotion departments became common in almost all trade publishing companies. In some cases, the department continued to function as an arm of the editorial group, but generally it was assigned promotion and sales functions. Subsequently, as reduction of budgets and the inflationary spiral of the 1970s made competition for the library dollar keener, the role of the library marketing department was expanded to include advertising and, in some cases, participation in decision making about whether or not to publish particular titles. These departments are the channels of communication to and about the library market.

The traditional patterns of library promotion can be divided into six separate kinds of activities. The nature of the publishing house and the kinds of books being promoted will determine the mix.

MARKETING BY DIRECT MAIL

The kind of information needed by librarians is different and generally far more specific than that required by bookstores. Retailers want to know an author's track record and the genre or theme of the new book. Most of all they want to see the cover art and hear about the promotion, publicity, and advertising support that the publisher will give the title. But the librarians are concerned primarily with bibliographic control and collection building, so they must have very detailed information about the contents of the book: number of pages, index, maps and other illustrations, and a complete description of the nature and level of the coverage. In addition to a listing of the author's previous books, librarians need to know the background and authority of the author and other contributors. If the promotional material can also include direct quotes from reviews and/or recommendations from known authorities in the field, it will be an invaluable aid to selection. In general, promotional copy for librarians requires fewer adjectives and less hype—just the facts will do.

Most trade publishers produce one or two seasonal catalogs that announce and briefly describe forthcoming titles, and these catalogs are used for both retailers and libraries. In addition, a complete catalog of new and backlist books is generally produced for library department's responsibilities because they are a primary reference source for school, public, and university libraries concerned with the development of subject collections.

The traditional backlist catalog will be supplemented, within constraints of budget, by other forms of printed materials. These can include four-color posters with illustrations from picture books, minicatalogs directed toward college subject specialists, author biographies, bookmarks, teachers' guides to the use of one or more books in the curriculum, brief announcements of reviews and recommendations, newsletters written for librarians, and any other combination of printed words that can be conceived of to promote the publisher's list.

REVIEW-COPY PLANS

The development of library promotion as an aspect of marketing was an attempt to meet and speed up the selection procedures primarily of public libraries, most of which until recently spent a great deal of time and money reviewing new books prior to purchase. The library's major problem was to identify titles and then receive copies early enough to allow for staff review, order, and processing before the book either became dated or went out of print. On the opposite side of the fence, publishers shared the belief that the book is its own best promotion—but couldn't program libraries' reviewing procedures into their schedule. From these two needs developed the Greenaway Plan, named for the noted library director whose brainchild it was.

Through Greenaway or similar plans, publishers send to major library systems one copy each of all or most of their new title output, at a discount that is considerably higher than normal. The books are usually sent direct from the bindery, in order to arrive about six weeks prior to publication date. Libraries cannot return these books even though they do not actually know in advance which titles they will receive. The most important decision for publishers in setting up the plan concerns which libraries warrant inclusion: They must be systems that would not purchase without reviewing and that would, if the book met their standards, purchase multiple copies and thereby justify the cost of the review copy.

It is the function of the library promotion department to devise a systematic approach to getting books to school libraries, and since very few school systems are budgeted for Greenaway-type plans, other kinds of review-copy programs have been developed. These include sending review copies to librarians who serve on award-designating committees, develop bibliographies, or simply carry weight within the profession. In the "good old days" it was not uncommon for 400 to 500 copies of a children's book (with a first printing of 7,500 to 10,000) to be distributed as library review copies. Whether that book succeeded often was a measure of how accurately the initial review copies were targeted.

In recent years, the Greenaway Plan has become less of a factor in public library selection. Budget cutbacks have made staff review of all new trade books virtually impossible, and there has been a shift in emphasis from acquiring the "best" to acquiring what is in demand. With the advent of paperbacks, the idea of spending money on ephemeral books to meet demand and not to become a permanent part of the collection has become prevalent. However, books for children and teenagers, as well as expensive, specialized books, will continue to require review—and when a publisher believes that a book is a potential award winner, there is no substitute for bringing it to the attention of the greatest number of librarians. Word of mouth in this profession, as in others, is the most effective promotion of all. And without question stalking prestigious awards is basic to library promotion. Committees of the American Library Association award the Newbury for the best-written and the Caldecott for the best-illustrated children's books of that year. Winning either coveted prize can result in a first-year sale of sixty thousand copies and a life span of several decades!

CONVENTIONS AND FIELD TRIPS

How do you find out who should receive review copies? Who are the next generation of influential librarians? What are the current concerns in the profession? What kinds of book needs are currently not being met? Library marketing specialists are only as effective as their communication with their marketplace, and this requires that they periodically go "on the road."

Conventions provide the best opportunity for face-to-face meetings, whether at the exhibition booth, in the bar, or in a hotel lobby. The booth is filled with books, catalogs, and posters and serves not only as a sales presentation but also as a backdrop for the garnering of information. The real value of conventions lies in the opportunity to meet many people, representing different areas of service. The responses to the books displayed can help you to target future promotions and may even provide editorial feedback for future projects. Committee meetings, idle chatter, and private talks can provide equally valuable information that ultimately determines the success of publishers' marketing strategies.

The annual meeting of the American Library Association draws 8,000–10,000 library registrants and close to 400 exhibitors. During a five-day period thousands of meetings and programs devoted to all aspects of librarianship will take place, and conference attendees will often begin their day with 7:30 A.M. breakfast meetings and end with an evening meeting or program. The business of the organization is conducted at this conference, and there are also substantive programs that generate innovative and creative approaches to service. This conference and the smaller state and regional meetings serve as inservice training grounds for the thousands of librarians who attend.

Conventions also provide a place where librarians get to see new products, and for many it is their only opportunity to see recently published books, because their library system is too small to warrant review copies. But it is generally agreed that the intangible contribution of interchange with other librarians, and with representatives of the companies who sell to librarians, is the greatest value of all.

Through most of the 1960s and into the early 1970s conventions were a primary library promotion activity. Publishers often attended a national meeting and six to eight state and regional library meetings each year, plus several in different education disciplines. Entertainment was lavish, including breakfasts, lunches, dinners, cocktail parties, and beer bashes, and many attendees could count on publishers providing more than half their meals. But in these days of escalating costs, the librarians and exhibitors who attend now are probably much more focused than in the past (there is less time spent socializing and greater emphasis on gathering specific information). Librarians attend fewer conventions, but the meetings continue to provide a unique and valuable forum.

Often a field trip was used to augment, or substitute for, conventions. Visits to librarians in their places of business can provide vast amounts of information about present conditions and future trends. It enables publishers to see full collections, to find out where their books fit within them, and to meet the working librarians who never attend conventions. Like conventions, the field trip allows librarians to react and interact with representatives of what many had thought of as an impersonal publishing establishment. However, the field trip too has become expensive, and most publishers today consider these personal visits to be harder and harder to justify.

ADVERTISING

In recent years, control of advertising for the library market has been the province of the library department, rather than the publishers' advertising department or agency. Decisions on which books to include in ads and on when the time is right to advertise rather than promote in other ways, as well as the actual writing of copy to appeal specifically to librarians, are aspects that logically are best handled by the group most familiar with the profession.

It is in the area of advertising that the most obvious differences between the responses of retailers and librarians can be seen: Advertising for the trade is written to titillate, to arouse interest in a book, to announce its arrival. Advertising for librarians, although obviously created for "selling" the book, must include substantial information about the nature of the book and the author in order to be effective. Publishers generally spend the greatest part of a book's trade advertising budget immediately upon publication and of a library advertising budget after the book has earned "quotable" reviews.

AUTHOR PROMOTION

Phil Donahue, Mike Douglas, Johnny Carson, the "Today" show— mention these talk shows and everyone verifies the impact on sales following an author's appearance on television. But years before the TV talk show, children's librarians testified to the impact of an author talking to a group of children in the library or classroom. For months thereafter the children would continually request books by the authors they had met. The same is true of authors speaking to groups of librarians—the impact on sales of that book to libraries can be magical. So among the many responsibilities of the library marketing department is the matching of an author's particular strengths to requests received from the institutional marketplace. For some children's book illustrators the appropriate format is a chalk talk; for some authors, a panel program devoted to the craft of writing for young adults; and for the more articulate and well known, a keynote or banquet speech. Despite bitter complaints and vexation about the amount of time spent on getting authors "out"— figuring plane schedules, making hotel reservations and arrangements for pickup, monitoring expense accounts, shipping books for autographing, and writing press releases for local newspapers—author promotion is a part of the job that reaps plentiful rewards.

REVIEWS

Where and how a book has been reviewed can have enormous impact on its sale to libraries, because—among other reasons—there are thousands of librarians selecting books who never receive a review copy. For them, reviews by other librarians or by a newspaper or magazine they trust is often the only way they can determine whether or not to purchase. The *New York Times Book Review, Time, Newsweek,* the *Washington Post Book World, Saturday Review,* and other consumer magazines and local press may or may not influence different groups of librarians. *Publishers Weekly, Library Journal, School Library Journal, Booklist, Choice, Horn Book, Bulletin* of the Center for Children's Books, and *Top of the News* are all professional publications that definitely carry weight. So too do *VOYA, English Journal, Language Arts,* the *Alan Newsletter* (Adolescent Literature Assembly of the National Council of Teachers of English), and other educationally oriented periodicals. General publicity departments are most frequently responsible for seeing that adult titles are sent to appropriate reviewers, but it is frequently the library department that must generate all publicity for books for children and young adults. This includes the creation of press releases and the systematic mailing of books to reviewers. The library department also maintains the necessary files so that review information can be included in future catalogs.

Reviews not only serve the needs of librarians in helping them make selections; they frequently provide direction to publishers for more effective advertising and promotion.

Distribution to Libraries

Although it is theoretically true that libraries and bookstores can buy either directly from the publisher or from a jobber, in actuality the more

viable way for libraries to operate is to use jobbers. Very few trade
publishers maintain a separate sales force to call on libraries, and many
do everything possible to discourage direct library orders. Therefore,
except for dealing directly with the few publishers who extend very
competitive discounts and/or to obtain titles not available elsewhere,
more libraries these days use jobbers for most of their purchasing. In
1982, library jobbers accounted for nearly 70 percent of all U.S. library
acquisitions, and that figure will undoubtedly increase as mass-market
paperbacks become a staple library purchase. Ordering books of many
publishers from a single source of supply is cost and time efficient and
is the logical approach to acquiring large numbers of diverse titles from
the myriads published each year.

What this can mean to publishers is a loss of control over their
product. In the first place, jobbers do not promote one book over another,
so there is a dislocation between the source of promotion and the source
of supply, possibly resulting in books being heavily advertised and
promoted but not readily available through local suppliers. And a second
and great concern is that if a book is not in inventory when it is ordered,
a library may authorize the supplier to substitute another, similar book
or may just cancel the order if it decides not to wait for the title to be
backordered. For this reason, and because they often receive the complaints
about poor service, library marketing specialists have developed close
ties to major jobbers, even though jobber responsibility is usually a trade
sales function. Part of this tangential relationship is to channel information
about new books of interest to schools and libraries, and part is to help
sales departments understand specific problems related to fulfilling library
orders.

As in many industries, distribution is truly the name of the publishing
game. Being able to get the book into the appropriate market channels
quickly has greater bearing on its ultimate success than does the nature
of the book itself. This is perhaps less true for children's books, which
have a longer life span generally than most adult books, but ultimately
distribution is of major consequence to all. As libraries become more
sophisticated about the ins and outs of the mechanisms of distribution,
they will undoubtedly save both time and money. But there is still a
considerable lack of sophistication concerning acquisitions among librarians who do not see the library as a "business." Traditional patterns
of library acquisition were developed during a period when balanced
collections of hardcover books were the norm, when selection decisions
were made by either a single coordinator or a small committee, when
criteria of excellence were an overriding consideration, and when patrons
were not looking to the library for the same kinds of service that
bookstores provide. Today, sometimes triggered by budget cutbacks or
the result of a changing view of the library's role, the traditional patterns

are disappearing. Speed in selection, purchase, and processing is now factored in when cost effectiveness is measured; decentralization in management has resulted in many more people making selection decisions; sophisticated systems of circulation and inventory control open doors to different forms of distribution. All have had, and will continue to have, enormous effects on marketing to libraries.

One of the major shifts in recent years is the result of the paperback explosion. For years, trade publishers devoted their attention to librarians because this was the primary channel for hardcover books. Now, as more of their product is paperbacks, marketing has been expanded toward the classroom teacher as well as the school and public librarian, and toward the college professor and bookstore as well as the university librarian. There is a growing awareness, especially within the children's publishing arena, that marketing to all outlets is interrelated. Bookstores, libraries, classrooms, student book clubs, and book fairs all bear on the success and life span of the book; there is, therefore, a growing realization within publishing that the people responsible for this success must become involved in all distribution and market planning. The attractiveness of paperbacks for libraries has expanded the function of the library marketing specialist, but even more important, it has modified the ways in which libraries evaluate materials and build their collections.

Idle Predictions

Several library marketing pros, in an informal survey, agreed that this area of publishing is changing drastically. Among the areas of agreement:

- Overall library budgets will not increase dramatically; unit purchases therefore will remain static or decrease, making it more urgent to open and maximize all markets.
- Decentralization in selection and publishers' own budget restrictions will inevitably lead to more depersonalization—less direct contact, more direct mail.
- Libraries will have to accommodate to publishers' financial realities and speed their ordering because publishers cannot hold books in inventory waiting for library orders.

Most important of all—we all agree that libraries will continue to be a major market for trade publishers and that developing tools and techniques to reach that market effectively and economically is the challenge of the 1980s.

CHAPTER SEVENTEEN

Wholesalers

FRANCIS HOWELL

Most items or goods manufactured in the United States are sold to the consumer through a distribution network of wholesalers and retailers. A wholesaler buys the product from the manufacturer, warehouses it in a strategically located facility, and resells it to retail stores or dealers in the local area. Manufacturers seldom sell directly to the consumer. However, book publishers sell to any and everyone, including the wholesaler, retailer, school, library, and book club, as well as directly to the individual consumer. Rarely does one find a distribution system as archaic, confused, unreliable, or complicated as that of the trade-book publishing industry. Figure 17.1 illustrates the varied avenues a book can take in the current basic pattern of book distribution.

One of the things that makes the system so complicated is the large number of titles readily available for purchase from publishers in the United States at any given time. This number, well over 500,000, remains relatively constant; each year about 50,000 new books are published and a nearly equal number of titles are dropped from publishers' lists. These books are published by thousands of different publishers, which further complicates the distribution system required to move books from the publisher to the ultimate consumer. The number of consumers is great, too: millions of individual book buyers, as well as thousands of school districts, libraries (both public and private), colleges and universities, all of which buy some of their books from the thousands of retail bookstores and book departments in the nation.

One of the ways books move from the publisher to the retail bookseller is through the facilities of a book wholesaler. As recently as twenty years ago, wholesalers in the United States sold primarily to the institutional market—that is, to schools, universities, and libraries of all kinds, rather than to the independent bookstore. At that time, the discount given by the wholesaler was not considered sufficient for the retailer's profit requirements. (It should be noted also that publishers' discounts to wholesalers did not encourage them to actively explore the retail bookstore marketplace.) Although service should be the determining factor in the

---

FRANCIS HOWELL is vice president of Ingram Book Company, Nashville, Tennessee.

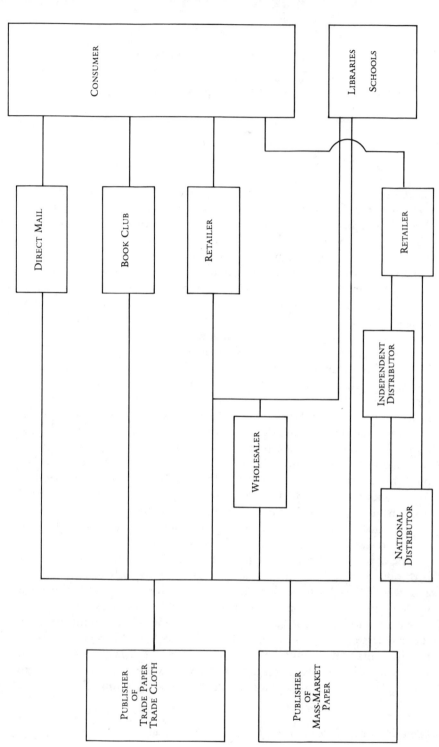

FIGURE 17.1 Channels of book distribution.

choice of a wholesaler by the customer, no significant effort was made by the wholesalers to deliver the books rapidly, nor did they provide a broad inventory selection. These were not critical points for schools and libraries, though, as they were willing to wait a reasonable time for the wholesaler to special-order those titles that were not regularly stocked. So the wholesaler's business was quietly accomplished, with something of an eye to the competition and with enough service to discourage the customer from ordering directly from the publisher.

Such factors as service, inventory availability, and discounts were considered important by retail booksellers, who were therefore forced to buy their books directly from the publishers. This caused an incredibly complicated ordering process. Figure 17.2 shows 10 bookstores ordering their books directly from 5 publishers. Imagine, if you will, enlarging this to 10,000 retailers and 1,000 publishers and remember the huge number of titles involved. Retailers found themselves spending more time administering the ordering procedure than the actual selling.

If the retail bookseller wants to create a reputation for fine service, those books not regularly stocked by the store must be ordered promptly for the impatient customer. Hence, there is a steady stream of orders flowing from retailer to publisher. The orders may be for single titles or combined with regular stock orders. To further complicate the matter, there is little standardization of policies among publishers. Each has a distinct discount schedule, freight policy, returns policy, and other peculiarities of doing business with the retailer. A retailer must order a certain minimum quantity of books in order to qualify for an adequate discount, and this creates problems when ordering frequently. Thus each day the retailer submits orders to many publishers, each requiring a separate purchase order or telephone call. Each order is a separate transaction, and the process continues with the opening of the shipments, checking of the packing slip, entering of the invoice, payment, and so on. Overstocked books that are eligible for return require separate letters to each publisher requesting return, and then, of course, when permission is received, the shipment must be made to each publisher.

Figure 17.3 graphically illustrates the reduction in administrative overhead for both publisher and retailer when a wholesaler becomes a part of the channels of distribution. Now the retailer can order from one source on one order form or with one telephone call books from hundreds of publishers and from a selection of thousands of titles. When the books are received, there is just one shipment to check in, one invoice to pay, one ledger entry, and so forth. Since wholesalers offer terms and policies similar to those of publishers, the problem of overstock returns is also greatly simplified. And since the retailer is generally closer

268

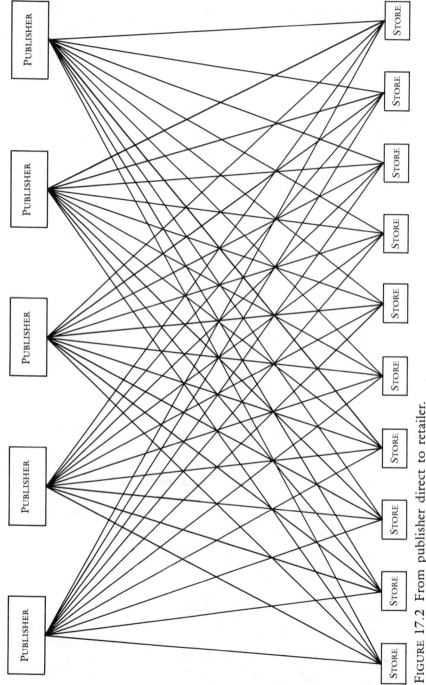

FIGURE 17.2 From publisher direct to retailer.

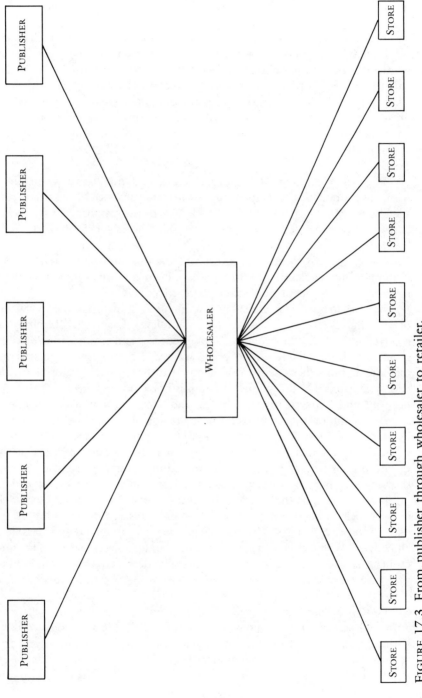

FIGURE 17.3 From publisher through wholesaler to retailer.

to the wholesaler than to the publisher, the shipping time and transportation charges are much less as well.

This is an obvious oversimplification inasmuch as no wholesaler can stock all of the books of each publisher, but it can be assumed that a wholesaler can supply about 80 percent of a retailer's needs, with the balance of special orders still requiring direct purchase from the publisher. There is no question that an efficient network of regional wholesalers greatly improves the distribution of books, improves the profitability of both publisher and retailer, and creates increased sales since the books are more likely to be available to the bookstore at the time the demand exists.

Today there are several aggressive, alert, and innovative wholesalers who have dramatically helped to change the process of distribution. Their services to the retailer as well as to the publisher have been considerably expanded. Recognition of the wholesaler's role and value has led most publishers to increase their discount, thus allowing the wholesaler in turn to offer a more profitable discount to the retailer. At the same time wholesaler inventories have been carefully tailored to meet the needs of the retail bookseller more effectively.

There are many other services now available from wholesalers. Certainly one of the greatest of these is the microfiche. Each week bookstores receive a microfiche that provides valuable current and advance information about the books likely to be most wanted by their customers. This includes a comprehensive list of scheduled author appearance on network and syndicated TV programs, upcoming book reviews in national publications and book tie-ins with movie and TV programs, titles that will appear on important best-seller lists in major newspapers, and regional lists of best-selling books for the booksellers' particular area based upon weekly sales in that area by the wholesaler. Important information is given on each title carried in stock, including complete inventory status showing the number of copies on hand, number of copies on order, publication date, author, title, and price. Other information includes out-of-stock notices and expected in-stock dates, delays in publication dates, and price changes. The microfiche listing is combined and classified alphabetically by title, author, publisher, and subject matter. The microfiche is used by placing it in a specially designed projecting reader that displays the information in an easy-to-read, oversized image on a viewing screen.

Phone ordering service, available from some wholesalers, now utilizes advanced computer technology and equipment and lets the buyer know with up-to-the-instant accuracy the availability of any book in the inventory at the wholesaler's nearest warehouse. A quarterly summary of purchases is available from some wholesalers that furnishes the retailer with information and proof of purchases so that the publishers will honor the store's cooperative-advertising claims.

For the individual interested in opening a new store or department, some wholesalers offer a program designed to assist in inventory selection. This is a computer print-out of those titles most in demand by wholesalers' customers located in a specific area; the suggested inventory is arranged by subject category. Within each category, the books in greatest demand are listed first, with other selections following in descending order. The current sales information for each title is computed when it is placed in this demand sequence by the computer. The title is listed first, followed by author, publisher, price, and publication date. Paperback titles are listed separately from hardcover. These inventory listings can also be tailored to any dollar amount requested. In short, the computer can be programmed to supply just about any combination of information needed for a new or expanding store.

As I have pointed out, the wholesaler can offer the retail bookseller some very immediate advantages over buying directly from the publisher. But there are some definite disadvantages as well to ordering from a wholesaler. No wholesaler can stock all of the books of a publisher, and this does necessitate special ordering from the publisher. The discount offered by the publisher can be greater than that offered by the wholesaler if the volume of books ordered is sufficiently large. Thus, in order to achieve maximum service and profitability, booksellers must constantly balance their ordering from both sources.

There are also several valuable services offered today by the wholesaler to the publisher. The microfiche service to booksellers previously mentioned is a great selling tool for the publisher, since it lists and describes promotional campaigns of many titles. Some wholesalers are also capable of preparing computer-generated listings of a publisher's sales state by state on a periodic basis, giving the publisher an excellent sales and marketing tool. The prime consideration of the publishers, of course, is the ability to have their books located in regional warehouses throughout the United States, closer to the retail bookseller and available for immediate delivery upon demand.

On balance, it seems clear to me that wholesalers of the 1980s will increasingly contribute to the overall well-being of the industry as booksellers and publishers continue to utilize their ever-growing services.

CHAPTER EIGHTEEN

Filling Customers' Orders

SANDRA K. PAUL

If a publisher's marketing efforts are successful, the result is the receipt of orders—many orders being the goal, of course. The order-fulfillment process starts with the receipt of that order—either in a publisher's own office or warehouse, at a warehouse that provides total order-fulfillment services for publishers, or at a data-processing service bureau that performs the paperwork functions necessary before book shipments can be made from a warehouse.

Steps in Order Fulfillment

The first step is to analyze the order to identify the customer. Before an order can be processed you need to determine whether the customer is one the company has dealt with in the past. If so, the current credit status of that customer is then reviewed; you would not want to ship more books to an account that the Credit and Collections Department feels is already financially overcommitted. Credit status includes consideration of the money owed by the customer, as well as the length of time it has been outstanding and the amount that this order will add to the current balance. If the customer is not one that the company has shipped to before, the Credit and Collections Department uses credit services and other sources to determine the limit it will establish for this new customer's balance. New customers with poor credit ratings may be asked to pay for books in advance of shipment.

Customer identification, particularly for the several "Book Nooks" and "University Bookstores" within the same city, can be difficult. However, a new device should help alleviate this problem. The SAN (Standard Address Number), a new standard of the American National Standards Institute (ANSI), has been assigned to every bookstore, wholesaler, library, publisher, school, and school system by R. R. Bowker, the maintenance agency.

SANDRA K. PAUL is president of SKP Associates, New York City.

SANs have been assigned to each different address of these and any other organizations regularly engaged in the buying and selling of books. Customers no longer have to deal with the many different "account numbers" publishers assigned to them and can preprint their SANs on their order forms, providing publishers with a direct link to the publisher's prior records for them.

Once the customer has been identified and credit status has been cleared, the next problem is to identify the specific titles on the order. Even when the order supplies the author's name and the full title of the book, this can still be a complex task. For instance, there are more than one hundred editions of *Gregg, Shorthand* published by McGraw-Hill—student editions, hardcover and paperback, instructor's manuals, workbooks, and so on. Unique, unambiguous identification of the specific title, edition, and binding the customer wants shipped is possible through the use of another standardized system—the International Standard Book Number (ISBN).

The ten-digit ISBN has four components. The first is a single digit that identifies the language of the country in which the book is published. All U.S. publications carry as their first digit 1, as do those published in other English-speaking countries. The next eight digits identify the publisher and title. The ISBN Agency (also housed at R. R. Bowker) assigns each U.S. publisher a prefix, the first part of this ISBN component. These prefixes take into account the publisher's expected title output. For example, a large publisher such as McGraw-Hill has as its prefix 07, leaving six digits that can be assigned to a total of 999,999 different titles before a new prefix will be required. Smaller publishers are assigned longer prefixes, providing them with fewer numbers to assign to their publications. Specific title numbers are assigned by the publishers themselves to each different title and each different binding (library, hardback, paperback, green, blue, and so on) of each title they publish, based on any logical—or illogical—scheme they consider appropriate. The final digit in the ISBN is a "check digit," a mathematical calculation that allows a computer to verify that the preceding digits are correct and to detect most inversions of numbers, the most commonly made error in transcribing numbers of this length. The check digit can be any possible number from 0 to 10. Since it was considered desirable that the ISBN always be ten digits long, if the check digit does have the value of 10, the Roman number X is used instead of the Arabic numeral 10.

If the customer ordering a book supplies an ISBN, the title, edition, and binding to be shipped are known; if no ISBN is provided on an order, you are left to determine this information on the basis of other data provided. For example, price can help you differentiate between the hardcover and paperback editions of the same title. Whatever the methodology, once you have determined which specific book is wanted, the next step is to check the inventory status to determine whether this customer's order can be filled. Through either manual records in small publishing houses or computer records in larger ones, the quantity available for shipment is compared with that ordered and the amount ordered deducted from inventory if there are enough to ship. If the books cannot be shipped, the customer is so advised, with the specific reason given for nonavailability. One of the following indicators would be used in each case:

- NOP—customers ordering books of another publisher are told that the title is "not our publication."
- OP or OOP—identifies out-of-print titles. If another edition of the same work is available, the *OP* may be followed by such information about the other edition as "paperback edition available at $1.95, ISBN 0-394-31135-X."
- OS—identifies out-of-stock books. If a title is *in stock,* but not in sufficient quantity to meet this customer's request, the customer is usually told that the book is *OS.* If the title is being reprinted, the *OS* will usually be followed by the date the publisher anticipates having new stock available in the warehouse.
- OSI—out of stock indefinitely. This means that the title is out of stock, is not being reprinted and probably will not be, but has not yet been officially declared out of print.
- NYP—indicates that the book is "not yet published." Again, the date books will be available for shipment usually is provided after this indicator.

If the customer instructs the publisher to back order, a record is retained of those books ordered that are out of stock or not yet published; the books are then shipped once they arrive in the publisher's warehouse. Usually, customers ordering future publications do so with the intention that the order be placed in the back-order file for shipment when books are first available. Customer policies vary on whether or not to back order backlist titles. Bookstores usually want a specific title and are willing to wait; libraries, whose funds must be spent within a given time period, may request "Do Not Back Order."

Now that you have identified the customer and titles, the next step is to create the paperwork necessary to complete processing of the order. This consists of a label (or several labels) to be affixed to the outside of the shipping carton; a picking list for the warehouse to use in picking the books ordered from the shelves; a packing list, to be inserted in the carton(s) and used by the customer to check off books received against those that should have been sent; and one or more copies of an invoice for the shipment.

One reason that there may be both a picking list and a packing list is the order in which the titles need to appear on those documents. Customers can specify if the packing list and invoice are to carry the titles in the same sequence as that shown on the order, in alphabetical order by author or title, or possibly in ISBN sequence. Publishers, however, attempt to minimize the time it takes to pick books from the warehouse shelves by arranging them in particular sequence—by ISBN, author, title, or possibly by rate of sale, so that fast-moving titles are located together, reducing the amount of territory a warehouse worker must cover to locate all of the titles on most orders. Therefore, the picking document may well be sequenced as the books are shelved, but the packing list sequenced as titles appear on the order.

The invoice would be inserted in the carton with the books unless the books were going to a "ship-to" address, but the customer asked for the invoice at a different "bill-to" address. Another exception would occur if the publisher is not using a prebilling system that calculates the shipping cost in advance and records it on the invoice, but has a postbilling system that requires that actual postage and shipping costs be recorded after the shipment has been completed.

Once the total order has been picked and checked, the books are packed for shipment. Postal regulations specify the strength of cartons appropriate for the mails, but publishers continue to investigate new materials and methods of packaging that provide the best protection for their books at the least expense.

Depending upon the weight of the shipment and the customer's instructions, the shipment is then sent at book or library rate through the U.S. mails, via United Parcel Service, or by private motor carrier. The increases in postal rates and inefficiencies of the postal system have recently led publishers to consolidate their shipments of books to the same customer (shipping back orders only once a month no matter when the reprints or new titles arrive from binderies, for instance) to gain sufficient weight to qualify for motor-carrier shipment. The traffic function performed by the individuals who determine the routing of incoming and outgoing book shipments is a complex one, worthy of a book on that subject alone.

The shipment of books, creation of an invoice, and addition of the amount due on that invoice to Accounts Receivable (A/R) ends the order-processing cycle for the publisher. However, a group of employees called Customer Service is assigned the responsibility of handling problems customers encounter when they do not believe the cycle is complete or consider that it was completed improperly. The Customer Service people act as the publisher's "complaint department," answering inquiries about orders not yet received by customers; shipments received with missing, erroneous, or damaged books; or invoices containing errors. In addition, Customer Service frequently answers requests for information about publication dates for not-yet-published titles or due dates for out-of-stock back-ordered books. It is up to the publisher to provide its Customer Service representatives with sufficient information to answer all of these requests intelligently and with the authority to reship missing books and issue credit for damaged books that are to be destroyed by the customer, rather than returned for credit.

Since most publishers give full credit for unsold trade books that are in print and returned to the publisher, the second most frequently encountered transaction in the distribution process is the processing of a returned book. Here the procedure is similar to the processing of an order in many ways. The first step is to identify the book and return it to the customer if it is "not our publication." Identifying your own titles is simplified if the ISBN is printed on the back corner of the jacket and/or cover. Most publishers are now doing so.

The next step is to determine the customer, based on the paperwork accompanying the return shipment. Then credit must be issued based on the discount at which the book was purchased. This rate is easily determined if the customer supplies a copy of the original invoice or an invoice number. If no invoice number is provided, the minimal discount is usually applied. Just as the creation of an invoice adds to a publisher's A/R, the issuance of a credit reduces receivables.

The final step in return processing is to determine if the book is resalable. Perfectly good books are returned to inventory. Books that are resalable except for a worn jacket are placed in "bad jacket inventory," awaiting a decision on the need to add another copy of that title to inventory. When a trade book has "died" and returns are pouring in, it may not make economic sense to spend the money rejacketing another copy that will not be sold. Unsalable (and bad-jacketed books not to be rejacketed) are placed in "hurt inventory," where they may be sold in "hurt assortments" to stores for their bargain tables. Customers who buy "hurt assortments" know only that they will receive either adult or juvenile books, the suggested list price range of the titles, the number of books in the assortment, and the fact that there will be no more than two copies of any one title in a carton.

Another type of bargain sale is made through the remaindering process. In this case the publisher decides that there is just too much inventory of a given title on hand and offers all or part of that inventory to the highest bidder, hoping that the price paid will equal the cost the publisher incurred to manufacture the books. The purchaser agrees to take all of the inventory offered, on a nonreturnable basis. Many publishers deface remaindered titles in some way, so that they can be detected if an attempt is made by a bookstore or wholesaler to return them for full credit.

Each of these steps in the distribution process yields a great deal of information of importance to the publisher. From records of sales and returns the publisher can determine (1) sales by title: for royalty calculations; for use when considering the next work of this type or by the same author; and for determining whether and when to go back to press, so as to remain "in stock"; and (2) sales by customer: for calculating commissions for sales representatives and as a managerial tool for the sales staff.

The amount of information provided, the timeliness of its receipt, and the ability of reports to highlight problem areas are the responsibility of the departments concerned with sales and those responsible for the company's manual and computer systems areas. The creative sales manager will make his or her needs known to the data-processing manager, so that all of the necessary information is captured during order processing and reports are delivered promptly and in the most usable form for that manager's needs.

Use of the Computer

The first application of computer technology to book publishing was to handle the basic process of order fulfillment. We are now beginning to see creative use of the computer to make the entire book-distribution process more efficient.

Most of the large book-buying customers have computers that are used to track their inventory and create orders for books they want to buy; most large publishers (and those using computer service bureaus) have computers into which those orders are placed after they have been deciphered as previously described and put into computer-useable form. To avoid the time-consuming and error-prone checking and inputting of orders by publishers and wholesalers, it was considered desirable for the purchaser's computer to have the capability of communicating with the computer of the vendor. To that end, a computer-tape ordering format has been developed by an ad hoc group of publishers and their bookstore, wholesale, library, and school customers. The group is known as BISAC— the Book Industry Systems Advisory Committee, and the format they developed has now been programmed for receipt by over seventy publishers. In return, these publishers are asked to provide computer-tape invoices and a monthly computer tape indicating price changes, books declared out of print, changes in anticipated publication dates, and new publications added to the list. The information is created on computer tape by a computer; the tapes are sent through the mails, introducing a delay it is hoped can be overcome by direct computer-to-computer transmission of the information.

The first format, developed by the data-processing managers of the companies who joined BISAC, was truly experimental. After problems with it had been identified, a second format was developed. This format also takes into consideration the emergence of what I call electronic middlemen. Such an organization is On-Line Computer Library Center (OCLC), the nation's largest bibliographic utility, providing over two thousand libraries with computer terminals through which they can locate information about over 8 million books and periodicals in the OCLC data base. OCLC, as well as other library networks, offers their member libraries an acquisition system that allows the library to determine the title it wants to buy by searching the computer data base and to place an order for the book by indicating on its computer terminal the vendor from whom the book is to be purchased. These orders are actually sent by OCLC to the wholesaler or publisher selected; OCLC is not expected to fill the order, receive the books, or pay for them. The R. R. Bowker Company developed a system in 1979 that provides libraries with the ability to review books in their books-in-print data base through a computer terminal and place an order for books that Bowker then sends on to the vendor of choice. It is anticipated that other organizations with computer power will perform such electronic middlemen functions for bookstores, libraries, and possibly school systems in the future.

I expect that the length of time it will take for customers to determine the ISBN of the title they want and to place an order for the book will be measured in seconds in the future, rather than the days or weeks involved in today's distribution system. Publishers will be pressured to maximize the speed of processing orders within their warehouses and to take whatever action they can to expedite the movement of books from one geographic location to another.

BISAC has also been involved in working with the retail trade in the area of machine-readable coding. Most Americans have become familiar with the bar codes on merchandise sold in grocery stores and the scanners at the checkout counters that interpret these codes and record the type of merchandise and its cost in the cash register. Those bars are called the Universal Product Code (UPC), and many mass-market paperback books sold in the supermarket, drugstores, and convenience-store market began carrying the UPC in January 1980. In department stores a different type of coding predominates. Called OCR-A (Optical Character Recognition, font A), it is readable by both the eye and a scanning device attached to an electronic cash register. Based on the need to scan books in department stores with the same scanners used for other merchandise and to scan other premarked merchandise sold in bookstores (e.g., T-shirts and beer mugs), BISAC negotiated with the National Retail Merchants' Association (NRMA), the organization that developed the OCR-A coding structure and asked for recognition of the ISBN as the item number to be encoded in OCR-A. After lengthy discussion, changes were made so that the N in ISBN triggers recognition of an ISBN in scanners programmed to meet the NRMA coding guidelines.

Since mass-market paperback covers are printed without knowledge of whether the book will reach a supermarket or bookstore, these books carry both the UPC and the ISBN printed in OCR-A. Hardcover books and trade paperbooks carry only the ISBN or OCR-A. Publishers who started printing these numbers in machine-readable font in 1980 can purchase their own scanners and will soon be able to use them to check in returned merchandise, as well as to reduce the effort of taking physical inventories of their warehouses.

Current demands for bar coding on hard covers from mass merchandisers has forced BISAC to rethink its earlier efforts in this area. They hope to develop a bar code symbology to meet the needs of this segment of the retail marketplace—and those of the traditional booksellers—in 1985.

It seems clear that future technological developments will continue to produce cost- and time-reducing mechanisms for both publishers and their customers. As this is written, these measures have not yet been implemented in many publishing, bookselling, and wholesaling offices. Those companies with the money to invest implemented them quickly; others, it seems clear, will do so during this decade. Once the various mechanisms have been implemented throughout the industry, we can expect to see reductions in the time it takes to process orders and an increase in more knowledgeable purchasing by booksellers. And, in the not too distant future, booksellers may be providing weekly information on title-by-title sales to an independent organization that will provide national and regional information on more than best-sellers to the industry as a whole and specific sales information to publishers in time for better reprint planning. Such information should also result in more informed decisions on new acquisitions. And we've only just begun to exploit this new technology.

PART FIVE

Some Major Categories of Publishing

CHAPTER NINETEEN

Children's Books

JAMES C. GIBLIN

One evening at a cocktail party, an editor of adult books from one publishing house was introduced to a children's-book editor from another. With the faint air of condescension that occasionally afflicts people when they meet someone working in children's books, the adult-book editor asked: "How do you like editing juveniles?" Not to be outdone, the juvenile editor replied, "I like it just fine. How do you like editing seniles?"

Actually there aren't as many differences between trade-book publishing for children and adults as that exchange may suggest. However, children's-book publishing does possess certain distinct characteristics that set it off from other types of publishing and make it unique. For one thing, children's-book publishing is relatively new as a specialty when compared with other trade-book publishing areas. The first separate department devoted exclusively to the editing, designing, and promoting of children's books was set up by the Macmillan Company shortly after World War I. Today children's books constitute an important element in U.S. publishing, both quantitatively and financially. In 1982, for example, 2,375 new children's books were issued out of a total for all types of publishing of 50,000 titles. Total U.S. book receipts in 1982 amounted to approximately $8.5 billion, of which children's trade books accounted for $256 million—no small amount.

For another thing, because most children's books are heavily visual, especially those aimed at younger children, editors of juvenile books need to have a strong sense of the visual as well as the verbal. The art director's role is more important than it is for adult trade books. Children's books also differ in the way they are marketed. Whereas most adult trade titles, at least initially, are sold through bookstores, over 80 percent of the sales of hardback children's books comes from the so-called institutional market—that is, public and school libraries.

The greatest difference of all, though, is obviously the audience. Of the annual U.S. output of children's books, at least two-thirds are directed at children under twelve, and some books are meant for babies as young

JAMES C. GIBLIN is editor and publisher, Clarion Books, Houghton Mifflin Company.

as one or two. To sense what this audience will respond to requires special aptitudes. The well-known illustrator and author Maurice Sendak probably defined it best when he said that those who write, illustrate, and publish children's books have to work from the thoughts and feelings of the children they once were, who are still alive within them.

Publishing books for this audience also puts a special burden of responsibility on editors and others involved in the field. What sorts of books should be offered to impressionable children and young people? Are some subjects and approaches taboo, or should they be? Where does responsibility to the child's undeveloped state end, and censorship begin?

Staff in a Children's-Book Department

In order to get a closer view of the field and the people who work in it, let's go behind the scenes of a medium-sized children's-book department. There we'll meet the key staff members and find out what each of them does.

This typical department publishes a wide range of books, from picture books for preschoolers to fiction and nonfiction for young teens—the so-called young adult audience. It issues approximately twenty new titles each season, forty a year. These, like most hardback juveniles, are published between February and May in the spring and between late August and early November in the fall, to coincide roughly with the semesters of the school year. Virtually no children's trade books are published in the summer, when most teachers and many public librarians are on vacation.

At the head of the department is the *editor in chief,* who may also be called the *editorial director* and/or the *publisher.* Like other trade publishing executives, he or she must be aesthetically responsive to the author's and illustrator's intentions, but knowledgeable about the business side of publishing, too. The director is usually responsible for establishing and maintaining the department's annual operations budget and for helping to formulate long-range plans for editorial programs and sales projections in conjunction with the firm's finance and marketing departments.

On the editorial side, the director is ultimately responsible for the critical and sales fate of all the titles the department publishes. A typical medium-sized children's-book department like the one we're visiting receives from 3,000 to 4,000 manuscript submissions a year and publishes, as I have said, 30 to 40. Most of these submissions come in directly from the author, though, rather than through a literary agent, so children's-book editorial departments, as opposed to some in the adult field, usually look carefully at all the unsolicited manuscripts they receive.

Once the director decides to take on a new project, the next step generally is to go over preliminary cost estimates with the production manager and then to negotiate the contract for the book with the author (or the author's agent, if one is involved). A contract is also negotiated with an illustrator if the project is a picture book. Standard royalties for children's books usually start at 10 percent of the list price as they do for adult books, but in the case of picture books they are divided 50-50, with the author and illustrator each receiving a royalty of 5 percent.

Advances against these royalties are generally much lower on children's trade books than on adult trade projects, but because they're lower, they are often earned back sooner. And once a children's book wins acceptance from librarians and teachers, it usually remains in print longer than the average adult trade title. So even though authors of children's books may not get as much money up front, they are likely to make as much or more from their books in the long run.

An effective editorial director often seems to possess invisible antennae that pick up changes in the audience and marketplace. Many of the most innovative ideas in children's-book publishing in the last twenty-five years—like Harper's I Can Read series of high-quality books for children just beginning to read and Crowell's Let's Read and Find Out series of well-illustrated beginning science books—originated in the forward-looking visions of their respective editor-publishers, Ursula Nordstrom and Elizabeth Riley.

Besides the editorial director, the department includes on its staff a *senior editor*, who works with authors and develops projects of her own, and an *assistant editor*, who reads manuscripts, writes jacket copy, and assists the editorial director and the senior editor with the flow of manuscripts through production. At the bottom of the ladder, but with a fine view of everything going on in the department, is the entry-level position of *editorial secretary*. This person—sometimes with the help of another secretary, sometimes alone—logs in and out the thirty-five hundred manuscripts that are submitted to the department each year, acts as first reader for many of them, and handles the correspondence of the editorial director and the senior editor.

In larger departments there may be additional editorial staff like an *associate editor*, who develops some books independently and assists on others, and a *managing editor*, who is responsible for the scheduling of all books and manages the traffic flow of edited manuscripts, galley proofs, and page proofs to and from authors, editors, and the production department. In smaller departments, one editor assisted by a single secretary may do the entire job.

The next person we will meet in the department—and one of the most important—is the *art director.* As soon as a new book is scheduled for publication, it is the art director, working in close collaboration with the editors, who selects an illustrator or jacket artist for it and answers any technical questions he or she may have about the assignment.

When a picture book goes on press, the art director usually travels to the printers and watches it run, making sure that the colors and balances are those the artist intended. The art director also supervises the typography of all books published by the department, either personally designing the books or farming them out to free lances. In her work, the art director must be careful to stay within the cost budget for each title and the operating budget established for the entire design area. The publisher wants to produce beautiful books, but doesn't want them to show up on the balance sheet as expensive losses.

The art director has one assistant, a recent art school student who helps with the more mechanical aspects of the job—paste ups, mechanicals, and so forth—and often interviews aspiring illustrators. Like the editorial secretary, the art assistant has an excellent opportunity to learn the design side of children's-book publishing from the bottom up.

In the medium-sized department we're visiting, the art director works with a *production manager* who is also responsible for the production of the firm's adult books. Because of the heavily visual nature of children's books, the production manager must be especially knowledgeable about color-printing techniques and the different kinds of paper that illustrated books require.

In larger firms that publish fifty to one hundred or more new children's books each year, the juvenile department may have its own production manager, along with several production and art assistants. In smaller firms, not only the production manager but often the art director is shared between the adult and children's departments, and sometimes the children's-book editor has to work with free lances.

Another key position in the department is the *director of publicity and promotion.* In some firms, this person may be called the *director of school and library promotion* or even the *marketing manager for children's books.* Whatever the title, the chief function of the job is the same: to make librarians, teachers, and parents aware of the new children's books the department publishes, and thereby to help increase sales.

The director of school and library promotion is responsible for the children's-book advertising, catalogs, review copies, free materials, and exhibits budgets. She coordinates the seasonal children's-book catalogs, writing the copy in conjunction with the editorial department and arranging for the mailing of the catalogs to librarians, teachers, and bookstores. This person also maintains the free copy list of more than three hundred opinion makers across the country who receive advance copies of each title the department issues for evaluation and review in the hope that they will recommend it for purchase in quantity.

Working with the editors and an advertising agency, the promotion director shapes the department's seasonal advertising schedules. Unlike adult trade-book advertising, which is concentrated in newspaper book-review sections and magazines aimed directly at the consumer, most children's-book advertising is placed in professional journals like *Publishers Weekly,* the *Booklist* of the American Library Association, and *School Library Journal,* which are read mainly by librarians and teachers.

Each year the promotion director organizes the department's exhibits at major national conferences like that of the American Library Association. She talks with librarians in the booth and often makes field trips to call on teachers and librarians in the surrounding area either before or after the conference in order to get a better sense of grass-roots trends.

The director of publicity and promotion has an assistant who helps with all the details of the job, from clipping and filing book reviews to typing correspondence. This is an excellent entry-level position for anyone interested in the varied and challenging field of children's-book promotion and marketing.

In some large houses, a *sales manager* is assigned to concentrate exclusively on children's books, but in most houses one sales department services both the adult and children's trade lists. Sales of subsidiary rights are becoming a more important element in the children's-book publishing picture, what with the growth in the number of juvenile paperback reprints, especially in the young adult area, and the widespread use of children's fiction as the basis for television films. Up until now, most sales of children's-book subsidiary rights have been handled by a firm's rights department rather than by a specialist in the children's-book division. However, as these rights sales increase, there may well be a demand in rights departments for more staff people with a special knowledge of children's books.

When deciding which area of children's-book publishing you'd like to get into, it's best to start with some self-examination. Are you most interested in helping children's books reach their ultimate audience via librarians, teachers, and parents? Then the publicity and promotion area would probably be the best for you. Does the look of a book and the way it's produced appeal to you the most? If so, you should aim for the art and production area. Or do you think you would derive the greatest satisfaction, and make the greatest contribution, by helping authors and illustrators to shape their manuscripts and dummies into handsome, well-developed books? Then direct your efforts toward the editorial area.

Associations

The most important association in the children's book field, to which more then sixty publishers belong, is the Children's Book Council. Founded in 1945 and dedicated to the promotion of children's books and reading, the Council maintains joint committees with such interested organizations as the American Library Association, the National Council of Teachers of English, and the International Reading Association. The Council also makes and distributes cassettes featuring discussions of various children's-book topics by outstanding authors, reviewers, professors, and librarians; issues a regular publication, *CBC Features;* and produces the posters, streamers, and bookmarks displayed in schools, libraries, and bookstores across the country in celebration of Children's Book Week in November.

Each member publisher is represented in the Council by two members-of-record. Generally these are the editor in chief of the children's-book department and the director of publicity and promotion.

Future of Children's Books

What new directions is children's-book publishing likely to take in the future? That's a difficult question to answer, but a few predictions can be safely risked on the basis of present-day trends. No doubt publishers will try to increase the percentage of children's books sold in the trade market via experiments in mass-market distribution through outlet stores and supermarkets.

As new developments occur in audiovisual technology and home entertainment centers become more common, children's books will probably play a significant role in family programming. Children's fiction titles may be accompanied by cassette recordings of selected chapters, read by professional storytellers or actors. Favorite picture books may be sold along with film cassette adaptations, utilizing the original illustrations, that can be played on television sets.

No matter what technological developments come about, though, everything will still begin in the imagination of an author who remembers what it was like to be a child. The author's story will be spotted, perhaps in the slush pile, by a perceptive editor and will be nurtured to life by all those in the publishing house—the art director, the promotion director, the salespeople—who are devoted to helping bring books and children together.

As long as there are children who like to hear or read words, and look at pictures, books for children will continue to be published with care, thoughtfulness, and love.

Bibliography

Bechtel, Louise Seaman. *Books in Search of Children: Essays and Speeches.* Edited by Virginia Haviland. New York: Macmillan, 1969.

Giblin, James C. "Children's Books in the 1980s: Changes Needed, Changes in the Works." *Publishers Weekly,* July 25, 1980, pp. 96–97.

_____ . "Honesty vs. 'Acceptability': How Does a Children's Book Editor Decide?" *Top of the News,* Spring 1979, pp. 243–246.

Gottlieb, Robin. *Children's Book Publishing in America, 1919–1976: An Annotated Bibliography.* New York: The Children's Book Council, 1978.

Karl, Jean E. *From Childhood to Childhood: Children's Books and Their Creators.* New York: John Day Company, 1970.

Varner, Velma V. "Thoughts on Children's Books, Reading, and Tomorrow." In Harold Tanyzer and Jean Karl, eds. *Reading, Children's Books, and Our Pluralistic Society.* Perspectives in Reading no. 16. Newark, Del.: International Reading Association, 1972, pp. 71–77.

CHAPTER TWENTY

College-Textbook Publishing

WILLIAM C. HALPIN,
WITH THE ASSISTANCE OF HERBERT J. ADDISON

College-textbook sales are estimated to have totaled $1.22 billion in 1983, representing the third-largest publishing component in the book industry after trade and professional. But its place in the overall cost of higher education is relatively small when this amount is divided by the total college student population of about 12 million. Each student spends an average of $79 per year on college texts, a small percentage of the total cost of a college education that includes tuition, room, and board.

A college textbook is generally defined in the industry as one that is written and produced primarily for use by students enrolled in college- and university-level courses. Such courses extend from those offered at junior and community colleges up through graduate schools. The books include those designed as central or basic texts, as well as those that can be used for supplementary reading. In fact, many college-textbook publishers also produce nonbook materials for the same market, particularly audiovisual items like tapes and films.

Most college textbooks are conceived and written by college professors who usually have extensive experience in teaching the specific course for which the book is designed. For the most part a college text combines a teacher's expertise in a given subject with a creative sense of what will engage and challenge students. In addition, the college-textbook publisher makes a contribution, particularly in the area of market research. El-hi texts, on the other hand, are often written by editors within the publishing house or by free-lance writers, often with the aid of a group of teachers.

College course offerings are much more diversified, the variations of individual curricula are much broader than at the elementary and secondary levels, and enrollments in each course are lower than in elementary and secondary schools. Thus college textbooks, with rare exceptions, do not sell in anywhere near the numbers of copies that el-hi texts do. Total

WILLIAM C. HALPIN was formerly executive vice president of Oxford University Press. HERBERT J. ADDISON is vice president and executive editor at Oxford University Press.

sales of an elementary-school series may run into millions of volumes per year, whereas very few college texts sell as many as 100,000 copies a year. In fact, the average successful college text is more likely to sell in the 5,000 to 7,000 copy per year range.

To describe the college-textbook publishing process, let's begin with the role of the acquisitions editor, for in many publishing houses the editor really acts as a sort of minipublisher of books in his or her area of responsibility—a responsibility that mirrors one or more fields in the standard college curriculum (such as English, history, and chemistry). The acquisitions editor is the one who recommends the books to be published and has overall responsibility for a project from the time of its inception until it goes out of print.

The editor's work begins when he or she first discusses an idea for a book with an author. If, after surveying the market and competing books, the editor decides that the idea will result in a book that will meet a course market need, the editor must convince the author that the editor's publishing house will do the most effective job of editing, producing, and marketing the book. The editor will also discuss contract terms with the author. The editor then prepares a proposal to the publisher that details the merits of the idea, contract terms, and a financial analysis of the costs and potential profit of the eventual book. Once the proposal is approved, the editor sends a contract to the author for signature.

In the time (sometimes years) following the signing of the contract, the acquisitions editor and other editorial experts in the house work with the author to develop the text to fit its market. The manuscript is sent out for review by professors teaching the course for which the book is designed, and these reviews are analyzed by editor and author so that the manuscript can be revised in accordance with the reviewers' suggestions. In the case of a major market course textbook (introductory psychology, for example), the publisher may assign development of the text to special project editor whose sole job for a year or more would be to work in detail with the author to assure that the book is right for its market.

As the manuscript nears completion, the acquisitions editor meets with the designer, the production and manufacturing people, the copy editor, and the marketing people to refine costs, schedules, design, and marketing plans. Each facet must be integrated to ensure efficient and prompt publication. Publication dates for college textbooks are particularly crucial because they must coincide with the times when adoption decisions are likely to be made.

Once the manuscript is in final form, the copy editor edits for spelling, punctuation, consistency, and style, and the author continues to be queried concerning these details. At the same time the designer begins work, usually with a duplicate manuscript, to prepare sample pages. Sample pages for a college text may be very elaborate because of the need to accommodate the bewildering number of elements that can go into such a book, particularly if it is one that is heavily illustrated. The acquisitions editor and sometimes the author also figure prominently in decisions concerning production and design.

While the composition, preparation of artwork, proofreading, printing, and binding processes are taking place, the marketing operation begins in earnest. The acquisitions editor and/or marketing manager presents the book, along with other new books on the list, to the college-textbook sales representatives at a national sales meeting. The primary purpose of this meeting is to present sales points that will help the sales representatives discuss the book in its best possible light when they make their calls on professors who teach the course for which the book is designed. College sales representatives must be familiar with the strengths and weaknesses of competitive books so they can convince professors that the book they are selling is the right one for the professor's course. After discussing the merits of the book with the professor, the representative arranges to have a complimentary copy of the book sent to the professor upon publication.

The sales representative is backed up by advertising and promotion efforts of other members of the marketing staff. Advertisements for the book are placed in the professional journals, and circulars are prepared and mailed to professors whose names appear on selected lists. Complimentary copies of the book are offered through the mail to those who may have been overlooked by the sales representative; as many as ten thousand complimentary copies of a college text may be sent out by the publisher. Although the average is a lot less, the high cost of complimentary copies is a significant factor in textbook pricing. Complimentary copies are, however, essential, effective selling tools because professors are unlikely to adopt books they have not had an opportunity to inspect.

The role of the sales representative (or college traveler, as he or she is often called) is thought to be pivotal by most college publishers, for personal sales calls, although expensive, are a vital part of the marketing operation. A representative needs to be very knowledgeable about the publisher's list and must be able to communicate effectively with college professors in all fields in which the publisher is active. Several years of selling college textbooks give the representative an introduction to the college-textbook business that can be achieved in no other way. Few college acquisitions editors are hired without college sales experience—

it is *the* entry-level job for most higher-level jobs in both the marketing and the editorial areas.

In addition to the sales, advertising, and promotion efforts mentioned above, the publisher attends annual and regional conventions of professional organizations like the American Historical Association, the Modern Language Association, and the Allied Social Science Association. Acquisitions editors and sales representatives exhibit the publisher's list of books in a given field, talk to professors attending the convention about the publisher's new books, and solicit promising manuscripts. Professional meetings give editors and salespeople access to large numbers of customers and authors in one place over a short period of time. The publisher's attendance is thus an effective and comparatively inexpensive editorial and marketing aid.

The adoption process begins when the professor receives the publisher's complimentary copy of the book. This is usually followed by a sales call by the traveler. On making a decision to adopt the book, the professor notifies the local bookstore, which places the order with the publisher. The publisher in turn ships the books in time to arrive at the bookstore at the beginning of a semester. During the first week of class the professor tells the students which books they are expected to study, and the students buy the designated books at the bookstore.

Prior to publication, a publisher's investment in a single text can be as high as $400,000 (for a large, heavily illustrated basic textbook), although a more usual figure might range between $30,000 and $50,000. These costs are of course reflected in the price the student pays for the book. A portion of this price goes to the bookstore as a result of the publisher's discount.

The rest of the money the student pays goes to the publisher. For every dollar the publisher receives from the bookstore, about six cents goes for editorial expenses, which include salary, travel, and entertainment costs incurred by acquisitions editors, copy editors, and special project editors. The publisher spends about twenty-seven cents of every dollar on design, production, and the manufacture of the book, which includes the cost of composition, artwork, printing, and binding. The marketing operation costs about fourteen cents and covers complimentary copies, advertising brochures, space advertisements, and the salaries of the marketing staff. Those who support the publishing operation—the accountants, shipping and warehouse people, customer service and computer people—cost the publisher about eighteen cents of every dollar received. Finally, about fifteen cents of the sales dollar is passed on to the author in the form of royalties. This leaves about twenty cents for taxes and profit, which can be estimated to be roughly equal. (These figures are based on the 1980 industry statistics gathered by the Association of American Publishers.)

Although the organization of a college-textbook department varies considerably among publishers, most are supervised by a general manager who has responsibility for both the editorial and the marketing functions. There may be an editorial director or executive editor who in turn supervises the work of the acquisitions editors and possibly the copy-editing staff. Smaller college departments may use the services of central copy-editing groups that have responsibility for in-house editing of all the publisher's books. A marketing director reporting to the general manager supervises a sales manager and the manager of advertising and promotion activities. Regional managers and sales representatives report to the sales manager. Larger college-textbook departments may have their own production and design capability, but smaller departments will probably use the services of a central group responsible for design, production, and manufacturing of all house publications. It is important to stress, however, that although the structure of a college department can be quite different from house to house, the element of teamwork is always present. Producing a successful textbook requires an ensemble operation of great complexity where editorial, marketing, design, production, manufacturing, and the business side interact repeatedly over the course of several years.

A word should be said about the revision process, for revisions of backlist titles are crucial to a successful college publisher's program. Because the initial cost of producing a college text is so large, the book may not make enough profit as a return on this investment until it has been selling for several years after publication. In addition, it is a characteristic of college books that sales decline from year to year as books become out of date and as new competitors appear. To keep books current with recent scholarship, and to reflect changes in the ways that college courses are taught, most college books are revised regularly—often as frequently as every three or four years. Planning for revisions can begin between author and publisher almost as soon as the ink is dry on the first edition. The nature of revisions can make it possible that the cost of composition (including artwork), usually a huge expenditure in basic texts, can be reduced dramatically in second and subsequent editions because only new material needs to be set. It is true, however, that every three or four editions—again, depending on the nature of the field—the publisher must incur the costs of having the entire text reset to keep up with new developments.

The college-textbook business, like the publishing industry in general, has changed dramatically since the golden years of the 1960s when college enrollments were increasing rapidly, costs were relatively low, money was readily available, and inflation was within bounds. Now the enrollment increase has slowed, and there has been a shift, perhaps temporarily, toward vocationally oriented courses at the expense of the humanities and social sciences. As a result, some publishers have changed the nature of their textbook programs. Some colleges, particularly those in the private sector, are in financial trouble; enrollment declines, inflation, and energy woes put some in imminent danger of having to close.

There are other stubborn problems, not the least of which is that bookstore managers maintain that they cannot run full-service stores on the discounts they receive from most college publishers. Higher discounts mean higher prices to students, however, since publishers must maintain a sufficient profit to finance future books. Finally, there is the used-book problem, which severely cuts into the publisher's sales. After the first year of publication of a new text, used books can account for a high percentage of the sale; the sale of a major introductory text usually drops off by from 25 to 50 percent the year after publication. Of course, the publisher receives nothing from the sale of a used book, and the author receives no royalties.

There are some encouraging trends, however. There is a growing interest in education by many segments of our society that have been underrepresented in higher education in the past—people over twenty-five, minorities, women, the handicapped, retired people, and foreign students. Community colleges have made a college education available to anyone who wants it. Finally, rapidly changing technology and the knowledge explosion have greatly expanded the need for new education-delivery systems. These developments present major challenges for our colleges and universities, and therefore also for college-textbook publishers.

CHAPTER TWENTY-ONE

El-Hi Textbooks

LOZELLE DELUZ

As John Tebbel points out in *Opportunities in Publishing Careers* (Skokie, Ill.: National Textbook Company, 1975), "textbooks are the cornerstone of our American society." And many of us who are employed in el-hi publishing indeed regard it as by far the most important part of the publishing industry—not only because of its size, but because the consumers of textbooks are the future market for all other areas of publishing.

El-hi has the responsibility of publishing textbooks and supportive audiovisual materials—film strips and cassettes, for example—that are sold directly to elementary, junior high, and high schools. The emphasis on direct sales to schools distinguishes el-hi materials from "over-the-counter" teaching materials marketed to parents, although some el-hi products are occasionally sold to parents as well as to educators.

El-hi texts may be published by a division within a large publishing house or by a specialty house. In either case, el-hi publishing differs significantly from other types of publishing in several respects, most notably in the vast scope of the market and in the unusually active involvement of in-house staff in the conception and development of the books.

The Market for El-Hi Books

The el-hi market is both enormous and well defined. The editors and publishers know their audience, and the market is as clearly outlined as a school-district map. The instructional materials they produce are designed and published specifically for classroom use by elementary and high school students and educators and occasionally, as noted, for parents to use with their children for instructional purposes.

The potential market for el-hi textbooks and materials is the number of students enrolled in elementary and high schools. According to the

LOZELLE DELUZ, formerly vice president of the school department at J. B. Lippincott Company, is president of DeLuz Management Consultants, Wilmington, Delaware.

U.S. Department of Education, in the academic year 1980-1981 there were approximately 28 million elementary pupils and 14 million secondary students enrolled in public and private schools in the United States.[1]

In spite of declining enrollments as a result of falling birthrates and in spite of increasing cuts in government allocations to education, el-hi textbooks continue to account for a sizable share of the instructional budgets of elementary and high schools. In 1983, for example, sales of el-hi textbooks amounted to more than $1.14 billion or approximately 13 percent of the total sales of the publishing industry. Further, for 1979 and 1980 the sales of such materials rose at a rate of 8 or 9 percent while sales of general trade, juvenile, religious, and paperback books declined.[2] It has been estimated—for example, by Nobel J. Kendrick, Jr., in "Textbook Publishing: Where It Is, Where It's Going"— that expenditures for books and other teaching materials will continue to match or exceed outlays for instructional staff.[3]

The implications of these figures are weighty. For one thing, there is understandably a great deal of competition among publishers for a share in this lucrative market. For another, since the potential for profit is so large, publishers are willing to spend considerable sums on the development, production, and marketing of their products. This means, among other things, that the staff of el-hi publishers or of the el-hi division of large general houses tends to be larger than that of other types of publishers.

What El-Hi Publishers Publish

The most remunerative and hence the most common form of el-hi publishing is a series of related materials in a given subject area—reading, language, literature, mathematics, social studies, music, art, or science— designed to be used at a sequence of grade levels. El-hi grade-level designations have been altered significantly during the past decade as a result of designations influenced by consistent changes in elementary and high-school organizational patterns at the local levels. Some publishers continue to use the traditional designations K–3 (the primary level), 4–6 (intermediate level), 7–9 (junior high), and 10–12 (high school), but others designate reading, math, science, literature, and social-studies materials as Readiness–8 and 9–12. These designations relate to the middle-school, junior-high, and high-school groupings used in a majority of school systems. Materials intended for use in high schools are usually produced in a separate division of the el-hi department. If the textbooks are accompanied by audiovisual materials intended for classroom use and sold along with the books, the series is potentially even more profitable. Special instructional aids to help teachers use the materials most effectively are usually part of the package. These are distributed at no charge, and the cost is absorbed as a part of the marketing budget.

Individual titles can also be profitable. The average print run at this writing is thirty thousand copies, and of course many books are produced in much larger quantities.

The largest el-hi publishers produce materials covering the full curriculum of elementary and secondary schools, but many successful publishers in this field concentrate on one or two subject areas or grade levels, producing, for example, a series or group of elementary language-arts textbooks.

Editing for the El-Hi Market

ACQUISITION

In all divisions of publishing, determining which books to publish and when to publish them is a crucial skill to be acquired and finely tuned by management-level staff. But unlike trade and professional publishers, for example, el-hi divisions frequently originate the idea for their publications rather than respond to a submission by an author or agent. In this respect, they are similar to reference-book publishers and, increasingly, to publishers of college textbooks.

A network of salespeople, curriculum specialists, and a variety of consultants retained by el-hi publishers plays a significant role in providing the information necessary to these publishing decisions. Such persons travel extensively to schools, attend national and regional meetings, keep up with the professional literature and with competing works, and maintain close contact with educators, always with an eye toward new trends, new developments, and new requirements. Through their personal and professional ties with those in teaching and education administration, salespeople and consultants are good resources for information about the demand for potential programs. Ideas and suggestions for new titles also come from authors already on the company's publishing list and sometimes from classroom teachers who submit recommendations for new programs and authors. From these and other sources the publisher garners as much information as possible about the size of the market and the sales, prices, and costs of competing books and series.

The authors of el-hi textbooks are generally selected from among well-known teachers and specialists in the subject matter being considered. These potential writers come to the attention of the publisher as a direct result of the careful monitoring of educational activities. If the publisher has originated the idea for the book or series, a prospective author may be identified from a published paper, a successful lecture series, or a presentation at a conference. An author may surface as a result of an editorial contact or through the recommendation of the publisher's consultants, teachers, or even other authors.

If the project includes a series of books and other components that will span several grade levels, the publisher may engage several writers. New authors may first be asked to write a sample chapter or two to enable the publisher to gauge their writing potential before they are employed to create a textbook. And in some instances, potential authors actually develop their own ideas for a new textbook and present the completed outline to the publisher for consideration.

The authors of an el-hi textbook or series generally receive a royalty of 6 percent of the publisher's received income, which in most cases is 75 percent of the list price of the books. The fact that this rate is somewhat lower than the royalty typically paid to the author of a college textbook or a trade book is justified by the usual degree of involvement of the publisher's editorial staff, the high cost of developing and marketing the books, and the high rewards the authors of successful books can expect.

The philosophy of the company plays an important role in determining the type of manuscript and author it selects. For example, a particular el-hi division or company may focus on reading materials based on a phonetic linguistic approach; another company may publish reading programs based on a sight approach. On rare occasions a publisher might publish competing series using different approaches. For example, Ginn and Company in the past was known for the sight approach to reading-skills development. Recently it has published a competing series using a phonetic/linguistic approach. Most publishers, however, do not publish competing books or series.

DEVELOPMENT

Regardless of how the author is chosen, the editorial staff in an el-hi division plays a key role in developing and producing the book, working closely with the author from the inception of the project to ensure the best possible presentation of the book and its components.

Entire programs are developed within el-hi divisions, sometimes including as many as sixty components. An executive vice president of the division, a managing editor, an editor in chief, an executive editor, one or two senior project editors, several senior associate and assistant editors, as well as a number of free-lance editors, assistant editors, and copy editors may work on a single program. The total staff involved depends, of course, on the scope of the project.

Once a book is under contract and a draft has been submitted, it is the responsibility of the senior project editor to review it carefully for content, style, and organization and to discuss needed revisions with the author. When the conceptual and substantive editing has been completed, the manuscript is then copyedited and prepared for design and production. The results of an informal survey reveal that editors, consultants, and salespeople currently employed in el-hi divisions typically come from education or education-related backgrounds. This is not often the case in college or trade divisions, although many editors of professional monographs are onetime instructors. In el-hi publishing, often several editors work with a particular manuscript. It is the senior project editor, however, who has the ultimate responsibility for overseeing the entire project from manuscript to bound books.

To remain informed, the project editor and other editorial staff must maintain close contact with educators. The senior project editor attends professional conferences and conventions, reads major educational publications, and keeps informed about the competition. At all stages he works closely with the product manager, a member of the el-hi marketing department whose responsibility it is to survey the field and determine what approach and format will appeal to the market. This information is passed on to the editorial department through the senior project editor.

The senior project editor and staff must also be aware of special-interest groups and lobbies that might affect the reception of the book and accompanying materials. Careful editing must ensure a balance among conflicting educational theories and an acceptable compromise between opposing views, such as those held by creationists and evolutionists. In most cases the goal is to produce a book that will be accepted nationally, while still fulfilling its educational purpose, but there are instances when publishers find it necessary or desirable to issue more than one version of a textbook in order to sell it in different parts of the country. Sometimes the el-hi editors must actually generate manuscript to provide the needed balance.

The senior project editor must work very closely in a coordinating role with the author, other editorial staff, the production and design department, the marketing department, and management to ensure that all are kept informed about progress on the manuscript. From the beginning to the end of a project, information is shared regularly in meetings with representatives of all departments. Communication and coordination are especially important in el-hi publishing because of its complex nature, involving many components and people.

Delays in completing a program as scheduled can be very costly to the publisher, and it is a major responsibility of the senior project editor and the managing editor to see that the author and others continue to transmit manuscript to the editorial department and then to production on a regular and timely basis. If there is slippage in the schedule, the project editor works out some system of making up for lost time with the production and marketing managers.

Consumer reactions to a book, conveyed by consultants and salespeople as well as in comments made directly to the publisher, often result in useful clues to desirable changes in textbooks. The editorial department keeps a correction file for future reprintings and a list of suggestions for revisions.

Production

Producing el-hi materials in many respects is a more complex operation than producing other kinds of books, because of the large number of elements that must be coordinated, the tight schedule that must be maintained, and the need to be constantly mindful of the changing demands of the marketplace and the competition.

Once the production manager receives the edited manuscript, the editing, production, and marketing staff attend regularly scheduled meetings to make decisions on trim size, binding, type of art, color, mode of composition, titles, covers, and press run, not to mention similar details concerning ancillary materials. Preliminary marketing plans and a target for bound-books delivery date are also agreed upon. After these decisions have been made, the progress of each book or component is monitored on a two-week tracking schedule. During the final stages of production weekly meetings are held. The production process for an el-hi textbook series, from the original concept to bound books, often takes several years and an outlay of $250,000 or even more. Obviously, the publisher must justify the high cost of production by the number of copies he expects to sell. Large press runs, which permit competitive pricing, are essential to the el-hi publishing enterprise. Even so, el-hi publishers tend to assume a higher risk than other publishers in that the books and their component parts take longer to produce. It therefore takes longer for a publisher to receive a return on investment. If the publishing company is undercapitalized, the result can be catastrophic.

Once a book has been published, the publisher must maintain large inventories to meet the projected demand, for failure to ship the books when they are required can jeopardize the sale of the whole series. A full warehouse further reduces the rate of return on the publisher's investment. Effective marketing is consequently a crucial factor.

Marketing and Sales

El-hi materials are sold by the publisher's representatives to state and local school authorities collectively, to textbook committees, and some-times to individual classroom teachers. El-hi publishers typically maintain a large sales staff. It is not unusual for a company to employ a marketing and a sales director, two national sales managers, four or five area or regional sales managers, and forty to sixty salespeople. Perhaps fifteen consultants may be part of this team, assigned geographically to sales territories that are known to differ in their interests, cultural patterns, potential for sales, and level of funding for textbooks. This last point is especially significant in that the sales of el-hi textbooks are highly responsive to the number of students enrolled and the level of state and local government funding for education.

El-hi textbooks are marketed mainly through educational institutions. However, before sales can be made, the textbook and its components must be examined and read by thousands of prospective customers: classroom teachers and others. Frequently this is done well before the book is published, through so-called field testing. This is a technique that not only alerts possible buyers to the merits of a new textbook but also unearths weaknesses that can be corrected prior to publication.

In field testing, page proofs of the book are sent to practicing classroom teachers who express a willingness to read and criticize them, usually for a modest fee. Field testing may also involve testing the skills of children before and after they have been exposed to a new book. Consultants and other outside readers are also sometimes employed to critique the book at this point. Obviously, time must be built into the production schedule for field testing of new projects and for mailing whatever changes are indicated as desirable.

As much as a year or two before the book is published, detailed descriptions, often lavishly produced, are widely distributed to potential buyers. Some advertisements may be placed in professional education journals such as the *Elementary School Journal, Instructor,* and *Grade Teacher.* Obviously the mass media are not used because they are not specifically targeted to the schools.

Once the book is published, free copies distributed to teachers, supervisors, and boards of education account for the major portion of the promotional budget of el-hi publishing. Usually one Teacher Resource

Teacher Kit per grade level is sent to designated schools. The kit may include, in addition to the textbook for the grade level, a student workbook, ditto masters, tests, and a teacher's guide.

The material designed especially for teachers may include a lesson-plan outline and a bibliography of suggested reading for the teachers and for students. Some el-hi publishers package this teacher material in a spiral-bound 8½-by-11-inch notebook, which contains reductions of pages from the textbook for easy reference. Student workbooks and duplicating masters are intended to reinforce vocabulary and skills developed in the text. An optional test to assist teachers in diagnostic, evaluative, and prescriptive measurement and filmstrips based on the text may also be part of the package.

The availability of new or revised el-hi textbooks and their components is also made known through the direct personal contact of salespeople and consultants who visit schools and display their materials at educational conferences and meetings.

Years ago, most states operated under an "adoption" plan whereby certain titles were approved by the state board of education and all school districts in that state were required to select books from the list in order to obtain state funds for the purchase of textbooks. Most states no longer exercise complete control over book selection, but there are still some that have official selection lists. Obviously, these "adoption" or "approved" lists are central to the marketing of el-hi textbooks. Most approved lists are effective for five years, a fact that probably influences the five-year revision plan used by some el-hi publishers.

Publishers whose books are selected by state boards have an obvious advantage, but they are still obliged to convince the local school districts that their books are the best of the five or six recommended titles in each area. Clearly, it is important to know the strengths and weaknesses of the competition. Presentations and demonstrations must be made to local school districts, individual schools, and sometimes even individual teachers. Here the salesperson's contacts play an important role. In states without an adoption plan or an approved list, the selling procedure is almost the same except that the competition is fiercer in a wide-open field.

Once the sale is made, salespeople and consultants must return to the schools to give demonstrations to the classroom teachers on how best to use the materials. Sometimes these demonstrations and workshops are required as part of the sale and are actually included in the sales contract.

In summary, el-hi publishing is a very profitable and important part of the publishing industry. The main source of revenue is heavily influenced by government policy toward funding for education. Although future projections show declining enrollments on the el-hi level during the next decade, it is predicted that federal funding for education will remain at approximately the same level.

Notes

1. U.S. Department of Education, *National Center For Educational Statistics* (Washington, D.C.: U.S. Government Printing Office, 1981).

2. Association of American Publishers, New York, 1983.

3. Nobel J. Kendrick, Jr., "Textbook Publishing: Where It Is, Where It's Going," *Book Production Industry* 56, no. 1 (January/February 1980), pp. 26–38.

CHAPTER TWENTY-TWO

The International Dimension of Publishing

FREDERICK A. PRAEGER

A Complex Market

The publishing industry in the United States, as elsewhere, is idiosyncratic, individualistic, and complex. Nothing in the industry is uniform or standardized. Within the average publishing house there are a great number of general and specialized units and subunits. International publishing is no less intricate: People who handle the import or export of books are part of a complex market consisting of a virtually infinite variety of nations and regions that differ in social, educational, political, and economic conditions; in their degree of development; in languages and language preferences; in censorship laws; and in the availability of foreign exchange for purchases of books.

Like our entire economy, the publishing industry operates in an unstable world. Sizable resources, including some of the industry's most capable people, are dedicated to crisis management, readjustment and realignment, and responding to financial constraints and technological pressures. Domestic sales and subsidiary income are no longer guarantees of survival—as in many other industries, international activities must provide additional revenue to strengthen the fabric of the industry and assure its stability.

The worldwide use of English as the lingua franca of trade, science, and technology; the strength and universal acceptance of U.S. science; and the traditional excellence of U.S. research and development efforts have created extensive overseas markets for U.S. scholarly and scientific books. Let us look at those markets and the tools and institutions employed to penetrate them.

FREDERICK A. PRAEGER is president and publisher, Westview Press.

Dimensions of the Overseas Market

Precise data on export sales are not available because the U.S. Department of Commerce records only bulk shipments (as opposed to orders from individuals for a small number of books). In addition, the relevant industry statistics—for instance, figures issued annually by the Book Industry Study Group (BISG)—are incomplete because not all publishers are members of or report their sales to BISG or the two main trade associations, the Association of American Publishers (AAP) and the Association of American University Presses (AAUP). A reasonable estimate would set export sales between \$800 and \$900 million annually, or somewhat less than 10 percent of total book sales. This figure represents book exports in the form of freight shipments and books sent by mail in all categories of publishing, including hardcover and softcover trade books; mass-market paperbacks; textbooks; encyclopedias; and books in special areas such as religion. According to Curtis Benjamin's study for the Center for the Book at the Library of Congress, sales of professional and reference books and college texts in 1980 constituted about 60 percent of the dollar value of all book exports, and general trade books (both hardcover and softcover) made up approximately 25 percent. Since the prices of scholarly and scientific books have experienced a higher rate of increase in the past few years than the prices of trade books, the current percentage represented by the sale of books in the scholarly sector is probably somewhat higher; a safe guess today would be slightly over 60 percent.

Each book in whatever discipline or category has its own particular export potential, the percentage of total sales that can be—sometimes must be—sold abroad, especially if the domestic market will not fully support the project. The export sales target varies from zero to about 60 percent of the print run of a specific title.

Development of the Overseas Market

The development of an international market for books in English was encouraged by the emergence of English as the primary tool of communication, the major language tying together countries and cultures. English is either the first or the second language spoken in the halls of diplomacy and in the world's universities and research institutions. Technological progress is rapid and, because everyone wishes to participate in it, requires a common language. In terms of international publishing, this has resulted in the new phenomenon of publishers in countries other than the United States and Great Britain—even those of the Soviet bloc, such as Hungary and Czechoslovakia—producing many of their scholarly books in English rather than in their native languages.

Historically, publishing has always had an international dimension. Its origin can be traced to the great German scholarly publishers, based primarily in Leipzig, who were most prominent from the sixteenth to the nineteenth century. The Leipzig Fair served as an annual international marketplace. Early in the twentieth century, London emerged as another focus for international publishing.

London's publishing structure is supplemented by long-established export wholesalers and specialist booksellers. It has traditionally been the intellectual center of the English-speaking world, and it has maintained close ties to the members of the British Commonwealth. Those ties have been eroded to some extent as the Commonwealth has dwindled during the past two decades. Nationalist ideologies, the desire for greater autonomy, and the strengthening of indigenous professional competence have led such countries as Australia and Canada to throw off their dependence on the London market. This decline in London's dominance has been accelerated by the actions of the U.S. Department of Justice, which objected to the restraint-of-trade aspects of U.S.-British distribution and publishing contracts. For example, if a U.S. publisher sold Commonwealth distribution rights to a British publisher, booksellers in Commonwealth countries such as Canada and Australia were required to purchase copies from the British publisher, rather than from the U.S. publisher, whose price was frequently lower. For this and a number of other reasons, dominance in international publishing began shifting to the United States.

Many U.S. publishers continue to conduct export operations not from their home bases but through subsidiaries or export agents in the greater London marketplace. It seems to be very difficult to depart from established practices. Some of the industry's giants—for example, McGraw-Hill, John Wiley, and Prentice-Hall—direct their exports from Great Britain rather than from the United States. The trend, however, is toward expansion into multinational structures with the primary New York–London operations supplemented by indigenous arrangements in countries and regions such as Mexico, Brazil, Japan (sometimes but not always including Korea, Hong Kong, or Singapore), India, Pakistan, and Australia (including New Zealand), plus various locations in Europe and Africa.

Most U.S. university presses, acting sometimes in concert and sometimes alone, have London sales offices or depositories that cover a large share of the world market. A depository—a "stockist" in British parlance—is a distributor who keeps multiple copies of a publisher's entire list on hand for distribution in a contractually defined territory. Orders or inquiries received by the publisher from customers in the distributor's territory are referred to the distributor for fulfillment.

Some U.S. publishers prefer to sell their books directly to British publishers; others opt for a mixed system involving a small export department in the United States, a depository in London (and often in Canada, Australia, Japan, India, or Pakistan), and the sale of certain titles to British or Dutch publishers, who issue the books under their own imprint, usually for sale in the entire world excepting the United States and Canada. The sale of a title is accomplished either by a transfer of bound books or of folded and gathered sheets (F&Gs) manufactured in the United States with the importer's imprint or by the sale of publication rights; in the latter case reproduction proofs or negatives are usually supplied to the foreign publisher, which manufactures its own edition.

Much of this international activity results from the leadership of the United States in scientific and technological research and its concomitant primacy in the publication of scholarly books. But this primacy is now being challenged; the Japanese, Germans, and Russians are matching or exceeding the United States in the percentage of gross national product devoted to research and development. Nevertheless, the world continues to regard U.S. science, and therefore scientific books produced in the United States, as the standard of excellence, the storehouse of essential information, and the harbinger of the future.

I do not mean that all scholarly books published in the United States are uniformly significant or that scholarly publishers in England and elsewhere do not produce outstanding books. Many excellent contributions, for example, are brought out in English by Dutch and German publishers such as Elsevier and Springer Verlag, and there is still universal acceptance for Oxford University Press reference books. Some U.S. reference books—for example, the *Encyclopaedia Britannica* and the major U.S. reference publications in chemistry and physics—retain their positions of primacy largely because they are the only such books available in English. The great German and French encyclopedias, although rigorously structured, thoroughly researched, and intellectually most satisfying, are unfortunately not viable in the international market because they are not in English.

Marketing

What are the methods by which a U.S. publisher markets products abroad? Some readers may bridle at the use of the word "product" in connection with books, pointing out that the book epitomizes our intellectual and cultural life and is therefore different from all other export commodities. In terms of marketing, it really is not. Each book must be assessed for its international potential, beginning with certain specific questions: Does it have any possible appeal to an overseas audience and if so, how much? How do we gauge that potential? Will the book travel easily by itself or does it need company in the form of other volumes in the same series, disciplines, or categories?

Next we must assess the world market in terms of the size, preferences, and absorptive capacities of its various sectors and subsectors so that we can pursue what might be called the logic of international marketing, including the logic of budgetary allocations. How much promotional money do we put where, and when? The various world markets can be classified roughly as (1) English-speaking countries; (2) industrialized nations where English is the second language, such as Japan, the Scandinavian countries, and Switzerland; (3) developing countries of the Third World where English is also the second language, such as some South Asian and Arab-world countries; (4) the Fourth World, comprising the really poor nations, where English as a second language and access to information and knowledge are still available only to a select few; and (5) the developing countries of the Soviet orbit.

With these general considerations about the book and its potential market in mind, let us now look at a hypothetical example, a comprehensive work on irrigation systems. It would seem logical to assume that it would be most useful in developing countries, especially in arid zones or areas where rainfall is unreliable or seasonal. Such a work would probably be marketable as well in countries with well-developed irrigation systems but somewhat limited access to modern irrigation technology or to advanced research, such as China, Southeast Asia, and some African and Latin American countries. In many of these countries, though, there is a tremendous imbalance between the need for information and the funds available to acquire it. It is necessary to seek support from government contacts, U.S. aid agencies, university exchange systems, or foundations or units connected to the World Bank in order to get important research to the end user. Such arrangements are occasionally part of the original publication contract, which in this case will include the terms of a purchase for distribution through the network of the sponsoring organization or an organization interested in wide distribution of the material. Westview Press (an independent publisher of scholarly books), for instance, produces works in cooperation with the International Agricultural Development Service (IADS) called the IADS Development-Oriented Literature Series. The service buys substantial numbers of books in the series for distribution in developing countries that otherwise would not be able to acquire them or distribute them effectively in the agricultural sector.

Marketing problems can arise because—in developing countries especially—the book is an important factor in economic and political growth: Planners and public officials in countries giving or receiving foreign aid are often distressingly shortsighted in their failure to recognize the indispensable role of the book in almost all areas of development. No progress is possible without supportive educational structures and meaningful increases in the level of technical and scientific skills. But the country most in need of a book on irrigation systems might also be one with little available foreign exchange, or none. It might be a country with a poorly developed book wholesale and retail structure, lacking trade channels and adequate financial resources. It might be a country with a library system that is more illusion than reality, one that does not have easy access to information about books or to books themselves. If the library does have access to information and books, it may not have the hard currency with which to purchase the books it would like. Often it will be prevented from improving its collections by the tendency of highly placed academics to appropriate scientific literature in order to improve their own private libraries and prevent their colleagues from obtaining the latest information: Knowledge is often perceived as power. The country's bureaucracy may be sluggish and unresponsive to book offerings; what book wholesalers there are may be accustomed to paying bills, not in thirty days, but in twelve months, or at some indefinite future time. An unstable political situation may even make it impossible to sell books altogether. There are as many variants on this situation as there are countries in need of books.

Departmental Structure

Most publishing firms, even small ones, have an export department that takes care of customer service and export promotion. These activities cannot be mirror images of domestic marketing but must relate to the characteristics of the complex international market. The job can be done in several ways, with a great variety of supporting and supplementary activities intertwined with the main approach. Let me outline some of the major ones:

- Some U.S. publishers simply direct all export activities from their main office.
- Some prefer to employ the expertise of a firm of export representatives such as Feffer & Simon, a U.S. firm that markets throughout the entire

world (sometimes excepting the United Kingdom/Commonwealth countries) and receives a commission for the sales it makes. Some export representatives finance their sales—usually paying the publisher in sixty days from the date of shipment, deducting a sales commission and a finance charge according to the prevailing rate of interest.

- Some firms prefer to appoint export agents, one of whom is usually based in or near London, with depositories at one or more additional locations worldwide. The agents buy "firm" (not on consignment) for their own accounts and market as independent distributors in their territories. For example, the R. R. Bowker Company in Epping, near London (a Xerox corporation subsidiary), is an independent operation representing a number of U.S. publishers. Most of its contracts reflect exclusive distribution arrangements.

- Other U.S. firms establish a branch office in London, sometimes tightly controlled by the parent company, sometimes functioning with a great deal of marketing and editorial independence. Often the London office is supported by subunits controlled from either London or the United States, operating in specific regions or countries. Depending on local laws, such units are fully or partly owned by the home office or the London subsidiary. Occasionally they are joint ventures utilizing supplementary indigenous capital. In cases in which there is a fair amount of editorial freedom, the local unit's books do not automatically flow back to the parent company but can be offered to other publishers for distribution in the U.S. market. In the case of large multinational publishers, each member of the structure would normally be expected to sell as much of the other members' production as possible. Indeed, in some of the largest U.S. publishing multinationals, sales of indigenous publications exceed the sales of books originally produced by the U.S. parent company. In fact, indigenous operations seem to be able to compete successfully with U.S. products in the world market.

- Some companies operate a system that contains a mixture of these elements. For instance, certain territories or regions may be served directly from the United States, others by export agents, and still others by the London office or by subunits.

- Some publishers work with a variety of independent agents, specialists, U.S. representatives of foreign distributors, and U.S. agents who purchase books for importers abroad.

The export system of U.S. publishers parallels similar systems that serve British, German, Dutch, Japanese, and other publishers. In recent years many foreign houses have founded bases of operation in the United States, sometimes by buying U.S. publishing units to take advantage of their established reputations and marketing strength. Some foreign companies now operating in the United States include Methuen, Routledge & Kegan Paul, Elsevier, Penguin, Springer Verlag, Butterworth, Longmans, St. Martin's Press (Macmillan London), and Allen & Unwin. Longmans purchased Viking and Elsevier bought several small U.S. houses, some of which were later sold.

IMPORTANCE OF DIRECT-MAIL MARKETING

The strategy and tactics of international marketing must, of course, be tailored to specific countries or regions. To some extent they are similar to the methods employed in the domestic market: promotion to bookstores, visits by the publisher's or distributor's representatives, direct-mail promotion to libraries and professionals, and locally or regionally initiated activities such as advertisements, newsletters, traveling exhibits, sampling of textbooks, and so on. For most developing countries, direct mail is often the only effective marketing method because of the absence of a workable book-distribution infrastructure. Mailing lists that include research institutes and government agencies can be developed from standard reference works such as *The World of Learning* (Europa Publishers, London; Gale Research Company, Detroit). Other academic and commercial lists can be obtained from various embassies in Washington. Often the original book proposal or the author's questionnaire will define export targets or provide specific mailing lists. Authors' questionnaires should be designed to make an author think about all possible channels and targets for marketing, especially when the book is aimed at developing nations, because of the difficulties of reaching buyers by other methods.

INTERNATIONAL BOOK FAIRS

The book world's great international marketplace and meetingplace, the Frankfurt Book Fair, is complemented by a host of local and regional fairs held at regular intervals in London, Moscow, Poznan, Cairo, Jerusalem, Bologna, Mexico City, Calcutta, and other even more exotic locations. The Frankfurt extravaganza almost defies description. It started in 1947 in two small rooms of the fledgling German National Library with fewer than one thousand books displayed. In 1984 there were over nine thousand exhibitors displaying millions of books to hundreds of thousands of visitors from both the industrialized nations and developing countries. It is a place where east and west, north and south, can meet, where representatives of the long-established firms encounter the book world's newest entrants. Although there is a good deal of cross-fertilization and stimulation, the frenetic atmosphere and shortage of time create considerable pressure. The atmosphere is also charged with hope, camaraderie, and the sense of belonging to an international institution devoted to communication and knowledge. The Frankfurt Book Fair is a marketplace not only of ideas and finished books but also of the cultural achievements that the various countries present through national exhibits. In sum, the Frankfurt Book Fair is a tremendous international cultural event with some elements of a county fair, a Paris boulevard cafe, an Oriental bazaar, a university seminar, and a designer's studio. It is both elitist and very democratic: Sometimes the large publishers deal only with each other, but it is also true that the fair makes it possible for the midgets of the international publishing world to meet the giants.

In terms of sales, the fair is perhaps not very cost effective. It is sprawling, somewhat overwhelming, and very expensive. Some very large deals are concluded, however, mainly by trade publishers, in its heady atmosphere. But there are many other reasons for the pilgrimage to Frankfurt: It is an entitlement perceived as an important status symbol; it is fun and it is informative; and it is the book world's favorite reason for travel. For publishers, hope seems to gush forth with renewed strength before fair time, and the threat of absence causes anguish and pain. A visit to Frankfurt can be a tremendous time-saver as publishers can take care of an enormous agenda in one place rather than traveling for weeks or months all over the world; thus, many transactions are made in Frankfurt that would not otherwise be concluded. The professional visitors there work very hard, and certainly the new contacts they make are important stimuli to the global book business.

TRANSLATIONS

So far we have discussed the international aspects of book publishing only in terms of exporting publications in the English language. But international publishing must also be seen in terms of the multidimensional flow of knowledge and information, literature, and entertainment through translations. Many books can be marketed much more effectively in translation than in their original English-language versions. Conversely, there is a market in the English-speaking world for books originally written in other languages.

Translation rights are handled by the subsidiary rights departments of both the buying and selling publishers. Sometimes these departments are fairly large operations; sometimes they consist of one person who handles an occasional contract. These departments may deal directly with the author and foreign publishers or operate through literary agents, who often work through local subagents. Agents can be very useful because of their knowledge of the local publishing industry, its foibles, capacities, and preferences, to say nothing of their ability to handle the foreign-exchange aspects of the transaction. The final contract, whether concluded by the publisher or an agent, is often the product of an intricate series of proposals, counterproposals, negotiations, letters, cables, telex messages, and phone calls. Publishers and agents frequently need the assistance of people who understand both the book's original and target languages.

Future Trends

As we have seen, international publishing is a complex business, subject to many influences. Technological progress, the emergence of new communication tools, and an information environment that is going through a metamorphosis in size, character, and efficiency will bring many changes, some of them impossible to anticipate, to the international book world and international science. The basic structure and configuration of the business will undoubtedly change. The book is losing its monopoly as the repository and carrier of knowledge and will have to share its role with electronic media and other information systems. Ultimately it will be possible to access information anywhere in the world immediately by means of facsimile transfer devices, digitized libraries on line, teletext, videotext, coaxial cables, satellite transmissions, and on-demand printers. A lone researcher in any country might obtain in minutes the latest in high-technology data from the National Technical Information Service in Washington, D.C., or from similar documentation centers in Great Britain. What, then, will become of the book?

Publishers are also affected by worldwide recessions that reduce sales to bookstores, libraries, and individual scholars everywhere. Even the traditional European markets, supported by numerous research institutes, have declined in the course of the past ten years. Library budgets have been reduced drastically, even in such major centers of learning as Great Britain and Germany. The Japanese market grew countercyclically in the past ten years, but it, too, has stopped expanding and shows the effects of reduced budgets and increased replacement of books by electronic information systems. The situation in the developing world is worse: When rising export-import imbalances and national budget shortfalls threaten the life of a nation, there is very little available for the purchase of books. The United States is certainly not a developing country, but we face the same problems here. Export shortfalls are particularly painful when we have just begun to rely on income from overseas markets.

Other factors threaten the survival of important sectors of the publishing industry in the United States. The rise of interlibrary loan systems, the distribution of information by wholesale photocopying, and the exponential growth of technological marvels that take over the storage and distribution of scientific knowledge and information certainly constitute short-range dangers to traditional publishing operations, but perhaps they will also provide long-range opportunities. The new world of publishing will probably consist of mixed systems, a blending of the traditional and the new, a mix of media to be used in different access and information distribution and storage situations.

The scholarly/scientific/informational book will continue to be published, but its importance will be sharply reduced, and editions of very specialized books and those in the forefront of knowledge will decline to the number needed to meet the basic requirements of regional documentation centers that will span the globe. Such publishing might become a social or governmental responsibility rather than the expression of the entrepreneurial spirit or the function of scholarly presses. It will be difficult to find sufficient funds to defray the cost of identifying literary contributions to civilization or to scholarship that also need to be edited, manufactured, and marketed internationally. The critical roles of the publisher in facilitating the flow of knowledge and providing entertainment in book form will need to be at least partially reallocated to authors, research institutions, and libraries. The traditional monopoly of the publisher will give way to multifaceted systems in which the publisher will often play a role complementary or even subordinate to electronic configurations.

The more complex the world becomes, the more intractable its problems, the more desperate is humanity's thirst for knowledge. Books will continue to fill this need, they will continue to be the world's major agent for knowledge transfer, but they will be linked to a host of communications devices that, in the aggregate, will make knowledge transfer more effective and efficient.

Acknowledgments

I am grateful to Beatrice Ferrigno-Lee and Barbara Ellington for their editorial help, their insistence on balance and completeness, and their many thoughtful suggestions.

CHAPTER TWENTY-THREE

Mass-Market Publishing: More Observations, Speculations, and Provocations

OSCAR DYSTEL

There is no way to talk about mass-market paperbacks today without discussing the whole world of trade publishing!

Pure mass-market paperback reprint publishing no longer exists—at least not as we learned to understand the term about forty years ago. It is a totally different business from what it was even in the mid-1960s and 1970s when paperback reprinters began to move up from their second-class position to join the rest of the industry as full-fledged original publishers.

Since then changes in editorial thinking, changes in the marketplace and marketing policies, changes in the ownership of mass-market companies, changes in management leadership—all these changes and more have become commonplace. Yet managing the process of change rather than submitting to it remains one of the greatest challenges we all face as trade publishers, whether we publish in soft covers or hard covers, in the mass market or in the more rarified atmosphere outside it. Moreover, the hierarchical distinction between the original hardcover house and the mass-market reprinter has begun to blur. We are witnessing a melding phenomenon in trade publishing, where the industry is moving from a horizontal, stratified business into a vertical, integrated *totality;* the increase and intensity of this melding process may prove to be the greatest change of all.

Today, mass-market paperback publishing has invaded the domain of hardcover publishing. Paperback publishers are producing their own hardcover editions with increasing pace and innovation. In turn, the hardcover side may soon invade the mass market by producing its own

OSCAR DYSTEL is former chairman of the board and chief executive officer, Bantam Books. This chapter originally appeared as the eighth of the new series of R. R. Bowker Memorial Lectures; © by R. R. Bowker Company. Reprinted here, with minor changes and updating, by permission of the R. R. Bowker Company.

rack-size paperback editions using the facilities of mass-market paperback organizations for manufacturing and distribution. In the past, hardcover and paperback publishers explored these avenues leading into each other's territory with little success and less confidence. Today, however, we *do* see a promise of success and some increasing confidence, and, as a result, I have little doubt that what was once a horizontally structured trade publishing universe in the United States will rapidly become vertical and integrated into hardcover and mass-market publishing entities.

Let me go back a few years to put this fascinating development into some perspective. Mass-market paperback publishing started solely as a merchandising operation. We bought the right to reprint hardcover books one year after hardcover publication and merchandised the paperback reprint better than any book had ever been merchandised before. We brought books to millions of people who never had access to them and at a low price that millions could afford. We opened up a market hardcover publishers had never penetrated before, including vast numbers of magazine readers. This marketing and merchandising feat became known as the "paperback revolution." And that revolution became one of the most stunning success stories in publishing history. But over the years the revolution turned into an evolution with perhaps predictable results: Growth slowed. Annual unit[1] sales stagnated and industry reactions to this situation were varied, to say the least.

With some mass-market publishers, the book became a product. The goal of editorial uniqueness became indifferent. And imitation was king. Others began to look for new directions, and today, as the cost of reprint rights for the headline-making blockbusters continues to climb, mass-market publishers are moving into new directions. The acquisition of volume rights and ventures into hardcover publishing is only one of them. More fundamental, I believe, will be the trend for mass-market publishers to acquire *all* the rights to a book and to merchandise these rights up and down as well as across: hardcover, trade paperback,[2] rack-size paperback, film rights, TV rights, foreign rights, cassettes; merchandising rights even in ways no one has thought of as yet.

Some hardcover houses may try to accomplish the same objectives. Already they are beginning to develop mass-market sophistication to a greater degree than ever before. And they will be building on some experience. Twenty years ago Walter Minton pioneered the idea by merchandising a mass-market edition of William Golding's *Lord of the Flies* with distinct success and recently Tom McCormick of St. Martin's Press has published a paperback edition of Gordon Liddy's book *Will,* using the Dell distribution system to achieve his mass-market sales objectives. In turn, paperback publishers are upgrading their editorial resources for their new total publishing effort. To achieve their objectives, they will need more talented editors with skills for shaping and pruning manuscripts into finished books, as well as skills in the acquisition of original material.

In short, mass-market houses will have to rebuild their own editorial support structure to match those of today's successful hardcover publishers. Hot merchandising ability will no longer be enough.

However, the first major confrontation between hardcover and paperback houses is not taking place on the hardcover shelves or in rack-sized paperback pockets. It is taking place in the trade-paperback area. Trade paperbacks have been around a long time, of course, but have only just begun to demonstrate tremendous mass-market potential. Some years back, many of us in the mass-market business (including me) looked askance at the trade paperback. We thought it had limited profitability, that it might interfere with rack-size volume.

Well, those of us who thought so were wrong. Sales of a million and more for some titles are now real possibilities. The phenomenal successes of *The Whole Earth Catalogue* and *The Joy of Sex* proved this. Just to give you an idea of how trade-paperback publishing has grown, industry trade-paperback sales in 1972 were reported at over 1 million units with dollar sales at almost 3 million. And in 1979 units were up to 37 million while dollar sales rocketed to about 70 million.[3] Today both mass-market and hardcover houses *can* and do sell trade paperbacks effectively. But I still think the mass-market houses have the edge. We have the facilities to reach a wider audience. We know more about the techniques of merchandising paperbacks regardless of their size and perhaps we sell a little harder.

Let me cite some examples. A few years ago Bantam licensed trade-paperback rights to Tom Robbins's *Even Cowgirls Get the Blues* to Houghton Mifflin, and it was a spectacular success. So successful, in fact, that with Tom Robbins's next novel, *Still Life with Woodpecker,* Bantam decided not to license the hardcover and trade-paperback rights elsewhere. Instead it decided to publish these editions itself with extremely successful results. Avon pioneered the hot historical romances in trade-paperback publishing that set sales records none of us believed possible. And now Bantam has introduced Louis L'Amour into the trade-paperback world.

Reverting Paperback Rights

But mass-market publishers are not alone. Increasingly, hardcover houses are tackling trade paperbacks as vehicles for a double market assault. I believe hardcover publishers will increasingly revert rights to highly successful rack-sized paperbacks when the paperback licenses expire,[4] in order to publish these titles in their own trade-paperback editions and perhaps eventually in their own rack-size editions. One recent example is Norman Mailer's *The Naked and the Dead*. It has not sold spectacularly in mass market over the last few years, but it has done well enough to persuade the original publisher to issue a trade paperback of his own rather than renew the mass-market license.[5] And as this trend goes further, the demands for longer paperback licenses from mass-market reprinters will become more insistent.

It's no secret. Much of the impetus for mass-market original paperback publishing comes from what we have *always* felt to be unfairly short licensing periods, as well as the economic impact of tremendous advances[6] we have had to pay for blockbusters. We need books to sell profitably, and with the greater risks now imposed on us by short licenses and high advances we *must* find and develop our own. As a result, the implications may be grim for hardcover trade publishers without paperback affiliations—and perhaps we will see more mergers in the offing.

Yet vertical integration of publishing is not the only imminent development. Author influence and power may also be shifting within publishing. Successful authors and their advisers are becoming entrepreneurs demanding a larger share of overall earnings—and not only through the competition for rights to books they sell. Instead, I believe we soon will be witnessing a trend to shared risk and shared equity, with authors demanding that their books be accepted as venture capital in separate or individual publishing partnerships. Indeed, I would not be surprised to soon see *successful* authors take the whole publishing risk and rent certain services from existing publishing companies.

To meet these new changes now beginning to spread throughout our business, mass-market publishers will have to retain a style of management loose enough to handle the surprises that lie ahead and flexible enough to risk failure. And this philosophy of management is perhaps the most important message I hope to leave with you. Without willingness to risk failure,[7] the achievements of the future may fall through our fingers. And unhappily I see less and less willingness to risk failure today, and more and more to bet on the tried and true; to follow what's left of innovation, not with more innovation, but with slavish imitation, until the last dollar has been squeezed from a promotional trend or editorial category that should have been buried long ago.

Yet the right to fail is fundamental to creative endeavor, and endemic to publishing, which is an activity built on risk and sometimes on long odds. We *must* take chances and encourage those who work for us to take chances. Playing it safe does not ensure greater profitability—because playing it safe is surely the kiss of death over the long haul. The right to fail is the catalyst of creativity. Give dedicated people the right to fail, and their enthusiasm will spark ideas that may seem fantastic and far out at first examination. Yet these ideas can be made real and successful with the help of a seasoned, understanding mentor and leader.

I am not, of course, suggesting that we allow every bright person in our publishing houses to run wild with earnest and probably unsalable ideas. Rigorous analysis of any publishing project is mandatory. But the real challenge to publishing management today lies in allowing the restless, roaming, searching editorial mind to create something exciting from the sum total of our analysis of trends—ideas that fire the whole publishing process, which begins with the visceral reaction to a piece of writing when editor and author work together, a process that reaches its zenith when the book arrives at the point of sale.

Need for Sensitive Management

The process is basic. Indeed *process* may well be the best word to define our business. Mass-market or hardcover trade publishing is too varied and too bewildering to readily accept anything more specific. Management based solely on computer printouts simply won't do. Only a management sensitive and responsive to creative people, with all their peculiarities and frequent eccentricities, can hope to succeed. Successful publishing management is a delicate balance rarely achieved and easily destroyed. Successful managements must deal with so many conflicting egos, and sometimes withstand so strong a torrent of abuse and criticism from the press, that those who practice the craft have sometimes been called men and women of steel.

Much too often publishers have unfairly been labeled as cultural desperadoes, people fired by greed and debased by incompetence. Yet for too long our business was cursed with the contradictory views of publishing as a gentleman's profession, a haven for proper young English majors, a hobby for the sons of the rich. It was a perception that bred the tired myth of the publisher in his tweed jacket sipping sherry in an oak-paneled office and puffing on a pipe while discoursing on literature and the life of the spirit. I don't think that myth had much reality back in the 1920s when publishers like Max Schuster, Dick Simon, and Leon Shimkin were looking for untapped markets with books of crossword puzzles, and salesmen like Mel Minton and Arthur Thornhill, Sr., were hustling up new territory. Nor do I share the critical perception of publishers as hungry barracuda feeding off the talent and lifeblood of poverty-stricken authors. The truth, I believe, lies elsewhere. Like many older and established businesses, trade publishing often ran a little behind the times and needed to be shaken up and shaken out.

And the paperback revolution did just that. In the mid-1950s when I took over at Bantam, new marketing skills were required for the titles we selected. We borrowed some of the ideas from the world of advertising, publicity, and public relations as well as from mass merchandisers. Then we applied them with an understanding of financial and administrative control. Today good trade publishing management continues to need all this expertise . . . and more. It needs an understanding of the publishing totality, an understanding of all aspects of the publishing process—and, most importantly, the editorial process.

Again, it is a matter of balance. Editorial sensitivity is basic to top-grade publishing management. It has to be. We sell books, and we have to know what's in them, how they are made, how they're put together. We should understand something of the agony inherent in the writing process, and we should even be able to work with writers if necessary. A good manager should be able to understand how a book is edited, should have respect for all varieties of writing, for design, graphics, art, and photography, all the visual arts; the typographic appearance, the feel and quality of paper, the physical impression of a book.

The way a book is produced and put together can make a tremendous difference at the point of sale. Again, that's where the balance comes in—at the point of sale. Understanding the psychology of the marketplace for a particular editorial work, whether it be scholarly, professional, or popular, is the vital switching station that enables the marketing process to function smoothly. Who out there is interested in this material? How do we reach these potential buyers?

The answer lies in a publisher's marketing experience, in the effective use of necessary technical skills, in the choice of appropriate media techniques and their successful application—a marketing orientation that even reaches down to the judgment of a selling brochure, the headline on a direct-mail piece, as well as a knowledge of discounts and of payment terms and a firm grasp of shipping policies. These are examples of what I mean by understanding the totality of the publishing process, an understanding so necessary in today's difficult competitive climate.

And the one managerial quality that ties all the others together, the quality that can make the difference between one company and another, is the amount of in-house enthusiasm and excitement for each publishing venture, all of which contributes to the environment of the company as a whole. . . .

The fact is—and it's almost embarrassingly obvious—in a book-publishing house, if you don't care about books and the people who *manage* the excitement of publishing, you just don't perform. Caring is crucial and that quality too has to come from the top. Creative management understands that difference. Creative management is participative management, where men and women of talent and ability are assured freedom of expression and where their contributions are eagerly sought and deeply respected. . . .

Numbers Are Not Enough

The book is what this business is all about. The successful book makes a balance sheet pleasant reading. Without books there are no profit-and-loss statements, no earnings per share, no systems, no movie deals, no inventory figures, no bank loans, no software, no hardware. Yet it is difficult to avoid the feeling sometimes that the systems environment in which we operate has taken on a life of its own. My concern is not the use of these systems. They are vital. They can make today's publishing activity more efficient, more profitable. But I am concerned about the overuse and the overemphasis of these systems, especially from the new breed of mass-market paperback stockholders, the conglomerate. . . .

Part of the myth attached to the conglomerate invasion of publishing in the 1960s and 1970s was based on the primacy of numbers, by the discovery of what looked like a hot new growth industry and by the dreams of easily increasing earnings per share with a fair amount of leveraging. Those dreams were fired dramatically in 1971 by the National General Corporation, Bantam's conglomerate stockholders. Against my advice at that time, National General offered 10 percent of its ownership to the public with a prospectus covering Bantam's financial condition and operating history.[8] As far as I know, no other mass-market company had ever revealed so much so quickly. Bantam's sizable profits and wide margins opened new vistas of the profit potential in the paperback industry, especially to other conglomerates looking for a hot new business. So it was only natural for several to ask, If Bantam can do it, why can't we, especially if we pour money and better management talent into a mass-market paperback company? It looked easy. Well, that's exactly what happened. Those conglomerates who already were in the mass-market paperback business decided to stay—and a new crop of conglomerate stockholders began to appear from the wings.

But many of these acquirers were soon disillusioned. The projected growth rates and the profits promoted by merger specialists could very often *not* be maintained. As an industry, our expansion turned sluggish and profits became more difficult to predict. So as a result, too many of the giants who "bought" into publishing found the going too slow. Many insisted on growth and profits beyond reasonable expectation—though, of course, the expectations seemed reasonable to *them* given the extravagant prices they paid. Too often acquisitions were made without careful study of existing realities. When these realities emerged, conglomerates showed little ability to reduce their profit expectations especially once inflationary pressures really closed in. Costs exploded and escalating cover prices could not make up the difference.

By the late 1970s our cash-rich days were over. Today we count nickels and dimes. Our margins are harder to maintain. Higher cover prices have flattened unit sales. More and more paperback companies are reporting net losses. We have bankrolled hardcover publishing too long, and I believe that trip is about over. Some mass-market houses are putting firm lids on bids, and others are simply walking away from auctions. Where big money bids *are* made, terms will be tougher. Money is too costly to settle for anything less. So the growing need for capital to stay in the mass-market business has soured conglomerates on mass-market publishing. . . ?

Odds are that many of these conglomerates would have done better investing in U.S. treasury notes and their management knows it. That's too bad. Too often management at the conglomerate top doesn't know how to read a mass-market publishing company's balance sheets and profit-and-loss statements correctly. And I don't mean the numbers. They're clear enough but their meaning often is not. . . .

Let me clear up one possible misunderstanding. No one can seriously quarrel with budgetary restraints the conglomerate parent imposes on a publishing subsidiary. Such controls are necessary and welcome. They become intolerable only when conglomerate executives interfere with publishing management's freedom of action and decisions on such matters as firing, hiring, and how jobs should be performed. . . .

The Role of Management in Marketing

Let me turn next to the role of top management in paperback marketing, a word that I will use as a catchall to include nearly all noneditorial activities: distribution, sales, advertising, promotion, publicity, even proper servicing of customers.

One of the most common complaints and questions I've heard over the years is why paperbacks aren't marketed like soap—and it seems as if the second most common complaint I've heard is that paperbacks *are* marketed like soap and shouldn't be. As usual, in contradictory situations such as this, everybody is right and everybody is wrong. By and large, books are not packaged goods or soap. Most books are unique and require individual handling. Having said that, let me add that some books indeed can, are, and should be marketed like soap. Intensive market-by-market advertising campaigns, sampling, back-of-the-book previews, and similar promotions—and even a magazinelike subscription campaign for continuity sales direct to the consumer—all these can work for certain category books like westerns and romances, mysteries, and even for science fiction and thrillers.

The Harlequin line is probably the most dramatic example of this kind of marketing success. It sells more units per year through book dealers and by subscriptions than does any other mass-market line in the world. These books *can* be sold like soap because Harlequin romances appeal to well-defined desires. Each title, each story is part of a brand name—uniform, homogenized, quality-controlled in the same way each bar of Ivory soap is quality-controlled. But a single work of fiction and a work of serious or popular nonfiction *cannot* be marketed that way. The markets are not as well defined, the "series" element not established, unless we are dealing with the vast following of some specific authors like John D. McDonald, Louis L'Amour, or Barbara Cartland. I do not believe it would be economically feasible, for example, to market a book as successful as *The Scarsdale Diet* like soap. It won't work for *one* book.

Nevertheless, the brand-name concept has a bright future in mass-market publishing. And it can take all shapes. The John Jakes Kent Family Chronicles and the Wagons West series *have* developed brand-name followings.[10] Customers will walk into stores and ask for them by name, the way they ask for Harlequin romances, and as science fiction fans ask for Del Rey books. Like most innovative ideas, however, the brand-name concept has some real disadvantages for the mass-market industry as a whole. Brand-name categories have joined super-sellers to dominate mass-market book displays and threaten to crowd out other books of merit and high salability.

Series like Wagons West, Harlequin, and Silhouette books, the hot historical romances, and the multiple display of the big best-sellers are creating a different impression of paperbacks at point of sale—a different look, which I believe will hurt us in the long run. The image of variety is no longer there in many locations, and I believe we are losing the paperback browsers who were once a key to multiple purchases.

Constant flogging of best-sellers probably has done *the most* to change retail display and crowd out other salable books. Again, I regret to say

Bantam pointed the way. We developed the concept of the super-seller. As long as we were alone, variety in title display did not seem to be affected because sales of *Valley of the Dolls* did not hurt our backlist titles. They sold *briskly* alongside the blockbuster. But when competitors picked up the idea, other titles began claiming equal sales status with *Valley of the Dolls* every week.

Even worse, I think, was the arrival of the brassy promoter, the illusionist, the superhype artist. He promised wholesalers and retailers[11] massive infusion of advertising dollars aimed directly at the consumer, as well as countless other promotional gimmicks—and all too often for a *nothing* novel. Even when he delivered on his promises the promotion failed to move the book, usually because the book didn't have what it takes to move off the shelves. And still superhype shows no slackening. The Hollywood syndrome of dubbing everything colossal and stupendous has spread through mass-market publishing like a fungus. What's more, the avalanche of imitation that follows one publisher's really innovative and successful promotional campaign has tended to debase the entire industry.

Yet intelligent publicity has leverage beyond price. Handled with style and grace, respectful of facts—and not of a company's exaggerated hopes for a book—it can make a major contribution to publishing success, perhaps more effectively than any other promotional activity. But such publicity is difficult to apply to books that don't deliver. Once your credibility is questioned, the selling message just doesn't work anymore. As an example, movie and TV tie-ins[12] can work very well—but not always. That's why blanket promises that any film or TV show will sell books can be harmful. As a matter of fact, most retailers today are probably more skeptical of movie tie-in selling power than of any other promotional device. And that doubt is the direct result of mindless hype.

Let's face it: Promotion works when it supports a worthy book in a cost-effective manner. While publishers must tailor each campaign to meet the specific market needs of the book, sometimes that campaign will fly and sometimes it won't—and sometimes we never will know the answer. Remember, this is a gambling business, and the right to fail is as essential to effective promotion of a book as it is to editorial judgment.

Author-Publisher Relations

Take the basics of our business, books. We need new books all the time, books that will sell, books by new writers. We have an obligation to find and nurture them, not because the future of literature depends on it, but because *our* future does. First novelists are the lifeblood of this business. Consider this list: Grace Metalious and *Peyton Place,* Jackie Susann and *Valley of the Dolls,* Norman Mailer and *The Naked and the Dead,* Frederick Forsythe's *Day of the Jackal,* and Judith Guest's *Ordinary People.* Most first novels lose money, but that cannot mean we'll stop publishing them or stop looking for authors to write them. Going out and looking—not sitting in our offices moaning that we can't afford to hire people to read the slush pile.[13] It's true, we probably can't. It's usually not cost effective. Looking for new writing talent in new ways, however, can be very effective. We ought to get editors to go outside into the towns and cities to find writers of promise through contacts with local media and the teaching world.

Let's say a young editor spends a week or two on the road and connects with writers of talent, looks at their material, and explores what else they can do in the way of a book project; takes that project back to New York and gets his colleagues excited about it. That's how novels are discovered. As well as judgment in writing talent, the mark of a good editor is feel for subject matter, market potential, and the ability to make a flawed manuscript work. The editor should be able to tell a copywriter in Indianapolis how to structure ideas for a funny novel on life in the Midwest, to explain the novelistic potential of an unsolved local murder to a young reporter covering the story in Des Moines. If we want new writers and new ideas that work, we will have to do more to generate them.

We're also going to have to find new ways of dealing with the established writers in our business. I mean the writers of super-sellers, the millionaire authors. I've already spoken about the new role I expect them to play in our business as entrepreneurs and co-owners. Now I'd like to discuss a controversial proposal about a more basic matter in publisher-author relations: the royalty rate. Today some authors are getting 15 percent of cover price, and I believe this royalty rate has to come down once the advance is earned out. Our costs have gone up—*all* our costs. That's why we're hiking cover prices the way we are. But the author's costs haven't gone up, beyond the increase in his cost of living— and that affects us all. As a matter of fact, a lower royalty would give us the needed cash to promote his titles more effectively, and a hundred other books as well. Another approach to making royalty structures more equitable could very well be to move our rates from a percentage of cover price to a percentage of net selling price. Royalties based on net selling prices would be a much fairer way to look at the relationship between author, agent, and publisher.

Solving the Problem of Distribution

Now I'd like to turn to the subject of mass-market paperback distribution. If management has been buffeted in editorial, corporate, financial, and promotional areas, it faces its most serious challenge and biggest opportunity as it attempts to solve its growing problems in mass-market distribution.

Let me try to make my point with some history. At the 1977 Mid-America Periodical Distributors Association (MAPDA) convention in Chicago, I described how the mass-market revolution started with the rack-size paperback that could be sold through magazine wholesalers in every drugstore and corner tobacco store in the United States and Canada. Magazine wholesalers gave paperback books tremendous reach. For the publisher, distribution seemed relatively simple. National distributors like Curtis and Independent News shipped paperbacks to magazine wholesalers on a fully returnable basis, and these wholesalers serviced retailers in the same way. Over the years, however, distribution became anything but simple. New national book jobbers competed with magazine wholesalers for retail accounts. Territories and channels were no longer exclusive. Bookstores that had shunned mass-market paperbacks began to buy directly from publishers, as well as from wholesalers and jobbers. You couldn't tell the players even with a score card.

Then in recent years, as the economy got tougher, our distribution problems grew even *more* intense. Costs rose. More capital was needed to finance inventories. Higher interest rates forced book jobbers, magazine wholesalers, and retailers to handle fewer titles and turn them over faster. Paperbacks had to make it in one, two, or at best three weeks, or they were off the shelves with covers back to the publisher for full credit. Returns skyrocketed and the magazine wholesaler became our number-one problem. As these wholesalers moved toward full computerization, they found paperback distribution difficult and cumbersome. Profits were better and easier in magazines. Where only five years ago paperback books accounted for 30 to 35 percent of a magazine wholesaler's total volume, these days volume can be down to 15 percent. The figures say it all. Wholesalers seem to have lost interest in paperbacks. Much of the trust that marked our relationship has gone—gone in just the few years since my Chicago speech.

Paperback book returns[14] are the single most important manifestation of the problem. Returns are a bigger headache for magazine wholesalers than they are for jobbers and retailers because magazine wholesalers are in other businesses besides books. The don't have the time or expertise to select books that sell. Too often they fall victim to superhype or the promise of better discounts.[15] As a result, too many wholesalers order indiscriminately. Paperbacks are shipped in and shipped out, and everybody hurts: the retailer, the wholesaler, and the publisher. Yet the control of returns is absolutely crucial to our future—even more so these days as we face rising manufacturing and shipping costs and narrowing margins. If we fail to master the returns problem, our whole business could go under.

And that's one reason I have always advocated placing separate responsibility for managing returns with a single important executive in a mass-market company, an individual with broad marketing and systems experience, someone who would live, eat, breathe, and sleep paperback returns. I understand the difficult political and practical aspects of such a decision, but an executive who surmounted these difficulties would be worth almost any price.

One idea such a manager might ponder is wider and more sophisticated application of the Universal Product Code (UPC) in paperback distribution. Most of us use UPCs on our books, but we're still years behind magazines in developing the kind of useful information that can be applied throughout the entire distribution chain, from publisher to distributor, to retailer, and ultimately to the consumer. What's more, wholesalers tell me they expect their own greatest growth over the next five years to come in paperbacks—provided publishers target sales through industry-wide adoption of UPC markings.

But it isn't all black. Many individual magazine wholesalers are continuing their own efforts to boost paperback sales—for example, their seven hundred paperback bookstores from coast-to-coast. And one of their most promising new ideas is the installation of a separate minibookstore within a supermarket. This one has real potential because it puts books where people are. The project began in the Farm Fresh Supermarket chain in Norfolk, Virginia, and is expanding elsewhere. What we have here is a store within a supermarket visited by twenty thousand people a week—a bookstore that carries magazines, children's books, mass-market best-sellers, and some hardcover books. The most significant marketing factor is this: In a research study, fully 50 percent of those who passed through the Farm Fresh minibookstore had never been in a bookstore in their lives. This could be a terrific new concept for paperback distribution. It was also amazing to learn what consumers are buying in these minibookstores—in variety, in amount, in price. It proves again that plenty of people want to read but it is up to us to make books accessible to them.

Convenience stores are another successful example of wholesaler expansion, but I believe we can *all* do more to find new outlets. Books can be sold virtually anywhere: sporting goods stores, liquor stores, hardware stores, wherever applicable titles can be placed.

Further, I don't believe existing retailers are putting enough *drive* behind their selling. Handled with imagination, discount retailing works. Discount stores in New York and Washington have shown that. But, in my opinion, the Barnes & Noble book merchandising philosophy is *still* not growing fast enough, even though cover prices continue to increase and retail dollar volume continues to go up.

Retailing books can also be a much more exciting business. As we have seen from recent book fairs in New York City and elsewhere, the theatrical aspect is easy to enhance. Today authors are celebrities, and celebrities draw crowds—like Louis L'Amour at the truck stops of America, for example, or at Shepler's in Denver and Kansas City, where hundreds waited patiently for up to two hours to have L'Amour autograph one of his western sagas.

These incidents certainly don't have to be isolated. Something should be happening at the retail level all the time. Store managers who can create events—author visits, seminars, contests around books they sell— can do better. Greater availability of magazines and newspapers can improve traffic and paperback sales. But for something to "happen" at the retail level all the time, bookstores have to change. Many of them are still too intimidating in layout, function, and style. The American Booksellers Association ought to do more to help retailers improve their merchandising thinking, planning, and expertise.

Many of the marketing and retailing techniques I have been trying to describe here would work in libraries as well. Libraries need much more showmanship—visits by major authors, more displays, and use of mass-market paperbacks. A more exciting use of mass-market poster material would be terrific. Get people accustomed to using libraries, get people feeling comfortable in them, using them more, and you end up with people more comfortable in bookstores and more willing to buy books.

One final word on distribution. I believe that in the future, certain mass-market paperback titles may be sold to the entire marketplace on a nonreturnable basis. Note I said *certain* titles. Obviously we are not going to reach a situation where returns are completely eliminated. That wouldn't be healthy either. But certain titles should work very well on a nonreturnable basis provided discounts and royalties are adjusted accordingly.[16]

Possibilities for Growth

Let me discuss now a series of provocations or new ideas—alternate futures if you will: different ways of looking at our growth possibilities.

We've only just begun to tell students how to prepare for a publishing career, and we need to do more to support educational programs for young people who are interested in trade publishing. Most people learn on the job and shift from house to house. By the time they get their third job they have some idea of the business, but too often they're also thirty years old and nowhere. I submit that's a terrible way to bring along bright people. We ought to have a college publishing program and an in-house apprentice system. Guidelines for study programs should be simple. Students should learn something about business, including basic accounting and financial management and to be able to read a balance sheet and a profit-and-loss statement. Courses in general economics, advertising, and marketing should also be required; and so should some grasp of journalism and public relations. Anyone we hire should demonstrate an ability to write clear, concise English. It would help if the applicant typed and knew the fundamentals of computers and word processors. Some formal training in the visual arts—photography, design, printing, and artwork—ought to be required. Knowing foreign languages can be helpful. And trainees should be conversant with literature, history, sociology, psychology, politics, and probably science, which is clearly a growing field of popular interest.

Not too far in the future, I think it's possible that we may publish books a little differently—for example in *newspapers*. The sale of bestsellers to newspapers for publication in a special supplement—the whole book in one or two weekend supplements—may be coming.

Suppose a mass-market paperback house and a specially formed group of newspapers formed a separate venture to acquire reprint rights to a major commercial novel with publication one year after hardcover in one or two special Sunday newspaper supplements (which of course would carry advertising)? And suppose further that the mass-market edition would follow immediately after the novel's appearance in the newspapers. Do you know something? I don't think its appearance in the newspaper supplement form would affect mass-market paperback sales all that much, and the potential financial rewards might be quite interesting.

Well, that's one example. Now let me try another. The United States is rapidly becoming a bicultural nation and a bilingual nation. There are 20 million Hispanics by the government's count and more like 30 million by unofficial estimates that include the millions of illegal aliens. Furthermore, I believe the number of Hispanics in this country is going to zoom. The population of Mexico City, some experts say, will reach 35 million by the year 2000. That's just the population of Mexico City. Where are those people going to go? Unless we build an Iron Curtain along the Rio Grande, how are we going to stop the influx of illegal aliens? The answer I'm afraid seems clear. We're not. So this country is going to have to live with the reality of a growing Hispanic minority—Spanish-speaking people who want to read paperback books in their own language. Already some efforts are being made. We have published some bilingual books in Spanish and English. True, it has been only sporadic. But I think we will see more of that as time moves on. Those mass-market publishers willing to pay some attention to the Spanish-language market will find it has *real* growth potential; but it will mean hiring bilingual editors fluent in both Spanish and English and with fingertips that can touch both cultures, as well as Hispanic executives with the distribution expertise to open up new markets.

In the near future, I also believe we are going to be looking far beyond our borders for new markets. If we seize the opportunities opening up now in mainland China, we may supply much of the reading matter so desperately needed there. English is China's second language, as it is in just about every other country in the world. I do not know what books the Chinese are likely to read or want to buy, or how much money they can spare for paperbacks. But any future-minded mass-market paperback publisher ought to think seriously about selling books to China. It may not be a bonanza tomorrow, but it could well be ten years from now, or twenty years from now, a time when those who bet their shirts on the "electronic revolution" replacing books may have no more shirts left to bet.

Nor is China the only market for English-language mass-market paperback books produced in the United States. Demand for English-language paperback books exists on the continent of Europe, in the Middle East, and in Central and South America. Yet there are few English-language paperback bookstores anywhere; certainly there isn't even *one* in Mexico City, a city of 9 million. We should therefore explore the possibility of joint ventures with British publishers for underwriting or supporting such stores in major cities abroad.

So you can see the range is wide—all the way to China, Europe, and bilingual publishing, and even children's books in mass-market paperback editions. Children's books are special, though I was never a great advocate. I worried about where children's paperbacks could be effectively displayed. I was wrong. Children's paperbacks *are* a promising field—doubly so because they instill lifelong reading habits in children, our mass-market audience of tomorrow.

And now I would like to discuss the use of advertising in paperback books as an editorial asset. I look for more experimentation with advertising in premium books: for instance, a sixteen-page advertising insert of tennis equipment in a mass-market paperback teaching one to play the game. The same kind of advertising "fit" could be tried in

travel paperbacks and cookbooks. Merchandise catalogs might offer a
whole new opportunity for mass-market publishing. Some are already
being produced in mass-market sizes. And with ingenious editorial
support, even *these* might find a successful home on the mass-market
rack. For instance, suppose one of us were to publish a Gadget Hunter's
Guide, a merchandise catalog filled only with paid advertising describing
and illustrating various gadgets and how they work. If a mass-market
paperback house were to try this project, it would charge the manufacturers
for the space; promote, distribute, and sell the guides; and become the
conduit for selling the products in the catalog on a mail-order basis. I
believe the idea might be especially successful if the catalog covered
really interesting gadgets difficult to find.

None of these ideas is the salvation of our business. No single idea
ever is. But I submit them as examples of the many directions we must
be exploring to stay in business and grow.

And so for all the reasons I have presented and despite the difficulties
that still lie ahead of us in mass-market paperback publishing, I'm not
at all pessimistic about the future. Opportunities are everywhere. Horizons
are wide. Books will survive. And we'll find a viable balance between
the upcoming electronic "retrieval and storage systems" and the book
as a means of speeding communication, entertainment, and education.
But I doubt that computer terminals will be as effective as books in
transmitting a continuous learning experience. Books and electronics
are going to live together—comfortably, I suspect—as long as we succeed
in our efforts to have more and more people read books . . . read
paperbacks. And *that,* I submit, is the real challenge of the 1980s. Mass-
market paperback books are versatile, informative, entertaining. And,
most important, mass-market paperback books will always be easily
available everywhere.

The State of Reading

Now let's take a few final moments to examine the state of reading in
this country. To say the least, it is precarious and needs extensive
nurturing. This means an active effort from all of us to encourage
reading at *every* level—from the reading of the classics to the reading
of romances. We must continue our work at the school level to promote
paperbacks as a supplementary and even primary educational tool. . . .
We cannot afford to let up the pressure, despite the changing financial
condition of the educational establishments across the country. For
example, I believe we should be doing more with teachers' colleges,

trying to train would-be teachers in the use of paperback books as a teaching tool. We should not let up on publishing books for the educational market—from dictionaries and texts to supplemental readings; and with cover prices moving up, students soon won't be able to afford anything but paperback books.

More ought to be done to recycle returns into the educational market. It certainly makes better sense to me to see that certain carefully selected returns find their way into the classroom rather than shredding[17] these books. They should be seeded into schools where social and economic conditions are poor and where this seeding can do the most good. And we should at least think about distributing returns to hospitals, prisons, and underprivileged neighborhoods. Paperback publishing, after all, could do with a stronger dose of social activism, especially in these times.

The Multiple Sclerosis (MS) Read-a-Thon is worth all the help we can give it. Supported by local Multiple Sclerosis Society chapters throughout the country, this national reading plan encourages children to read and helps raise money to fight the tragic results of this disease. As a matter of fact, I understand that recently about 1 million children across the country read more than 12 million books under this very worthwhile program.[18]

New York City has a small but effective effort to help its estimated one million functional illiterates. An organization called Literacy Volunteers has used trained volunteers to tutor students for the last ten years. It is worth our support. . . .

I want to stress the urgency of this problem. Functional illiteracy is a major national issue. If reading is not actually declining, it is surely static, and I see no evidence of any reversal in this situation.

Yet I believe our potential audience for mass-market paperbacks is growing all the time. In absolute numbers, there will be millions more of us in the years ahead. And somehow our government will not let our people down despite our continuing difficulties with functional illiteracy. So the market is there for trade publishing—hardcover, trade paperback, mass-market paperback. The market is there, and it is ours to exploit—with prudence and caution, with innovation and excitement, or rapaciously and uncaringly. The choice is clear—and it is ours to make.

Acknowledgments

First, I should like to thank Paul Carnese, publisher of *Publishers Weekly,* for his invitation to give the lecture on behalf of the R. R. Bowker Company and the Columbia University School of Library Service.

But its ideas really could not have been as clearly presented without the writing talent of Tom Weyr, who spent countless hours helping me prepare it, and without the diligent, efficient, and loyal support of my assistant, Barbara Stevens-Essick, who retyped draft after draft without complaint.

Among the many friends and associates who were especially helpful in listening, guiding, and making important suggestions were Stuart Applebaum and Paige Mitchell. But I should also acknowledge the aid of many others, including John Choi, Richard Conway, Linda Cunningham, Alun Davies, Robert DiForio, Heather G. Florence, Ernest Hecht, Lawrence Hughes, Robert Keegan, Esther Margolis, Roy Newborn, Patrick Newman, Angela Rinaldi, Jack Romanos, William Sarnoff, Louis Satz, Roger Scherer, Alberto Vitale, and Dwight Yellen.

And finally my appreciation goes to all those in trade publishing, in mass-market publishing, and in distribution who over the past twenty-five years helped me form the basis for the viewpoints I expressed in the preceding pages.

Notes

1. Units are books.

2. Trade paperbacks are an amalgam between hardcover books and traditional mass-market, rack-size paperbacks. They vary in size, use better paper and stiffer covers than mass-market volumes, and are usually priced in between hardcover and softcover books.

3. These trade-paperback numbers are taken from a speech by Alberto Vitale, October 18, 1980, at the first International Paperback Conference, Como, Italy.

4. Paperback publishers purchase the right to publish books from the hardcover proprietor for a limited time only. Licenses usually run from five to ten years. The license must be renegotiated at the end of that time or the rights revert to the hardcover publisher.

5. Holt editor in chief Thomas Wallace, in *Book Digest,* January 1981, p. 10.

6. Advances are money paid "up front" against royalties to be earned out later. Paperback advances of $1 million and more were relatively common in the 1970s but much rarer in the leaner 1980s.

7. I must credit the talented Paige Mitchell who brought this term and the concept to my attention during several conversations we had about the publishing process.

8. The prospectus was prepared by the Wall Street firm of Loeb Rhoades, which floated the stock issue in 1971.

9. In fact, in the early 1980s, four paperback houses—Fawcett, Popular Library, Ace, and Playboy—were spun off from their corporate umbrellas, or went under.

10. The series was developed by Lyle Kenyon Engel in his upstate New York "writing factory" and is one of the more interesting new developments in mass-market publishing.

11. Wholesalers take shipments of books from the publisher and distribute the books (as well as magazines) to their network of retailers by truck. Retail outlets for paperback books include drugstores, supermarkets, airport newsstands, and specialty stores.

12. Movie and TV tie-ins are promotional devices that allow a paperback book to feed

off the publicity given a TV miniseries or a hit film. Publishers will often market a special edition of the book on which the film or TV show is based.

13. The slush pile is the trade name for unsolicited manuscripts that pour into publishers' offices every day in great volume. With what often seems like half the population convinced it can write a best-seller, manuscripts can pile up in stacks far too great for even the richest publisher to handle. Manuscripts are occasionally pulled out of the slush pile and some, like *Ordinary People,* become smash hits. Most don't even get looked at and are returned to the author unread.

14. *Returns:* Retailers and wholesalers may return unsold books for full credit to the publisher. Some outlets don't even bother to open the crate in which the books came before returning them for full credit. Returns are a major financial headache for all publishers, but especially for paperback publishers.

15. *Discounts.* Publishers knock down prices for retailers and wholesalers in exchange for taking a set number of copies. Discounts are an important part of any publishing business.

16. This idea is being implemented today by Harcourt Brace Jovanovich and other companies. It should prove an interesting and informative test of the thesis.

17. *Shredding:* Paperback books are often destroyed upon being returned from the retail outlet where they have not been sold.

18. For further information on the MS Read-a-Thon, contact the MS Society, 205 E. 42 Street, New York, N.Y. 10017

CHAPTER TWENTY-FOUR

Professional and Scientific Books

ANDREW H. NEILLY, JR.

Professional publishing accounts for a substantial and growing part of the U.S. book industry and of international publishing as well. Of an estimated $10.8 billion total U.S. book industry sales in 1983, more than $1.2 billion were derived from professional books and journals. These are defined broadly as publications for an educated audience ranging from post–high school through the higher levels of professional training in business, the sciences, engineering, the social sciences, medicine, nursing, and law. Formats range from basic practical books to advanced texts, references, and treatises. They include professional encyclopedias, handbooks, data books, and, on a more specialized level, research journals and monographs.

Professional publishers are entrepreneurs trafficking in ideas, in the results of research and development. They are risk takers, and a significant number of projects fail in the marketplace. They seldom enjoy the success of a best-seller, although some titles may have a steady sale over many years. They have no single product line, no "season." They deal with small market segments. They operate in a time span unacceptable in most investment circles, and the cost of every stage in the process and all materials involved is increasing. Their companies are not known to every household, nor are their activities widely reported in the media. Nevertheless, this part of publishing has an inordinate influence on education, the arts, and international trade and in the dissemination of information throughout the world.

A basic function of society is the storage, processing, and retrieval of information. J. M. Ziman, writing in *Nature,* the British journal of science, said,

> the invention of a mechanism for systematic publication of fragments of scientific work may well have been the key event in the history of science. A journal (or book) carries from one research worker to another the various

---

ANDREW H. NEILLY, JR., is president of John Wiley & Sons.

observations of common interest . . . this technique of soliciting many modest contributions to the store of human knowledge has been the secret of Western science since the 17th century.

Lewis Thomas noted that "exploring in science is a largely meditative business . . . but always, sooner or later, before an enterprise reaches completion, as we explore, we call to each other, communicate, publish; present papers, cry out on finding."

A career in professional publishing involves the anticipation of discovery, an opportunity to be "present at the creation," or at least close by. It involves finding, organizing, and distributing information that will enable a reader to solve a problem, to broaden his or her knowledge of a subject, to further a career, or even sometimes to improve the quality of life.

This part of the book industry predates Gutenberg and is as old as publishing itself. It probably began with the early dictionaries of the Greeks and Romans. Plato's *Republic* was written in the fifth century B.C. The *Censure and Judgement* of Erasmus was published in 1550. Galileo published *Dialogue on the Two Principal Systems of the World* in 1632, for which he was censured by the church and placed under house arrest. His *Dialogues on the Two New Sciences* appeared in 1638. Lavoisier's *Elements of Chemistry* appeared in 1789, and Darwin's *Voyage of the Beagle* and *Origin of the Species* in the 1850s, by which time England, as a function of the Industrial Revolution and its flow of new ideas and developments, became a center of publishing—as did France, Germany, and Holland to some degree.

In the United States, Lea & Febiger was founded in 1785, J. B. Lippincott in 1792, and John Wiley in 1807. Wiley's first technical book was *The American Practical Brewer and Tanner* by Coppinger, published in 1815. Most U.S. publications were then based on the practical sciences—civil engineering, mechanics, agriculture, railroad engineering—and many came from the faculties of the land-grant colleges that later became our state universities.

U.S. and European professional publishers developed along distinctly different lines prior to World War I. Publishers are fond of the idea that Europeans published for authors while Americans published for readers, which is to say that the European scientists talked to each other, and in the United States the more practical engineers instructed their students. The years following 1918 saw the beginning of the integration of these two schools when, for example, some German scientists came to work in our chemical industries. With the advent of Hitler's regime in 1933, European refugees moving to the United States included publishers and booksellers who founded some now prestigious U.S. firms:

Frederick Ungar opened his company in 1940; Eric Proskauer and Maurits Dekker founded Interscience Publishers that same year; Walter Johnson and Kurt Jacoby the Academic Press in 1942. They brought with them a concept of scholarly editors and multiauthored books and research journals. After 1945 they prospered as English became the international language of science and the United States the world center of research and development. New learned societies and professional groups began to publish their own journals, and European teaching and publishing followed their practitioners into U.S. colleges.

Professional Markets

In the United States in 1982, according to the Bureau of Labor Statistics, there were approximately 3.1 million professionals in the business world, 3 million in scientific and technical activities, 3.4 million in the health occupations, and slightly over .5 million social scientists. The projected growth rate of this population between 1982 and 1995 ranges from 24 percent in the social sciences to 35 percent in health occupations. This large group of potential buyers, the envy of European publishers, is, however, fragmented and every year more specialized, limiting the market for many projects and creating cost, distribution, and decision-making problems ("Can we afford to do this book?") for publishers. One New York publisher with 10,000 active titles has only about 100 that sell over 10,000 copies a year; another 150 sell from 5,000 to 10,000; the remaining titles sell in lesser quantities.

Much of the market for these books is institutional: sales to business, to government agencies, and to academic and industrial libraries. There has been, until recently, less reliance on bookstores as distributors in the United States than in foreign countries. Direct-mail sales have grown substantially, primarily to individuals. Depending on the subject areas, international sales may account for 35 to 50 percent of the total and can often make the difference between profit and loss.

In an industry that normally relies on larger print runs to bring down unit costs and therefore prices, this kind of short-run publishing presents unique problems. There is usually little elasticity in the market for specialized books; thus, given the finite size of an audience, there is not much prospect for increasing unit sales by holding down prices. The information either is of value to the customer or it is not. If we add to these concerns the element of high composition costs for mathematics or chemistry, for example, it becomes easier to understand that prices for these books will be higher than those of trade or school-book publishers. It is perhaps surprising, therefore, to find that professional publishing is one of the more profitable segments of the industry.

The Professional Author

Authors are found in many places, and the publisher's search for them is as constant as the scientist's pursuit of discovery. Many are faculty members in colleges and universities, particularly those with research and graduate programs. Many are in industry—in the laboratory of Exxon or DuPont—or in government agencies such as the National Institutes of Health, Bureau of Standards, or the National Aeronautics and Space Administration (NASA). Both the authors and their readers are, in a sense, the products and beneficiaries of research and development funds that have increased substantially in this country since 1945. Over $75 billion was budgeted in 1982 by both the public and private sectors for research and development, an amount, nevertheless, judged to be inadequate for the national purpose.

Authors of business books are often found in banking, auditing firms, or industrial consulting. Authors of books on health care include many physicians who conduct research in conjunction with teaching in university hospitals. But discovery is not always a group activity, and there is still the individual researcher hidden in the laboratory of a small college or hard at work in the basement of his home developing some new theory or project or hoping for a new industry to be born.

The Editor

It is difficult for one with a career in marketing to admit that the key person in program development is the editor, but that happens to be the case in scientific and professional publishing. The editor in charge of a physics, chemistry, or engineering list is responsible for maintenance of the backlist, processing of manuscripts through editorial and production, and liaison with all elements of marketing and sales. Editors are the principal and permanent liaison between the company and its authors, but their primary duty is program development: the planning of a list for their assigned fields, the acquisition of projects, and the negotiation of contracts. They may also contribute to such other activities as the creation of new journals, handbooks, and data books whose publication may be the responsibility of others.

Editors come from many backgrounds. Some are former college

representatives; others have been teachers. An editor may have an advanced degree in engineering, an M.B.A. or a Ph.D. in chemistry, anthropology, or some other specialty. Some have had no formal training in a specific field but become editors through the experience gained in a series of assignments within the company.

A successful editor must have a real sense of what is happening in his or her field, where research and development is leading, who the top young professionals are, which companies or universities are its research centers. Essential to this information gathering are professional society activities, such as annual meetings and regional events. About 40 percent of an editor's time should be spent in the field.

A program editor generally does not edit a manuscript. Outside advisers, with whom editors meet frequently, counsel on program planning and help to build a stable of consultants for expert reviews prior to publishing decisions and for manuscript development later on. An experienced editor is recognized by advisers and authors as a colleague who understands the literature and the markets and who can develop publishing ideas from often unorganized data. In larger companies editors are assigned a program with sales on the order of $2 million per year in one or several disciplines, depending on markets and the size of the list. As with any research and development operation, management has the difficult problem of balancing the contributions that creative editors can make in developing important publishing ideas against their potential performance if promoted to administrative positions.

Production

The copy-editing process is unusual for the professional book in that it is regarded as part of production. A copy editor reads for clarity, style, usage, and organization but will not attempt to judge the accuracy of most scientific and technical material. That is the responsibility of the authors and professional manuscript reviewers. Illustrations, which must be clear, informative, and keyed specifically to the text, are often of great importance. They may be supplied as photographs, drawn from authors' sketches, created in-house or by free-lance artists, or reprinted with permission from other publications. They range from simple line drawings to complex graphics, air brush renderings, computer-generated charts, equipment photographs, or photomicrographs. A good illustration department is a major asset and often makes the difference in the competition for authors.

Composition is a high-cost item in professional publishing. A simple page of type cost $13 to $25 to be set in early 1983, whereas type with

TABLE 24.1 COSTS OF AN AVERAGE BOOK

Costs	Quantities		
	2,250	5,000	25,000
Fixed costs			
Composition	$10,240	$10,240	$10,240
Author's Alterations	1,500	1,500	1,500
Illustrations			
(reproduction)	642	642	642
Plates	1,213	1,213	1,213
Makeready	562	562	562
Variable costs			
Paper	1,928	4,113	19,833
Printing	517	1,148	5,740
Binding	1,900	3,700	15,000
Cover	507	765	2,640
Total costs	$19,009	$23,883	$57,370
Unit cost	$8.45	$4.78	$2.29

Note: Trim size is 6⅜-by-9¼ inches.

mathematical formulas ranged from $30 to $45; a full page of organic chemistry could run as high as $65. The physical dimensions of the book and number of columns per page directly affect the final cost. Composition and other fixed costs—plates, illustrations, "make-ready," and authors' alterations—remain the same regardless of the number of books to be printed. Variable costs—paper, printing, and binding—will change depending on the number of units: that is, the more printed, the lower the unit cost. Table 24.1 shows fixed and variable costs as they apply to an average book. In this sample, a printing of 2,250 copies costs the publisher $8.45 per copy, whereas in a printing of 25,000 the unit cost drops to $2.29. The unit cost is naturally a crucial element in the pricing calculation for a book, and editors are often tempted to project a larger sale in order to hold to a retail price they consider reasonable. They are generally constrained by the cynics in marketing from doing so.

Marketing

If books are to reach their sales potential, marketing must be involved from the outset. Marketing managers estimate the number of customers, create a market plan and budget, and are responsible for carrying out the plan. As pointed out earlier, for most titles there is a measurable audience in each discipline—a known universe of chemists, statisticians, or financial managers—and the marketing program must be designed to reach this group at reasonable cost. It will involve a mail-order campaign using in-house lists or a purchased list from another source. A professional publisher's list may consist of a million or more names in a computer-based system, broken down by specialty, geographic location, and frequency of purchase, and it is continually up-dated. Well-maintained lists are essential to successful marketing.

The marketers will include coverage of industrial and government customers and libraries. U.S. libraries can account for up to 60 percent of a professional publisher's sales. A trade sales campaign is developed for domestic booksellers by way of sales representatives. Many houses have some variation on an "agency plan" that involves a bookstore's commitment to stock a required number of titles in selected subjects. Wiley has approximately 500 such agencies. In the last five years more stores in cities and suburban shopping centers have begun to stock professional books, and there are also approximately 150 large college stores that maintain professional sections.

International sales are an essential component of professional publishing. Wiley sells about 35 percent overseas. This business is often handled by a division or a separate company responsible for worldwide distribution, and that unit may also direct the original publishing of overseas subsidiaries or joint ventures including special editions for the Third World markets.

The international pipeline is designed to take original products from the parent company and its subsidiaries and joint ventures and to distribute them to customer outlets around the world. In Wiley, for example, we publish in New York, Toronto, Brisbane, Chichester (England), New Delhi, Mexico City, Rio de Janeiro, and Singapore. There is an interchange of promotion and sales among these entities. The international division is also generally responsible for the management of a translation program, which can generate considerable subsidiary income. Our company currently has contracts for books to be translated into forty-six different languages.

$$* \quad * \quad *$$

The electronic age will change much of professional publishing, and every company is attempting to evaluate the threats, opportunities, and timing of current technological developments. The whole publishing cycle—from an author's concept to a product for the reader—will be compressed in time and cost effectiveness. Word processing for authors, on-line editing, computerized composition and production, and rapid delivery of final product—whether in hard copy, display, or printout—are all in use on some projects and will soon become standard.

Some observers foresee that every professional will someday be able to become his own publisher, freely transmitting personal cries of discovery on networks via satellite to peers around the world. But it would be depressing to contemplate such a world of undifferentiated "noise," lacking in the editorial or critical analysis necessary to orderly development of a discipline. Knowledge and understanding do not come from images; few of us would argue that daily exposure to TV news, immediately accessible but superficial in content, has made us better informed about the complexities of the world.

There is more acquirable knowledge available to us than ever before; the question is how it can be reasonably managed. Publishers must keep in mind that their real function is to identify, organize, and distribute material in a useful form. It will still be necessary to create a body of literature from the results of research. The flow generally runs from the researcher to industry, to graduate schools, and then to undergraduate courses—each with its special needs and formats.

The excitement of professional publishing involves participation in all the stages of this process. The search is endless and generally hopeful. Modern research has shown us how little we know even from the most recent discoveries and how infinitely more complex the world is than we believed it to be. We are on the verge of a new age of discovery, and I expect that the professional publishers will be there to report it.

CHAPTER TWENTY-FIVE

University Press Publishing

ARTHUR J. ROSENTHAL

Except for a few knowledgeable authors, booksellers, and readers, a university press is usually viewed as a combined printing plant and book distributor that deals with dry-as-dust Ph.D. theses and faculty monographs. These wares are acknowledged to be "scholarly"—whatever that abused word means—and a moment of silence is often forthcoming after their mention, as if one were in the presence of some compelling force.

The facts are quite different. A primary purpose of a university press is to function as a natural outlet for information, theory, speculation, and methodology that will influence human endeavor and enrich understanding in generations to come. Elusive as this goal may seem, university-press editors in the 1980s are beginning to recognize that perhaps they alone will be able to publish the seminal works of our culture—whether a yet unrecognized *Interpretation of Dreams* or a *Das Kapital*. For as economic pressures continue, and as bookstores are less and less able to stock a range of titles, it is only natural that the increasing burden of the risk of publishing books that are at the intellectual frontier should be assumed by presses that are nonprofit by charter.

Of course, this is not an entirely new trend. An examination of the eighty-five Phi Beta Kappa Book Awards from 1951 through 1984 reveals that fifty-five of these prestigious citations have gone to university presses. This is a startling confirmation of the cultural worth of the presses, particularly when measured against the actual size of the book industry. Of the forty thousand new books published each year in the United States, about one in twelve bears a university-press imprint, accounting for barely 1.5 percent of the industry's total sales.

The first university press, it is said, was established at Oxford in 1478, one year after William Caxton issued the first book printed in England. There are conflicting dates and claims for the first university press in the United States, but there is no denying that publishing in America

ARTHUR J. ROSENTHAL is director of Harvard University Press.

started at Harvard when its first president, young Henry Dunster, married the affluent Widow Glover and thereby acquired for the college her late husband's printing press, the first in the colonies. For fifty years, from the 1640s to the 1690s, the press in the Yard produced psalmbooks, Latin broadsides, catalogs, and almanacs, as well as a Bible in the language of the local Indians.

Since 1878, when the Johns Hopkins University Press was started, more than eighty presses have been established. More often than not, they began as publication offices serving the printing needs of the parent university and gradually evolved into what we know as the university presses of today.

As part of the university whose name it bears, a press is an essential academic unit of the institution and should strive to be just as intellectually central to its purpose and communication as the library or the political-science department. One would expect the director to be a senior member of the faculty, and like other members of the faculty he or she would want to be active in the committee work and other internal activities of the institution. But this status is not conferred automatically. It is only recently that faculty members have come to recognize that there is a difference between the publishing arm of their alma mater and the printing plant or facility that is usually located at some other part of the campus. The senior professor still finds it hard to accept a refusal to publish his student's revised dissertation, and it requires exceptional skill in diplomacy and public relations to say no without antagonizing faculty members who may be central to the success of an editorial program.

It is not easy to succeed in the gray area that marks the crossroads between editorial independence and the "oneness" of being part of a special community. Those who are most successful at it often discover the key in the recognition and acclaim their list of publications achieves outside the university. Several years ago a committee set up to investigate what is probably the greatest publishing house in the world voiced the dilemma: "The problem," according to the Waldock Report on Oxford University Press, "is one of striking the correct balance between the role of the press as a press of this university and its role as a national and international publisher responsible not only to the university but to the world of learning at large."

Fortunately, almost all university presses have a group of allies in charting this perilous course, and without question the most important of these is an editorial committee, usually composed of leading members of the faculty chosen from those disciplines that represent the strengths of the university. At Harvard this committee, chaired by the director, consists of twelve men and women who meet monthly to discuss ten to twelve manuscripts proposed by the staff of the press. A week before the meeting, board members receive an agenda, which includes a description of the special contribution of each manuscript, written by the editor responsible for the book; one, two, or sometimes three detailed readings by leading scholars outside the author's university, experts in the subject area of the manuscript being considered; and usually a response by the author. The committee discussion is started by the board member most familiar with the subject area, and this presentation is often based on a detailed reading of the manuscript. Discussion of the book is sometimes brief, sometimes exhaustive, but almost never includes financial, sales, or marketing considerations.

Such a separation of financial and editorial assessments would be an act of sacrilege at Random House or McGraw-Hill. But in the case of a university press it frees the editorial committee for its unique function: to decide the question of publication on intellectual merit alone. It is also no small advantage, both for the editors of the press and for the author-to-be, to have the kind of help an active editorial committee can give in suggesting ways to strengthen a manuscript. The main disadvantage of the system is the length of time it can take to secure expert readings. It is imperative that, in those cases where a valued author is unwilling to wait for several months, the board have special rules in place for a rapid decision.

Financial oversight—monitoring the cash flow, setting up budgets, attention to size and turnover of the inventory, pricing policy, helping to chart strategies for the press—often falls in the domain of an administrative vice president for the smaller presses and of a board of directors for a larger press. Harvard's board of directors consists of the director of the press, the press's financial officer, the president of the university, six faculty members, and two commercial publishers. Much as with boards of public companies, its role has expanded in the past ten years from that of financial watchdog to include long-range planning.

Compared to the commercial world, university presses are very small. Even the three largest—California, Chicago, and Harvard—published only some 150 new hardcover books a year. And of the seventy-five presses reporting their statistics to the Association of American University Presses recently, more than two-thirds publish fewer than 30 books a year. Size, then, is a crucial factor in understanding the similarities and differences between university-press operations and those outlined earlier in this book for the general publisher.

The smaller press, publishing perhaps a dozen books a year, will have considerable flexibility of staff, with a director acting quite often as the editor in chief, one copy editor, and a person who combines the functions of promotion and sales. For the person who loves books, small *is* beautiful, and it is not surprising that the small university press (sales of $400,000 or less) has published books that would be welcomed by the most successful publishing giant. In addition to sound scholarship and the occasional book that may "break through," many of these presses have exploited a new genre of publication, the regional title—a book that may cover the geography, history, lore, or special attributes of a press's local area. It is particularly with the regional title that a small press may overcome some of the marketing handicaps of its size.

The larger presses tend to use commercial publishing as their organizational model, having, for example, a publicity department that cares deeply about the number of reviews it is securing in the *New York Times Book Review*, and a subsidiary rights person concerned with the adoption of its titles by book clubs.

But this broader focus is a double-edged sword and can lead to a certain amount of internal turmoil. It is quite likely that a large university press will have from three to six leading trade titles each season that could have a respectable place on the list of a general publisher. These titles need an inordinate amount of editorial attention and promotion money and often drain staff energy that is needed by the forty or fifty other books on a seasonal list. Yet without these leading titles the total mission of the press is not accomplished. For these are the books that can be found in major bookstores, that provide the possibility of give-and-take with publishers in other countries, that get the kind of wide distribution and attention that bring special prestige and make it possible to attract top authors to the list.

I like to think of these leading titles as extension books, making the research and thoughts of a scholar accessible not merely to a narrow circle but, as university teaching itself does, across the corridor to interact with neighboring disciplines and out to the wider world of intelligent men and women generally. While simply the tip of the iceberg, these books provide many of the joys and satisfactions of being part of the "real" publishing scene and are a useful training ground for the skills the marketing group can apply to the broad range of other titles.

Yet it is in the editorial role of a university press—large or small—that its true separateness from the rest of the industry is most visible. When an editor is required to guarantee that a book will make a profit before a contract can be signed—as is true in an increasing number of commercial firms—it is natural for editors to select titles in subject areas that have had a proven record of success. Editors know that a self-help book is certainly a safer bet than a study of how psychology became a real discipline in Germany before World War I; a biography of John Lennon is preferable to a series of volumes of the letters of William Lloyd Garrison; studies in Byzantine art and first volumes of poetry cannot compete with books on the solar house or coffee-table books on Picasso.

University-press editors, concerned to a large extent with books whose subject matter is shunned by their for-profit colleagues, can no longer take it for granted that the world will buy enough copies of a scholarly book of average merit to enable it to break even. Now a book must be acclaimed as outstanding by the relevant journal before it will be found on a library shelf or in a reader's hand. The editor who is successful at finding such books is a very special person. Quite likely he or she will have considerable postgraduate grounding in one or two disciplines and will have built over the years a network of authors and academic advisers who place special confidence in the ability of that editor to recognize a path-breaking title as opposed to the simply solid and reliable one. And such an editor will show a vigilant concern for the successful editing, design, production, and marketing of the book. That editor must also be able to tolerate failure if it occurs, and a successful press director must encourage the kind of boldness that may lead to failure and be able to live comfortably with it.

Certainly, in these times, failure in terms of sales as opposed to editorial value is not a sometime thing for a university press. To date, sales volume has tended to hold steady or increase not because of new or more intense marketing strategies but rather because of simple price increases. Many of us are not content with this and are searching for ways to increase unit sales while trying to hold down soaring expenses.

One answer lies in cooperation. The Massachusetts Institute of Technology and Harvard, for example, built and share a warehouse facility in Littleton, Massachusetts. Columbia University Press has taken over the marketing functions of New York Unversity Press and several others. The Johns Hopkins University Press provides shipping, order fulfillment, and data-processing services for a number of university presses. Cooperation among presses for marketing in the United Kingdom and Europe and around the world is in effect in a number of different forms.

Another answer lies in greater sharing among members of the Association of American University Presses, the cooperative centerpiece in the continuing effort of its ninety members to expand their intellectual influence and marketing abilities. In addition to performing the normal activities of any professional association, the AAUP has a special marketing subsidiary that maintains a classified listing of more than 500,000 college and university faculty members in the United States and Canada and can also make available similar lists of faculty members throughout the world. The Educational Directory, as it is called, also acts as a broker for over 400 lists of subscribers to scholarly journals and members of learned societies. Its lists may be rented by all publishers, not merely university presses.

Usually subvention takes priority even over cooperation as a press tries to balance its books before the end of the fiscal year. Subsidies can come from the government—in diminishing amounts today; from foundations for specific titles or translations; and, most important, from the university itself. Such support is essential if presses are to stay true to their mission. It was Daniel Coit Gilman, the first president of Johns Hopkins, who put into words the justification for this support. He believed that a great university has three vital functions: teaching, research, and dissemination of the results of research. "It is one of the noblest duties of a university to advance knowledge," Gilman wrote in 1878, "and to diffuse it not merely among those who can attend the daily lectures . . . but far and wide." Today this "far and wide" rests largely on the books and journals that make up the staple of university-press publication.

CHAPTER TWENTY-SIX

Reference Books for Libraries

DEDRIA BRYFONSKI

Reference publishing produces the encyclopedias, indexes, dictionaries, directories, bibliographies, handbooks, readers' guides, biographical sources, and similar research tools that the user consults not to be amused, converted, entertained, emotionally moved, or spiritually advised but to be informed. Occasionally a reader might be mildly tickled by a reference book—for instance, when reading in Gale Research Company's ongoing biographical series *Contemporary Authors* that Ray Bradbury, whose fiction offers vivid descriptions of space and time travel, has never flown in an airplane and, in fact, has never driven a car. But this is icing on the cake. Reference-book editors are generally satisfied if their books provide timely, accurate, and comprehensive information in a convenient, well-organized format.

Reference books are as widely used and well known as the H. W. Wilson Company's index *Readers' Guide to Periodical Literature* and as specialized and esoteric as the R. R. Bowker Company's bibliography *Magic as a Performing Art*. A trait common to all reference books, however, is their function as information sources. An information source can lead the user to many kinds of facts—about people, as in Marquis's *Who's Who in America;* about places, as in Bowker's *American Library Directory;* about things, as in Bowker's *Books in Print;* even about ideas, as in Macmillan's *Encyclopedia of Philosophy.* Depending on the tool, research can be a one-step or a two-step process. Dictionaries and encyclopedias are direct reference sources, typically providing the user with the fact or definition being researched. Conversely, indexes and bibliographies are the first step in a two-step process; they instruct the user where to go to find, for example, a book review of *Absalom, Absalom!* or an essay on existentialism.

At this point it is useful to separate nonsubscription reference books, which are the focus of this chapter, from subscription reference books. Probably the most familiar titles in the latter group are general ency-

DEDRIA BRYFONSKI is senior vice president and editorial director, Gale Research Company.

clopedias such as *Encyclopaedia Britannica, World Book,* and *Encyclopedia Americana.* These reference sets are designed for home, as well as institutional, use and are therefore sold door-to-door and through direct promotional mailings to individuals, as well as to libraries and educational institutions. Back in the 1960s subscription reference books enjoyed an impressive share of the publishing marketplace. Although this share has fallen somewhat with the declining birthrate, it remains significant. The number of editors and assistants, contributors and compilers, researchers and consultants required to produce or revise a multivolume encyclopedia translates into an enormous investment. Therefore, it is only after exhaustive research and painstaking planning that a new encyclopedia is launched.

Unlike subscription reference books and trade books, nonsubscription reference books have as their primary market institutions, not individuals. Although some reference books are bought by individuals, generally through a specialized bookstore or through direct mail to a carefully selected list, they are most often purchased by libraries and other institutions. Thus, the typical buyer is the librarian, general and specialized, and this profoundly affects the kinds of book the reference publisher offers, how these books are assembled, and how they are marketed. Most reference books are tools for librarians—either to answer patrons' questions or to perform their own jobs. In thinking about the specifics of reference publishing—the editing process, marketing strategies, and economics—it is important to keep in mind the central fact that we are providing professionals with job-related tools.

Editing

In reference publishing we are compiling and formatting information—sometimes masses of it—and thus we need a sizable staff of in-house information gatherers rather than a few authors laboring at home on a royalty basis. Waves of questionnaires, elusive facts that need nailing down—the reference-book editor is confronted by both magnitude and minutiae. Unlike other types of editors who work with authors and agents, the typical reference editor is both author and editor of the book.

The major reference tools are not one-time publishing ventures but parts of series. Some series, such as directories, are published in editions, with the latest book superseding earlier ones. For example, the 1983 edition of Bowker's *Literary Market Place* provides a thorough updating of the information in the 1982 edition. Other series, such as most indexes, are published in open-ended sets, with each new volume adding fresh information to the series. Gale's *Book Review Index* is published bimonthly, with each issue indexing approximately eighteen thousand new book reviews. Although indexes are often cumulated for one-year, five-year, and ten-year periods for the users' convenience, each separate issue contains new information.

Each series typically has its own editor and staff, who are, or quickly become, specialists in the field covered by the series. Each series in a publishing house thus forms its own cottage industry. Jobs with the same title vary widely from series to series: Editing an encyclopedia, which often requires reviewing and revising lengthy essays for grammar, knowledge of subject, and writing style, is substantially different from editing an index, which generally entails checking to see that basic bibliographical citations have been accurately recorded by compiler and computer. However, certain generalizations can be made.

The positions of editorial assistant, assistant editor, associate editor, and editor are the usual stepping-stones in the editorial hierarchy. Let's see what these positions involve on one particular series, Gale's *Contemporary Authors,* making some generalizations along the way. *Contemporary Authors* is a bio-bibliographic guide to more than seventy-seven thousand current writers. A staff of thirty-two people researches and processes information on approximately four thousand new authors per year.

If there is a one-word summary of most reference editorial assistants' jobs, that word would be *research*. In this case, the research focuses on tabulating questionnaire responses. Figure 26.1 shows a questionnaire filled out by writer Wayne Dyer for his *Contemporary Authors* sketch. For *Contemporary Authors,* as for many reference books, the questionnaire is the most important research tool. The editorial assistant's duties in relation to this questionnaire might be to scan a variety of sources for authors not already in the series, to research addresses of eligible authors, to mail questionnaires, and to do research directed by an editor to unearth bibliographical and biographical information on authors who do not return their questionnaires or supplementary information to be used in the "Sidelights" section.

From this questionnaire and supplementary information, an assistant editor wrote the sketch in Figure 26.2. Whatever specific functions assistant editors perform for reference series, most are engaged in assimilating researched information and translating it into a useful format.

Associate editors usually come from the assistant-editor ranks. They have teaching skills and have been staff members long enough to have a thorough knowledge of the departmental style sheet. They frequently

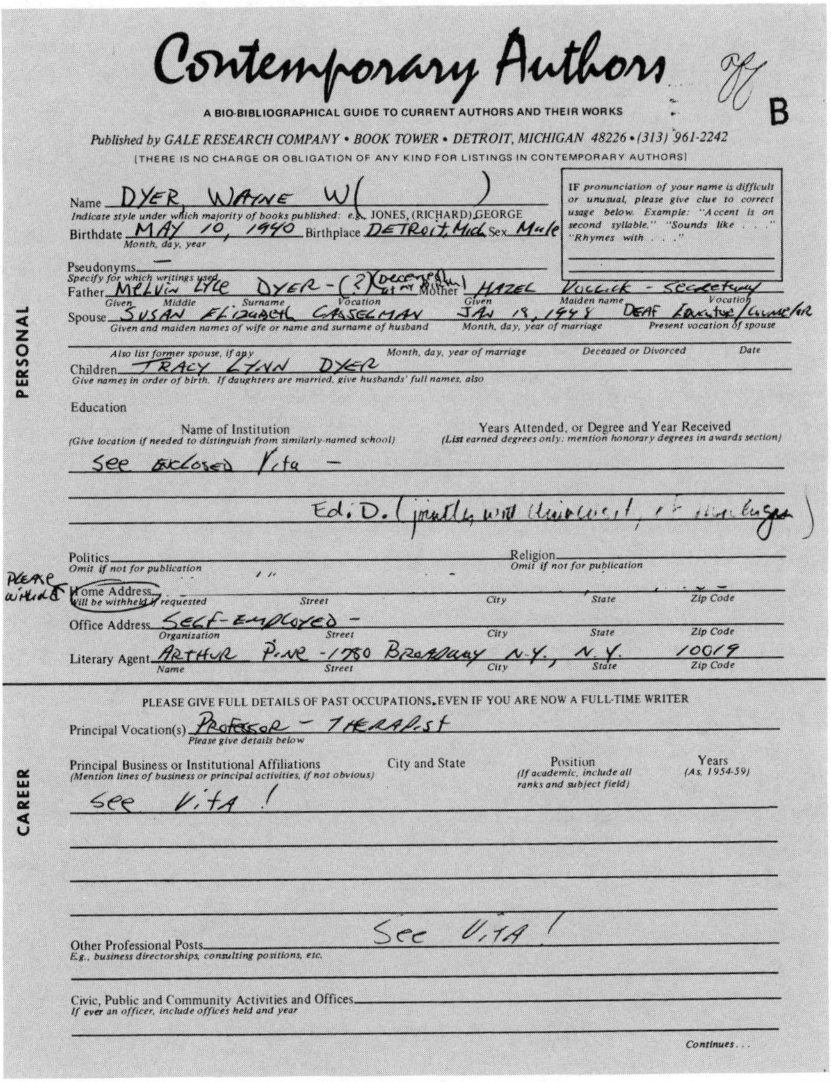

Contemporary Authors

B

A BIO-BIBLIOGRAPHICAL GUIDE TO CURRENT AUTHORS AND THEIR WORKS

Published by GALE RESEARCH COMPANY • BOOK TOWER • DETROIT, MICHIGAN 48226 • (313) 961-2242

[THERE IS NO CHARGE OR OBLIGATION OF ANY KIND FOR LISTINGS IN CONTEMPORARY AUTHORS]

IF pronunciation of your name is difficult or unusual, please give clue to correct usage below. Example: "Accent is on second syllable," "Sounds like . . ." "Rhymes with . . ."

PERSONAL

Name DYER, WAYNE W( )
Indicate style under which majority of books published: e.g., JONES, (RICHARD) GEORGE

Birthdate MAY 10, 1940 Birthplace DETROIT, Mich. Sex Male
Month, day, year

Pseudonyms —
Specify for which writings used

Father MELVIN LYLE DYER – (?) (Deceased) Mother HAZEL VOLLICK – Secretary
Given Middle Surname Vocation Given Maiden name Vocation

Spouse SUSAN ELIZABETH CASSELMAN JAN 19, 1948 DEAF Counselor/Counselor
Given and maiden names of wife or name and surname of husband Month, day, year of marriage Present vocation of spouse

Also list former spouse, if any Month, day, year of marriage Deceased or Divorced Date

Children TRACY LYNN DYER
Give names in order of birth. If daughters are married, give husbands' full names, also

Education

Name of Institution
(Give location if needed to distinguish from similarly-named school)

Years Attended, or Degree and Year Received
(List earned degrees only; mention honorary degrees in awards section)

See ENCLOSED Vita –

Ed. D. (jointly with University of Michigan)

Politics
Omit if not for publication

Religion
Omit if not for publication

PLEASE WITHHOLD Home Address
Will be withheld if requested Street City State Zip Code

Office Address SELF-EMPLOYED –
Organization Street City State Zip Code

Literary Agent ARTHUR PINE – 1780 BROADWAY N.Y., N.Y. 10019
Name Street City State Zip Code

CAREER

PLEASE GIVE FULL DETAILS OF PAST OCCUPATIONS, EVEN IF YOU ARE NOW A FULL-TIME WRITER

Principal Vocation(s) PROFESSOR – THERAPIST
Please give details below

Principal Business or Institutional Affiliations
(Mention lines of business or principal activities, if not obvious)
City and State
Position
(If academic, include all ranks and subject field)
Years
(As, 1954-59)

See Vita!

Other Professional Posts See Vita!
E.g., business directorships, consulting positions, etc.

Civic, Public and Community Activities and Offices
If ever an officer, include offices held and year

Continues . . .

FIGURE 26.1 Author's questionnaire.

354

CAREER (Continued)

Military Service and Awards _See V.tA_
Mention whether Army, Navy, etc., inclusive dates of service, highest rank held, decorations received

Memberships _See V.tA_
List current professional societies, associations, clubs, etc.; indicate in ( ) any offices held, and inclusive dates

Awards, Honors and Prizes _See V.tA_
If awards are for specific works, please indicate which works; mention names of groups bestowing awards; give dates of awards

WRITINGS

| Titles of Books | Publisher | Year Published |

Please give **complete list of books**, including dates of all revised editions, and substantial separate monographs. If you are co-author, please mention collaborators' names; if editor or translator, please so indicate; indicate pseudonyms for individual books, if used.

See V.tA —
Your Erroneous Zones — N.Y. Times, Publisher weekly,
Los Angeles Times, etc. Number one (1) Non-Fiction
Best Seller in the U.S. Sept., Oct, 1976!

Other Writings, Editorships
Plays, TV and motion picture scripts, journals edited, journals contributed to, regular columns, etc.

(Attach supplementary material, if additional space is needed)

WORK IN PROGRESS

Research or Literary Activity in Progress   Mention current research interest, even if no publication is expected to result. Give subjects   of book manuscripts in process, with proposed titles and expected completion dates.

① _Book For T.V. Oswell — "Sizing up Your culture" subtitled —_
Stop Being a "Knee-Jerk" Victim — ② Book — "Hered Your
Toys". A Guide to Self-Actualization For Children —
(Attach supplementary material, if additional space is needed)

SIDELIGHTS
Please do not hesitate to reply at length.

In this section, please comment on motivation, circumstances, etc., important to your career, to a specific book, or to your writing generally. Add comments indicative of your viewpoint on subjects you consider vital.

ALSO: Please mention major areas of vocational interest, avocational interest, travels and expeditions, foreign languages in which you have competence, etc. • Illuminating personal data are valuable. Please do not hesitate to reply at length.

Working on National T.V. Show Based on Your Erroneous Zones —
Regular Appearances on Today Show, Tonight Show, Good
Morning America — Host on Radio and T.V. Variety Shows.
"I feel a mission to change the mental health of our country —
Far too many people are addicted to tranquilizers, anti-depressants,
(Attach supplementary material, if additional space is needed)
Alcohol, etc... Looking for answers every place but within themself.
We need to return to a No-Nonsense common-sense approach to

BIOGRAPHICAL/CRITICAL SOURCES _mental health & begin to take responsibility_ _For our own lives rather_
List articles or books about you (omit reviews of individual books), and give exact date of issue. Also list directories, Who's Who, etc. in which you are included. _than blaming others."_

* _Feel Free to contact Ms. Donna Gould_
at Funk + Wagnalls, For a detailed press   Prepared by _Wayne W. Dyer_   9-26-76
kit on myself — 212-489-4618   Name   Date

FIGURE 26.1, cont.

DYER, Wayne W(alter) 1940-

PERSONAL: Born May 10, 1940, in Detroit, Mich.; son of Melvin Lyle and Hazel (a secretary; maiden name, Vollick) Dyer; married Susan Elizabeth Casselman (a teacher of the deaf and a counselor); children: Tracy Lynn. *Education:* Wayne State University, B.S., 1965, M.S., 1966, Ed.D. (jointly with University of Michigan), 1970. *Residence:* Fort Lauderdale, Fla. *Agent:* Arthur Pine, 1780 Broadway, New York, N.Y. 10019.

CAREER: High school teacher and counselor in Detroit, Mich., 1965-67; Mercy High School, Farmington, Mich., director of guidance and counseling, 1967-71; St. John's University, Jamaica, N.Y., assistant professor, 1971-74, associate professor of counselor education, 1974-76; on promotional tour, 1976—. Counselor and therapist in private practice, Huntington, N.Y., 1973—. Staff consultant to hospitals, school districts, and public health agencies in the United States and Germany. Wayne State University, instructor, and practicum supervisor, 1969-71, member of summer school faculty, 1970-73, professor of counselor education in overseas program in Berlin, West Germany, and Istanbul, Turkey, 1974. Has made numerous guest appearances on national radio and television programs. Lecturer. *Military service:* U.S. Navy, 1958-62.

MEMBER: American Personnel and Guidance Association, Association of Counselor Educators and Supervisors, National Vocational Guidance Association, Association for Specialists in Group Work, New York Personnel and Guidance Association, New York Association of Counselor Educators and Supervisors.

WRITINGS: (With John Vriend) *Counseling Effectively in Groups,* Educational Technology Publications, 1973; (with Vriend) *Counseling Techniques that Work: Applications to Individual and Group Counseling,* American Personnel and Guidance Association Press, 1974; (with Vriend) *Group Counseling for the School Practitioner,* American Personnel and Guidance Association Press, 1976; *Your Erroneous Zones: Bold but Simple Techniques for Eliminating Unhealthy Behavior Patterns,* Funk, 1976; *Pulling Your Own Strings,* Crowell, 1978.

Also author of professional tapes, tapes series, and testing material. Contributor to professional counseling and guidance journals. *Educational Technology,* contributing editor, 1971—, co-editor of special issues, January and February, 1973.

WORK IN PROGRESS: A television show based on his book *Your Erroneous Zones;* a guide to self-actualization for children, *Hoard Your Toys.*

SIDELIGHTS: Wayne Dyer's best-selling book, *Your Erroneous Zones,* has been described as an indictment of what he calls the "psychological establishment." Dyer told R. Allen Leider: "Psychology as practiced today is all off-center. It tells people to look for the reasons for their unhappiness, upsets, hangups, and illnesses in terms of outside places and events—how their parents treated them, how their friends reacted to them, etc. That's looking backward for answers. Those explanations are gimmicks—slick gimmicks. Mental health is not complex, expensive or involved, hard work. It's only common sense."

He told *CA:* "I feel a mission to change the mental health of our country. Far too many people are addicted to tranquilizers, anti-depressants, alcohol, etc. . . . looking for answers every place but within the self. We need to return to a no-nonsense, common-sense approach to mental health and begin to take responsibility for our own lives rather than blame others."

Dyer explains that his philosophy is "based on the reality that you can be whatever you want to be by going out there and making it happen." He defines erroneous zones as areas of self-defeating behavior which result in a person's immobilization. Immobilization, Dyer told an interviewer, "is any state in which you are not functioning the way you would like to be." His solution to immobilization is to eliminate these erroneous zones by living for the moment. He says in *Celebrity* magazine: "Anxiety is nothing more than the avoidance of 'now.' If you live each moment as it comes, you can't be anxious or neurotic."

Dyer's own life can be seen as proof of the success of his theories. He says that until ten years ago, he was "just as messed up as everyone else." According to *People* magazine, when Dyer became convinced that he had to be in control of his own life, "he learned to stop worrying about being bald or feeling guilty about his divorce from his first wife. . . . He no longer depended upon other people's opinions of him. In sum, he began deciding for himself, minute by minute, how he would live his own life."

Then Dyer decided to write a best-seller. The first draft of *Your Erroneous Zones* was completed in thirteen days, after two years of research, and the book has been near or at the top of most national best-seller lists for more than eleven months. He left his teaching position and lucrative private practice, bought a new car, loaded it with copies of his book, and set out on what *People* called "a self-marketing tour-de-force."

In four months, Dyer had visited forty-eight states promoting the book, and had done more than 600 radio and television interviews. He told a *Newsday* reporter of the tour: "I never had a day when I didn't do an interview. Sometimes I'd do a dozen in one day. No, I didn't get tired. Each interviewer was a chance to meet someone new. I would tell the listeners that they could buy the book at such and such a bookstore. Then, in the morning, I'd go to the bookstore, and tell the manager, 'Here's 25 copies, but you better put in a big order because you're going to need them.' I went to all the bookstores. It just began to mushroom."

Dyer's book has received criticism for trivializing substantial problems. His response to a *Newsday* reporter: "I know it all sounds too simple to some people, but what's the other choice? To be unhappy with yourself? That's the least effective choice of all."

BIOGRAPHICAL/CRITICAL SOURCES: Miami News, July 13, 1976; *Deseret News,* August 10, 1976; *Newsday,* November 18, 1976; *Miami Herald,* December 14, 1976; *Chicago Tribune,* December 19, 1976; *Celebrity,* December, 1976; *People,* January 10, 1977.

* * *

FIGURE 26.2 Author's sketch.

train new employees, checking their work for compliance with the series style sheet as well as for errors in grammar or composition.

Above them are editors, who typically combine a solid knowledge of their series' subject with organizational, managerial, and business skills. They should also be good detail people. It helps to be a competent instructor and a discerning interviewer, for, given the turnover rate in publishing, much of an editor's time is spent hiring and training staff. Editors tend to concentrate more on long-range planning than on day-to-day preparation of material, although the latter is certainly an important element. Schedules for reference series are planned years in advance. It falls to the editor to translate these schedules into timetables for research, compilation, editing, typesetting, and printing. And, when a book falls behind schedule, it is up to the editor to troubleshoot the various alternatives to determine where lost time can be made up. Enlarging the scope of a series, adding a new feature, and changing a format to improve legibility or attractiveness are other concerns of editors. Since making a change in an existing reference tool is an expensive procedure, any change must be carefully researched and the advantages and disadvantages documented. Most editors complain that their days are so filled with writing memos, attending meetings, and listening to and trying to solve problems that there is precious little time left for the editorial work that originally attracted them to publishing. A colleague has the editor's dilemma summed up succinctly in a cartoon on her bulletin board: "When you're up to your ass in alligators, it's hard to remember your initial objective was to drain the swamp."

It is clear, from these job descriptions, that although they share the same title, reference-book editors and editors of trade, text, and scholarly books have very different jobs, requiring different skills and styles. The trade-book editor, for example, is involved in a lot of one-on-one interchanges—courting hot new authors, going to the mat with agents in contract negotiations, eloquently championing an author's interests to the sales department. The reference-book editor, on the other hand, generally directs a large staff toward specific goals. Those who do this most successfully are adept at such general supervisory skills as time and personnel management and training.

Systems management is the arena where many reference editors exercise their special wiles and ingenuity. Given the importance of the computer to reference publishing, and particularly to that aspect of it that has come to be known as data-base publishing, an effective systems manager is generally an intelligent computer user. This doesn't mean that he or she is a programmer or even has mastery over the computer terminal keyboard. It does mean that reference-book editors need to know enough

★4140★ HALT - AN ORGANIZATION OF AMERICANS FOR **LEGAL**
REFORM (HALT-ALR)
201 Massachusetts Ave., N.E., Suite 319 Phone: (202) 546-4258
Washington, DC 20002 Paul T. Hasse, Chm.
Founded: 1977. Members: 30,000. **Staff:** 10. Citizens of diverse socio-
economic and age groups dedicated to legal reform. Purposes are: to educate
the public about law, legal procedures and legal services; to develop and
support alternative means for resolving legal disputes; and to improve the
quality and reduce the cost of available legal services. Compiles data on the
cost and nature of legal services nationwide, on alternative dispute resolution
and legal service delivery systems and on model reforms in probate, real
estate and other areas of law. The acronym HALT stands for Help Abolish
Legal Tyranny. **Publications:** (1) Americans for Legal Reform (newsletter),
quarterly; (2) Action Alerts (bulletins), irregular; also publishes Citizens Legal
Manuals which teach consumers how to avoid unnecessary legal counsel and
how to find competent legal service, at reasonable prices, when necessary.
Formerly: (1979) HALT - Help Abolish Legal Tyranny.

FIGURE 26.3 Entry in sixteenth edition of *Encyclopedia
of Associations.*

about computers to understand how the computer can most effectively
assist them.

A data base is simply a collection of related facts stored together with
a minimum of repetition. Data-base publishing involves formatting these
facts, usually through computer programs, in ways that provide useful,
logically arranged information. Data-base publishing is especially efficient
where the same information is to be arranged in several ways for multiple
access. This frequently occurs in the same book: For instance, the main
section of a reference book on research centers could be programmed
so that subject, executive, and geographic indexes are generated with
no additional input. In the case of some mammoth data bases, several
books can be drawn from the same base. An example of this is Bowker's
Books in Print data base.

The computer is also a valuable tool when it comes to updating an
edition with the most current information. An example from Gale's
recent history demonstrates the impact computers have had on this area
of publishing. In 1974 it took two years to produce the *Encyclopedia of
Associations* using a keypunch card system. Today it takes less than half
that time to produce a 2,774-page, three-book set, plus three supplements
published between editions. Figure 26.3 shows an entry from the sixteenth
edition of the *Encyclopedia of Associations;* Figure 26.4 shows that entry
as it was revised for the seventeenth edition, with the parts that were
changed underlined. Before the series was computerized, the entire entry
would have been rekeyboarded. Now the assistant editor can call up the
old entry on his or her VDT (video display terminal), type in only the
part that has been changed, and store the material. When all entries
requiring revision have been altered, a tape containing the stored in-

★4393★ HALT - AN ORGANIZATION OF AMERICANS FOR LEGAL REFORM (HALT-ALR)
201 Massachusetts Ave., N.E., Suite 319   Phone: (202) 546-4258
Washington, DC 20002   Paul T. Hasse, Chm.
Founded: 1977. **Members:** 30,000. **Staff:** 10. Citizens of diverse socio-economic and age groups dedicated to legal reform. Purposes are: to educate the public about law, legal procedures and legal services; to make consumers sophisticated shoppers of legal services and increase their self-reliance and ability to handle their own affairs; to simplify the language of the law; "to focus public attention on the legal profession's undue influence in federal and state legislatures and the American Bar Association's (see separate entry) indirect control of judiciary committees;" to develop and support alternative means for resolving legal disputes; and to improve the quality and reduce the cost of available legal services. Works on reform legislation in probate, divorce and real estate at the state and federal levels; encourages increased citizen participation on attorney grievance committees. Maintains constant pressure on the Federal Trade Commission to further its investigation of bar associations' restrictive trade practices; supports measures to reduce incidence of unnecessary litigation including establishment of no-fault accident insurance. Compiles data on the cost and nature of legal services nationwide, on alternative dispute resolution and legal service delivery systems and on model reforms in probate, real estate and other areas of law. Maintains Judicial Integrity Program. Produces educational materials. The acronym HALT stands for Help Abolish Legal Tyranny. **Publications:** (1) Americans for Legal Reform (newsletter), quarterly; (2) Action Alerts (bulletins), irregular; also publishes Citizens Legal Manuals which teach consumers how to avoid unnecessary legal counsel and how to find competent legal service. **Formerly:** (1979) HALT - Help Abolish Legal Tyranny.

FIGURE 26.4 Entry in seventeenth edition of *Encyclopedia of Associations.*

formation is sent to a typesetter for setting. The savings in time is significant. The use of the computer throughout the reference-book industry has been directly responsible for the increasing availability of very up-to-date information.

Some projects are not done in-house. Sometimes, particularly with a one-time publishing venture like a specialized bibliography or a manual relating to some specific aspect of library science, there is no one within the company with the required expertise. Sometimes an author comes to a publishing house with an attractive proposal that he or she is uniquely suited to create. In these instances the reference publisher enters into contractual agreement with the author. There is usually no agent. involved, and the advance, if any, is generally adequate only for research or manuscript preparation.

Marketing

In marketing books to librarians, reference publishers keep in mind that they are selling professional tools. A hard-sell marketing approach is generally neither necessary nor effective. The marketing department is usually service oriented, expending most of its energy in helping librarians sort out any difficulties with their orders. Sales are generally made through direct mail, and brochures are characteristically low-key and filled with specific facts about the book being marketed. The reference publisher's direct-mail campaign generally results in relatively small orders, perhaps only one or two copies of a book for each library placing an order. However, direct mail provides the publisher with a record of the purchase and a profile of the buyer, which the marketing department can use in many ways, inputting the lists of who has bought what onto a computer. This information is invaluable for informing libraries of a new edition of a book they have previously purchased, and it also can be used to identify libraries that are likely to buy a new series by examining the orders they have placed in the past.

Although one measure of success in trade publishing is the best-seller list, reference publishers have a different method of quantifying success— a yardstick calibrated in standing orders for books in a series. The advantages of this system for both buyer and seller are considerable. Standing orders cut down on paperwork for librarian and publisher, enabling the publisher to discount the book for standing-order customers. In turn, the standing orders for a successful series give a company the financial base from which to launch new projects.

Economics

Given the tremendous cost of researching, compiling, editing, and producing a new series, it usually takes several years before it begins to break even. Depending upon the size of the staff required, the length of time spent in preparation, and the cost of research materials and computer time, the expenses involved in launching a new project can be considerable. Since a reference book rarely makes a profit in its first months of publication and often doesn't make one in the first few years following publication, good reference publishers, with a feel for what is needed, will frequently stay with a fledgling reference tool through another edition or volume to give it a chance to become established. Happily, once the book becomes established, it can go on forever, adding new editions or volumes and building up standing orders. This is a very strong reason why reference publishers look for books that are not restricted to one-time publishing ventures.

There is a great deal of variation from house to house, and even within houses, as to how profits and losses are calculated. What follows is only one approach, but it does give a clear picture of two important facts about reference publishing: (1) Almost all the expenses on a book prepared in-house, including editorial, production, and some of the promotional expenses, show up before publication; and (2) it is often not until several years after publication that a title begins to show a profit.

Suppose ABC Reference Book Publisher has these projections on a new title: Editorial preparation will cost $36,000 over a two-year period; printing and binding 7,000 copies will cost $70,000; ABC is willing to spend 15 percent of anticipated revenue on promotion and plans to spend 5 percent of revenue on fulfillment (some houses set absolute dollar rather than percentage numbers for either or both of these cost categories); and revenue (net of discounts and returns) should average $50 per copy. ABC anticipates that sales will be zero in years one and two (prepublication period). After that it is estimated that sales will be:

3,000 copies × $50 =	$150,000	in year	three
1,200	60,000		four
600	30,000		five
400	20,000		six
350	17,500		seven
300	15,000		eight
250	12,500		nine
200	10,000		ten
150	7,500		eleven
100	5,000		twelve
0	0		thirteen and thereafter

Over the entire cycle of the book, all costs must be charged off, regardless of what conventions are used in capitalizing or expensing prepublication expenses. The conventions affect the timing of the write-offs but, one way or another, full cost absorption will apply over the life cycle. The foregoing assumptions might produce a full-cycle profit-and-loss statement that looks like the one in Table 26.1.

Year by year, reported results can vary depending on how prepublication expenses are treated. Following is a year-by-year table showing results on three different approaches: (1) a pure cash or checkbook basis (an approach that would be of interest to the treasurer of the house), in which inventory is charged off when purchased; (2) profit-and-loss statement with prepublication costs expensed (written off as incurred); and (3) profit-and-loss statement with prepublication expenses capitalized (carried into inventory from work in process and written off as inventory is sold).

CUMULATIVE $ (IN 1,000S)

Year	(1)	(2)	(3)
one	(18)	(18)	0
two	(106)	(36)	0
three	14	52	72
four	62	87	100
five	86	105	115
six	102	117	125
seven	116	127	133
eight	128	136	140
nine	138	143	145
ten	146	149	150
eleven	152	153	153
twelve	156	156	156

In (2) above, inventory is written off as it is sold, but inventory value excludes prepublication expenses. In (3) above, inventory is written off as it is sold, and inventory value includes prepublication expenses.

The table indicates that a contribution in excess of $100,000 is generated by this title. Suppose, however, that actual sales are only half of forecasted levels. Instead of $156,000, the life-cycle contribution—as shown in Table 26.2—would be $25,000. This slim result would preclude subsequent editions or volumes in most houses.

Given the expenses and risk involved, new projects are undertaken only after extensive research into the market. The most fruitful and accurate research on new projects comes directly from reference-book buyers—librarians. The organization most important to reference publishers is the American Library Association (ALA). ALA conventions

TABLE 26.1 PROFIT-AND-LOSS STATEMENT

	Prepublication Capitalized	Prepublication Expensed
Net sales	$327,500	$327,500
Cost of sales (COS)	(106,000)	(70,000)
Gross margin	221,500	257,500
Promotion and fulfillment	(65,500)	(65,500)
Prepublication expenses	included in COS	(36,000)
Contribution to profits	$156,000	$156,000

TABLE 26.2 PROFIT-AND-LOSS STATEMENT AT LOWER SALES LEVEL

	Prepublication Capitalized	Prepublication Expensed
Net sales	$163,750	$163,750
Cost of sales (COS)	(106,000)	(70,000)
Gross margin	57,750	93,750
Promotion and fulfillment	(32,750)	(32,750)
Prepublication expenses	included in COS	(36,000)
Contribution to profits	$25,000	$25,000

provide all publishers with the opportunity to showcase their new books, remind librarians of the backlists, and solicit candid and informed opinions on books under consideration. Many reference houses have advisory panels, sometimes formal ones that meet several times a year with a definite agenda, but more often simply a network of librarians who are willing to have their brains picked from time to time. No matter how formally or casually it's accomplished, the goal is the same—to get librarians to respond meaningfully.

The Essence of Reference Publishing

Earlier in this chapter I talked about the magnitude and the minutiae of reference publishing; it's this thought that I'd like to return to in conclusion. Reference books are valued as information sources, and the accuracy of each small piece of information is essential to the integrity of the whole. The specific functions involved in publishing a reference book—mailing out tides of questionnaires, checking and rechecking endless pieces of information, inputting data, proofing printouts—may in themselves seem unimpressive, even at times prosaic. It's when we look at the larger picture, realizing that we are feeding an information-hungry society, that reference publishing becomes meaningful and satisfying. I'm reminded of a very old story: A traveler stopped by a construction site where three men were working. He went up to the first man and asked him what he was doing. The man answered, "I'm mixing these materials together and making some bricks." The traveler asked the second man the same question and was told, "I'm carrying these bricks from this place to that place." The traveler posed the same question to the third man, who was mixing mortar, and the man answered, "I'm building a cathedral."

CHAPTER TWENTY-SEVEN

Information Systems and New Technology

MARGARET KNOX GOGGIN

In our reading, TV viewing, and radio listening these days we're constantly invited to join the information revolution, to understand the information industry, to be ready to receive on our home computer all kinds of information from The Source, a new computerized store. We're told we must manage information, access information, retrieve information, share information—and that more than half of us will be working in some part of the information industry during this coming decade.

An Information-Based Society

Recognition of the growing importance of information in national planning was evident by the early 1970s when the Conference Board (an organization of leaders of industry, transportation, banking, education, labor, religion, politics, and government) issued a two-volume report, *Information Technology,* that presented testimony to support the conclusion that the United States could not succeed and continue to maintain its leadership role in the world unless it moved from an industrial base to an information base.[1] At the same time, the Organization for Economic Cooperation and Development stated: "Information is the key to man's future . . . society must learn to use it effectively,"[2] and a Japanese White Paper concluded:

> Japan has to change its goal from industrialization to informationalization to prevent social and economic problems such as dollar shock, pollution, and congestion in urban areas, which have been caused by the extension of industrialization. . . . We propose that the final national goal be a new information society which will bring about a general flourishing state of

MARGARET KNOX GOGGIN is former dean and professor in the Graduate School of Librarianship and Information Management, University of Denver.

human intellectual creativity by the year 2000 with 1985 the medium goal year of the plan.[3]

Futurists and those studying societal changes have pronounced that we have, indeed, moved from the industrial society into what noted sociologist Daniel Bell calls a post-industrial society, that is, an information-based society in which knowledge and information are the "strategic and transforming resources of the society." As Bell describes the changing patterns of this new age, "the dependence upon information to create innovation and change places a high premium on the ability of nations to access and use information to create advances in society."[4]

A report submitted to the president in 1976 by the Domestic Council's Committee on the Right of Privacy, recommending "that the United States set as a goal the development of a coordinated National Information Policy,"[5] explicated some of the factors that have brought us to this information age. First, there is the explosion of information, the exponential growth of this body of books, articles, reports, data—a massive amount to store and retrieve in the traditional systems. Second, the development of computer technology in the last twenty years, coupled with the rapid advances in communication technologies—and the fusing of the two to tackle information storage, retrieval, and transmission problems—has almost catapulted us into the development of new systems for information retrieval and delivery.

It is not only the nation that is shifting to an information base; individuals within society are finding their lives and their livelihoods dependent upon the availability of certain information necessary for daily decisions. Survival or success may depend upon a person's ability to access the exact information at the moment of need. Does this sound overly dramatic? Let me illustrate.

A young girl in California was so physically handicapped that she could not move, dress, or feed herself and existed only with the help of an aide who gave her constant attention. Her mind, however, was alert, and with great perseverance and determination she managed to gain an education and fit herself to become a contributing member of society. When she finally persuaded an employer to overlook her physical condition and hire her to work at a job she could do with the aid of her companion, the Social Security Office declared her ineligible for funds to pay her companion, without whom she could not exist. When all avenues of appeal for relief of that ruling failed, the young girl committed suicide. In her story told on the television show "60 Minutes," the interviewer asked the officer at the Social Security agency if he and his staff had known that several weeks earlier the California legislature had passed a relief bill for those denied funds under these conditions and that, in fact, the girl could have held her job and received from the state the money to pay for her companion, her lifeline. The answer was that there was so much information that his staff could not be expected to keep up with it. Survival may indeed depend on accessing the right information at a critical time.

Access to information is important to the business and professional community, both individuals and corporate bodies. Pertinent information at the critical decision-making moments may enable the business to flourish, may assist the professional in a career advance, may make the difference between success and failure of an enterprise or an individual.

What does all this mean for publishers and those entering the publishing field?

R. R. Bowker—publisher of *Publishers Weekly, Library Journal,* and other reference sources for the industry—identified its role in a full-page ad in one of its journals that declared in large black letters "Information: A New Industry That's 5000 Years Old." Charging that "in a democracy there must be, in addition to freedom of information, efficient and convenient means of obtaining that information," Bowker staked a claim to a role in the world of information suppliers: "We remain at the center of the industry with a vast data base plus the experience to use it. . . ."[6]

In *Publishers Weekly* during the fall and winter of 1979-1980, there was announced a one-day seminar, "An introduction to online for reference-book editors and data-base editors." Why would a publisher sponsor such an activity? The reason stated was that "it is essential that today's editors and product managers be familiar with this dynamic new tool [online information retrieval system]."[7]

The Information Cycle

Let us see what we mean when we say that publishers are an integral part of the information system. A diagram of the information cycle would start with the creator of information, the person who develops the ideas, the concepts, the creative thinking. The publisher takes the creative work and packages it so it can be shared with others—as a book, in a journal, on a videocassette, or in some other form. It is thus the publisher who translates the created thoughts and information into a transportable commodity, serving as the bridge between the creator of information and those who would use that information.

Once the package is produced and made available, the indexers and abstractors specify the terms by which the book can be identified and index the contents in such a manner as to allow for retrievability. In many instances abstracts of the material are written to more precisely identify the subject matter covered. *Books in Print* is a familiar example, an index to the books published and currently available in the United States, enabling a person to identify the book by author, title, or subject. Public- and school-library card catalogs are such indexes, as are periodical indexes like *Chemical Abstracts, Readers' Guide to Periodical Literature,* and *The Humanities Index*—that is, they identify packaged information in order that the package or its contents may be located and used.

Having been created, packaged, and indexed, the information is then stored. The most familiar location for the storage of books and journals is the library—the public library, the school media center, the university or college library, the large research or special library. A bookstore houses books for a limited period, the amount of time depending upon the nature of the store and its clientele. Information agencies, often created for a single purpose or a specific area of knowledge, may also house publications as may museums, associations, and federal agencies. And some information may be stored in computers to be retrieved in hard copy only when someone needs it.

The chief purpose in storing information is to enable people to access the material, retrieving that information necessary for the purpose at hand. Therefore the next step in the cycle is the retrieval process accomplished by the individual seeker or by an intermediary. Once retrieved, the information is delivered to the person who needs it, and the cycle ends with the user. But it really does not end there, for the user may correlate the information with previous knowledge, may add new ideas and new insights, and thereby create new information that needs to be published, indexed, stored, retrieved, delivered, and used. Thus the cycle is a continuous one (see Figure 27.1).

The information cycle is not new. What *is* new is the application of sophisticated technologies to the processes, thus dramatically changing our ability to access information more rapidly and with greater economy and precision.

INFORMATION STORAGE

A major breakthrough in the ability to store bibliographical data in computers was the development by the Library of Congress of the Machine Readable Catalog (MARC) format, a structure by which the distinct parts of a bibliographical citation—the author, title, imprint, collation, and subject descriptors—are entered into the computerized data file. This MARC format became the national standard for the exchange of bibliographical data starting in 1969, and since that time adoption of the format internationally has made great progress.

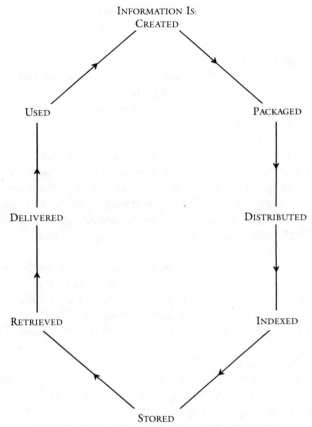

FIGURE 27.1 The information cycle.

What does this mean? It means a possible worldwide compatability of data files so that the same structure for the description of a book or a document will be followed in all data files.

The MARC record of books received by the Library of Congress and cooperating libraries since 1968 formed the base for the On-Line Computer Library Center (OCLC) data base, now used by thousands of libraries to identify their acquisitions and to catalog them. The same tapes helped Stanford University develop its data base, which now in expanded size is the data base of the Research Library Information Network (RLIN). These two organizations are examples of the new "information utility" that provides its customers with a variety of services all aimed at expanding their ability to access information.

The emergence of machine-readable data bases is making revolutionary changes in the methods of providing information. The decade of the

1970s saw a dramatic growth in the number of data bases; indeed by 1984 over twenty-one hundred are commercially available, with new ones added monthly. The majority of these are bibliographical—that is, they will provide users with a list of articles, books, and reports to read on a subject. The chart of representative data bases indicates the wide subject coverage of the data files (Table 27.1).

Many of the files are a by-product of the printed indexes and abstracts that are familiar tools in any library's reference collection. CA Search is *Chemical Abstracts*, Compendex is the *Engineering Index, Psychological Abstracts* and PAIS are in both printed and computer formats. Some, such as INFORM (in the field of business and management), have no counterpart in print, but are designed solely as a computerized data base; others, such as the *New York Times* Information Bank, are a combination of printed index and the indexing onto computer of the contents of additional sources (about sixty current-events magazines and newspapers for the *Times* bank).

Computerized data bases are revolutionizing information retrieval for two reasons. First, the computer can run through an enormous number of citations and select the pertinent ones in a matter of seconds, thus saving the searcher time; second, the computer in its search can look for a number of different elements or terms at the same time. The human mind cannot do this, and thus the person must search the file for one or two terms at a time.

Nonbibliographic data bases are growing in number and in importance to information seekers. These data bases provide the answer to a question, give a fact or figure or present the entire text of a journal or document rather than a citation to another source. The Smithsonian Science Information Exchange is an example of such a data base, providing the names and addresses of those persons who are engaged in research on specific topics. If you are editing a manuscript in the rapidly changing field of solar energy, you may wish to corroborate the author's up-to-dateness or verify his analysis of the research in the field. Through a search of this data base, you may find that a certain doctor has just completed a research project on that topic or that a team of researchers has a contract to experiment with a specially designed solar system, and you can then contact those experts for further assistance.

There are also numerical or statistical files. The U.S. census is recorded in a data base, allowing you to retrieve all kinds of demographic data. For example, you might seek data on book production as it relates to book-selling markets, educational status of people, and housing facilities. In another area, Predicasts provides international as well as domestic statistical data, market data, wholesale and retail figures, stock market

TABLE 27.1 REPRESENTATIVE DATA BASES

Data-Base Name	Subject Coverage
ABI/INFORM	Management
Accountants' Index	Finance
AGRICOLA (CAIN)	Agriculture
ASI	Statistics
BIOSIS/PREVIEWS	Life sciences
CA SEARCH	Chemistry
CANCERLIT	Cancer
Child Abuse and Neglect	Child abuse
Congressional Information Service (CIS)	U.S. Congress publications
COMPENDEX	Engineering
ENERGYLINE	Energy
EPILEPSYLINE	Epilepsy
ERIC	Education
GEOREF	Geology
INSPEC	Physics, electronics, computers
LIBCON(E)	English language materials, cataloged by Library of Congress
Magazine Index	Popular magazine literature
MEDLINE	Medicine
NASA	Aerospace
NTIS	U.S. government–sponsored research
New York Times Information Bank	News, current events
PAIS	Public affairs
Predicasts	Statistics
Psychological Abstracts	Psychology
SPORT	Sports and recreation
SSCI (Social Science Citation Index)	Social sciences

quotations, and other data. Other files give comparative shopping information, menus from restaurants in the city, and theater schedules with provision for making reservations by computer.

Whatever kind of information you are seeking, the first question should be "Is there a computerized data base available in this area?"

INFORMATION RETRIEVAL

An information-retrieval system consists first of the various data bases I have been discussing and second of a computerized data-base vendor, which buys the data bases, makes them available from its computer, services them, and offers training to those who wish to access their services. Of the over 350 vendors in operation in 1984, 3 dominate the U.S. field, providing the majority of data bases: Bibliographical Retrieval Service (BRS), Lockheed using the software called Dialog, and Systems Development Corporation with its Orbit.

The route from the user to the specific data base is a simple one. The user starts with his library, information agency, or information broker. Consultation with a data-base directory will help in the selection of the appropriate data base for the task at hand and the appropriate vendor to use. The link between the computer terminal at the library or information agency and the computer at the vendor's location is made by long-distance telephone. Several companies now exist that provide for the sharing of long-distance commercial lines, reducing the cost of the telephone link to that of a local call. Telenet and Tymnet are the two commercial networks most popularly used.

With all the parts of the information-retrieval network now identified, let us look at an example of the process of retrieval. Suppose a junior editor with Doubleday has been asked to work with staff on the idea of publishing a series of books aimed at the growing elderly population. The publisher has asked, "How can we cater to and expand sales of books to this group?" The junior editor, recognizing a need to do some quick reading on the subject in order to contribute to the discussion, goes to the company's information manager/librarian or calls the public library. An interview with the librarian helps to delineate the question: "Are the reading interests of the aged different from those of the general adult population, and, if so, in what ways?"

The ERIC data base is chosen as the most logical source for articles and reports on the topic, and the librarian consults the thesaurus or guide to the terms used in the ERIC files. Terms selected are *reading, reading interest or interests, reading habit or habits,* and possibly *reading behavior.*

Since the computer can handle and search many terms at one time, the librarian will use the language for adding terms (*OR*), for combining terms (*AND*), and for omitting terms (*NOT*). Thus the search strategy will tell the computer to select everything on Reading *AND* (Habit *OR* Habits *OR* Interest *OR* Interests *OR* Behavior). Every citation identified through this search must have *Reading* and any one of the other terms. To refine the search further, the searcher will tell the computer to search the files for articles on Aged *OR* Elderly *OR* Older Adult. Wishing to eliminate articles referring to the sight-impaired elderly, the searcher tells the computer to search for Visually Handicapped *OR* Visual Impairments *OR* Sight Impaired.

Then the command is given to identify all those items that combine Reading *AND* (Interests *OR* Habits *OR* Behavior) *AND* (Aged *OR* Elderly *OR* Older Adult) *NOT* (Visually Handicapped *OR* Visual Impairments *OR* Sight Impairments). The result is a total of ninety-one citations.

At this point, the editor and the searcher may decide to see which articles are being retrieved and may ask the computer to print in brief form the first twenty items (see items 4/3/1–3 on the computer printout, Figure 27.2). If the contents are not clear from the titles, the editor could request a printout of the abstracts along with the citations (see 4/5/1 and 4/5/2 on Figure 27.2). Finally, deciding that the articles are relevant, the editor may ask for all of the citations to be printed on-line—that is, while the editor is connected to the computer by telephone—or may request that the citations be printed and mailed, saving the long-distance charges for the printing time.

If the editor wishes to have Selective Dissemination of Information (SDI) service on this topic, it is possible to request a monthly update of the articles published on this topic to receive a printout of abstracts of articles that have appeared during the month. From those a user may select items to read in full.

INFORMATION DELIVERY

We've now seen how the information-retrieval process is accomplished. The next step is the information-delivery process. Delivery systems have been time-consuming operations, involving the location of the physical book or journal wherever it is stored and the transportation of the reader to the book or the book to the reader.

Traditionally the process started at the local library, where a search of the card catalog might lead the reader to the shelf location for the title. If the item needed was not owned by the home library, it could be borrowed through a system of interlibrary lending, governed by a mutually agreed upon code of borrowing/lending policies. Identification of the library owning the needed title depended upon the librarian's knowledge of other libraries' collections, the use of printed catalogs and union lists, and communications with colleagues. The title located was then delivered to the borrowing library by mail, and the reader was called to the library to pick up the item. In recent years the teletype machine has helped to speed up the requesting process.

In the mid-1960s, the U.S. government gave great impetus to a

```
@C 213 170


213 170 CONNECTED


ENTER YOUR DIALOG PASSWORD
████████  LOGON File1 Mon 30jul84 13:46:20 Port85A


File1*:ERIC - 66-84/Jun
        Set Items Description
        ───── ───── ───────────
? S READING AND (HABIT? ? OR BEHAVIOR OR INTEREST? ?)
            44557 READING   ((NOTE: USE A MORE SPECIFIC TERM IF POSSI
             4525 HABIT? ?
            45225 BEHAVIOR   (THE AGGREGATE OF OBSERVABLE RESPONSES O
            23176 INTEREST? ?
        1   7208  READING AND (HABIT? ? OR BEHAVIOR OR INTEREST? ?)
? S S1 AND (ELDERLY OR OLDER ADULT? ?)
             1865 ELDERLY
             4444 OLDER ADULT? ?
        2     68  S1 AND (ELDERLY OR OLDER ADULT? ?)
? S VISUALLY(W)HANDICAPPED OR VISUAL IMPAIRMENTS OR SIGHT(W)IMPAIR?
              874 VISUALLY(W)HANDICAPPED
             2202 VISUAL IMPAIRMENTS   (VISUAL LOSSES THAT INTERFERE
                4 SIGHT(W)IMPAIR?
        3   2378  VISUALLY(W)HANDICAPPED OR VISUAL IMPAIRMENTS OR SIGHT(W)IMPA
IR?
? C 2 NOT 3
        4     67  2 NOT 3
? T4/3/1-5
4/3/1
EJ289244
  Literacy and Social Milieu: Reading Behavior of the Black Elderly.
  Heisel, Marsel; Larson, Gordon
  Adult Education Quarterly, v34 n2 p63-70 Win
  1984
  Available from: UMI


4/3/2
EJ240288
  Does Literacy Really Enhance the Lives of the Elderly?
  Kingston, Albert J.
  Reading World, v20 n3 p169-71 Mar
  1981
  Available from: Reprint: UMI


4/3/3
EJ238136
  Older Adults and Reading, the Effect of Residential Lifestyles.
  Murray, Martha S.
  Lifelong Learning: The Adult Years, v4 n5 p17,31 Jan
  1981
  Available from: Reprint: UMI


4/5/1
EJ289244  CE513905
  Literacy and Social Milieu: Reading Behavior of the Black Elderly.
  Heisel, Marsel; Larson, Gordon
  Adult Education Quarterly, v34 n2 p63-70 Win      1984
  Available from: UMI
  Language: English
  Document Type: RESEARCH REPORT (143)
  Reports on a study that examined the literacy behavior of 132 elderly
Blacks in a large city environment with a high   concentration   of
undereducated adults. Found that the group developed the necessary literacy
skills to meet the demands of their social environment. (JOW)
  Descriptors:   *Adult Literacy;   *Blacks;   *Educationally Disadvantaged;
Functional Literacy;  *Older Adults;  *Reading Habits;   Reading Skills;
*Social Environment; Urban Environment
```

FIGURE 27.2 The search as accomplished through Lockheed's Dialog.

4/5/2
EJ240288 CS713597
  Does Literacy Really Enhance the Lives of the Elderly?
  Kingston, Albert J.
  Reading World, v20 n3 p169-71 Mar   1981
  Available from: Reprint: UMI
  Language: English
  Document Type: JOURNAL ARTICLE (080); POSITION PAPER (120)
  Argues that adult literacy programs should be structured so that reading
becomes a genuine means of enhancing the lives of the elderly. (FL)
  Descriptors: *Adult Literacy; Improvement; Lifelong Learning; Literacy
Education; *Older Adults; Program Improvement; Quality of Life; *Reading
Habits; *Reading Skills

4/5/46
ED198502 CS005904
  The   Preferences of a Selected Group of Older Readers for Five
Biographical Short Stories.
  Drotter, Molly Wilson
  Dec 1980   16p.; Paper presented at the Annual Meeting of the National
Reading Conference (30th, San Diego, CA, December 3-6, 1980).
  EDRS Price - MF01/PC01 Plus Postage.
  Language: English
  Document Type: RESEARCH REPORT (143); CONFERENCE PAPER (150)
  Geographic Source: U.S.; Idaho
  Journal Announcement: RIEJUL81
  The reading interests of a group of older adults were examined. Subjects
were 16 adults between the ages of 50 and 85 who read five stories from
"Readers' Digest" short story collections and who responded to a
questionnaire about their preferences for the stories, their reading habits
and interests, and the appealing elements of the stories. The results of
the study of preferences for the five stories showed that participants
preferred happy stories with moral characters.   Overall, the subjects
indicated a wide variety of reading interests and a continuing interest in
reading into older adulthood. Two problems indicated by the respondents
were the legibility of print and the trouble they had in finding
interesting things to read. In terms of Erickson's developmental theory,
these subjects seemed to be in the stage of integrity versus despair,
wherein they questioned whether they had had full and productive lives,
whether their lives had made a difference. Reading about characters who had
met with success in living and who had been rewarded for it was seemingly
very appealing for this age group. (RL)
  Descriptors: Adult Development; Characterization; Developmental Stages;
Literature Appreciation; Middle Aged Adults; Older Adults; Reading Habits;
*Reading Interests; Reading Materials; *Reading Research;   *Recreational
Reading; Self Esteem

? B1
          30jul84 14:05:22 User7222
   $4.79 0.319 Hrs File1* 18 Descriptors

FIGURE 27.2, cont.

movement to speed up the sharing of library resources by enacting the Library Services and Construction Act, which provided funds to state libraries to establish and maintain networks for interlibrary cooperation. Since that time, all fifty states have developed a systematic and planned network that connects libraries within the states for the purposes of sharing resources, providing bibliographical assistance, and delivering documents.

The networks have many different configurations and programs, but each one is working to assure that all citizens have access to the information they need regardless of where they live, where their businesses are located, or how remote they are from resources. Thus, a person could set up a publishing house in Flagstaff, Arizona, and receive the information needed to make decisions by sending the request through the local public library to the library in Arizona where that information is available.

Communications throughout the network are generally maintained by telephone or teletype, with the document delivered by postal service or, in urban areas, by courier. Hundreds of specialized networks have been developed, some very formal and others merely informal agreements and protocols. For example, the National Library of Medicine has a well-established, far-flung network of medical libraries and hospital libraries for the sharing of health-related information. Networks, therefore, are one newer system for the delivery of information and documents. "Can you borrow what I need through your network or networks?" is a question to be asked when trying to locate a title.

The use of a computerized data base for the location of titles and the processing of borrowing requests is another new development. OCLC has an interlibrary lending system whereby the searching of its data base of over 4 million records reveals up to five locations in libraries for each title. The borrowing library selects, in order of preference, the libraries to be used, and the system automatically translates the title to a borrowing form and forwards the request via computer to the first potential lender, with an automatic referral to the second and succeeding choices as needed. Responses are immediately transmitted to the borrowing library, and the documents are shipped from the lending library via mail. This system has proved to be an excellent time saver for the libraries and the patron since it eliminates the correspondence and speeds up the location process.

Another system to speed document delivery for those who wish to purchase the material is the on-line document-ordering service of Dialog, called DIALORDER. Under this plan the searcher identifies the items needed at the time of the data-base search, and the order is automatically copied from the file and transmitted to one of a growing number of suppliers. The supplier obtains the document and mails it to the requester with a bill.

These last two systems speed the location of the documents and the ordering process, but the delivery of the actual pages relies upon mail services, which may take from three days to as long as several weeks unless express mail is used. What is being done to try to speed the transmission of materials?

Telefacsimile may be one of the answers. Telefacsimile or "telefax" is a means of reproducing documents at a distance through the use of special equipment at the sending and the receiving stations, which are connected by telephone. Since the process was first demonstrated in the 1920s, changes in the technology have brought improvements in the clarity of the copy (resolution) and in speed of delivery, so that today telefax is a viable method of delivering information and/or documents.

I conducted a demonstration of this technology to test the state of the art as of 1979-1980. This was done with William E. Rapp at the University of Denver's Graduate School of Librarianship and Information Management. Financed by the Office of Telecommunication Policy of the Department of Health, Education, and Welfare (HEW), Talinet (Telefax Library Information Network) was a network of public libraries in five western cities with headquarters at the U.S. National Oceanic and Atmospheric Administration Library in Boulder, Colorado, and through it a link to the Federal Library Network of some fifteen government libraries in all parts of the United States. All libraries had two pieces of telefax equipment—Quip 1200, transmitting an 8½-by-11-inch sheet in four to six minutes, and a Rapifax 100, sending pages at thirty-five seconds, forty-five seconds, and ninety seconds per page. Perhaps one incident in the Talinet project will suffice to demonstrate the process and the potential of this new technology.

One morning an urgent telephone call came into the Talinet office. In a hospital in Rapid City, South Dakota, lay a young man whose right foot had turned purple, a condition diagnosed by his doctors as gangrene. As three surgeons discussed the amputation necessary to stop the progress of the infection, one of them remembered reading of a case in which the combination of diabetes, high blood pressure, and a certain drug caused a purplish color in a patient's extremities with symptoms similar to gangrene, but treatable through medication. The surgical team agreed to delay the operation for one hour to allow the doctor to verify this.

The article could not be located in Rapid City, and the surgeon was calling for help through the local public library. The Talinet staff found the article at the medical library in Denver; as they were transporting the article to the Talinet office, the doctor was traveling to the Rapid City Public Library. The article was sent at thirty-five seconds per page over the telefacsimile equipment, the doctor reading each page as it came off the machine. The article did describe the young man's symptoms and specified the drug the patient had taken. The operation was canceled, and the young man is walking around today on two good legs.

A dramatic story of information found and delivered in a time-critical situation? Yes. And a demonstration of the use of telefacsimile to overcome distance and disparity of local resources.

The telefax scene is changing rapidly as new technologies are applied and new equipment is produced that speeds up the time of delivery, improves on the quality of the copy, and decreases the cost of the process. For example, during the year of the Talinet demonstration, Quip II was marketed, which cut in half the time of transmission as compared with the Quip 1200. We are learning daily of new possibilities, such as the FAX-COMP, an add-on box that can reduce the six-minute-per-page transaction to under thirty seconds, or the Optical Character Reader combined with the telefax equipment. Indeed, by the time one writes about the newest telefax situation, the information is outmoded by newer modifications. Denis Krusos, president of Panafax Corporation, has predicted that "within the next two decades, facsimile will be home-affordable, available to the individual consumer and smallest entrepreneur."[8]

No discussion of delivery systems would be complete without recognizing the great potential of satellites for transmitting information. We accept as commonplace the reception on our home television sets of the sports and news events of the world, transmitted via satellite. Over twenty commercial satellites are in orbit today, delivering messages for worldwide business and industry. Numerous other satellites are conducting research, providing weather information, providing information for the defense needs of many countries, and conducting experiments in all fields of endeavor. One example of the commercial use of satellites in publishing is the transmission of daily copy of the *Wall Street Journal* from its headquarters computer in New Jersey via satellite to its computer in Orlando, Florida, where copy is printed for distribution to the southeast.

Noncommercial usage of the satellite—for health services, education, and the public good—has been guided in experimentation by the National Aeronautic and Space Administration (NASA) and a variety of government funding agencies. Projects on the Applied Technology Satellite (ATS-6) and the Communications Technology Satellite (CTS) demonstrated the power of satellites to deliver medical education, health care, educational offerings between campuses, career information, and continuing education programs. Teleconferencing via satellite was successfully demonstrated by the Westinghouse Corporation and the National Library of Medicine, and the WAMI Corporation showed that doctors in Seattle, Washington, could diagnose illness in Alaskans located in isolated communities where health-care facilities were not available. To further the development of public, noncommercial use of satellites, agencies such as the Public Service Satellite Consortium have been formed and are active in promoting new ways of delivering information.

There are three reasons why satellites provide great promise for future delivery systems. First, satellite cost is not dependent upon distance. Unlike the telephone system, the cost of satellite is only the cost of accessing a channel. The message transmitted may reach anywhere within the footprint of the satellite.

Second, the bandwidth of the satellite channel is much greater than that of telephone lines, enabling more users to send more messages. One observer illustrated the channel capacity of satellites twenty years. from now (if certain advances are made) by predicting the availability of 22,000 channels, so that "if every man, woman and child in the U.S. spent four hours a day transmitting messages on a teletype terminal, the resulting message traffic would just fill those 22,000 channels."[9]

A third reason for a promising future for satellite transmission is the increasing power of the satellites being built and launched, which means that the earth stations needed to receive the messages can be reduced in size and therefore in cost. It may indeed be possible (as the same futurist has described) that a time will come when each person will be able to wear a small satellite transmitter on his or her wrist, a so-called wristwatch telephone.

Information-delivery systems are changing rapidly, promising new and innovative transmission systems for the individual wherever located.

$$*\quad*\quad*$$

We can access data bases in seconds or minutes, we can receive a printout of citations to books and articles in minutes, we can receive statistical data upon which to make decisions, we can order copies of articles in an instant, we can request hard copies of articles and have them sent by telefacsimile in seconds or minutes per page. But our problem is that we can only do these things for people who know that these services are available, who can articulate their needs, and who can afford the services.

Notes

1. Conference Board, *Information Technology,* Reports 537 and 577 (New York: Conference Board, 1972).

2. Organization for Economic Cooperation and Development (OECD), *Information for a Changing Society: Some Policy Considerations* (Paris: OECD, 1971).

3. *Computer White Paper* (Tokyo: Japan, Computer Usage Development Institute, 1970).

4. Daniel Bell, "Communications Technology—For Better or for Worse," *Harvard Business Review* 57, no. 3 (May-June 1979), p. 24.

5. U.S. Domestic Council Committee on the Right of Privacy, *National Information Policy* (Washington, D.C.: National Commission of Libraries and Information Science, 1976), p. vi.

6. *Library Journal* 104, no. 16 (September 15, 1979), p. 1741.

7. *Publishers Weekly* 217, no. 7 (February 22, 1980), p. 84; and other issues from October 1979 to March 1980.

8. Howard Anderson, "What Is Electronic Mail. . . ?" *Telecommunications* 12, no. 11 (November, 1978), p. 31.

9. Joseph P. Martino, "Telecommunications in the Year 2000," *The Futurist,* April 1979, p. 98.

CHAPTER TWENTY-EIGHT

Tools of the Trade

ELIZABETH A. GEISER

Bibliographies, "books about books," reference tools—whatever label you give to them, they sound less than glamorous and maybe even dull, until you stop and realize what these tools can mean to you in publishing. And their applications are endless!

Whatever side of publishing you may be in or interested in—be it editing, design, production, advertising, promotion, publicity, or sales— you have one main goal in mind: to see that books reach as many people as possible, to be sure that books are so effectively marketed that wherever there is an inquiry—in a bookstore in New Mexico or a major library in New York—the inquiry brings nods of recognition, not blank stares. Publishers have many ingenious ways of getting books known, but most titles are given minimal sales attention. And even for those that do get the full-scale blitz, the effect is usually fleeting. Newspaper ads go out with the garbage, the TV talk shows fade from the tubes, and brochures end up in the wastebasket. Unless there is some permanent record that the book has been born—and of who published it—it can languish in the warehouse never finding its readers.

And that is where the bibliography comes in—providing that valuable record of what is available and where it can be found. The "book finders" or major bibliographies serve an important two-fold purpose for all publishers: They are depended upon by libraries and booksellers worldwide and thus are an unsung source of promotional power for the titles they list, and additionally they serve publishers as an invaluable key to competitors' output.

Book Finders

BOOKS IN PRINT
Books in Print (*BIP*) is the annual guide to just about every available U.S. book. When you want to know whether a title you're considering

ELIZABETH A. GEISER is senior vice president of Gale Research Company and director of the University of Denver Publishing Institute.

has been used before, want to find publication details about a competing book, or simply need a full list of a particular author's works complete with the names of all his publishers, you can turn to *Books in Print.* This annually revised, six-volume reference work, published each October, includes information on almost every *currently available* book of more than 13,500 U.S. publishers. Three volumes are indexed by author, the other three by title; all kinds of books are covered: trade, text, adult, juvenile, paper. Each entry includes (when known) author's name, title of book, publisher or distributor, price, series, date of publication, International Standard Book Number (ISBN), and Library of Congress catalog number. A complete list of publishers with addresses is also included. To get your books listed in *Books in Print* and the other bibliographic services described here, write to Department of Bibliography, R. R. Bowker Company.[1] You will be placed on a mailing list to receive a supply of Bowker's Advance Book Information (ABI) forms. If you fill these out on a regular basis, information about your books will be included in Bowker's data base, which produces *Books in Print* and all of its derivative products. Thus entries of your titles will automatically appear in a number of other Bowker bibliographies that are issued regularly and are designed to serve libraries, bookstores, researchers— all those in search of current book information. For a free catalog explaining how to use the *Books in Print* family of products (on-line, fiche, hardcopy), write to the Marketing Department, R. R. Bowker Company.

Forthcoming Books, an important bimonthly periodical, provides the same kind of comprehensive author-title information for all books due to be published in the coming five-month period, plus a continuing cumulative index to books published since the last *Books in Print* appeared. With *Forthcoming Books,* and its companion, *Subject Guide to Forthcoming Books,* you can research books months back as well as months ahead and also keep up with postponements, price changes, and cancellations and locate recently published titles not yet listed in *BIP.*

Books in Print Supplement appears annually in April, mid year between the annual editions of *Books in Print,* and completely updates *Books in Print* and *Subject Guide to Books in Print.* Some thirty thousand new books of all kinds published since July of the preceding year (closing date for editorial preparation of the base volumes) and through July of the current year are listed by author, title, and subject. Price changes and out-of-stock and out-of-print titles are also recorded.

To help users find books in special areas, Bowker annually publishes the following "book finders" that provide information to those with interests in particular subjects.

Subject Guide to Books in Print, a two-volume set published annually in October indexes 500,000 books of 13,500 U.S. publishers and distributors under sixty-two thousand Library of Congress subject headings. It enables publishers to check the coverage of a certain field, see who the authors are, establish the date of the latest publication—and identify gaps.

Children's Books in Print provides author-title-illustrator indexes to some forty thousand in-print children's books from preschool to grade twelve, and provides a directory of the fourteen hundred publishers and distributors represented. Entries include price, publisher, grade level, binding, and illustrator. An annual companion volume, *Subject Guide to Children's Books in Print,* lists fiction and nonfiction under Sears and Library of Congress subject headings. It is published annually in November.

El-Hi Textbooks in Print, published annually in the spring, lists approximately thirty-five thousand textbooks and related teaching materials under 239 subject areas and provides a directory to the 420 publishers represented. Entry information includes author, title, grade level, series affiliation, publication date, binding, ISBN, price, Library of Congress number, and publisher.

Large-Type Books in Print indexes over fifty-five hundred titles available from seventy-five large-type publishers and associations by subject, author, and title, with a directory to the publishers represented. Includes textbooks and books for general reading printed in fourteen-point type and larger. The publication itself is in eighteen-point type to facilitate independent reader selections. It is published biennially.

Medical Books and Serials in Print, which is put out every June, indexes by author, title, and subject some fifty thousand monographs, texts, and other in-print books of all kinds dealing with all areas of medicine, dentistry, and psychiatry. A directory of publishers and distributors is included.

Paperbound Books in Print indexes all available paperbacks by author, title, and subject; each entry includes full bibliographic data. The three-volume set is issued biannually: the first set each spring; the second set each fall.

Religious Books and Serials in Print indexes 50,000 books and 4,500 serials under 4,600 subject areas. It includes a separate sacred works section, including 71 Bible versions and 800 book titles, author and title indexes, separate indexes for children's and religious fiction, and a directory to the eighteen hundred book publishers represented. Another feature is the Subject Area Directory, which arranges the 4,600 subjects by broad topics derived from the Library of Congress Classification Scheme. It is published biennially.

Scientific and Technical Books and Serials in Print indexes more than

80,000 books by author and title and by some 12,370 subjects. It also indexes about 17,000 serial entries by subject and title and includes a directory to all twenty-five hundred publishers represented. It is issued annually in December.

A WORLD LIST OF BOOKS IN ENGLISH— THE CUMULATIVE BOOK INDEX

Whereas *Books in Print* covers only books published and distributed in the United States that are in print, the *Cumulative Book Index (CBI)*, subtitled *A World List of Books in the English Language,* is the only single-alphabet author, title, and subject index to books published in the English language from all over the world. Fifty thousand to sixty thousand books are indexed each year. Author entries include complete bibliographic information: full title, series note, paging, price, ISBN if available, publication date, publisher, edition, and Library of Congress card number. When the work is published or available in more than one country, additional publishers or distributors are given. Dictionaries, grammars, phrase books, readers, editions of foreign classics, and other aids to language learning are included in *CBI* if they contain some English. Government documents, inexpensive paperbound books, music scores, and material of local or ephemeral nature are not included. It is published monthly except August with quarterly cumulations and permanent bound annual cumulations. *CBI* is published by the H. W. Wilson Company.

INTERNATIONAL BOOKS IN PRINT

Covering over ninety-five countries, part 1 of the third edition (1983) of *International Books in Print* lists over ninety thousand available titles in English published outside the United States and the United Kingdom by three thousand publishers. Entries give title, author, publisher, year of publication, country of origin, ISBN, price, and more. Part 2, new with the 1983 edition, is a country- and Dewey-classified arrangement of the fiction and nonfiction works in part 1. It is published by K. G. Saur Verlag and is available in the Western Hemisphere exclusively from Gale Research Company.

THE CATALOG OF CATALOGS

Booksellers and librarians the world over depend upon the *Publishers' Trade List Annual (PTLA)* when they want to check out a particular publisher's complete list, find that publisher's discount information, and check all titles in a series. *PTLA* compiles—in one annual six-volume edition—the catalogs and trade lists from some 2,250 publishers arranged alphabetically and bound in permanent volumes. It includes a special supplement of firms with catalogs of fewer than four pages and a subject index to publishers to help quickly identify their editorial emphasis. To include your catalog, write *PTLA,* R. R. Bowker Company.

Book Trade Magazines—To Publicize Your Books and Keep You *au Courant*

Publishers Weekly (*PW*) is the comprehensive journal of the U.S. book industry, keeping people in the book world informed about the immediate news and long-range trends of every branch of the industry. Published weekly, each issue contains articles, analyses of trends, exchanges of opinion, interviews, and news about personnel, new books, publishers, booksellers, and others. The forecasts section gives concise advance reviews of general fiction and nonfiction titles (hardcover books, paperbacks, and children's books). Twice a year, spring and fall, giant announcement issues tell readers what will be published in the season ahead. Among other services, there are two feature issues per year for children's books and two for religious books, frequent roundups of industry statistics, and numerous feature issues about the book trade abroad and in regions of the United States. For information on advertising costs or to enter a subscription, write to *PW,* R. R. Bowker Company.

AB Bookman's Weekly is a weekly magazine that lists books that are either "wanted" or "available" on the second-hand market—out-of-print books, particular editions, specialized books. For a small fee you can list the item you want to find, and chances are you will get a bid from one of the many buyers and sellers who use the magazine. Write to *AB Bookman's Weekly.*

American Bookseller, issued by the American Booksellers Association the first week of each month, is aimed directly at booksellers and their needs with practical articles on the business of bookselling, feature stories, and regular departments. For information on advertising rates or to enter a subscription, write to *American Bookseller.*

Christian Bookseller is a monthly trade magazine serving religious bookstores, general bookstores with religious-book departments, Christian camps and conference bookstores, and other outlets of church and Sunday school supplies. Includes articles on unique methods of merchandising, managerial articles on the "how to" of store operation, personnel articles on training, interviews with authors, and so on. For information on advertising rates or to enter a subscription, write to *Christian Bookseller.*

Library Journal provides news, trends, and views of the library profession and its members, a comprehensive book-review service, and many special issues providing indexes to the season's forthcoming books. Published semimonthly except July and August, when it is published once a month. For information about advertising costs or to enter a subscription, write to *Library Journal,* R. R. Bowker Company.

School Library Journal, published monthly August through May, provides news, trends, views, and reviews devoted exclusively to school libraries, public libraries for children, and young-adult library services. For information about advertising or to enter a subscription, write to *School Library Journal,* R. R. Bowker Company.

Wilson Library Bulletin reports the events, trends, and ideas of organized librarianship in the United States and around the world. Addressing itself to an audience of school, public, special, and academic librarians, the *Bulletin* is also read by publishers, information brokers, network directors, government officials, and educators. Published monthly except July and August. For information about advertising costs or to enter a subscription, write to *Wilson Library Bulletin,* H. W. Wilson Company.

For Information About Publishers

The *Literary Market Place* (*LMP*) provides facts on over twenty-five thousand firms and individuals in U.S. and Canadian book publishing and numerous related fields. It lists names, titles, addresses, phone numbers, and data reflecting recent mergers, realignment, and personnel changes in the book business. Tells who's where among book publishers, authors' agents, promotional services, review media, art, design and manufacturing facilities, editorial and translation free lances, courses, conventions, radio and TV outlets, exporters, government bodies, and book trade and other associations. It is issued annually in December. Send information for *LMP* to R. R. Bowker Company.

Book Publishers Directory is a guide to new and established, private and special interest, avant-garde and alternative, organization and association, government and institution presses. It provides users with detailed information on a broad range of publishing houses that are not listed in traditional sources. The fifth edition (1984) includes 9,300 publishers, and its supplement adds over 1,500 more. Entries give, where appropriate, name, address, phone number, date founded, ISBN prefix, affiliation, principal officers and managers, number of titles published per year, brief description, discount and returns policies, imprints, divisions, articles about, selected titles, and more. It is published annually each fall with supplements each spring by Gale Research Company.

International Directory of Little Magazines and Small Presses is a guide to small and independent magazines and presses. It contains such data as name, address, phone, editor(s), price, circulation, frequency, type of material used, payment rates, rights purchases, discount schedules, size, personal statements by editors, and number of issues/titles published in previous year and projected in coming year. It is published annually by Dustbooks.

International Literary Marketplace provides a guide to publishers and allied organizations in 160 countries of the world. The eleven thousand entries include some nine thousand publishers. It is published annually in May by R. R. Bowker Company.

Publishers and Distributors of the United States: A Directory lists editorial and fulfillment addresses and telephone numbers for over eleven thousand book publishers in Bowker's Publisher Authority Database. Includes indexes by *Books in Print* abbreviation. It is published annually in November by R. R. Bowker Company.

Publishers' International Directory lists some 130,000 active publishers in Europe, the Americas, Africa, Asia, and Oceania. Each entry gives the firm's name, address, and phone number, publishing specialties, and ISBN prefix. The ninth edition was published in 1982 by K. G. Saur Verlag and is available in the Western Hemisphere from Gale Research Company.

Who Distributes What and Where: An International Directory of Publishers, Imprints, Agents and Distributors. Lists over 4,520 publishers, agents, representatives, and distributors from Argentina to Zambia. It includes a main index alphabetically arranged by company or agent name and a geographic index alphabetically arranged by company or agent name within country. Entries include company name, sales address, country, telephone number, telex number, cable address, contact name and title, distribution address, imprints, ISBN prefix, parent company, and subsidiary company. It was published in 1981 by R. R. Bowker Company.

For Information About Authors— and Their Works

Author Biographies Master Index, a two-volume work, is a consolidated guide to biographical information concerning authors living and dead as it appears in nearly 150 biographical dictionaries devoted to authors, poets, journalists, and other literary figures. The first edition, in 1978, indexed 416,000 sketches on about 238,000 different authors. The 1980 supplement added more than 182,000 citations. It is published by Gale Research Company.

Children's Authors and Illustrators is a master index to sources of collective biography. It provides 100,000 citations to biographical sketches of over twenty thousand children's authors and illustrators in 150 biographical dictionaries and other reference sources. The third edition was published in 1981; Gale Research Company is the publisher.

Contemporary Authors is a bio-bibliographical guide to current writers in fiction, general nonfiction, poetry, journalism, drama, motion pictures, television, and other fields. Biographical sketches provide not only basic personal and career facts but also such valuable features as extensive bibliographies, work in progress, personal sidelights, and biographical/critical sources. A cumulative index appears in every other new volume; it has about six hundred pages per volume. It is revised regularly and published by Gale Research Company.

Contemporary Issues Criticism is a new series that gathers excerpts from a wide range of criticism on the works of today's key nonfiction writers. It is published by Gale Research Company.

Contemporary Literary Criticism contains excerpts from criticism of the works of today's novelists, poets, playwrights, and other creative writers. Complementing *Contemporary Authors,* this continuing work contains excerpts from contemporary criticism and evaluations of both new and established authors now living (or deceased since 1960). Each author entry contains excerpts from one to a dozen or more appraisals taken from major and minor reviewing media. Companion series available are *Twentieth-Century Literary Criticism* (covers 1900–1960), *Nineteenth-Century Literature Criticism, Literature Criticism from 1400 to 1800,* and *Shakespearean Criticism.* All are published by Gale Research Company.

The *Dictionary of Literary Biography* is an ongoing series of literary scholarship in which each volume provides biographical, critical, and bibliographical details for leading writers in a specific movement or period. It is illustrated with author portraits, manuscript facsimiles, and more. Gale Research Company is the publisher.

Something About the Author (*SATA*) presents facts and pictures about authors and illustrators of books for young people. Provides bio-bibliographical information on authors and illustrators of children's books from all eras with focus on those who are still living or deceased since 1960. For each writer covered, *SATA* furnishes an extensive bibliography that includes works the author illustrated as well as wrote. It also includes career and personal data, works in progress, and reference sources to further biographical and bibliographical information. It is published by Gale Research Company.

Reader's Adviser, A Layman's Guide to Literature, is a literary reference book that gives background information and reading lists on nearly every subject, every type of book, every period and literary form, every noted writer from antiquity to today. It was published in three volumes 1974–1977, by R. R. Bowker Company.

World Authors: 1950–1970 covers nearly one thousand authors, most of whom came to prominence between 1950 and 1970. In addition to the biographical (and often autobiographical) material on each author, evaluative comments indicate the critical consensus on his writing. Coverage of the book is worldwide with selections based in part on literary importance and in part on exceptional popularity. Photographs are included. It was published in 1975 by H. W. Wilson Company. A companion volume, *World Authors: 1970–75,* covers 348 writers, most of whom came into prominence after 1970. It also includes photographs and was published in 1979 by H. W. Wilson Company. Other titles in the Wilson Author Series are as follows:

American Authors: 1600–1900 covers almost 1,300 biographies of American authors (1938).

British Authors Before 1800 provides biographies of 650 authors from the dawn of English literature to Cowper and Burns (1952).

British Authors of the Nineteenth Century includes more than 1,000 biographies of British authors from William Blake to Aubrey Beardsley (1936).

European Authors: 1000–1900 contains biographical sketches of 967 continental European authors (1967).

Greek and Latin Authors: 800 B.C.–A.D. 1000 contains biographical sketches of 373 authors writing in Greek or Latin from the time of Homer to the Middle Ages (1979).

The Junior Book of Authors provides biographical and autobiographical sketches of 289 authors and illustrators of books for children (some with portraits) (1951). Also in this series: *More Junior Authors,* 268 biographical sketches (1963); *Third Book of Junior Authors,* 255 sketches, some with portraits (1972); *Fourth Book of Junior Authors and Illustrators,* 243 authors and illustrators (1978).

Twentieth Century Authors contains 1,850 biographical and autobiographical sketches of authors throughout the world whose works have been published in English. Includes 1,700 portraits (1942). *Twentieth Century Authors,* First Supplement, contains 700 biographical and autobiographical sketches of authors who have become prominent since 1942 (1955).

Writers for Young Adults is an index to biographical sketches of young-adult authors and popular lyricists appearing in 265 biographical dictionaries. Provides about forty-three thousand citations to biographical sketches of over ninety-six hundred different young-adult authors, those writing for grades 7–12. The first edition was published in 1979 by Gale Research Company.

Marketing Tools

American Book Trade Directory is a geographically arranged guide, by state and city, to over seventeen thousand U.S. and Canadian book outlets in some forty-four hundred cities, with a guide to the special type of stock carried. Also includes wholesalers, paperback distributors, remainder dealers, auctioneers, appraisers, and exporters. It is published annually in October by R. R. Bowker Company.

American Library Directory provides data on public, county, and regional systems; academic libraries; junior-college libraries; special libraries; libraries operated by private organizations, clubs, and institutions; government libraries; armed-forces libraries; library networks; library schools; and libraries for the handicapped. Entries are arranged alphabetically by state and city and include names of key personnel, number of volumes, book budgets, subject interest, and so on. It covers 29,600 libraries in the United States and its territories and about 2,679 in Canada and is published annually by R. R. Bowker Company.

Book Marketing Handbook: Tips and Techniques for the Sale and Promotion of Scientific, Technical, Professional, and Scholarly Books and Journals, by Nat G. Bodian, describes in detail virtually every aspect of the marketing process, from bound book to ultimate sale. Ideas, techniques, approaches, case histories, rules, models, formulas, and guidelines are offered throughout, providing the nuts and bolts that are essential to a strong, well-constructed marketing program. Volume 1 was published in 1980. Volume 2, published in 1983, contains new material in all areas covered by volume 1 and adds eleven new chapters. It is published by R. R. Bowker Company.

Directory of Directories is a reference volume covering business and industrial directories, professional and scientific rosters, and other lists and guides of all kinds. The third edition provides entries for more than seven thousand directories all thoroughly indexed under nearly twenty-one hundred detailed subject headings and cross-references ranging from Accountants, Alternate Culture, and Automobile Racing to Yoga Groups and Zoologists. Listings include titles and subtitles, full publisher addresses, description of coverage, analysis of information in a typical entry, arrangement, type of indexes, number of pages, frequency, editor's name, price, and whether data base is machine readable. The most recent edition was 1984. *Directory Information Service,* a periodical supplement, provides new directory information between editions. Both are published by Gale Research Company.

Directory of European Associations (Part 1, third edition, 1981; Part 2, second edition, 1979) and *Directory of British Associations and Associations in Ireland* provide much the same kind of information for those parts of the world as is found in *Encyclopedia of Associations.* They are published by CBD Research and are available from Gale Research Company.

Directory of Special Libraries and Information Centers, Volume 1, 1983, provides information on the holdings, services, and personnel of over sixteen thousand special libraries in the United States and Canada. This eighth edition includes data on computerized services and a list of seven hundred networks and consortia. The libraries provide in-depth information on over twenty-five hundred topics. Volume 2, *Geographic and Personnel Indexes,* was published in 1983. Volume 3, *New Special Libraries,* is a periodical supplement covering the period between editions of the base volume. They are published by Gale Research Company.

Subject Directory of Special Libraries and Information Centers includes every entry contained in the basic *Directory* but in a convenient subject arrangement in five separate, easy-to-handle volumes: Volume 1, *Business and Law Libraries;* Volume 2, *Education and Information Science Libraries;* Volume 3, *Health Sciences Libraries;* Volume 4, *Social Sciences and Humanities Libraries;* Volume 5, *Science and Technology Libraries.* The eigth edition was published in 1983 by Gale Research Company.

Encyclopedia of Associations includes detailed descriptions of over sixteen thousand active organizations in the United States: names, addresses, and telephone numbers for contact and information on publications, membership lists, special committees, and conventions. It is divided into seventeen sections such as Trade, Business and Commercial, and Scientific, Engineering, and Technical. A separate volume provides geographic and executive indexes, and there is an interedition supplement service, *New Associations and Projects.* The 19th edition came out in 1984; it is published annually by Gale Research Company.

Research Centers Directory is a guide to university-related and other nonprofit research organizations established on a permanent basis and carrying on continuing research programs. The ninth edition (1984) includes 7,500 entries that provide information on advanced study in hundreds of fields. It is published by Gale Research Company.

World Guide to Libraries provides detailed information on 42,200 national libraries, university libraries, and public libraries as well as on scientific and specialized libraries in all fields in 167 countries. It is organized by type of library within country sections. The sixth edition was published in 1983 by K. G. Saur Verlag and is available in the Western Hemisphere from Gale Research Company.

For Information About Magazines and Newspapers

Ayer Directory of Publications lists editor, publisher, circulation, advertising rates, subscription price, size, and addresses of newspapers and periodicals in the United States, Philippines, Panama, Puerto Rico, Virgin Islands, Bermuda, Bahamas, and Canada. It is published annually by Ayer Press.

Standard Periodical Directory provides access to more than 20,000 magazines, 8,000 newsletters, and 5,000 journals plus house organs, directories, government publications, and so on. It covers 244 subject categories. The eighth edition, 1983–1984, is available from Oxbridge Communications.

Ulrich's International Periodicals Directory provides information about some sixty-five hundred periodicals from all over the world. Arranged alphabetically according to 375 subject headings, the entries include frequency of issue; name and address of publisher; circulation; languages used in text; year first published; whether advertisements, reviews, bibliographies, illustrations, and so on are carried; and the assigned International Standard Serial Number with country code and Dewey Decimal Classification number (ca. 2,200 pp.). It is published annually in August (quarterly supplement available) by R. R. Bowker Company.

For Guides to Book Reviews

Book Review Index is a guide to approximately 80,000 reviews of 40,000 books that appear each year in over 400 widely read periodicals. It appears bimonthly with annual hardbound cumulative volumes and covers 1965 to the present. It is published by Gale Research Company.

For Excerpts from Book Reviews

Book Review Digest is an index to reviews of current fiction and nonfiction appearing in seventy periodicals and journals. It lists approximately six thousand books a year. Each book is entered by author (or title, if appropriate), with price, publisher, year of publication, descriptive note, citations for all reviews, ISBN when available, and excerpts from as many reviews as are necessary to reflect the balance of critical opinion. Published monthly, except February and July, with quarterly cumulations and a permanent bound annual cumulation. It is published by H. W. Wilson Company.

Notes

1. Addresses for all companies mentioned in this chapter are in the list of publishers at the end of the book.

CHAPTER TWENTY-NINE

Careers in Publishing

CHESTER LOGAN AND ANN PELLER

No single activity—except sleeping—consumes a greater portion of most people's time than work does. Choosing a job involves making a decision that influences a person's entire life-style; friends, home, financial status, even attitudes are affected by career choice. Publishing has been called "the accidental profession" because in the past it was a profession for which there was very little training or specific education available. But decisions about career choice should be no accident; they ought to involve critical self-assessment, careful research, analysis, and thought.

Facts About Publishing Opportunities

The selection of book publishing as a career will be less accidental if one has first looked at both the alternatives and at oneself. It is important to try to gain an understanding of how any business works and how one's skills, interests, and personal characteristics fit the various job functions in order to make sound career decisions. Beyond that, a love of books and a strong interest in the art and skill of communicating are prime requirements for many jobs in publishing.

Because book publishing offers a diversity of career opportunities those who are seriously considering it will be wise to learn some specifics about the business so that they can be prepared to make choices such as the following: whether to be in a small house or a larger one; whether to go into educational, trade, or professional publishing; whether to learn skills in editorial, production, marketing, business management, or distribution; and where to work and live. All these choices must be made in the context of a relatively small industry that cannot provide unlimited opportunity for all the bright and ambitious people who are attracted to it.

There are an estimated sixty-five thousand people employed in book publishing in the United States. Because publishing as we now know it

---

CHESTER LOGAN is vice president, personnel, at Harper & Row Publishers. ANN PELLER was formerly assistant director, personnel, at the same publisher.

is a relatively mature industry, many forecasters expect little or no overall growth in the decade of the 1980s. The same economic pressures that affect many other U.S. businesses will make it increasingly difficult for publishers to expand, so that in the foreseeable future, job opportunities are more likely to come from normal staff turnover and from shifts of emphasis in the industry than from the creation of new jobs.

Still, it will certainly be possible to enter the industry, and newcomers should be able to improve their odds by focusing on where the jobs are most likely to be. A recent Association of American Publishers (AAP) survey revealed that, contrary to the popular perception, most publishing jobs are not editorial; as the statistics below indicate, approximately 85 percent of the people in book publishing do something else:

Publishing Category	Percentage of Employees
Editorial	15
Production & Design	10
Marketing (including sales)	26
Fulfillment (billing, warehousing)	34
Office and Administration	15

The distribution of sales volume among the various categories of publishing provides an indication of how many jobs are likely to be found in each area. The AAP sales volume breakdown is: Mail Order/ Book Clubs, 15 percent; Educational (elementary, high school, and college), 27.5 percent; General Publishing (fiction, nonfiction, children's, religious), 21.9 percent; Professional and Reference, 17.1 percent; and Scholarly/University Press, 1.2 percent. From this we see that the two most publicized categories—educational and general publishing—each contribute about one-third of the sales volume. At the risk of oversimplifying, one could estimate that 5 percent of the jobs are in general editorial, 2 percent in professional reference production and design, and 8 percent in educational marketing, for example. Rough though these figures may be, they can be useful in realistically assessing opportunities. Clearly there will always be a need for first-rate editors who can develop the books and related materials that the market demands, but there is likely to be a need for a greater number of production, marketing, distribution, and financial professionals to see that those publications reach the markets for which they are intended.

All of these jobs call for a wide range of skills and experience. Like other modern businesses, publishing companies require people with specific business skills and experience—including law, accounting, and financial analysis. Many people with professional training in these fields are attracted to publishing, but an interesting development in recent years has been the growing number of people who have discovered their interest in these aspects of the business of book publishing on the job, and then have acquired additional training in order to assume less traditional professional management responsibilities.

Education for Publishing

Book publishing relies heavily on a kind of apprentice system for filling its professional ranks. In the key functional areas of editorial, production, and marketing, a love of books and ability to learn on the job often carry more weight than specific skills or preemployment training. In entry-level positions—as editorial assistants, advertising and promotion assistants, or sales trainees—people learn their publishing skills on the job. Although most people in editorial and marketing management have begun their careers this way, it is necessary to understand that—unlike many larger, more highly structured professions—there are no fixed career paths or guarantees of advancement in publishing. Publishing is an entrepreneurial sort of business, a business in which people with curiosity and initiative can often shape their own careers. Some encouraging examples include

- a liberal arts undergraduate who progressed from secretary to business manager and associate publisher in less than ten years
- a journalist who switched to publishing and eventually became cofounder of a new publishing house in about fifteen years
- a textbook editor who earned degrees in psychology and became a career counselor and training director in publishing in about ten years
- several college-textbook sales representatives who have become directors of university presses
- a clerk/typist who earned an M.B.A. at night and became a marketing manager

Even though publishing abounds with case histories such as these, one must also look at the other side of the coin. In all probability the industry will continue to need more assistants than chiefs, and inevitably some able and ambitious people will experience disappointment and even frustration. For those who cannot achieve their financial and career goals within their own time frame, the best solutions usually involve change—a different job function, another company, another city, perhaps even another business.

An important factor that works in favor of the entry-level employees in book publishing is that most professional and management jobs are filled by promotion within the ranks or by mobility within the industry. Added to this advantage is the fact that the size of this industry makes it easier for people with proven skills and good experience to discover job opportunities where they may put their talents to work.

Publishing provides a variety of training programs for employees seeking career advancement. These range from on-the-job training provided by supervisors to formal courses at the college or graduate level. Some supervisors are better teachers than others, and new employees are well advised to discuss learning opportunities with their supervisors at the start—to avoid disappointments. Often employees who have learned all they think they can in their first jobs can benefit from lateral transfers in which they expand their range of experience and skills, thus improving their chances for advancement. Needless to say, one should exercise good judgment in doing this; too much mobility can be counterproductive for everybody concerned.

Many publishing houses offer informal educational programs of their own. A major purpose of those programs is to help members of the staff understand what goes on in other parts of the company—for example, how books are shipped, the difference between the work of children's-book editors and college-textbook editors, and how books are designed and manufactured. There are often training programs in specific skills, such as copyediting or sales techniques. Most companies supplement their in-house training by encouraging employees to enroll in outside programs.

Many colleges and several industry groups sponsor formal courses that range from information about publishing to "hands on" training in specific skills. There are several first-rate summer institutes for people interested in entering publishing—such as those at Radcliffe, University of Denver, and New York University—and many after-hours courses— such as City University of New York and New York University—for those already at work. A number of publishers provide generous tuition assistance for employees who take such courses.

How a Publishing House Is Organized

The organization of every publishing house reflects its own history, its business and publishing priorities, its size, and the style of its management (see Figure 29.1). Some companies focus on editorial priorities, others on financial marketing goals.

There are thus many possible variations of staff organization. For example, art and design may be found in the editorial group of a college-

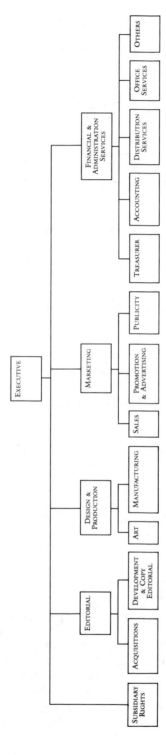

FIGURE 29.1 Publishing house organization.

textbook house or division, and sales may have a separate reporting line from other marketing functions. The smaller the organization, the more likely it is that a manager will be responsible for more than one function. This can be an advantage in that it provides more opportunities for people to use their own particular talents without being too rigidly confined to organizational structure. Some people thrive in such loose and flexible organizations; others miss the security of specific job descriptions and defined career paths that more highly structured companies provide. Those planning to enter publishing should therefore think about the kind of structure in which they might best fit.

Entry-Level Positions

Bearing in mind that jobs in publishing companies may be more or less well defined, let us look at some possible entry-level positions.

EDITORIAL

In the editorial departments of general publishing companies the most common beginning positions are those of editor's assistant and copy editorial trainee. In the position of editor's assistant, (which may be called editorial secretary, editorial assistant, or some similar title), there is usually a substantial secretarial component because most editors have a lot of correspondence, and therefore typing and other office skills are usually required. It is therefore extremely important for anyone seeking an editorial career to learn first to type well. An editor's assistant must also help the editor in coordinating the flow of the publishing process from manuscript to finished book and thus can have some interaction with production and marketing functions. An editor's assistant may progress to a higher-level assistant or associate position with relatively more editorial and fewer clerical responsibilities. Many acquisitions editors in general publishing began their careers as assistants, whereas managing editors are more frequently drawn from the copy editorial ranks.

The patterns are different in educational publishing. Because of the necessity of matching materials to curriculum, school-textbook editors often have a background in teaching or academic training in education in addition to their on-the-job experience. College-textbook sponsoring— that is, acquisitions—editors are usually recruited from the sales ranks because of the importance of market planning in developing texts. College developmental editors, who work closely with the authors on the content of basic texts, often have prior experience in copy editorial or production editorial jobs.

It is not easy to find patterns in the editorial careers of those in professional publishing. Although some technical background can be an asset, a firm grounding in language and writing seems more important. People in educational publishing can sometimes find interesting ways to transfer their knowledge of specific academic disciplines to professional publishing.

DESIGN AND PRODUCTION

As the technology of book manufacturing changes, jobs in the production and design areas offer continuing challenges to find new and better ways to get things done. Formal education in graphic arts is normally required for jobs in design, and training in printing technology is usually needed for professional and managerial jobs in production. However, the apprenticeship system works here, too; people can begin at the assistant level and expand their technical knowlege and skills on the job. Some familiarity with electronic technology is becoming increasingly important as the computer becomes a growing factor in design and production.

MARKETING

Jobs in marketing require increasingly diverse skills as the world's economy affects publishing marketplaces. Apprenticeship continues to be a major ingredient, providing entry-level opportunities that may lead to further career development in any of the marketing functions: sales, advertising, promotion, and publicity.

Each of these areas demands a high level of professionalism. Quantitative skills are required for projecting and assessing results. Creative skills are needed to develop effective approaches to the changing marketplace. So although publishers continue to employ relatively untrained people for entry-level jobs in sales and other marketing positions, advancement to managerial levels will depend increasingly on the individual's demonstrated ability to apply analytical and communications skills to marketing objectives. Since such skills are difficult to identify in advance, publishers probably will continue to build marketing staffs on the apprenticeship system, but will expect candidates for promotion to have records of measurable accomplishment.

The Job Search

Armed with as much information about the industry as can be obtained, a job seeker in book publishing needs to review some personal priorities.

The job search cannot be conducted intelligently if one compartmentalizes personal and professional concerns. A good assessment—one that will hold up over the long haul—must provide an integration of one's life goals and job choices.

For example, the environment in publishing houses can vary every bit as much as published materials do. Ambiance and style, location and personnel are important elements to consider when looking for a job. Before beginning to job hunt, one should consider one's long-range career objectives, the sort of coworkers one hopes to encounter, whether one prefers to work primarily alone or as part of a team, one's willingness to commute or one's desire to live very near the job, and whether work comes first, or whether other aspects of one's life are more important.

It is critical to assess the pace of a work environment. In publishing, as in other industries, both hares and tortoises are necessary. However, it is important to know—in advance—whether a particular job requires someone who likes to work very intensively over a relatively shorter period of time with breathers in between; or whether a more steady, methodical, and less erratic pace is likely to be the rule. One needs to be clear about one's own personal style and try to determine whether it dovetails with expectations of the work environment. Many unfortunate job situations stem from a failure to take this factor into account.

The job search is, basically, a sales campaign in which the product— in this case, the applicant—is packaged and presented to best advantage. To "close a sale," one needs to keep both personal objectives and the audience in mind. The entry-level opportunities one seeks should fit into long-range career goals, and the working environment should "feel" right. At the same time, one should try to assess the contribution one can make to the desired organization and be able to communicate those assets clearly to the individuals conducting job interviews.

To obtain an interview, one needs to prepare a résumé that presents appropriate credentials in the most attractive manner. A great deal of thought, careful research, and selective editing needs to be done. Consult your local library for some of the many good books that can help in preparing a résumé.

Whether to pursue a career in publishing is of course a personal decision. But the more one knows about one's own priorities and the publishing business the better decision one is likely to make. The industry is small and unlikely to grow substantially in the near future; on the other hand, publishing presents diverse opportunities in an usually stimulating and creative environment where people are continually challenged to think and grow. The choice, itself, is something to challenge the mind.

CHAPTER THIRTY

Courses to Assist Newcomers Entering the Book-Publishing Industry

ELIZABETH A. GEISER

Education-for-publishing programs are available at colleges and universities throughout the United States. What follows is a listing of some of the best-known courses. Note that a comprehensive listing is available in *Guide to Book Publishing Courses* (Princeton: Peterson's Guides, 1979).

Introductory Programs

DENVER PUBLISHING INSTITUTE
A four-week program combining "hands on" workshops in editing, marketing, and production with lecture/teaching sessions covering every phase of the book-publishing process. Concentrates just on books. Ten reading, research, and writing assignments must be completed prior to course. Accepts eighty-five students; most are college graduates, although occasionally those without degrees but with commensurate working experience are admitted. Admission competitive with selections made by a committee of three. Six hours of graduate credit granted by Graduate School of Librarianship and Information Management, University of Denver. Director actively works on job placement. Founded in 1976. Held annually. Contact: Elizabeth A. Geiser, Director, University of Denver Publishing Institute, 150 East 50th Street, New York, New York 10022.

The major part of this chapter has been excerpted with permission, with minor changes, from "Education for Publishing," by Elizabeth A. Geiser, which appeared in the April 1983 issue of *Scholarly Publishing;* © 1983 by *Scholarly Publishing.* Reprinted here by permission of the University of Toronto Press.

HOWARD UNIVERSITY PRESS BOOK PUBLISHING INSTITUTE

A five-week program examining four major aspects of the publishing process—editorial, design and production, marketing, and business. Concentrates just on books. One reading and one written assignment must be completed prior to attending program. Accepts thirty students with college degrees and also accepts students who have completed the junior year of study. Admission competitive with selections made by a committee of three. Provides placement service. Founded in 1980. Held annually. Contact: Janell E. Walden, Program Administrator, Howard University Press Book Publishing Institute, 2900 Van Ness Street N.W., Washington, D.C. 20008.

NEW YORK UNIVERSITY BOOK
AND MAGAZINE PUBLISHING INSTITUTE

A six-week session covering both books and magazines, involving lectures, workshops, seminars. Students prepare a prototype of a new magazine including editorial and business plans. Six assignments are sent to students prior to program. Accepts sixty students on a first-come-first-served basis. Selection by a committee of two. Provides placement service. Founded in 1978. Held annually. Contact: Director, Center of Publishing, School of Continuing Education, 2 University Place, Room 21, New York, New York 10003.

RADCLIFFE PUBLISHING PROCEDURES COURSE

A six-week program covering both books and magazines. The first half concentrates on books; the second half deals with magazines, with students divided into publishing staffs, each creating and producing a prototype of a new magazine. Fifteen reading, research, and writing assignments to be completed prior to program. Accepts eighty-five students with college degrees. Admission competitive with selections made by a committee of ten. Director actively works on job placement. Founded in 1947. Held annually. Contact: Frank Collins, Course Administrator, Radcliffe Publishing Procedures Course, 6 Ash Street, Cambridge, Massachusetts 02138.

THE RICE PUBLISHING PROGRAM

A four-week course divided between books and magazines, concentrating on trade-book publishing. For books, students are organized into mock publishing houses, with students holding different positions. For magazines, students create a prototype for a new magazine, much as in the Radcliffe program. Emphasizes regional/specialized publishing. Admits fifty to eighty students with college degrees but will also accept promising students who have completed the junior year. Admission competitive with selections made by a committee of three or four. Founded in 1978. Held irregularly. Contact: Patricia S. Martin, Director, The Rice Publishing Program, Box 1892, Houston, Texas 77251.

Continuing Education Programs

The late 1970s saw the development of a number of introductory programs for those seeking an entrée into the business; those already at work in the field who want to enhance and enrich their knowledge also have some good choices. Here are some of the best known.

CITY UNIVERSITY OF NEW YORK, GRADUATE CENTER, EDUCATION IN PUBLISHING PROGRAM

Evening sessions conducted each spring and fall with a curriculum based on the guidelines developed by the Association of American Publishers Education for Publishing Committee. Each course meets two hours once a week for ten weeks. Typical courses: computer technology in publishing; book-editing workshop; economics of publishing for the nonspecialist; marketing specialized books. A special effort is made to review applicants' credentials and place students in appropriate courses. Approximately $155–$175 per course. Founded: 1978. Contact Coordinator, Education in Publishing Program, Graduate Center, City University of New York, 33 West 42nd Street, New York, New York 10036.

COALITION OF PUBLISHERS FOR EMPLOYMENT (COPE)

This workshop teaches design and production and also covers the overall publishing process. It is designed for minority-group students within publishing who seek advancement through new skills and knowledge. Accepts thirty students who work in teams to produce four to six books a year. Funds and materials are contributed by the publishing community. Founded in 1970. Classes held at Cooper Union, New York, New York, every year from early October to mid-February. President of COPE is James Mairs, vice president, W. W. Norton & Co. Contact: Ms. Terry Hulley, Personnel Department, The Macmillan Co., 866 Third Ave., New York, New York 10022.

GEORGE WASHINGTON UNIVERSITY, PUBLICATION SPECIALIST PROGRAM

A 240-hour evening program awarding a certificate to those completing two sixteen-week semesters (fall and spring) and an eight-week summer session. Fall and spring semesters are each divided into two eight-week periods during which certificate students normally take two courses, each meeting once a week for three hours. Certificate students must take seven required courses and may choose from fifteen electives, including association publishing; computer publishing; creative editing, finance, and accounting; magazine design and production. Students can also apply for individual courses. Founded: 1974. Contact: Sharon W. Block, Director, Publication Specialist Program, George Washington University, Suite T409, 801 22nd Street N.W., Washington, D.C. 20052.

New York University,
Center for Publishing (credit courses)
Diploma Program in Magazine Publishing, designed for junior-level personnel, offers four evening courses in the fall and five evening courses in the spring. Students may apply for entire program or enroll in individual courses. Topics include magazine publishing management; advertising, sales, and promotion; magazine manufacturing management; magazine editing. Grants eighteen college credits. Contact: The Director, Center for Publishing, School of Continuing Education, New York University, 2 University Place, New York, New York 10003.

New York University,
Center for Publishing (non-credit courses)
The School for Continuing Education also offers twenty-five to thirty noncredit courses, workshops, and seminars in book and magazine publishing each fall and spring semester, covering such topics as international publishing, free-lance indexing, copyediting and proofreading, the information industry. Approximately $200 per course. Founded: 1946. Contact: Director, Center for Publishing, address above.

Stanford Publishing Course
A two-week program covering books and magazines for experienced professionals who want to learn about components in the process other than their own specialty. Designed for those edging into middle management, but has also attracted heads of houses. Students must complete six case studies before the course. Accepts about 150 students who are divided into two tracks, magazines or books, with several general sessions for all. Founded: 1978. Contact: Della van Heyst, Director of Publications, Bowman Alumni House, Stanford University, Stanford, California 94305.

UNIVERSITY OF CALIFORNIA,
CERTIFICATE PROGRAM IN PUBLISHING

A certificate program spanning the academic year. Those seeking the certificate must take three required courses and eleven units of electives. Courses include editorial workshop; printing techniques; publish-it-yourself; microcomputers for authors, editors, or publishers; introduction to typographic tools and techniques. Founded in 1978. Prices range from $90 to $150 depending upon credit granted. Contact: Ruth Majdrakoff, Director, Certificate Program in Publishing, University of California Extension, 2223 Fulton Street, Berkeley, California 94730.

For those seeking a degree with a concentration in publishing, there are two programs.

HOFSTRA UNIVERSITY

The Publishing Studies Program provides English undergraduate majors with a concentration in book publishing. Students must take thirty-nine credits in publishing and literature and three credits in history. They have opportunities to serve internships in publishing houses between their junior and senior years. Built around a two-semester core program on book editing, the course covers every aspect of the publishing process. Courses toward a certificate may be taken by those not admitted to the university. Founded in 1976. A master's program in under development. Contact: Arthur Gregor, Director of Publishing Studies, English Department, Hofstra University, Hempstead, New York 11550.

NEW YORK UNIVERSITY'S (NYU) GALLATIN DIVISION

The Oscar Dystel Fellowship in Book Publishing is a graduate program leading to a master's degree in book publishing. It combines courses selected from the many schools within NYU with a tutorial led by participating publishing executives. The program is individually tailored to the interests and needs of the student and provides opportunities for internships and independent study. Established through an endowment from Bantam Books to honor its former president and first awarded in the fall of 1982. Winner of the fellowship receives approximately $2,000–$2,500 toward the total cost of about $6,000. Contact: Joan Goulianos, Director, M.A. Degree Program, New York University, Gallatin Division, 715 Broadway, New York, New York 10003.

More Help for Students
and the People of Publishing

Employees and students of book publishing now have a new resource center—the William H. and Gwynne K. Crouse Library for Publishing Arts that has been established at the Graduate Center of the City University of New York through the generosity of the Crouses. Designed especially for those employed in the publishing industry, the library is expected to become the authoritative source of publishing materials in the field. It is the first and only comprehensive collection of materials pertaining to the book-publishing industry that is fully open to all users and available in the evening as well as during working hours. Mr. and Mrs. Crouse, in describing their dreams for the library, said that they see it as providing the opportunity to bring "some of the best and brightest people into the publishing business, to help them and to keep them in it, because they are satisfied, learning, growing." Crouse is the author of more than fifty books published by McGraw-Hill.

Books About the Book Industry

CHANDLER B. GRANNIS

This is the third edition (1984) of a list prepared in its original form in 1977 for the Education for Publishing Program of the Association of American Publishers (AAP) and distributed by the organization.

A number of the books named appeared not to be in print at the time this revision was completed. They are listed, however, because they are important and because they can be obtained in library collections, through the used-book trade, or through on-demand facsimile, primarily through University Microfilms International, Ann Arbor, Michigan. Books known to be out of print are indicated by *o.p.* in the entry.

A list of publishers, with their addresses and telephone numbers, appears at the end of this bibliography. It includes publishers cited earlier in the book as well as in this bibliography.

Book Industry: Education and Practice

Bailey, Herbert S., Jr. *The Art and Science of Book Publishing*. New York: Harper & Row, 1970; Austin: University of Texas Press, 1980 (paperback).
   The financial realities of an industry characterized by a creative mix of "irrationality and rationality"; some sections addressed to management, some to students. By the director of Princeton University Press.

Bodian, Nat G. *The Book Marketer's Handbook*. New York: Bowker, vol. 1, 1980; vol. 2, 1983.
   The promotion and selling of scientific, technical, scholarly, and professional books and journals; hundreds of instructions and tips on advertising, direct mail, trade exhibits, professional meetings, copy writing, sources of lists, reviews, ways to reach libraries and other institutions, professional workers, industries, and businesses.

Bohne, Harald, and Harry van Ierssel. *Publishing: The Creative Business*. Toronto: University of Toronto Press, 1973 (paperback).
   Specifics of the business operations of publishing management; major housekeeping functions; accounting for all operations; wise financial procedures.

Book Publishing and Distribution: Legal and Business Aspects. New York: Practising Law Institute, 1978 (available from AAP).

Produced as a course handbook on practical problems in publishing and distribution, including First Amendment matters. Contains contract forms, court decisions.

Cain, Michael Scott. *Book Marketing: A Guide to Intelligent Distribution.* Paradise, Calif.: Dustbooks, 1981.

Informal, concise, interesting views; includes twenty-page "revisionist history" of U.S. bookselling.

Carter, Robert, ed. and coauthor. *Trade Book Marketing Handbook.* New York: Bowker, 1983 (hardcover and paperback).

Sixteen chapters contributed by specialists in the varied aspects of marketing trade books: the market environment; marketing in relation to editors; hardcover books; paperbacks; selling to the trade; rights; advertising, promotion, and publicity; sales channels including wholesale, retail, library, club, direct response, special sales, and premium sales.

Dessauer, John P. *Book Publishing: What It Is, What It Does.* 2d ed. New York: Bowker, 1981 (hardcover and paperback).

Basic facts and advice about management and operation in virtually every phase in the sequence of book publishing under current conditions.

Follett, Robert J. R. *The Financial Side of Book Publishing: A Correspondence Course in Business Analysis for the Non-Accountant.* New York: Association of American Publishers, 1982 (loose-leaf).

Nineteen detailed self-study lessons in basic accounting and financial skills. Accompanied by a hardbound textbook by the same author, who is chairman of the Follett firm: *How To Keep Score in Business: Accounting and Financial Analysis for the Non-Accountant.* Chicago: Follett, 1980.

Grannis, Chandler B. *Getting into Book Publishing.* 3d ed. New York: Bowker, 1983 (pamphlet from book publicity department).

For students and others who may want to enter the industry; sketches the varieties of book publishing, basic functions, and jobs; short reading list; institutions offering courses, coast to coast.

―――――, ed. *What Happens in Book Publishing.* 2d ed. New York: Columbia University Press, 1967.

Twenty chapters by experts in the principal functions of book publishing and its major branches.

Greenfeld, Howard. *Books: From Writer to Reader.* New York: Crown Publishers, 1976.

Description of every step in general book publishing, from author to agent to bookseller and reader; informative illustrations; meant for aspiring or new employees.

Hackett, Alice Payne, and Henry James Burke. *Eighty Years of Best Sellers, 1895–1975.* New York: Bowker, 1977.

For each year, the fiction and nonfiction best-sellers are tabulated, with notes on their social and historical settings. Supplementary indexes, topical listings, statistics.

Henderson, Bill, ed. *The Publish-It-Yourself Handbook: Pushcart Press's Revised Edition.* New York: Harper & Row, 1979 (paperback).

Pieces by writers and others who have put out their own books without commercial or vanity publishers. Unconventional procedures; facets of contemporary literary history.

Huenefeld, John. *How To Make Money Publishing Books.* Bedford, Mass.: Huenefeld Co., 1978 (loose-leaf with binder).

Detailed, comprehensive guide for managing small book-publishing houses.

Naggar, Jean V., ed. *The Money Side of Publishing: Fundamentals for Non-Financial People,* report of a 1976 conference sponsored by the Association of American Publishers' General Publishing Division. New York: Association of American Publishers, 1976 (paperback).

Topics include working capital, cash flow, operating statement, controlling production costs, and negotiating a contract.

One Book, Five Ways: The Publishing Procedures of Five University Presses. Trade ed., rev. Los Altos, Calif.: William Kaufmann, 1978.

An Association of American University Presses (AAUP) project; five presses provided memos, forms, sketches, and specifications for the editing, design, production, and marketing they would have used for a certain proposed how-to book.

Publishers Weekly Yearbook. New York: Bowker, 1983 (paperback and hardcover; later issues titled *The Book Publishing Annual*).

First issue of an annual collection of statistics and specially written articles on the current scene in the book industry.

Reading: Old and New. New York: Bowker, 1983 (paperback and hardcover).

Mainly from Winter 1983 issue of *Daedalus;* about twenty articles on the backgrounds and contemporary conditions of criticism, readers, readership, and how readers are served.

Smith, Datus C., Jr. *A Guide to Book Publishing.* New York: Bowker, 1966.

Fundamentals expressed in simple, step-by-step style, with special note of the needs of the book trade in developing countries.

Smith, Roger H., ed. *The American Reading Public: What It Reads, Why It Reads.* New York: Bowker, 1961 (o.p.).

Mainly from Winter 1961 issue of *Daedalus.* Twenty authorities examine schools, commercial publishers, university publishing, the reader and the book, mass media, and book reviewing.

Tebbel, John. *Opportunities in Publishing Careers.* Skokie, Ill.: National Textbook Co., 1975 (paperback).

A concise, brightly written outline of the nature of book publishing, its main branches, jobs available, and how to get started.

To Be a Publisher: A Handbook on Some Principles and Programs of Book Publishing Education. New York: Association of American Publishers, 1979.

Information prepared by AAP Education Committee on organizing and conducting education and training; course outlines for basic and advanced study; thirty job descriptions.

Book Industry: Analysis and Statistics

Altbach, Philip G., and Sheila McVey, eds. *Perspectives on Publishing.* American Academy of Political and Social Science, *Annals,* Sept. 1978; Lexington, Mass.: Lexington Books, 1976 (hardcover).

A full issue of *Annals* presenting important articles on publishing today; changing trends in the book industry in the United States and abroad.

Arthur Anderson & Co. *Book Distribution in the United States: Issues and Perspectives.* New York: Book Industry Study Group, 1982 (distributed by Bowker).

Trends, areas of possible improvement, the book-ordering process, physical movement of books, inventory control, and returns.

Association of American Publishers (AAP) *Industry Statistics.* New York: AAP, annual.

Figures compiled by Touche Ross & Co. showing overall sales of books and instructional materials, marketing and operating costs, and profit ratios and other data for trade and religious publishing, professional books (technical, scientific, business, medical, other), mass-market paperbacks, book clubs, mail order, school, and college. For AAP members.

Benjamin, Curtis G. *A Candid Critique of Book Publishing.* New York: Bowker, 1977.

A former president of McGraw-Hill Book Co. digs into numerous issues important to the book industry; challenging, controversial.

The Bowker Annual of Library and Book Trade Information. New York: Bowker, annual.

Over seven hundred pages of reports: the year's events in the book and library worlds, legislation, funding, essays on trends and services, library education and employment, book-trade and library statistics and research, directories of library and related organizations.

Bowker Lectures on Book Publishing. New York: Bowker, 1957 (o.p.).

The first seventeen of the Richard Rogers Bowker Memorial Lectures, each by an authority reviewing a specific area of the book industry. (Later lectures are available as pamphlets from Bowker for $2.50 postpaid; see also Knopf entry under Backgrounds.)

R. R. Bowker Memorial Lectures. 2d series. New York: Bowker, mostly annual (pamphlets).

Available from Bowker's New York office. Titles: (1) Harriet F. Pilpel, *Obscenity and the Constitution;* (2) Barbara A. Ringer, *The Demonology of Copyright;* (3) Frances E. Henne, *The Library World and the Publishing of Children's Books;* (4) Samuel S. Vaughan, *Medium Rare, A Look at the Book and Its People;* (5) Herbert S. Bailey, Jr., *The Traditional Book in the Electronic Age;* (6) Peter Mayer, *The Spirit of the Enterprise;* (7) Richard DeGennaro, *Research Libraries Enter the Information Age;* (8) Oscar Dystel, *Mass Market Publishing, More Observations, Speculations and Provocations;* (9) Robert Giroux, *The Education of an Editor;* (10) Lowell A. Martin, *The Public Library: Middle Age Crisis or Old Age?*

Cole, John Y., ed. *Responsibilities of the American Book Community.* Washington, D.C.: Library of Congress, Center for the Book, 1981 (paperback).

Papers from two Library of Congress seminars; a PEN N.Y. symposium; and a Senate hearing on concentration in publishing and bookselling. Also statements by industry leaders, authors.

Compaigne, Benjamin. *The Book Industry in Transition: An Economic Study of Book Distribution and Marketing.* White Plains, N.Y.: Knowledge Industry Publications, 1978.

An important compendium of facts and figures.

Coser, Lewis A., Charles Kadushin, and Walter W. Powell. *Books: The Culture and Commerce of Publishing.* New York: Basic Books, 1982.

Provocative analysis and opinions about hard realities in three divisions of the American book industry: adult trade, college text, and scholarly. Authors are noted sociologists.

Dessauer, John P., ed. *Book Industry Trends.* New York: Book Industry Study Group, annual (distributed by Bowker).

Massive economic analysis; indispensable for both management and researchers in book publishing. Narrative studies plus extensive tables of current and projected figures on dollar and unit sales by types of publishers and markets.

Ehrlich, Arnold, ed. *The Business of Publishing: A PW Anthology.* New York: Bowker, 1976.

Forty-five articles, 1972–1976, from the book industry journal, *Publishers Weekly,* on issues and operations.

Jovanovich, William. *Now Barabbas.* New York: Harper & Row, 1964 (paperback).

Incisive, thoughtful essays on the publisher and editor and their relation to writers, readers, sellers, reviewers, government, and the public interest; by the head of Harcourt Brace Jovanovich.

Kazin, Alfred, Dan M. Lacy, and Ernest L. Boyer. *The State of the Book World.* Washington, D.C.: Library of Congress, Center for the Book, 1980 (paperback).

Papers presented at a Library of Congress symposium ("The Book Revue," "Publishing Enters the Eighties," "The Book and Education.")

Kujoth, Jean Spencer, comp. *Book Publishing: Inside Views.* Metuchen, N.J.: Scarecrow Press, 1971.

Trends and issues in publishing, 1962–1970, in fifty articles by experts and observers of the book industry.

U.S. Book Publishing Year Book and Directory. White Plains, N.Y.: Knowledge Industry Publications, annual (paperback).

Business chronology; assorted statistics; publishing costs; salary trends; finances of publicly reported firms; leading publishers and associations.

International Book Trade

Altbach, Philip G., and Eva-Marie Rathgeber. *Publishing in the Third World: Trend Report and Bibliography.* New York: Praeger, 1980.

Succinct but incisive analyses of publishing in Asia, Africa, and Latin America in different settings and stages of development.

Benjamin, Curtis G. *U.S. Books Abroad: Neglected Ambassadors.* Washington, D.C.: Library of Congress, Center for the Book, 1982 (paperback).

Important, fact-filled study of U.S. book export trends, assistance programs, and proposed action for expansion.

International Literary Market Place. New York: Bowker, annual (paperback).

The 1983–1984 edition is described as an authoritative, comprehensive, and current source on all aspects of international trade in books; publishers, retailers, libraries, trade organizations, library and literary groups, periodicals, and book import, export, and rights regulations; key contacts.

Lottman, Herbert R. *Book Publishing World Wide.* New York: *Publishers Weekly,* 1979 (paperback, distributed by circulation department).

Compilation of lengthy reports in *Publishers Weekly* on the book trades of Scandinavia, Germany, Portugal, Spain, Australia, Soviet Union, and Japan, by the Paris-based international correspondent of *Publishers Weekly*. See also his continuing reports in the magazine on Great Britain, France, Netherlands, and other important markets.

Smith, Datus C. *The Economics of Publishing in Developing Countries.* Paris: United Nations Educational, Scientific, and Cultural Organization, 1977 (paperback, distributed by Unipub, New York).

Clearly stated analysis of Third World publishing, its problems and prospects, by the longtime head of the technical-assistance agency Franklin Book Programs.

Editors, Agents, and Authors

Appelbaum, Judith, and Nancy Evans. *How to Get Happily Published.* New York: Harper & Row, 1978; New York: New American Library, 1982 (paperback).

Cheerfully written, practical guidance on writing, how publishers make decisions, and how authors and publishers can work successfully together.

Balkin, Richard. *A Writer's Guide to Book Publishing.* New York: Hawthorn, 1978; rev. ed., New York: Dutton, 1980.

Systematically describes standard operations, contracts, negotiations, and the handling of manuscripts.

Belkin, Gary, *Getting Published: A Guide for Businesspeople and Other Professionals.* New York: Wiley, 1983 (paperback and cloth).

A different, important approach to publisher-author relations and getting into print.

Berg, A. Scott. *Maxwell Perkins, Editor of Genius.* New York: Dutton, 1978; New York: Pocket Books, 1979 (paperback).

Sympathetic biography of the great Scribner editor. For other views, see letters and biographies of Thomas Wolfe and others.

Burack, A. S., ed. *The Writers Handbook.* Boston: The Writer, 1979.

Collection of articles by authorities about writing, writers, and their relations with publishers and audiences.

Commins, Dorothy, ed. *What Is an Editor? Saxe Commins at Work.* Chicago: University of Chicago Press, 1978 (hardcover and paperback).

The late, deeply gifted Random House editor's letters and notes; memories of him; how he worked with O'Neill, Faulkner, Irwin Shaw, many others.

Gross, Gerald, ed. *Editors on Editing.* New York: Grosset & Dunlap, 1962 (paperback).

The editor in action, shown in twenty-five articles, speeches, and sets of letters portraying the thinking and functions of editors in many branches of book publishing.

Henderson, Bill. *The Art of Literary Publishing: Editors on Their Craft.* Wainscott, N.Y.: Pushcart Press, 1980.

Contemporary outlook and problems. Two dozen articles from varied sources by outstanding editors and acclaimed authors.

Hill, Mary, and Wendell Cochran. *Into Print: A Practical Guide to Writing, Illustrating and Publishing.* Los Altos, Calif.: William Kaufmann, 1977 (paperback).

The creation of a successful publishing project; gives detailed attention to illustrations, graphs, tables, and publisher-author-artist relations.

Madison, Charles A. *Irving to Irving: Author-Publisher Relations, 1800–1974.* New York: Bowker, 1974.

Specific cases show, often amusingly, how contracts, copyright agreements, and other business arrangements among authors and publishers have evolved.

Reynolds, Paul R. *The Writing and Selling of Fiction.* Rev. ed. New York: Morrow, 1979.

Addressed to authors, but equally valuable for publishers. Covers author-publisher business matters.

Design and Production

Chappell, Warren. *A Short History of the Printed Word.* New York: Alfred A. Knopf, 1970; Boston: Godine, Nonpareil Books, 1980 (paperback).

A handsomely illustrated account of top events and personalities in printing history, by a distinguished designer and artist.

Craig, James. *Designing with Type: A Basic Course in Typography.* Rev. ed. New York: Watson Guptill, 1980.

Updated version of a widely used and very comprehensive textbook, reflecting the many developments of recent years.

_____ . *Photo Typesetting: A Design Manual.* New York: Watson-Guptill, 1978.

Comprehensive, heavily illustrated; companion to *Designing with Type;* what the designer has to know.

_____ . *Production for the Graphic Designer.* New York: Watson-Guptill, 1974.

Details the designer needs to know about each stage in the production of printed matter: typesetting, mechanicals, imposition, paper, ink, printing, folding, binding. Glossary of more than one thousand entries.

Grannis, Chandler B., ed. *Heritage of the Graphic Arts.* New York: Bowker, 1972.

Illustrated lectures by or about twenty-three masters of modern typography and book design. From a series arranged by Robert L. Leslie.

Klemin, Diana. *The Illustrated Book: Its Art and Craft.* New York: Clarkson N. Potter, 1970 (distributed by Murton, 1983).

A survey of the work and methods of seventy-four book artists, with examples and commentary, by a distinguished art director and designer.

Lee, Marshall. *Bookmaking: The Illustrated Guide to Design/Production/ Editing.* 2d ed. New York: Bowker, 1979.

Heavily revised, greatly expanded edition of the standard, comprehensive manual on the making of books; new technology and equipment treated fully; major new section on editing; job guidance; index-glossary.

Meynell, Sir Francis, and Herbert Simon, eds. Fleuron *Anthology.* Boston: Godine, 1980 (paperback).

Twenty-three articles (with their illustrations) chosen from the famous 1923–1930 journal devoted to the history of printing and the brilliant modern typographic revival in typography.

Rice, Stanley. *Book Design: Systematic Aspects* and *Book Design: Text Format Models.* New York: Bowker, 1978.

Systematic Aspects is a heavily illustrated manual on essential, permanent elements of book design. *Text Format Models* provides visual alternative specifications (mechanics and style) for all aspects of front and back matter, text, legends, and so on.

Updike, Daniel Berkeley. *Printing Types: Their History, Forms and Use.* 2 vols. New York: Dover, 1980 (paperback).

The classic, definitive work on letterforms in printing; 1,072 pages and more than 300 illustrations of types over a 500-year span. First issued by Harvard University Press, 1922.

White, Jan V. *Editing by Design: A Guide to Effective Word and Picture Communication for Editors and Designers.* 2d ed. New York: Bowker, 1980.

Stresses integration of text and images in solving design problems in periodicals and, more and more, in books.

Children's Books

Bader, Barbara. *American Picture Books From* Noah's Ark *to* The Beast Within. New York: Macmillan, 1976.

Spirited, definitive eighty-year history of children's illustrated books and their artists, authors, and publishers; changing styles, standards, and approaches. Lavishly illustrated, largely in color.

Colby, Jean Poindexter. *Writing, Illustrating and Editing Children's Books.* New York: Hastings House, 1967; 1974 (paperback).

Describes all aspects of children's-book publishing; covers editor-author-artist relations; deals with diversity of the field.

Klemin, Diana. *The Art of Art for Children's Books.* New York: Clarkson N. Potter, 1966 (distributed by Murton, 1982).

Pages from more than sixty contemporary books with comments on how the artists complemented the texts.

Lanes, Selma G. *Down the Rabbit Hole.* 2d ed. New York: Atheneum, 1976 (paperback).

Subtitled *Adventures and Misadventures in the Realm of Children's Literature,* this volume is one of the most informative and stimulating books assessing contemporary children's literature.

Sutherland, Zena, and May Hill Arbuthnot. *Children and Books.* 5th ed. Glenview, Ill.: Scott, Foresman & Co., 1977.

Heavily illustrated, extremely comprehensive work on children's needs and interests in reading; analyses of books and authors.

Turow, Joseph G. *Getting Books to Children: An Exploration of Publisher-Market Relations.* Chicago: American Library Assn., 1979 (paperback).

Factors that determine editorial selection and distribution patterns in publishing children's books for two major markets—library ("literary") and mass. Good information, not fully obscured by its turgid socioeconomic jargon.

Mass-Market Paperbacks

Davis, Kenneth. *Two-Bit Culture: The Paperbacking of America.* Boston: Houghton Mifflin, 1984 (paperback).

An examination of the mass-market "paperback revolution," its backgrounds, development, and consequences—literary and cultural.

Petersen, Clarence. *The Bantam Story: Thirty Years of Paperback Publishing.* 2d ed. New York: Bantam Books, 1975 (paperback).

A sparkling account of the largest firm in the field, its history and current practice. Also includes overall U.S. paperback-publishing development.

Smith, Roger H. *Paperback Parnassus.* Boulder, Colo.: Westview Press, 1976.

A broad, detailed survey of the mass-market paperback industry, its current condition and structure, and its relations with the rest of the book industry and with authors.

Scholarly Books

Harman, Eleanor, and Ian Montagnes, eds. *The Thesis and the Book.* Toronto: University of Toronto Press, 1976 (paperback).

Some practical aspects of scholarly publishing and its responsibilities and procedures.

Hawes, Gene R. *To Advance Knowledge: A Handbook on American University Press Publishing.* New York: American University Press Services for AAUP, 1967 (paperback).

A full guide for workers in or entering scholarly publishing; examines objectives, history, problems, audiences, economics, and authors.

Horne, David. *Boards and Buckram.* Hanover, N.H.: University Press of New England, 1980 (distributed by American University Press Services, New York).

Humorous essays that deal seriously with practical aspects of scholarly press operations and relations with authors and the scholarly market.

Nemeyer, Carol A. *Scholarly Reprint Publishing in the United States.* New York: Bowker, 1972.

Development, structure, audiences, economics, and other aspects of a special field, highly important in the library market.

Scholarly Communication: The Report of the National Enquiry. Baltimore: Johns Hopkins University Press, 1979 (paperback).

Report of a lengthy examination of how the results of ever-proliferating research are disseminated, the growing problems and shortcomings in the process, and recommendations for remedy.

Textbook Publishing

Cole, John Y., ed. *Television, the Book and the Classroom.* Washington, D.C.: Library of Congress, Center for the Book, 1978 (paperback).

Symposium: papers by Mortimer J. Adler, Frank Stanton, and others, with discussion.

Cole, John Y., and Thomas G. Sticht. *The Textbook in American Society.* Washington, D.C.: Library of Congress, Center for the Book, 1981 (paperback).

A two-day symposium; papers by eighteen writers, educators, critics, and publishers on textbooks in relation to literacy, school curricula, and publishing.

Fitzgerald, Frances. *America Revised: History Schoolbooks in the Twentieth Century.* Boston: Little, Brown, 1979; New York: Random Vintage, 1980 (paperback).

Challenging analysis of the writing, editing, and publishing policies and forces involved in textbooks; contends many books sidestep the "why and how" of events, so blandness dominates.

Translation

Congrat-Butler, Stefan, comp. *Translation and Translators.* New York: Bowker, 1979.

Growth and recent developments; organizations, centers; awards, fellowships, subsidies; training; codes of conduct; contracts; copyright; journals, register of translators; marketplace directory.

The World of Translation. New York: PEN American Center, 1971.

Compilation of thirty-nine conference papers on world problems of translation of literary manuscripts and on author-translator-publisher relations.

Copyright

Johnston, Donald. *Copyright Handbook.* 2d ed. New York: Bowker, 1982.

Full account of the 1976 copyright law, with texts and with explanations especially for the book industry; newest interpretations and procedures.

Photocopying by Academic, Public, and Nonprofit Research Libraries. New York: Association of American Publishers, 1978 (paperback).

Jointly prepared by AAP and the Authors League; describes policies about photocopying, fair use, and so on, and gives answers to questions frequently asked by librarians and others.

Freedom to Publish and Read

Berninghausen, David K. *The Flight from Reason: Essays on Intellectual Freedom in the Academy, the Press and the Library.* Chicago: American Library Association, 1975 (paperback).

By a long-active leader in the field of library concerns for intellectual freedom.

DeGrazia, Edward, author and comp. *Censorship Landmarks.* New York: Bowker, 1969.

Compilation of dozens of important court decisions and dissenting opinions marking the development of censorship adjudication and changes, with a brilliant introductory essay by the author—attorney in several key defenses—tracing evolving legal ideas. (DeGrazia is also coauthor of the definitive *Banned Films,* Bowker, 1982.)

Haight, Anne Lyon. *Banned Books.* 4th ed., rev. and enlarged by Chandler B. Grannis. New York: Bowker, 1978.

Chronology of censorship of books on political, religious, and moral grounds, from 387 B.C. to A.D. 1978; U.S. legal changes, 1957–1978, analyzed by attorney Charles Rembar; types of censorship; excerpts from report of U.S. commission on obscenity.

Jenkinson, Edward B. *Censors in the Classroom.* Carbondale, Ill.: Southern Illinois University Press, 1979.

Reviews the impact on schools and libraries of the rising tide of censorship; the groups and psychology behind it; legal rulings; the need to defend free inquiry and an open society.

Lewis, Felice Flannery. *Literature, Obscenity and the Law.* Carbondale, Ill.: Southern Illinois University Press, 1976; 1978 (paperback).

Clearly stated, well-organized, and comprehensive account and analysis of all aspects of the problem.

Oboler, Eli M., ed. *Censorship and Education.* Vol. 23, no. 6 of The Reference Shelf. New York: H. W. Wilson Co., 1981.

Selection of twenty-three recent articles offering interesting expression of differing positions in the climate of censorship, the censors themselves, censorship in schools and libraries, major court decisions.

Perrin, Noel. *Dr. Bowdler's Legacy: A History of Expurgated Books in England and America.* Hanover, N.H.: University Press of New England, 1969.

Entertaining account of books that were not banned, simply expurgated or bowdlerized, as one Dr. Bowdler did to Shakespeare's presumably bawdy passages.

Rembar, Charles. *The End of Obscenity.* New York: Random House, 1968.

The trials of *Lady Chatterley, Tropic of Cancer,* and *Fanny Hill* described by the lawyer who defended them.

Libraries

The Future of Books in Libraries. New York: Association of American Publishers, 1979.

Summary of a conference of the AAP General Publishing Division's Libraries Committee; papers and comments by six authorities.

Mathews, Virginia. *Libraries for Today and Tomorrow.* New York: Doubleday, 1976 (paperback); New York: Octagon, n.d. (reprint).

American library services, their nature, how they came about, how they are funded, the problems they face. Strong political views, but useful.

Backgrounds

U.S. AND GENERAL

Anderson, Charles, B., ed. *Bookselling in America and the World.* New York: Times Books, 1975.

History of U.S. and world bookselling and of the American Booksellers Association (ABA), by several authorities, with many literary excerpts on the subject; prepared for ABA's seventy-fifth anniversary.

Bliven, Bruce. *Book Traveler.* New York: Dodd, Mead, 1975.

Account of the working life of a well-known book sales representative who calls on booksellers on behalf of several publishers. A *New Yorker* "Profile."

Burlingame, Roger. *Endless Frontiers: The Story of McGraw-Hill.* New York: McGraw-Hill, 1959.

Foundations of today's enormous business, technical, educational, and international publishing firm; some major names absent.

_____ . *Of Making Many Books: A Hundred Years of Writing and Publishing.* New York: Scribner's, 1948.

The greatest years of the famous Scribner company; emphasis on its role in twentieth-century U.S. literature.

Canfield, Cass. *Up & Down & Around: A Publisher Recollects the Time of His Life.* New York: Harper's Magazine Press, 1971.

A publisher for major literary artists, statesmen, and other public figures since the mid-1920s recounts his dealings with them in succinct essays.

Cerf, Bennett. *At Random: The Reminiscences of Bennett Cerf.* New York: Random House, 1977.

Oral and written recollections, edited by the late publisher's widow and associates, reflecting an exuberant career that deeply influenced U.S. book publishing.

Comparato, Frank E. *Books for the Millions.* Harrisburg, Pa.: Stackpole Books, 1971.

History of book manufacturing; decisive inventions, especially for binding.

Daigh, Ralph. *Maybe You Should Write a Book*. Englewood Cliffs, N.J.: Prentice-Hall, 1977; 1979 (paperback).

Breezy, unabashedly commercial advice to authors, based on Daigh's own colorful career in mass-market publishing.

Doran, George. *Chronicles of Barabbas 1884–1934*. 2d ed. New York: Holt, Rinehart & Winston, 1952.

A great publisher tells of the pains, fun, and achievements of his profession, with many anecdotes of a brilliant period.

Doubleday, F. N. *The Memoirs of a Publisher*. New York: Doubleday, 1972.

Frank Nelson Doubleday recounted here, in 1926, his early years with Scribner's, the founding and growth of Doubleday, work with famous persons, problems of the industry; with essay by Christopher Morley.

Exman, Eugene. *The House of Harper*. New York: Harper & Row, 1967.

Entertaining, authoritative account of a major firm's 150 years, its ups and downs, mistakes and successes.

Ford, Hugh D. *Published in Paris*. New York: Macmillan, 1975; Wainscott, N.Y.: Pushcart Press, 1980 (paperback).

Important literary and publishing history, subtitled *American and British Writers, Printers, and Publishers in Paris, 1920–1939,* describing a bold, imaginative, creatively influential group of people.

Gilmer, Walker. *Horace Liveright: Publisher of the Twenties*. New York: David Lewis, 1970 (o.p.).

The meteoric career of a flamboyant publisher who presented many outstanding new writers to a large public and whose firm was the training ground for several later leaders of the industry.

Gross, Gerald, ed. *Publishers on Publishing*. New York: Grosset & Dunlap, 1961.

The background of today's publishing told in thirty-six articles and excerpts by British and U.S. publishers, mostly modern; arranged according to the functions of publishing.

Hale, Robert, Allan Marshall, and Jerry M. Showalter, eds. *A Manual on Bookselling*. 4th ed. New York: Harmony Books–Crown for American Booksellers Association, forthcoming (paperback).

Again a major revision; experts cover every aspect of modern bookselling for systematic instruction and for reference by all persons in the book industry.

Hart, James D. *The Popular Book: A History of America's Literary Taste*. Berkeley: University of California Press, 1961 (paperback).

Reprint, from 1950 edition, of a literary historian's broad-scale review of popular authors and their books; a cultural more than a publishing-business history.

Haydn, Hiram. *Words and Faces.* New York: Harcourt Brace Jovanovich, 1974.

The sometimes bitter, angry memoirs of a top editor who worked in widely different situations at Bobbs-Merrill, Harcourt, and Atheneum.

Knopf, Alfred A. *Publishing Then & Now: 1912–1964.* New York: New York Public Library, 1964 (pamphlet).

Reminiscences, contrasts, and notes on a famous career in publishing. (One of the Bowker Memorial Lectures; see entry under Book Industry: Analysis and Statistics.)

Lehmann-Haupt, Hellmut, Lawrence C. Wroth, and Rollo G. Silver. *The Book in America.* Rev. ed. New York: Bowker, 1951.

The definitive single-volume history on the making and selling of books in the United States, 1630–1950.

Lippert, Jack E. *Scholastic: A Publishing Adventure.* New York: Scholastic Book Services, 1978.

An unusual education publisher and its founding genius (Maurice Robinson); development from periodicals to a range of books and innovative materials.

Moore, John Hammond. *Wiley: 175 Years of Publishing.* New York: Wiley, 1982.

Well-illustrated account of the firm's books and authors in science, industry, and education; international role.

Mott, Frank Luther. *Golden Multitudes.* New York: Bowker, 1960; orig. Macmillan, 1947.

Comprehensive publishing and literary history of best-sellers, 1662–1945; anecdotes, economics, various lists.

Regnery, Henry. *Memoirs of a Dissident Publisher.* New York: Harcourt Brace Jovanovich, 1979.

Though a general publisher, Regnery gave special attention to books by strongly conservative authors.

Steinberg, S. H. *Five Hundred Years of Printing.* Rev. ed. New York: Penguin, 1974 (paperback).

The leading, handy, one-volume work on the subject, especially on the printing of books, including twentieth-century production.

Stern, Madeleine B. *Books and Book People in 19th Century America.* New York: Bowker, 1978.

Studies of representative episodes in publishing history; includes anniversary history of *Publishers Weekly,* 1872–1947.

————. *Imprints on History: Book Publishers and American Frontiers.* New York: AMS Press, 1976 (reprint of 1956 ed.).

The pioneering activity of seventeen publishers on various U.S. frontiers, including some that became important in the twentieth century.

Targ, William. *Indecent Pleasures.* New York: Macmillan, 1975.

Short, outspoken, often witty observations, recollections of famous writers, and advice about publishing by a top editor and publisher.

Tebbel, John. *A History of Book Publishing in the United States.* Vol. 1, *The Creation of an Industry, 1630–1865;* Vol. 2, *The Expansion of an Industry, 1865–1919;* Vol. 3, *The Golden Age Between Two Wars, 1920–1940;* Vol. 4, *The Great Change, 1940–1980.* New York: Bowker, 1971–1981.

The most extensive history of American publishing; thorough, but entertainingly written.

Thompson, Susan Otis. *American Book Design and William Morris.* New York: Bowker, 1977.

Discloses vital aspects in the publishing, design, and typographic history of the first third of this century.

Unwin, Sir Stanley. *The Truth About Publishing.* 7th ed. New York: Bowker, 1960.

An outspoken, widely respected English publisher produced this classic textbook of sound publishing practice.

BRITISH

Hodge, Sheila. *Gollancz: The Story of a Publishing House 1928–1978.* London: Victor Gollancz, 1978.

The nonconforming, innovative, vigorous patron of left and avant-garde writers; covers U.S. connections.

Howard, Richard L. *Jonathan Cape, Publisher* London: Cape, 1971.

Account of a leading London general publisher; includes relations with United States.

Morpurgo, J. E. *Allen Lane, King Penguin: A Biography.* London: Hutchinson & Co., 1979.

Lively account, by a book-industry scholar and former Lane associate, of a primary creator of the modern English-language paperback industry.

Sutliffe, Peter. *The Oxford University Press: An Informal History.* Oxford and New York: Oxford University Press, 1978.

Five hundred years of publishing; changes in British and world book trade; includes Oxford U.S. branch.

Reference: Editorial

Bernstein, Theodore M. *Miss Thistlebottom's Hobgoblins.* New York: Farrar, Straus and Giroux, 1971.

A guide for writers aimed at exposing inhibitions on language that turn out to be based on personal prejudice or misguided pedantry.

The Chicago Manual of Style. 13th ed. Chicago: University of Chicago Press, 1982.

Much-heralded revision and enlargement of this major authority in book industry and scholarly usage. New material on manuscript markup for current technology, indexing, composition, printing, binding, copyright, and so on.

Glaister, Geoffrey. *Glaister's Glossary of the Book.* Berkeley: University of California Press, 1979.

Much more than a glossary; earlier U.S. edition was better titled: *Encyclopedia of the Book.* Fully defines topics, processes, and terms of bookmaking and publishing; also historical and biographical entries.

Jordan, Lewis. *The* New York Times *Manual of Style & Usage.* New York: Times Books, 1982 (paperback).

A leading reference that sets high standards for journalistic style; updated.

Skillin, Marjorie E., and Robert M. Gay. *Words into Type.* 3d ed. New York: Prentice-Hall, 1974.

One of the references most favored by book editors.

Strunk, William, Jr., and E. B. White. *Elements of Style.* 3d ed. New York: Macmillan, 1978 (paperback).

This short manual is recognized as the outstanding guide to clear, straightforward expression.

United States Government Printing Office Style Manual. Rev. ed. Washington, D.C.: U.S. Government Printing Office, 1984.

Major and thorough reference, especially valuable in handling information about government.

Reference: Book Trade Tools

The American Bookseller. New York: American Booksellers Association, monthly.

Journal of the principal organization of book retailers; statistics, bookstore operations, industry problems, meetings, exhibits.

American Book Trade Directory. New York: Bowker, annual.

The twenty-eighth edition in 1982 gave geographic listings of over 17,000 retailers and 1,000 wholesale book outlets in the United States and Canada. Entries include stock carried, size, and specialities. Other lists name paperback and remainder distributors, auctioneers, appraisers, former publishers and imprints, and so forth.

Book Buyer's Handbook. New York: American Booksellers Association, annual.

Distributed only to ABA bookseller members; complete loose-leaf directory of all publishers' terms and arrangements.

The Bookseller. London: Whitaker, weekly.

A magazine for the book industry of England with trade news, trends, notes on people, and so on.

Books in Print. New York: Bowker, annual.

Three volumes each of author and title indexes of all books from 13,500 U.S. publishers; over 590,000 titles. Companion publications include *Subject Guide to Books in Print, Paperbound Books in Print, El-Hi, Religious, Sci-Tech, Business & Economics, Medical, Children's, Large-Type,* and bimonthly *Forthcoming Books.*

The Christian Bookseller. Wheaton, Ill.: Christian Life Missions, monthly.

Journal of a major segment of the conservative, evangelical, fundamentalist Christian book trade. Store operations, industry data, meetings, reviews, lists, notes on sales promotion.

The Horn Book. Boston: Horn Book, bimonthly.

The definitive journal of children's-book editing, illustrating, writing, and publishing.

Hubbard, Linda, ed. *Book Publishers Directory.* Detroit: Gale, annual.

Detailed listings of 9,000 private, special-interest, alternative, organization, association, government, and institutional publishers.

Literary Market Place with Names and Numbers. New York: Bowker, annual (paperback).

Extensive directory of publishers and their personnel; also dozens of other categories—associations, agencies, trade services, manufacturers, review media, and so on; "yellow pages" list of most names, with addresses and telephone numbers.

Peters, Jean, ed. *The Bookman's Glossary.* 6th ed. New York: Bowker, 1983.

Even more significantly enlarged than the fifth edition in 1975, which was a complete revision of earlier ones. Covers nearly sixteen hundred terms used in publishing, bookselling, composition, printing, the rare- and fine-book trade, and contemporary technology of copy preparation and book production.

Publishers Weekly. New York: Bowker, weekly.

The comprehensive magazine of the book industry; trade news, trends, personnel notes, and advance reviews of about five thousand trade books per year.

Scholarly Publishing. Toronto: University of Toronto Press, quarterly.

This "journal of authors and publishers" covers the broad range of North American editing and publishing while focusing on university and other learned presses.

List of Publishers

AB Bookman's Weekly
Box AB
Clifton, NJ 07015
(201) 772-0020

AMS Press, Inc.
56 East 13th St.
NYC, NY 10003
(212) 777-4700

American Academy of Political
& Social Science
3937 Chestnut St.
Philadelphia, PA 19104
(215) 386-4594

American Booksellers
Association
122 East 42nd St.
NYC, NY 10017
(212) 867-9060

American Library Association
50 East Huron St.
Chicago, IL 60611
(312) 944-6780

American University Press
Services, Inc.
One Park Ave.
NYC, NY 10016
(212) 889-6040

Association of American
Publishers
One Park Ave.
NYC, NY 10016
(212) 689-8920

Atheneum Publishers
597 Fifth Ave.
NYC, NY 10019
(212) 486-2700

Ayer Press
1 Bala Ave.
Bala Cynwyd, PA 19004
(215) 664-6203

Bacon's Publishing Co.
14 East Jackson St.
Chicago, IL 60604
(312) 922-8419

Bantam Books, Inc.
666 Fifth Ave.
NYC, NY 10019
(212) 765-6500

Basic Books Inc., Publishers
10 East 53rd St.
NYC, NY 10022
(212) 207-7057

Bobbs-Merrill Co.
4300 West 62nd St.
Indianapolis, IN 46206
(317) 298-5400

Book Industry Study Group,
Inc.
160 Fifth Ave.
NYC, NY 10010
(212) 929-1393

R. R. Bowker Co.
205 East 42nd St.
NYC, NY 10017
(212) 916-1600

Jonathan Cape Ltd.
30 Bedford Square
London WC1B 3EL
ENGLAND
(01) 636-5764

Center for the Book
The Library of Congress
Washington, D.C. 20540
(202) 287-5108

Christian Bookseller
Christian Life Missions
396 East St. Charles Rd.
Wheaton, IL 60187
(312) 653-4200

Clarion Books
52 Vanderbilt Ave.
NYC, NY 10017
(212) 972-1190

Columbia University Press
562 West 113th St.
NYC, NY 10025
(212) 678-6777

Crain Books
740 Rush St.
Chicago, IL 60611
(312) 649-5250

Crown Publishers, Inc.
One Park Ave.
NYC, NY 10016
(212) 532-9200

Davis Publications, Inc.
380 Lexington Ave.
NYC, NY 10017
(212) 557-9100

Dodd, Mead & Co.
79 Madison Ave.
NYC, NY 10016
(212) 685-6464

Doubleday Publishing Co.
245 Park Ave.
NYC, NY 10017
(212) 953-4561

Dover Publications
180 Varick St.
NYC, NY 10014
(212) 255-3755

Dustbooks
Box 1000
Paradise, CA 95969
(916) 877-6110

E. P. Dutton Inc.
2 Park Ave.
NYC, NY 10016
(212) 725-1818

Editor and Publisher
575 Lexington Ave.
New York, NY 10022
(212) 752-7050

Farrar, Straus & Giroux
19 Union Sq. West
NYC, NY 10003
(212) 741-6900

Gale Research Co.
Penobscot Building
Detroit, MI 48226
(313) 961-2242

Gebbie's Press
P.O. Box 1000
New Paltz, NY 12561
(914) 255-7560

David R. Godine, Publisher
306 Dartmouth St.
Boston, MA 02116
(617) 536-0761

Victor Gollancz Ltd.
14 Henrietta St.
Covent Garden
London WC2E 8QJ
ENGLAND
(01) 836-2006

Grosset & Dunlap, Inc.
200 Madison Ave.
NYC, NY 10016
(212) 576-8900

Harcourt Brace Jovanovich, Inc.
757 Third Ave.
NYC, NY 10017
(212) 888-4444

Harmony Books: See Crown
Publishers

Harper & Row, Publishers, Inc.
10 East 53rd St.
NYC, NY 10022
(212) 593-7000

Hastings House, Publishers, Inc.
10 East 40th St.
NYC, NY 10016
(212) 689-5400

Hawthorn Books, Inc.
260 Madison Ave.
NYC, NY 10016
(212) 725-7740

Holt, Rinehart & Winston
383 Madison Ave.
NYC, NY 10017
(212) 688-9100

The Horn Book
Park Sq. Bldg.
31st St. & James Ave.
Boston, MA 02116
(617) 482-5198

Huenefeld Co., Inc.
119 The Great Rd.
Bedford, MA 01730
(617) 275-2280

The Hutchinson Publishing
Group
3 Fitsroy Square
London W1P 6JD
ENGLAND
(01) 387-2888

Irvington Publishers, Inc.
551 Fifth Ave.
NYC, NY 10017
(212) 697-8100

Johns Hopkins University Press
Baltimore, MD 21218
(301) 338-7875

William Kaufmann, Inc.
95 First St.
Los Altos, CA 94022
(415) 948-5810

Alfred A. Knopf, Inc.
201 East 50th St.
NYC, NY 10022
(212) 751-2600

Knowledge Industry
Publications
White Plains, NY 10604
(914) 328-9157

Lexington Books
125 Spring St.
Lexington, MA 02173
(617) 862-6650

Little, Brown & Co.
34 Beacon St.
Boston, MA 02106
(617) 227-0730

McGraw-Hill Inc.
1221 Avenue of the Americas
NYC, NY 10020
(212) 997-1221

Macmillan Publishing Co., Inc.
866 Third Ave.
NYC, NY 10022
(212) 935-2000

William Morrow & Co., Inc.
105 Madison Ave.
NYC, NY 10016
(212) 889-3050

Murton Press
26 Anderson Rd.
Greenwich, CT 06830
(203) 869-4434

National Textbook Company
8259 Miles Center Rd.
Skokie, IL 60077
(312) 679-4210

New American Library
1633 Broadway
NYC, NY 10019
(212) 397-8000

Newmarket Press
3 East 48th St.
NYC, NY 10017
(212) 832-3575

New York Public Library
Fifth Ave. & 42nd St.
NYC, NY 10018
(212) 340-0849

Oxbridge Communications
150 Fifth Ave.
NYC, NY 10011
(212) 741-0231

Oxford University Press, Inc.
200 Madison Ave.
NYC, NY 10016
(212) 679-5892

PEN American Center
47 Fifth Ave.
NYC, NY 10003
(212) 255-1977

Peterson's Guides
Box 2123
Princeton, New Jersey 08540
(609) 924-5338

Practicing Law Institute
810 Seventh Ave.
NYC, NY 10019
(212) 765-5700

Praeger Publishers
521 Fifth Ave.
NYC, NY 10175
(212) 599-8400

Prentice-Hall Inc.
Englewood Cliffs, NJ 07632
(201) 592-2000

Publishers Weekly
R. R. Bowker Co.
205 E. 42nd St.
NYC, NY 10017
(212) 916-1600

Pushcart Press
Box 380
Wainscott, NY 11075
(516) 524-9300

Random House Inc.
201 East 50th St.
NYC, NY 10022
(212) 751-2600

Scarecrow Press Inc.
52 Liberty St.
Metuchen, NJ 08840
(201) 548-8600

Scholastic Inc.
730 Broadway
NYC, NY 10003
(212) 505-3000

Scott, Foresman & Co.
1900 East Lake Ave.
Glenview, IL 60025
(312) 729-3000

The Scribner Book Companies
  Inc.
597 Fifth Ave.
NYC, NY 10017
(212) 486-2700

Southern Illinois University
  Press
Box 3697
Carbondale, IL 62901
(618) 453-2281

Stackpole Books
Box 1831
Cameron & Kelker Sts.
Harrisburg, PA 17105
(717) 234-5041

Standard Rate and Data Service
5201 Old Orchard Rd.
Skokie, IL 60076
(312) 256-6067

Text-Fiche Press
540 Drexel Ave.
Glen Cove, IL 60022
(312) 835-1952

Times Books
3 Park Ave.
NYC, NY 10016
(212) 725-2050

University of California Press
2223 Fulton St.
Berkeley, CA 94720
(415) 642-4247

University of Chicago Press
5801 Ellis Ave.
Chicago, IL 60637
(312) 962-7700

University of Toronto Press
St. George Campus
Toronto, Ont. M5S 1A6
CANADA
(416) 978-2239

University Press of New
  England
2 Lebanon St.
Hanover, NH 03755
(603) 646-3348

Viking Press
40 W. 23rd St.
NYC, NY 10010
(212) 807-7300

Watson-Guptill Publications
1515 Broadway
NYC, NY 10036
(212) 764-7300

Westview Press, Inc.
5500 Central Ave.
Boulder, CO 80301
(303) 444-3541

John Wiley & Sons Inc.
605 Third Ave.
NYC, NY 10158
(212) 850-6000

H. W. Wilson Co.
950 University Ave.
Bronx, NY 10452
(212) 588-8400

The Writer, Inc.
8 Arlington St.
Boston, MA 02116
(617) 536-7420

About the Book and Editors

The Business of Book Publishing:
Papers by Practitioners

edited by Elizabeth A. Geiser
and Arnold Dolin, with Gladys S. Topkis

This book is aimed at the beginner—the person who knows very little about publishing and aspires to a career in the field, or has recently launched that career, or simply wants to know more about the publishing business. It is based on the curriculum developed at the University of Denver Publishing Institute, now entering its tenth successful year, and includes among its contributors many of the industry's leaders who have served on the faculty of the Institute. The book covers every phase and function of the book publishing process as well as specialized types of publishing.

Elizabeth A. Geiser is a senior vice president of the Gale Research Company and director of the University of Denver Publishing Institute. From 1982 to 1985 she was a member of the Board of Directors of the Association of American Publishers and also served on its executive committee.

Arnold Dolin is vice president and editor in chief of New American Library. He has been a member of the Denver Publishing Institute faculty since its inception, where he directs the popular editing workshop with Gladys Topkis, a senior editor at Yale University Press.

Index